Cities and Housing

THE GRADUATE SCHOOL OF BUSINESS
UNIVERSITY OF CHICAGO

FIRST SERIES (1916–1938)
Materials for the Study of Business
Edited by DEAN LEON CARROLL MARSHALL and
DEAN WILLIAM HOMER SPENCER

SECOND SERIES (1938–1956)
Business and Economic Publications
Edited by DEAN WILLIAM HOMER SPENCER

THIRD SERIES (1959–   )
Studies in Business and Society
Edited by DEAN W. ALLEN WALLIS
and DEAN GEORGE P. SHULTZ

Cities and Housing

The Spatial Pattern of Urban Residential Land Use

Richard F. Muth

The University of Chicago Press
Chicago and London

International Standard Book Number: 0–226–55413–9
Library of Congress Catalog Card Number 69–13201

THE UNIVERSITY OF CHICAGO PRESS, CHICAGO 60637
THE UNIVERSITY OF CHICAGO PRESS, LTD., LONDON

To My Parents

Contents

vii

PART III   CONCLUSIONS AND IMPLICATIONS

List of Tables

List of Figures

Foreword

The paramount concerns of a university—the discovery and promulgation of knowledge—are sovereign concerns also of the Graduate School of Business. Here scholars drawn from many disciplines bring their varied approaches and methods to bear in performing research on special problems of business and society.

The truth is sought assiduously wherever the search may lead, and the findings are articulated both in the teaching programs of the School and in published works that make knowledge available to all who have the need and capacity to use it.

This volume is the most recent expression of a significant publishing program inaugurated by the School more than half a century ago. A series of publications, *Materials for the Study of Business*, was initiated in 1916, under the editorship of Dean Leon Carroll Marshall, and was continued by Dean William Homer Spencer. Fifty titles were published, and many became classics in their fields. In 1938 a second series, *Business and Economic Publications*, was launched; under the editorship of Dean Spencer, thirteen titles were published. In addition, in the two decades prior to 1948 the School published some seventy monographs under the general title, *Studies in Business Administration*.

The third (current) series, *Studies in Business and Society* (formerly *Studies in Business*), was initiated in 1959 under Dean W. Allen Wallis, who edited the first six volumes.

The present volume resulted from research largely carried on by Professor Muth at the Graduate School of Business from 1959 to 1964, and supported in part by a grant from the RELM Foundation. In this volume Professor Muth presents an analysis of the operation of the price system in urban housing and residential land markets. A primary aim of the book is to develop a substantive theory of the spatial pattern of demand and supply of housing and residential land in different parts of a metropolitan area. The implications of the economic theories of consumer behavior and of the business firm for the determinants of the location of households by income, the consumption of housing, and the intensity of residential land use are drawn and tested empirically. These implications are shown by Professor Muth to be quantitatively consistent with a wide range of characteristics of American cities in 1950 and 1960. The book's second major aim is to investigate alternative theories of the determinants of housing quality in cities and to ascertain whether the residential segregation of racial minorities raises housing prices for them and lowers the quality of the housing they inhabit.

The work has a number of important implications for today's urban problems; it brings new understanding to such matters as the determinants of urban blight and metropolitan decentralization, the varying roles of private initiative and collective action, and the relation between income and housing quality.

I congratulate Professor Muth on having produced a distinguished work in an area that urgently needs such illumination.

George P. Shultz, Dean
Graduate School of Business
University of Chicago

Preface

In the Preface to the first edition of his *Principles of City Land Values*,[1] Richard M. Hurd wrote in 1903:

When placed in charge of the Mortgage Department of the U.S. Mortgage and Trust Co. in 1895, the writer searched in vain, both in England and this country, for books on the science of city real estate as an aid in judging values. Finding in economic books merely brief references to city land and elsewhere only fragmentary articles, the plan arose to outline the theory of the structure of cities and to state the average scale of land values produced by different utilities within them.

My own experience was quite similar to Hurd's. When I first joined the Graduate School of Business of the University of Chicago nine years ago, to prepare for the research in urban economics I was to do and direct, I too made an extensive search of the literature in the field. I did find several textbooks and a variety of articles on urban land economics and real estate. These, however, were largely descriptive and contained little application of economic analysis, still less empirical estimation and testing. Indeed, when coming upon Hurd's book, I was struck by how favorably it compared with most other writings then available. Like Hurd, I set out to improve the theory of city structure and land use.

This monograph presents the results of my efforts to develop a theory of the spatial pattern of the housing market in cities. It is addressed primarily to the professional economist, though I have tried to include, for other readers, intuitive explanations of some of the technical analysis. The theory developed is based largely upon the generally accepted economic theories of consumer and firm behavior. It has been modified and further developed along lines suggested by rather extensive empirical testing. Unlike many writings on urban housing, the book aims to explain the actual operation of these markets rather than how they should be made to operate. My study suggests to me that many widely accepted policies for dealing with

---

[1] New York: The Record and Guide, 1903.

urban housing problems are seriously deficient because the theories upon which they are based have little or no empirical support.

In organizing the material I initially thought of presenting the theory, its testing, and their interactions and modifications in the same sequence as they evolved in my research. While doing so would undoubtedly have provided the reader with a better basis for evaluating the theory and the evidence bearing upon it, I rather quickly realized the monograph would have been far too unwieldy if organized in this way. In placing the theoretical and empirical material in separate parts, however, I have tried to indicate in several places, especially at the end of Chapter 2 and throughout Chapters 4 and 12, how the original theoretical analysis was modified by subsequent empirical testing.

In presenting my empirical findings I have tried to be as objective as is consistent with readability. Thus, the comparisons in Part II are largely presented in the order in which they were made, both within and among chapters. The major exception is the analysis of central-city population and urbanized-area land area, which, though done last, seemed most closely related to the analysis of central-city density gradients. Where additional variables or different methods of comparison are used to correct results that at first seemed unsatisfactory to me or to colleagues with whom I discussed them, I have tried to indicate the reasons as well as to show the initial results. Finally, I have tried to report on all of the hypotheses tested. It would, of course, have been tedious to show every regression equation calculated. I have, however, retained in the final regression equations shown most of the variables used, even those which were unsuccessful.

The research on and writing of this monograph were largely done during the period 1959 through 1964. After the first draft was circulated for critical comment, the manuscript was rather extensively revised and additional material was added during the first half of 1966. Since the first draft of the manuscript was written, the literature on urban economics and problems has expanded rapidly. The latter no doubt reflects the great upsurge of interest in this field among economists which has occurred in the past decade. In revising the manuscript I largely decided against referring to these later works, preferring instead to cite only those materials which were available to me when the bulk of my research was done. The major exceptions to this practice were, in each case, added references to empirical materials which have a bearing upon important issues I discuss and which supplement my own evidence. I wish to emphasize that my failure to refer to other recently published work in no way reflects an adverse judgment of mine upon it.

Some of the material of this monograph, especially summaries of my empirical findings, has previously been published in article form. For several reasons, however, it seemed desirable to include this previously published material. I gratefully acknowledge permission to reprint the following articles, kindly given by their original publishers. The first section of Chapter 7 and the material through Table 7.7 in the second originally appeared in an article titled "The Spatial Structure of the Housing Market," *Papers and Proceedings of the Regional Science Association* 7 (1961): 207–20; the latter part of the first section of Chapter 4 and most of the 1950 comparisons in the latter part of Chapter 7 are contained in my "The Distribution of Population within Urban Areas," *Determinants of Investment Behavior*, edited by Robert Ferber, Conference of the Universities' National Bureau Committee for Economic Research (New York: National Bureau of Economic Research, 1967), pp. 271–99. The second half of Chapter 8 as well as a brief summary of many of my other findings appear in my "Urban Residential Land and Housing Markets," in *Issues in Urban Economics*, published in 1968 by The Johns Hopkins Press for Resources for the Future, Inc. A summary of my findings in Chapter 9 and equations (9.42) and (9.45) in Table 9.13 were first published in my "The Variation of Population Density and its Components in South Chicago," *Papers and Proceedings of the Regional Science Association* 15 (1965): 173–83. Finally, a brief survey of the argument of Chapter 6 and a summary of the findings of Chapter 10 were presented in my paper "Slums and Poverty," in *The Economic Problems of Housing*, published for the International Economics Association by Macmillan and Company, Ltd.

Many colleagues have contributed importantly to my work, and I am happy to acknowledge my indebtedness to them. Jerome L. Stein of Brown University, John Meyer of Harvard University and the National Bureau of Economic Research, and Hugh O. Nourse of the University of Illinois carefully read the first draft. Their comments on it, especially where they disagreed with my interpretation or presentation, were most valuable to me in revising the manuscript. Margaret G. Reid of the University of Chicago originally suggested the comparisons of Chapter 11 to me. She and Beverly Duncan of the University of Michigan carefully read an earlier version of this material and suggested several additional comparisons, and Harry V. Roberts of the University of Chicago made many helpful suggestions for interpreting and presenting my findings on this delicate issue. I also appreciate the opportunity to present, and thus refine, my ideas to students in courses at the University of Chicago and Washington University; to seminars at the University of Chicago, the University of California at Los Angeles, the University of Illinois, Case Institute of Technology, the Institute for Defense Analyses, Washington University, and the University of Indiana; and to the conferences and professional society meetings at which the papers noted in the above paragraph were presented.

I am especially indebted to my close friend and valued colleague Martin J. Bailey, who, during our association at the University of Chicago and later at the Institute for Defense Analyses, discussed many theoretical and empirical issues with me during the progress of my research and read and made valuable comments on my first draft, especially Chapters 6 and 10. I alone, however, am to be held accountable for the shortcomings of this monograph.

I am also very grateful to many persons who assisted in the preparation of this monograph in a variety of other ways. Ruth Campbell and Navinchandra Amin, while my research assistants at the University of Chicago, gathered data and made preliminary calculations pertaining to comparisons presented in Chapters 7 and 10, respectively. Harold Fibish at the University of Chicago, Evelyn Douglas at the Institute for Defense Analyses, and Marilyn Thompson and Carol Martin at Washington University supervised the typing of the manuscript. Miss Thompson also prepared the Table of Contents, Lists of Figures and Tables, and helped in the preparation of the figures themselves, while James Cantwell of Washington University prepared the Glossary of Variable Names. I wish especially to acknowledge the generous financial support of the RELM Foundation and the exemplary interest and encouragement to follow my own research interests of its secretary, Richard A. Ware. Finally I owe an especial debt to my wife Helene for her frequent assistance in several aspects of writing the manuscript as well as for her continued reassurance and understanding.

RICHARD F. MUTH

Saint Louis, Missouri
June, 1968

I *Introduction*

Urban problems are among the most vital domestic issues of today. Hardly a day passes in which a newspaper, public official, businessman, or scholar fails to voice concern over suburban sprawl, urban blight, racial segregation, the city's finances, or a host of similar problems. Despite the widespread public concern over urban problems and the intensive investigation given such problems by other social scientists, economists have paid little attention to them. The economists' lack of concern for urban problems probably stems in large part from the great urgency of such nation- or worldwide problems as depression, inflation, and economic development during the thirties, forties, and fifties. Economists' neglect of urban problems may also result from the belief, held by those few economists who, prior to the past decade, had given much serious study to housing and urban land markets, that the usual methods of economics are not very helpful in understanding these particular markets.

The following statement is an excellent summary of prevailing popular and most scholarly views on urban problems:

> ...the plight of the urban communities has resulted from the lack of planning and collective control of their physical development in the public interest. On the fuzzy-minded but comfortable assumption that, in the use of urban land as well as in almost everything else, economic action motivated by virtually unbridled self-interest would always promote the public interest, the cities and towns have been allowed to drift into their present sorry state.[1]

Diagnoses such as this one seldom go beyond asserting that chaos results from unregulated individual activity in urban land markets. In their crudest form, statements such as that quoted above reflect the widespread belief that unregulated individual behavior in any sphere of economic life fails to serve the public interest. Happily, the science of economics has demonstrated that, as a general proposition, the chaos hypothesis has little validity. The failure of economists to give much attention to the operation

---

[1] Guy Greer, "City Replanning and Rebuilding," in *Postwar Economic Problems*, ed. Seymour E. Harris (New York: McGraw-Hill Book Co., 1943), p. 207.

of the market mechanism in housing and urban land markets, however, has even led some professional economists to accept uncritically this crude form of the chaos hypothesis when applied to urban land markets.

Most professional economists who accept the chaos hypothesis would probably subscribe to a more sophisticated and intellectually respectable interpretation of the quotation above. They would argue that external economies and technical imperfections are so all-pervasive and of such quantitative importance in urban land markets that a far greater degree of social control over them is necessary than over other markets to insure socially desirable results. While this may be true, it is an entirely different matter to assert that our major urban problems result from faulty workings of the price system in urban land markets.

There has never been, to my knowledge, a clear and detailed statement in either the scholarly or popular literature of how shortcomings in the market mechanism have given rise to today's urban problems. By putting together bits and pieces, though, one can arrive at the following, which would probably be accepted as describing their views by most adherents to the second version of the chaos hypothesis. The older parts of our central cities were not properly planned and regulated when they were initially developed. As a result, the demand for housing in the older parts of central cities by middle- and upper-income persons has declined, and these groups have largely moved to the suburbs. The decline in demand, in turn, has reduced the returns to owners of buildings in the older parts of cities, and these owners have allowed their properties to deteriorate. The deterioration of buildings has reinforced the flight to the suburbs. The older parts of cities have thus come to be inhabited largely by lower-income persons, who are the unfortunate victims of past mistakes and the failure of the private market to provide them with decent housing. While it would be socially desirable to redevelop large areas of our central cities, external economies and market imperfections prevent private individuals and firms from undertaking this redevelopment.

The policy implications of the chaos hypothesis, unlike the theory behind them, are usually quite explicitly stated. Government intervention is necessary to provide decent housing for the unfortunate victims of slums, to correct the mistakes of the past by rebuilding vast areas of the central city along socially desirable lines, and to attract middle- and upper-income persons back to the central city, which is their rightful home.

I believe the views described above are almost completely wrong. Contrary to the belief of many housing and urban-land economists, the theoretical and empirical techniques of modern economic analysis yield highly fruitful results when applied to housing and urban land markets, provided that, as in any applied field of economics, account is taken of a few special features of these markets. Contrary to the implications of the crude form of the chaos hypothesis, the distribution of population within cities and the quality of their housing exhibit strong regularities and are highly predictable. Contrary to the more sophisticated version of the chaos hypothesis, our urban problems arise for reasons almost totally unrelated to external economies, market imperfections, and the lack of planning and governmental control. Problems certainly do exist in urban areas, but the real nature of these problems is not well understood. Many current governmental programs in the housing and urban fields for this reason are at best of little value and may do real harm.

This monograph is concerned with the operation of the price system in urban housing and residential land markets. Its primary purpose is to develop a substantive body of propositions suggesting how these markets operate in allocating households to locations in urban space and in determining the number of people, the consumption of housing per household and the quality of housing consumed, and the output of housing per unit of residential land in different parts of the city. Part I contains five chapters which set out my theoretical analysis. The empirical testing of this analysis follows in Part II. While my major concern is not with policy proposals for urban problems, my analysis does have important implications for many of these problems. In Part III, therefore, the implications of my work for the nature of and solutions to certain urban problems are discussed.

The Pattern of Urban Land Uses and Values

The pattern of urban land uses and values is highly complex and varies considerably from city to city. Still, certain regularities can be discerned, and it is the task of theory to provide an explanation for these regularities. In this section I shall first sketch out some of the important features of the location of the various types of economic activity in cities and the accompanying pattern of land values. I shall then describe briefly several theories or generalizations of city structures which have been offered as explanations of these tendencies.

The region of heaviest concentration of buildings and economic activity within a city[2] is known as the Central Business District (CBD). It consists almost exclusively of commercial, financial, retail, and service establishments. It is generally the region of greatest employment per unit of land,

---

[2] Throughout this study when I speak of the city I mean a region of relatively dense concentration of labor and non-land capital in space. Such concentrations consist almost exclusively of non-extractive economic activity. Thus, the term "city" as I use it corresponds to the urbanized area concept of the Bureau of the Census rather than to an area governed by a particular political unit—the Chicago area instead of the City of Chicago. When referring to the largest political city of an area I will use the term central city.

and few residences are located within it. Almost without exception it contains the major railroad and intercity bus terminals, and it is the hub of the intracity transportation system. Around its outer limits there frequently exists a region of small manufacturing and wholesaling firms.

Outside the center, housing is by far the most important type of land use. This residential part of the city, however, is by no means uniform. Close to the center, the multistory apartment building is by far the most important kind of structure. Near the edges of the city, however, housing is usually provided mostly in the form of single-family units. In between, the heights of buildings decline and lot sizes increase, as does the proportion of single-family homes. Finally, beyond the city itself lies the region devoted primarily to agriculture. But in the agricultural region, too, the intensity of land use tends to decline with distance from the city center.[3]

Thus, in broad outline the spatial pattern of land uses in cities is essentially annular, with non-farm, non-residential uses predominating in the innermost annulus and agricultural tending to predominate in the outermost one. But their boundaries may be very irregular, and many exceptions to the annular structure are to be found. Manufacturing areas are scattered about here and there, primarily along rail lines and truck routes and near harbor areas. Clusters of retail and service establishments, or shopping centers, of various sizes are located in a fairly regular hierarchical pattern within the residential annulus, often at the intersections of major streets. The CBD is the largest of these centers. Finally, there are many clusters of specialized establishments surrounding institutions such as hospitals and universities.

The pattern of land values within a city is quite similar to that of building heights. Land values reach very high peaks near the center of the CBD and decline rapidly to its edges. Corresponding to the residential annulus is a region of less rapid decline in land values. Finally, in the agricultural area outside the city proper, land values continue to decline but at a still slower rate. But as with the pattern of land uses, there are many exceptions to the annular pattern of differential decline in values. Local peaks of values of varying heights occur near shopping centers and around special-purpose institutions such as hospitals and universities. Also, ridges or valleys of value may exist along the waterfront, rail lines, major streets, and elevations of land which are especially desirable for residences because of their topography.[4]

---

[3] For evidence on this point see Otis Dudley Duncan, *et al.*, *Metropolis and Region*, pp. 184–96.

[4] For a more detailed description see Homer Hoyt, *One Hundred Years of Land Values in Chicago*, chap. 6.

There are three traditional theories or principles of the internal structure of cities: the concentric-zone theory, the sector theory, and the multiple-nuclei theory. All three are primarily inductive generalizations rather than a set of propositions deduced from prior principles. All contain elements of truth from a purely descriptive point of view, but because of their purely descriptive character none offers much help in predicting behavior not yet observed. I shall give a very brief description of each of them below. This is followed by an equally brief summary of Thünen's theory of agricultural location and a discussion of its relation to recent theoretical analyses of the internal structure of cities.

The oldest theory of the internal structure of cities is the so-called concentric zone theory, generally attributed to the sociologist Burgess.[5] Burgess asserted that the characteristics of any town or city vary radially from its CBD or first zone. There follow in reverse order of distance from the center: an area in transition, which contains the poorest-quality residences and is being invaded by business and light manufacturing, the zone of "independent workingmen," the better residential area, and the commuter's zone. Burgess gave little rationale for the assignment of activities to areas and did not discuss the behavior of land rents as between the different zones. He was primarily interested in sociological phenomena and appears to have been especially interested in the process of growth and change.

Homer Hoyt, after examining patterns of residential rentals in 142 American cities in 1934, concluded that levels of housing rentals tended to conform to a pattern of sectors rather than concentric rings.[6] He noted that no two cities appear to have high and low rental areas of the same size or shape or in the same location relative to the CBD. But none of the cities examined by Hoyt appeared to have an upward gradation of housing rentals from the CBD to the edges of the city in all directions. Rather, the highest rental areas of the city tended to be located in one or more sectors, the location of which varied from city to city, and rentals tended to decline from these high-rental areas in all directions. Hoyt, however, gave virtually no explanation of why the sector pattern of rentals exists.

Harris and Ullman have argued that economic activity is built around

---

[5] Ernest W. Burgess, "The Growth of the City," in Robert E. Park, Ernest W. Burgess, and Roderick D. McKenzie, *The City*, pp. 47–62.

[6] *The Structure and Growth of Residential Neighborhoods in American Cities*, pp. 72–78. Observe that Hoyt examined the rental value of dwellings rather than the rental value of land. The rental value of a dwelling depends upon both the price per unit of housing and the quantity of housing contained in the dwelling. The rental value of dwellings of given quality, or quantity of housing per dwelling, and the rental value of land might each vary quite differently.

several centers or nuclei rather than a single center, the CBD.[7] These nuclei generate financial, retail, manufacturing, or residential districts; other clusters of activity may exist around cultural centers, parks, outlying business districts and small industrial centers. Some such nuclei have existed from the time of origin of the city, while others developed as the city grew, but generally the larger the city the more numerous and specialized are the nuclei. The existence of nuclei and differentiated districts is attributed to the fact that certain groups of activities require specialized facilities, certain groups profit from cohesion, and certain dissimilar activities are detrimental to each other. Like the sector pattern of housing rentals and some other phenomena, the pattern of multiple nucleation varies from city to city.

The first economist to take a serious interest in the spatial distribution of economic activity and to make an important contribution to the subject was Thünen. His theory of the organization of agricultural production, which is over one hundred years old, is very much like the concentric zone theory of Burgess. But Thünen's work differs from the concentric zone theory in that its conclusions were derived by deductive means from certain postulates about economic behavior and the nature of space. Thünen's model consisted of a single, large city in the center of a fertile plain without navigable waterways and surrounded by wilderness. He showed that products such as milk and fruits, for which transport costs are greatest, would be produced nearest the city and that other products would be produced in concentric rings in order of decreasing transport costs. Thünen also concluded that the price of a product in the city must be high enough to cover the costs of the most distant producer, including his transport costs, and that less distant land would earn a rent attributable to its location, equal to the sum of production and transport costs to the city at the most distant producing location minus the sum of these costs at the less distant location.[8]

Within the past decade several economic analyses of urban land use and city structure have appeared, all of which are quite similar to and inspired by Thünen's theory of the spatial distribution of economic activity.[9] In these the CBD plays the role of the isolated city of Thünen, and the land

---

[7] Chauncey D. Harris and Edward L. Ullman, "The Nature of Cities." This work also contains a good description of the concentric zone and sector theories.

[8] The above brief description was abstracted from Erich Roll, *A History of Economic Thought* (New York: Prentice-Hall, 1942), pp. 359–62.

[9] Among these are: William Alonso, "A Theory of the Urban Land Market"; John F. Kain, "The Journey-to-Work as a Determinant of Residential Location"; Herbert Mohring, "Land Values and the Measurement of Highway Benefits"; Richard F. Muth, "Economic Change and Rural-Urban Land Conversions," and "The Spatial Structure of the Housing Market"; and Lowdon Wingo, Jr., *Transportation and Urban Land*.

surrounding the CBD is used for residential and other non-agricultural purposes. Since the CBD is the point of maximum accessibility to the city as a whole and may have other advantages, transport costs tend to be lower for producers who locate there. As a result of competition for scarce locations near the city's center, those producers for whom transport costs are greatest or for whom the use of space is least important locate in or near the CBD, and conversely. For households, the CBD is the most important, though not necessarily the only, place of employment and the purchase of goods and services, and the costs of transporting people for work or shopping tend to be lowest close to the CBD. As with business firms, those households for whom transport costs are greatest or for whom the consumption of space is smallest tend to locate near the CBD, while for households for whom the opposite is true the best location is near the edge of the city. The difference in land rents between any two locations devoted to the same type of use depends upon the difference in costs, primarily transport costs, associated with the two locations.

The reader will soon realize that much of this study is an elaboration of the Thünen type of analysis and the three principles of city structure discussed previously in this section. It differs from them and other recent economic analyses of city structure in two important respects: first, my main concern is with the way land is used for residential purposes; and second, the present work contains much more extensive empirical analysis, particularly multiple regression analysis, than other such studies have done.

A Brief Summary of the Study

In the remainder of this chapter I wish to present a brief overview of the theoretical argument of this book and some of its main empirical findings. While so doing I will make no attempt at rigor or completeness, a deficiency which I hope the body of the work itself will correct. I begin by considering the influence of accessibility to the CBD upon the location of households, their consumption of housing, and the intensity of residential land use by producers of housing. Following this I consider the effects of the age of neighborhoods and preference factors associated with the incomes of their inhabitants on the production and consumption of housing services in different parts of the city. Finally, I consider the residential segregation of Negroes and the determinants of housing quality or condition.

In order that a household in space with a member employed in the CBD maximize its utility, two conditions must hold. The first, that housing and all other commodities be consumed in such quantities that the marginal utility per dollar spent is the same for all, is quite well known. The second, that no small move can increase the household's real income, implies that housing prices must decline with distance from the CBD if the marginal cost of transport is positive. The second condition also implies that the relative rate of decline in housing prices must vary directly with the marginal cost of transport and inversely with a household's expenditures on housing. The two conditions together imply that the consumption of housing services by otherwise identical households must increase with distance from the CBD. Empirical evidence presented in Part II suggests, indeed, that housing prices declined at the rate of about 2 percent per mile on the average in American cities in 1950. As would be anticipated from a unit-price elasticity of housing demand, per household expenditures on housing were roughly constant, however, once the effect of income differences was removed. The empirical evidence also gives strong support to the proposition that the relative rate of decline in housing prices varies directly with the marginal costs of transport, as they are reflected by their inverse relationship with car registrations per capita.

For the location dictated by the second of the conditions described above to be a stable one, it is sufficient that the net savings on the quantity of housing purchased and transportation decline with distance. If the latter condition did not hold, any household could continually increase its real income by moving farther from the CBD, and no recognizable city would exist. Provided, as seems sensible, the marginal costs of transport do not increase with distance, housing prices must decrease by decreasing absolute amounts with distance. In fact, if the price elasticity of housing demand is −1 or smaller, housing prices must decline at a non-increasing relative rate with distance. This same stability condition also implies that the equilibrium location for households whose housing expenditures are higher relative to their marginal transport expenditures must be a greater distance from the city center.

Because of the great variation among households in income levels at a given time and the fact that, at annual growth rates of 2 to 3 percent per year, average income for a city as a whole can increase by from 22 to 35 percent in a decade, the effect of a household's income on its best location is a question of substantial quantitative significance. The greater a household's income the greater its expenditures on housing tend to be; hence the smaller must be the price gradient at, and the greater the distance from the CBD of, its equilibrium location. However, household income differences arise largely because of differences in the hourly earning opportunities of its members and, consequently, the value they would place on their travel time. Thus, on a priori grounds alone, the effect of income differences upon a household's optimal location cannot be predicted. Empirically, however, it seems likely that increases in income would raise housing expenditures by relatively more than marginal transport costs, so that higher-income CBD worker households would live at greater distances from the city center.

The average expenditure on housing would, of course, increase with distance because of the increase in income.

When I examine the median income level of a census tract in various cities, I find a strong, positive simple correlation with distance from the CBD. However, when the age of dwelling units in the tract is added to the analysis, the association between median income and distance vanishes, while that between age and income is strongly negative. The failure of census-reported money income to increase with distance once the effect of age of dwellings is removed can be explained by considering the effects of distance upon the money incomes of locally employed workers. The latter by definition, incur no transportation costs. But, since workers locally employed at greater distances from the CBD pay lower prices for housing, their money wage incomes must be lower if they are not to have higher real incomes. The reported money incomes in a census tract include those of CBD and locally employed workers, and the increase in the money incomes of the former group with distance from the CBD tends to be offset by the decline in money incomes of the latter.

The decline in housing prices with distance from the CBD implies that the rental value of land used for residential purposes must likewise decline if firms producing housing services are to earn the same incomes regardless of their locations. Since payments to land are probably only around 5 percent of the value of housing services produced, the relative rate of decline in land rentals is of the order of twenty times that of housing prices. The decline in land rentals in turn leads producers of housing services to use more land relative to other factors of production at greater distances from the city center. Empirically, it appears that the value of housing services produced per square mile of land tended to decline at a relative rate of about 30 percent per mile on the average for American cities in 1950. The intercorrelation of age of dwellings and income of their inhabitants is responsible for only a little of this decline. It is far more important than the increase in per household expenditures on housing in accounting for the decline of population densities with distance from the CBD, once the influence of age of dwellings is removed.

The relative rates of decline in land rentals and the value of housing produced per square mile at different distances from the CBD are subject to two opposing forces. First, as was suggested earlier, the relative rate of decline in housing prices with distance probably becomes smaller at greater distances, causing the relative rates of decline in land rentals and housing output to become smaller as well. Secondly, however, the decline in land's share in the value of housing output with distance means that both become more responsive to a given change in housing prices. As a result, the declines in both land rentals and the value of housing services produced per square mile tend to be at roughly constant relative rates. Since the increase in housing expenditures per household with distance is small once the effects of age of dwelling units are eliminated, the tendency for population densities to decline at roughly constant relative rates in cities is largely the result of the offsetting effects of the two forces just noted on the rate of decline of housing output.

The greater responsiveness of housing output to price changes at greater distances from the city center has important implications for the growth of cities. With an increase in population or in income per family, the aggregate demand for housing services and their relative price tend to increase. Because of a unit-price elasticity of housing demand, the price rise has no effect on expenditures per family and thus on the relative rate of decline of housing prices. The greater elasticity of housing output at greater distances means, however, that, in response to equiproportional price increases everywhere, housing output and thus population tend to grow more rapidly at greater distances from the center. Empirically, it would appear that with a 10 percent increase in population the relative rate of population density decline falls by about 5 percent. Roughly half of this decline can be attributed to the greater responsiveness of housing output to price changes at greater distances. It appears that the decline in the fraction of the central city in the urbanized area's population and the marked increase in the land area the latter occupies which occurred for American cities during the 1950's can be almost wholly accounted for by the effects of reduced transport costs on the one hand and increases in urbanized area population on the other. Conversely, there is little evidence that the decline of the central city's share in an urbanized area's population or the increase in the land area occupied by the latter has come about to any practically significant extent because of undesirable physical or social conditions in the central city.

While distance to the CBD is of crucial importance in determining the intensity of residential land use, the age of dwellings and the income of their inhabitants also have an important influence. Because the marginal costs of transport for workers commuting to the CBD were greater prior to the automobile and, incomes being lower, expenditures on housing services per family were smaller, the rate of decline in housing prices was almost certainly greater. For this reason, the output of housing per square mile was probably greater than its equilibrium for the auto era near the city center, and conversely in its outer parts. After the development of the automobile, the demand for housing and housing prices fell in the central parts of the city relative to its outer parts. Because of the long lag in the adjustment of the intensity of land use to changing conditions, especially where reductions are called for, one might anticipate that population density and the output of housing per square mile of land would be greater than otherwise in those central parts of the city developed prior to 1920.

For 1950, at least, one does indeed find a decided tendency for population density to be greater the higher the proportion of older dwellings in a census tract. Quite surprisingly, however, there was little tendency for the value of housing output per square mile to be greater the higher the proportion of older dwellings. This is probably the case because housing prices are lower in comparably located older areas. For the proportion of dwellings in one-unit structures—which varies inversely with the physical intensity of housing output—was indeed smaller in the older areas. Empirically, the direct association of population density with age of dwelling arises mainly from smaller housing expenditures per household in older areas, which itself results mostly from the inverse relationship between age of dwelling and the income of its inhabitants. The best explanation for the latter, I believe, is that older housing is more cheaply converted to occupancy by lower-income households than is newer housing.

There are a variety of reasons apart from a differential effect of income on housing expenditures and marginal transport costs why higher-income households might tend to live at greater distances from the CBD and at lower population densities. Stronger preferences for privacy or for space relative to structural features of housing is one frequently cited example. Empirically, therefore, it is quite surprising to find that population densities are no smaller, and, if anything, the value of housing produced per square mile of land is higher in comparably located higher-income areas. This probably results from so-called neighborhood effects, which raise housing prices and residential land rents in higher-income areas, for one does not find a higher proportion of dwellings in one-unit structures in comparably located higher-income areas.

Residential segregation or separation occurs for a variety of groups of persons variously defined. Segregation of the Negro population, however, is one of its most striking instances and is of great current public interest. The segregation of Negroes is frequently attributed to a unique aversion on the part of landlords and real estate agents, which is not shared by the community at large, to dealing with Negroes as tenants or buyers. The major shortcoming of this explanation is the economic incentive for those landlords or real estate agents who have an aversion to dealing with Negroes to sell out to others without such aversions. The segregation of Negroes is also sometimes attributed to a conspiracy on the part of landlords, real estate agents, and perhaps others such as mortgage lenders to profit from higher Negro housing prices. Such a conspiracy, though, would be quite difficult to organize and would almost certainly break down if it did, for a time, succeed in raising Negro housing prices. A much more satisfying explanation is that whites have a greater aversion to living among Negroes than do other Negroes.

Segregation need not imply higher housing prices relative to marginal costs for Negroes. Indeed, if prices in the interiors of the white and Negro residential areas were the same, the greater aversion by whites to living among Negroes would imply that prices on the white side of the boundary separating the residential areas of the two groups would be below those on the Negro side. The Negro area would thus expand, and in the process prices in the interior of the Negro area would fall relative to those in the interior of the white area. Thus, only if the Negro demand for housing grows faster in relation to the white demand than the Negro residential area will prices in the interior of the Negro area exceed those in the interior of the white area. Empirically, housing expenditures per family by non-whites appear to be a third or more higher at a given current money-income level than those of whites. Such a result is frequently interpreted as demonstrating that Negroes pay higher prices per unit of housing. But with a unit or elastic housing demand with respect to price, higher prices per unit would leave unchanged or reduce expenditures for housing, not increase them. When I examine physical indicators which one would expect to reflect price variations, such as population densities, crowding, the proportion of dwellings substandard, and the proportion which are in one-unit structures, the differences as between non-white and white census tracts are small. My examination of changes in average contract rents of tenant-occupied dwellings during the fifties between areas shifting from white to non-white occupancy and those remaining in white occupancy also suggest that the Negro housing price differential is small, at most of the order of 5 percent for renters.

Most explanations for the expansion in slum or poor-quality housing in central cities in recent years are based upon forces which influence the supply schedule of poor-quality housing. In many, the increase in the supply of poor-quality housing in the central city as a whole has resulted from a decline in the demand for better housing in certain parts of it. A variety of reasons, such as the development of automobile transportation, physical obsolescence, poor initial planning, and the failure of local governments to supply a proper level of municipal services, have been suggested to account for the decline in demand. Other explanations stress market imperfections, external economies, or shortcomings in property taxation, as forces increasing the supply schedule of poor-quality housing directly. Whatever the reason for the increase in the supply of poor-quality housing, because lower-income households might be presumed to have less of an aversion to living in poor-quality housing than higher-income ones, the deteriorated areas have come to be inhabited largely by lower-income groups.

While certain of the factors just discussed may have some empirical relevance, all theories which attribute the increase in the absolute numbers of slum dwellings to increased supply are either inconsistent with or, at best, fail to provide an explanation for three simple, empirical facts. These are: (1) that slum housing would, if anything, seem to be especially expensive in relation to its quality; (2) that urban renewal projects lose money; and (3) that during the 1950's the proportion of dwellings which were substandard in American cities declined sharply. These three facts, however, are readily explainable by the hypothesis that the growth in the number of poor-quality dwellings is the result of an increase in the demand for poor-quality housing in cities in the United States. Income per family is probably the most important determinant of housing demand. Viewing quality, space per person, and other features as inputs into the production of the commodity called housing, one would expect a growth of the lower-income population to increase the demand for poor-quality housing and for smaller dwellings. In consequence, dwellings would be converted to smaller units and allowed to deteriorate in quality. Since quality deterioration takes a longer time than conversion to smaller units, many persons have mistakenly inferred that crowding causes deterioration.

Empirically, one finds a close association between housing quality and income and a large quantitative response of the former to the latter. Whether making comparisons among census tracts within a given city in 1950 or 1960 or among central cities in 1950, the elasticity of the fraction of dwellings which are substandard with respect to median income averages about -3.5. One also finds an elasticity of the same magnitude but of opposite sign with respect to construction costs among cities. The similarity of the magnitude of these income and price elasticities provides fairly strong support for the hypothesis that variations in the proportion of dwellings substandard primarily reflect variations in demand. Previous estimates of mine suggest that the income and price elasticities of housing demand are about equal numerically. Apart from a strong negative association with age of dwellings in 1950, though not in 1960, there is little direct evidence for any of the hypotheses relating to the increased supply of slums. In addition, my estimates suggest that dwelling-unit condition is of negligible importance upon the location of households by income. For this reason, the increased-supply-of-slums hypotheses cannot account for the close association between dwelling-unit condition and income. If anything, my evidence suggests that the private market has not carried the production of slum housing far enough. On the south side of Chicago in 1960, I find that net population density, the value of housing output per square mile of residential land, and crowding all tended to be greater, and the proportion of one-unit dwellings to be smaller, the higher the proportion of substandard dwellings. These findings all suggest that the price per unit of housing service is higher in slum areas than in other comparably located areas.

The findings of this monograph strongly suggest that many actual and proposed governmental policies will have little effect upon urban decentralization and housing quality. What effects they have will probably tend to make these problems worse. Public policy has sought to reverse the tide of decentralization largely through improving the physical condition of the central city, especially through the federal urban-renewal program. My findings suggest, first, that the location of households by income and the distribution of population between the central city and its suburbs is little affected by physical condition. Secondly, however, slums are largely the result of the poverty of their inhabitants; urban renewal does little or nothing to remove poverty—it merely removes buildings in which poor people live.

To the extent, of course, that the relative supply of poor-quality dwellings is less than perfectly elastic, urban renewal or demolition under other programs will tend to reduce the fraction of substandard dwellings. But it will also raise the price of poor- relative to good-quality housing, reduce the real income of the poor, and lead the poor to consume poorer quality housing and less space on the average. At the same time, the building of urban express highways, largely aided by federal funds, has undoubtedly contributed greatly to the urban decentralization of the fifties. The building of subsidized rapid-transit systems is likely to have the same effect. In a similar vein, surburban development policies, such as proposals for subsidizing the building of new towns, like the federal income tax advantage to home-ownership and federal mortgage programs will encourage further decentralization by reducing the price of housing to consumers in the outer parts relative to the inner parts of cities.

PART I

Theoretical Analysis

2 · The Equilibrium of the Household in Urban Space

In this chapter I begin my analysis of residential land use by considering the equilibrium of the consumer. The equilibrium of producers of housing is considered in the following chapter, while in Chapter 4 the behavior of consumers and producers are fitted together and some testable implications are drawn. The analysis of this chapter is restricted to the implications of spatial uniqueness for the locations of different types of households in urban space and for the spatial pattern of housing consumption at different points. Additional considerations, such as the effects of the age of buildings and neighborhoods and preference of households for different types of housing on their location and consumption of housing, will be considered in Chapters 5 and 6. While the latter kind of consideration may be of greater importance in understanding certain aspects of the urban housing market, spatial uniqueness has important implications for variations in housing consumption which have never been considered very thoroughly. In addition, spatial uniqueness is, I believe, of crucial importance for understanding the spatial pattern of the production of housing in cities. To understand the latter it is first necessary to understand the influence of spatial uniqueness upon the spatial pattern of housing consumption and housing prices. In this and the following two chapters I shall follow the time-honored practice of beginning with what I believe to be the crucial aspects of the problem and then relaxing various assumptions in turn in order to determine the effect these have on the analysis. In the discussion of my empirical results in Part II, I shall attempt to call attention to those points for which relaxing my admittedly simple and restrictive assumptions seems to make a difference for explaining real-world behavior.

INITIAL ASSUMPTIONS

My initial assumptions may be classified under three headings: those related to housing, to transport costs, and to centers of non-residential economic activity. In discussing urban household behavior I shall divide commodities into two groups which are meant to be mutually exclusive and exhaustive, housing and all other commodities except transportation but including the money value of time not spent in work or transit, or simply leisure. Since I shall assume throughout that the prices of all commodities other than housing and transport are the same everywhere in the city, I can lump them into a composite commodity which I call dollars of other expenditure. By housing I mean the bundle of services yielded both by structures and also by the land or sites on which they are built. I emphasize that, in this monograph, by phrases such as consumption or production of housing and expenditures on housing I refer to the flow of services and the satisfactions they yield per unit of time from residential real estate, not to activities associated with newly constructed assets of this type. The reader should also note that in my framework the demand for residential land is treated as derived from the demand for housing rather than as a demand at the consumer level, as in other studies.[1] I do so because it seems likely to me that space and quality or land and structures are closely related commodities in consumption. Treating them as inputs into the production of housing is an analytically convenient and, I believe, empirically fruitful manner of handling their interrelatedness. In addition, this treatment is consistent with the more usual analysis of other economic activity such as agriculture. However, in Chapter 5 I shall consider some exceptions, particularly the possibility that, as income increases, the demand curve of the consumer for land shifts upward more rapidly than that for structures.

In line with my treatment of land and structures as inputs into the production of a commodity I call housing, by the price per unit of housing I mean the expenditure needed to obtain a composite bundle of services of land and structures. Again I refer to the price of a flow of services from housing, not the price of the asset, when I use the term housing price. Obviously, different parcels of residential real estate provide different intensities of flow of a large number of features of housing such as size, quality, and layout of rooms as well as location, to name only a few. Thus, when I speak of housing prices or the price of housing of given quality, I really mean an index of the prices of all those items one generally includes under the rubric housing. My usage of the term price of housing is perfectly analogous to the meaning more readily attached to the term price of food, namely the expenditure required to obtain a given "market basket" of food and related items. I realize, of course, that an index number problem

---

[1] For example, Lowden Wingo, Jr., *Transportation and Urban Land.*

exists, since there need not be a unique ratio of the prices of, say, space and quality at all locations within a city, but I shall generally ignore this problem. Note, too, that, in my language, a consumer's expenditure on the services of any particular dwelling is the product of the price per unit of housing and the number of units of housing the dwelling contains. Failure to realize this distinction as well as the distinction between the price of housing and the price of land can lead to considerable confusion.[2] While it would be very difficult to measure the price of housing as I have defined it, my analysis has implications for the behavior of other much more easily measured phenomena, such as population densities and expenditures for housing.

In my analysis, the behavior of individuals as consumers is limited to their consumption of housing and other commodities. Owners of houses or apartment units in which they reside are treated as both consumers of and producers of housing, and individual behavior under the latter heading is considered in Chapter 3. The distinction between income property and property for owner occupancy is pointless for most purposes, despite the fact that this distinction is frequently belabored in real estate textbooks and monographs. Now, of course, exemption from the federal income taxation of the income from owner-occupied housing and the federal mortgage insurance and guarantee programs have no doubt had important effects on urban housing markets. Where these have important effects for my purposes I shall try to note them. However, apart from favorable tax treatment and interest rates, I can think of no compelling reason why renters and owners need separate analytical treatment. Finally, I shall initially neglect differences among consumers in tastes for different kinds of housing and for location. But several effects of tastes and differences in them will be examined in various places throughout Part I.

Another set of assumptions of my analysis relates to transport costs incurred by consumers. I shall assume throughout that the costs per trip consist of a fixed and a variable part. Fixed costs would include time spent walking to a bus stop and waiting for a bus, parking charges, and bus fares where independent of distance traveled. Variable costs refer to the cost of time spent in transit as well as variable bus or train fares or the variable costs of automobile ownership and operation. If anything, traffic generally moves more rapidly at greater distances from the CBD; less time in transit

---

[2] For example, see the contribution of Duane F. Marble to William L. Garrison, et al., *Studies of Highway Development and Geographic Change*, chap. 8, where house values are confused with land values.

is thus spent per mile, and vehicles, up to a point, operate at more economical speeds with less stopping and starting. Therefore, I assume that the variable portion of transport costs increases at a non-increasing rate with distance from the CBD or any other center of activity.

Time costs are a major item of transport costs, and savings in time an important part of the benefits of investment in highways and transit facilities.[3] But little is known about the value consumers place upon the time they spend in urban travel, and attempts to measure this value have generally had to use data that are not readily available and rather expensive to collect. Clearly, time costs of a particular household are related to the wage rates earned by its workers, since additional work is an alternative foregone by time spent in travel, but need not be equal to the wage rate unless on balance there are no non-pecuniary advantages or disadvantages of time spent in transit. In what follows I shall simply assume that time costs are a function of the wage rate; also, I include travel time costs in trip costs and the money value of travel time in the income variable in the consumer's budget constraint. I will then suggest a way of measuring transport costs using census housing data.

In what follows I shall assume initially that the household makes a fixed number of trips to and from the CBD per unit of time, regardless of location or any other consideration. I can then express transport costs as a given function of location and the wage rate or income. I suspect that this is a reasonably good approximation since most CBD trips are work trips—witness the problem of rush-hour congestion in any major city. The number of work trips made is not likely to vary much over time or as among groups of workers within rather wide limits. However, later on in this chapter the assumption of a fixed number of CBD trips is relaxed, and the number of trips is taken as a variable to be optimized by households. I show that, while the analysis is considerably complicated, the assumption of a variable number of trips does not change my earlier conclusions materially. I also assume, initially, that transport costs to and from the CBD are the same in all directions. This enables me to specify location vis-à-vis the CBD with a single variable, distance. In Chapter 4, however, I consider the effects of differences in transport costs to the CBD that result from expressways and rapid transit facilities. As this analysis demonstrates, if one substitutes the more general term accessibility for distance, the initial analysis is formally unchanged. Therefore, the

---

[3] See William C. Pendleton, "The Value of Accessibility," chap. 1. The valuation of time is discussed more fully in Leon N. Moses and Harold F. Williamson, Jr., "Value of Time, Choice of Mode, and the Subsidy Issue in Urban Transportation."

assumption that transport costs are the same in all directions is not very restrictive.

There may be many nuclei or centers of economic activity, accessibility to which may be desirable for different households. However, I shall begin by assuming that only one such center exists, the CBD. The CBD is quite obviously the single most important employment and shopping center in the city, even though it has been declining in relative importance in recent years. Initially, I assume that all employment is concentrated in the CBD. Later in this chapter this assumption will be relaxed and the effects of non-concentrated local employment discussed. In Chapter 4 I consider the effects of concentrations of employment other than the CBD. With regard to retail and service centers, I initially assume that all purchases are made either locally or in the CBD. In the former case, no site is different from any other in terms of transportation costs for local shopping trips or any similar trips. In the case of the CBD, sites differ with respect to transport costs for non-work trips in the same manner as for work trips. Transport costs, as I have already defined them, are assumed to include the costs of non-work CBD trips. In Chapter 4 the existence of other retail and service centers, as well as special purpose centers such as universities or parks, is considered.

The Conditions of Household Equilibrium

As is typical in economic analyses of consumer behavior, I assume that the household acts in such a way as to maximize an ordinal utility function subject to a budget constraint. Under the assumptions discussed in the preceding section the utility function may be written $U = U(x, q)$, where q is consumption of housing and x is dollars of expenditure on all commodities except housing and transportation but including leisure. The budget constraint can be written as:

$$g = x + p(k)q + T(k, y) - y = 0.$$

Here p is the price per unit of housing, a function of location or distance from the CBD, k; T is the cost per trip, a function of location and income, y, multiplied by a given number of CBD trips for the household (which need not be the same for all households). Income could be broken down into non-wage and wage income, where the latter includes the money value of travel and leisure time. For simplicity, however, I prefer to use a single variable and let $T_y = 0$ for non-wage income and $T_y > 0$ for wage income, etc.

The necessary or first-order conditions for household equilibrium are found by equating the first partial derivatives of the Lagrangian function $L = U - \lambda g$ to zero.[4] These derivatives are:

$$\frac{\partial L}{\partial x} = U_x - \lambda = 0 \tag{1}$$

$$\frac{\partial L}{\partial q} = U_q - \lambda p = 0$$

$$\frac{\partial L}{\partial k} = -\lambda(q p_k + T_k) = 0$$

$$\frac{\partial L}{\partial \lambda} = y - \{x + p(k)q + T(k, y)\} = 0$$

The last of equations (1), of course, merely expresses the condition that the consumer's expenditure on everything must exhaust his income. The first two of equations (1) together imply the usual condition

$$U_x = \frac{U_q}{p(k)}, \tag{2}$$

which states that, irrespective of location, the household consumes housing and other commodities in such relative amounts that the marginal utility per dollar spent is the same for all commodities. Location influences the household's consumption only through its effects on the price of housing, since I am provisionally neglecting the effects of tastes and preferences.

The third of equations (1) implies

$$-q p_k = T_k \quad \text{or} \quad p_k = -\frac{1}{q} T_k < 0. \tag{3}$$

This equation states that in the equilibrium location, the household's net savings on the purchase of a given quantity of housing and transport costs which would result from a very short move—either toward or away from the CBD—would be equal to zero. Stated differently, the household is unable to increase its real income by any change of location. The term $-q p_k$ is the reduction in expenditure necessary to purchase a given quantity of housing that results from moving a unit distance away from the market; the term T_k, of course, is the increase in transport costs occasioned by such a move. Since by assumption $T_k > 0$, equation (3) can be

---

[4] Throughout this monograph I assume that the various functional relationships possess the necessary differentiability properties to permit the differentiation I perform.

satisfied only if the price of housing declines with distance from the CBD, or $p_k < 0$. If the price of housing were the same everywhere but the marginal costs of transport increased with distance, any move toward the CBD would increase the real income of any household, and everybody would try to live as close to the center as possible. Such a situation is, of course, absurd, and the market would not sustain it. Rather, the price of housing in the vicinity of the CBD would be bid up, while housing prices in more distant locations would be bid down.[5]

One other property of the necessary conditions of consumer equilibrium is worth noting at this point. Equation (3) may also be written as

$$(pq)\left(-\frac{p_k}{p}\right) = T_k, \tag{3'}$$

or, in words, the household's monthly expenditure on housing multiplied by the relative change in housing prices per unit distance in absolute value is equal to the monthly marginal costs of transport. It is relatively simple to obtain information on expenditures for housing from the housing census or other sources. Furthermore, in Chapter 3 I will show how the relative change in housing prices can be inferred from data on variations in the output of housing per unit of land, also using housing census data. Thus, observation of consumer location choices along with other data permits measurement of the valuation of transport costs by consumers.

The nature of household equilibrium in urban space can be illustrated as in Figure 1. Figure 1a shows a usual indifference curve, the coordinate axes being consumption of housing and x, which is everything except housing and transportation. The budget line, B_1, for a household located at k intersects the x-axis not at y but at $(y - T(k))$. At the location k, the bundle (q_1, x_1) maximizes utility, for at this point the slope of the budget line is equal to the slope of the indifference curve I_1. Now, consider the effect of moving a very small distance farther from the CBD. As the household does so, the origin of the budget line on the x-axis shifts downward by the amount of the increased transport costs and the budget line becomes

---

[5] In discussing the influence of access, Hoover states that: "Of course, we cannot expect access to appear all by itself as a determinant of location. If access to work were the sole factor operating, everyone would live where he worked and commuting time would be zero." Edgar M. Hoover and Raymond Vernon, *Anatomy of a Metropolis*, p. 143. Interpreted quite literally, of course, the statement is correct. But access to work plus utility maximization is sufficient to account for the fact that not everyone lives where he works. While factors such as age of buildings and neighborhoods, desires for spacious living, etc., which Hoover discusses so ably, might be important in explaining observed consumer location patterns, they are not logically necessary. I will consider these other factors in Chapter 5, below.

flatter, reflecting the fall in the price of housing. If the new budget line is, say, B_3, the consumer is at a location such as k_1 in Figure 1b; here the savings in expenditure necessary to purchase the quantity of housing, q_1, consumed at the initial location exceed the increase in transport costs. Hence, the consumer can increase his real income by making the move. If, however, the consumer is initially at his optimal location, which is k_2 in

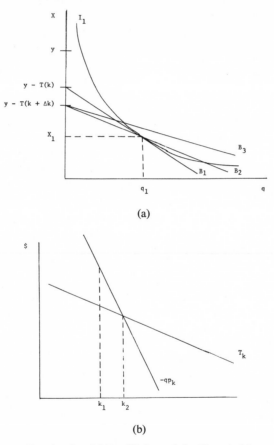

(a)

(b)

FIG. 1.—Spatial Equilibrium of the Household

Figure 1b, the new budget line is B_2 in Figure 1a, which passes through the point (q_1, x_1). Thus, the savings in housing expenditure are exactly equal to the increased transport costs, and the move leaves the real income of the consumer unchanged.

In order that the equilibrium location described above not be an unstable one, the net savings on the quantity of housing purchased and on transportation must not increase with a move a short distance farther from the CBD. Differentiating equation (3),

$$-qp_{kk} - p_k \frac{\partial q}{\partial k} - T_{kk} \leq 0. \tag{4}$$

Since, as was demonstrated in the paragraph above, in the neighborhood of the household's equilibrium location its real income is constant with a small change in location, the change in housing consumption with such a move is given by the household's real-income compensated housing demand curve. Where $(\partial q/\partial p)_c$ is the slope of this demand curve,

$$\frac{\partial q}{\partial k} = \left(\frac{\partial q}{\partial p}\right)_c p_k.$$

Thus, upon substituting in (4),

$$p_{kk} \geq -\frac{1}{q}\left\{\left(\frac{\partial q}{\partial p}\right)_c p_k{}^2 + T_{kk}\right\} > 0, \tag{5}$$

so long as the compensated demand curve for housing is not perfectly inelastic.[6] On the assumptions I have made, then, in order that the household's equilibrium not be an unstable one, housing prices must not decrease at a numerically increasing rate with distance from the CBD. The inequality (4) can also be written as

$$E_{q,p;c}\left(\frac{p_k}{p}\right) + \left(\frac{p_{kk}}{p_k} - \frac{T_{kk}}{T_k}\right) \leq 0, \tag{6}$$

where $E_{q,p;c}$ is the real-income compensated price elasticity of housing demand. I shall return to the interpretation of (6) later in Chapter 4. In terms of Figure 1*b*, (4) states that the curve $-qp_k$ must cut the curve T_k from above, in which case the household possesses a unique best location, or that the two curves must coincide. In the latter case the household's equilibrium is a neutral one, and it would be indifferent to any locations about which the two curves in Figure 1*b* coincide. Alternatively, if the curve $-qp_k$ cuts the curve T_k from below in Figure 1*b*, a move farther from the market increases real income and the household would not remain at k_2. If there is a single point of intersection but $-qp_k$ increases more

---

[6] In my earlier paper, "The Spatial Structure of the Housing Market," p. 208, I suggested that a negative exponential price-distance function is the simplest one analytically which satisfies the first- and second-order conditions of locational equilibrium. In Chapter 4, below, I shall demonstrate that the negative exponential function is the only kind of function which will satisfy them under certain rather simple conditions.

rapidly than T_k, then the equilibrium location is at the outer edge of the city—if indeed the city would have an outer edge under these conditions. Since this clearly cannot be the case for all consumers under any empirically sensible conditions, I shall assume in what follows that (4) holds.

I now wish to examine the locational changes which result from a displacement of the initial equilibrium. Such displacements can result from changes in any of the conditions taken as given by any particular household: its income, transport costs, and the price of housing in various locations. However, many different kinds of changes in these factors are possible. Income, for example, may increase either because the wage rate earned by a working member of the household has increased or because of an increase in its non-wage income. In the former case, both T_y and T_{ky} are positive, while in the latter they both are zero. With an increase in either source of income, the household's consumption of housing at the old equilibrium location changes by an amount $(\partial q/\partial y)\, dy_R$, where dy_R is the change in the household's real income. If the increase in income results from an increase in the money wage rate earned by one of its members in the CBD, the opportunity cost of time spent in travel by this household member increases even if the household remains at its old location. Hence, the household's real income rises only by

$$dy_R = (1 - T_y)\, dy. \tag{7}$$

Equation (7) is illustrated in Figure 2*a*, in which the increase in real income is the difference in the ordinates of the budget lines B_1 and B_2. The first of these is that appropriate to the initial equilibrium, while the second shows the budget line facing the household if it remains at the old equilibrium location following the increase in its income. However, with a rise in its income and thus its housing consumption, the household's old location need not remain its equilibrium one. If not, a shift in location results, and this shift induces a change in the price of housing services the household pays. This last point is also illustrated by Figure 2*a*, where the budget line appropriate to the new equilibrium location is B_3. Thus, in contrast to the well-known income effect of a change in the money price of a commodity, when one considers the locational equilibrium of the household there is a price effect of a change in income.

The location and housing consumption of households is also influenced by the functions $p(k)$ and $T(k, y)$. Both may change either because of a change in their level or in their slope at any given distance, k. Thus, where

$$p(k) = p_0 + \int_0^k p_v \, dv,$$

and p_0 is the level parameter of housing prices or the price of housing services when extrapolated to the city center,

$$dp = dp_0 + \int_0^k dp_v \, dv + p_k \, dk, \tag{8}$$

$$= \Gamma + p_k \, dk.$$

In (8) Γ is the change in the price of housing services at the old location. Such a change has, of course, both an income effect and a substitution

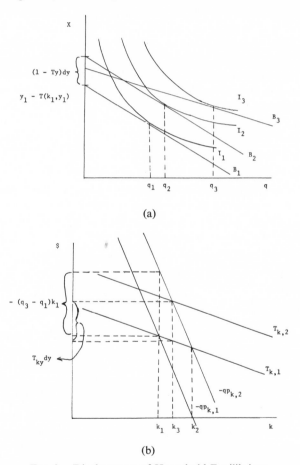

(a)

(b)

Fig. 2.—Displacement of Household Equilibrium

effect, as is well known from the general theory of consumer demand. By changing the quantity of housing services consumed, Γ would also induce a change in the household's location. The change in location, in turn, would induce a further change in p, equal to $p_k \, dk$ in (8). Furthermore, changes in the slope of the price-distance function may be either exogenous or induced by changes in location; that is,

$$dp_k = \gamma + p_{kk}\, dk. \tag{9}$$

In the former case, denoted by γ in (9), a change in slope of the price-distance function has a direct effect upon the household's equilibrium location and may induce a change in housing consumption.

The situation is quite similar when considering the effects of changes in transport costs. Let

$$T(k, y) = T_0 + \int_0^k T_v\, dv,$$

where T_0 refers to the fixed component of transport costs and the second term in the right member to the variable component. Then, holding money income constant,

$$dT = dT_0 + \int_0^k dT_v\, dv + T_k\, dk \tag{10}$$
$$= \Delta + T_k\, dk.$$

The term Δ in (10) tends to reduce the real income of the household and thus its consumption of housing services. For this reason a change in location is induced, which leads to a further change in the transport costs incurred by the household denoted by the term $T_k\, dk$ in (10). Similarly, the change in the marginal costs of transport may be written as

$$dT_k = \delta + T_{kk}\, dk + T_{ky}\, dy. \tag{11}$$

An exogenous change, δ, in T_k leads directly to a change in location and induces a change in housing consumption.

To determine the effects of a change in any one of the factors just described on the household's location and consumption of housing, one could differentiate the system of equations (1) and solve as is usually done in the analysis of consumer demand. Armed with the results of the conventional demand analysis, however, it is simpler to differentiate only the third of equations (1), the condition of locational equilibrium, and then to make the appropriate substitution for the change in the consumption of housing. In differential form the condition of locational equilibrium becomes

$$-q\, dp_k - p_k\, dq - dT_k = 0, \tag{12}$$

where

$$dq = \frac{\partial q}{\partial y}\, dy_R + \left(\frac{\partial q}{\partial p}\right)_c dp.$$

Making the appropriate substitutions already described in equations (7) through (11), one can then determine *dk* and *dq* rather easily. Because equation (3) holds for all households under all conditions, (12) must hold between different times and given conditions for the same household or between different households facing different given conditions at a given time. Everything said above about the effects of changes in the given conditions to a particular household, of course, applies equally to differences in these given conditions among households. In the following two sections I shall develop some of the implications of equation (12) which are important for my empirical analyses in Part II.

The Effects of Income Differences on Location

First I want to inquire into the effects of differences in the money income of households on their equilibrium locations and their consumption of housing. For simplicity let us consider two households which are identical in all respects except that one has a larger money income than the other. Suppose tentatively, however, that both are located the same distance from the CBD. So long as the higher-income household remains at this common location, its consumption of housing exceeds that of the lower-income household by an amount which depends upon the shift in their common demand curves for housing per dollar change in real income multiplied by the difference in their real incomes. The difference in their real incomes is given by (7). If, now, a change in location is permitted, and one assumes that the initial common location is the equilibrium one for the lower-income household, the higher-income one will move if the difference in the housing expenditures of the two households is not exactly equal to the difference in the marginal costs of transport to them. Under the assumptions made at the start of this paragraph, of course, such differences can occur only because of differences in the valuation of travel time by the two households. If the higher-income household changes its location, the price per unit that it pays for housing changes. Therefore, the difference in housing consumption, *dq* in (12), is

$$dq = \frac{\partial q}{\partial y} (1 - T_y) \, dy + \left(\frac{\partial q}{\partial p}\right)_c p_k \, dk \qquad (13)$$

upon substituting (7). If, in addition to (13), equations (9) and (11) are substituted into (12), upon rearranging, one has

$$\left\{ -q p_{kk} - \left(\frac{\partial q}{\partial p}\right)_c p_k{}^2 - T_{kk} \right\} dk = \left\{ p_k \frac{\partial q}{\partial y} (1 - T_y) + T_{ky} \right\} dy.$$

This last is more understandable if written in elasticity form. With a little simple manipulation it becomes

$$- \left\{ E_{q,p;C} \left(\frac{p_k}{p} \right) + \left(\frac{p_{kk}}{p_k} - \frac{T_{kk}}{T_k} \right) \right\} dk \qquad (14)$$

$$= \{ E_{q,y;R} (1 - \rho_T E_{T,y}) - E_{T_k,y} \} \, dy^*,$$

where asterisks mean the natural logarithm of the variable so designated, $E_{q,y;R}$ is the real income elasticity of demand, ρ_T the proportion of income as I have defined it which is spend on travel, and $E_{T,y}$ and $E_{T_k,y}$ are the elasticities of total and marginal transport costs, respectively, with respect to money income.

The meaning of equation (14) becomes more clear upon referring to Figures 2a and 2b. The initial equilibrium of the lower-income household is characterized by a rate of housing consumption q_1 in Figure 2a and location k_1 in Figure 2b. So long as the higher-income household's location is also assumed to be at k_1, its budget line, B_2, is parallel to B_1. The quantity of housing consumed by the higher-income household is q_2 in Figure 2a. But, because of the difference in housing consumption, the condition of locational equilibrium may not be satisfied for the higher income household. In Figure 2b, the curve $-qp_k$ for the higher-income household would lie above that for the lower-income one by an amount $-(q_2 - q_1)p_k$ as measured along the vertical or dollar axis so long as both are at k_1. On account of its greater housing consumption alone—empirically there is no doubt about the sign of the income elasticity of housing demand—the higher-income household could increase its well-being by seeking out a location more distant from the CBD.[7]

If the difference in income is wholly due to non-wage income or in the unlikely event that the elasticity of the marginal cost of transport with respect to the wage rate is zero, there is no more to the story. For the higher-income household the equilibrium location is given by the intersection of the curves $-qp_{k,2}$ and $T_{k,1}$, which is k_2 in Figure 2b. As the household moves to the location k_2 the appropriate budget line is now B_3 in Figure 2a. B_3 cuts the x-axis at a point below that of B_2 because of the increase in transport costs incurred due to the greater distance traveled. But the flatter slope of B_3, resulting from the fall in the price of housing which accompanies the move from k_1 to k_2, more than compensates for the increased transport costs. The higher-income household, therefore, moves to

---

[7] This would seem to be the essence of the argument given by Alonso, "A Theory of the Urban Land Market," p. 156, which originally suggested this point to me. Note, however, that there is more to the argument. I failed to spell this out in my "Spatial Structure of the Housing Market," p. 208.

the indifference curve I_3 by changing its location and in final equilibrium consumes the quantity of housing q_3. The movement from q_2 to q_3 in Figure 2*a*, which accompanies the change in equilibrium location, is partly what might be termed a price-effect of the income difference and partly the result of the increased real income which results from the move to k_2. With the move to k_2 the curve $-qp_k$ for the higher income household shifts upward to the position shown in Figure 2*b*.

The argument is essentially identical if we compare two consumers, I and II, with different preferences for housing versus other consumption. Let consumer I consume q_1 at k_1 and II consume q_2 because of differences in their indifference curves. If, then, k_1 is I's equilibrium location, the relevant $-qp_k$ curve for II in Figure 2*b* is $-qp_{k,2}$. Hence, II's best location is at a greater distance from the CBD than I's, and II consumes more housing than I. Thus, households with stronger preferences for housing will tend to live at greater distances from the CBD. However, little can be said about the empirical importance of this phenomenon unless something is known about the distribution of preferences for housing vis-à-vis other consumption among households.

If the difference in money incomes occurs because of a difference in money wage rates, and if this difference affects the marginal cost of transport because of a difference in the valuation of travel time by the two households, the analysis is more complicated. The effect of a difference in the marginal cost of transport is shown as a shift in the T_k curve in Figure 2*b* from $T_{k,1}$ to $T_{k,2}$ for the higher-income household. An upward shift in the T_k curve tends to counteract the effect of increased housing consumption on the household's location. In fact, if the elasticity of the marginal costs of transport with respect to the wage rate were large enough relative to the real income elasticity of demand for housing, the higher-income household's equilibrium distance from the CBD might even be less than k_1. On empirical grounds, however, I believe the latter would be unlikely. Work by Margaret G. Reid and by me suggests that the income elasticity of housing demand is at least equal to one and may be as large as two.[8] Since time costs are generally only a fraction of the total and marginal costs of transport, the elasticities of total and marginal transport costs with respect to the wage rate would be less than one if the money value of travel time were equal to the wage rate. The term $(1 - \rho_T E_{T,y})$ by which $E_{q,y;R}$ in (14) is multiplied is likely to be close to one. If the consumer's wage rate is $2 per hour, then his income, which includes the value of his travel and leisure time, is $48 per day plus his non-wage income if it is assumed that the money value of travel and leisure time is equal to the wage rate. If, further,

---

[8] See her *Housing and Income* and my "The Demand for Non-Farm Housing."

he spends one hour per day in travel and incurs $1 non-time costs in travel per day, then $\rho_T \leq \$3/48 \simeq 0.06$. The effects of increased housing consumption on location, then, might conceivably be just about offset by increased transport costs. If not, it would seem most likely that the former outweighs the latter in establishing the consumer's new equilibrium location. Therefore, in Figure 2*b* I show the shift in T_k to be smaller than that of $-qp_k$ so that the equilibrium location for the higher-income household is at $k_3 \geq k_1$. Of course, as in the case discussed earlier, the household consumes a larger quantity of housing, q_3, at its new equilibrium location than at its old one.[9]

The coefficient of dy^* in equation (14) is the difference in the net savings on housing expenditure and transport cost as between the two households when evaluated at a given location. For the reasons discussed in the preceding three paragraphs, dy^*'s coefficient is likely to be non-negative. The coefficient of dk in (14) is the change in the net savings on the purchase of housing and transport cost incurred at the given location. As was argued in connection with (4) in the preceding section, for each household to have a uniquely determined location this coefficient must be negative. Assuming the latter to be the case, one can write

$$\frac{\partial k}{\partial y^*} = -\frac{\{E_{q,y;R}(1 - \rho_T E_{T,y}) - E_{T_k,y}\}}{\left\{E_{q,p;C}\left(\dfrac{p_k}{p}\right) + \left(\dfrac{p_{kk}}{p_k} - \dfrac{T_{kk}}{T_k}\right)\right\}} \geq 0. \tag{15}$$

The numerator of (15) gives the extent of the shift in the $-qp_k$ curve in relation to that of T_k in Figure 2*b*, which results from an income change of 1 percent. The denominator indicates the amount by which the difference between the ordinates of these curves diminishes per unit distance. Their ratio, then, is merely the difference in distance accompanying a difference in income of 1 percent. Equation (15) also demonstrates the point shown by Figure 2*b*, namely that the effect on location of an income difference depends upon its relative effects upon housing consumption and upon transport costs.

The relation of income to the optimal household location is important largely because of its implications for the per household consumption of housing in different parts of the city at a given time. Clearly, income is one of the most important determinants of housing consumption, if not the most important. The relation of housing consumption to income implied

---

[9] If the shift in T_k were greater than that of $-qp_k$, the budget line B_3 would intersect the x-axis at a point above the intersection of B_2, and B_3 would be steeper than B_2. Movement to the new equilibrium location closer to the CBD would still enable the household to reach a higher indifference curve than I_2, but in this case q_3 is less than q_2.

by my model and illustrated in Figure 2 can be readily evaluated. When written in elasticity form, equation (13) becomes

$$dq^* = E_{q,y;R}(1 - \rho_T E_{T,y})\,dy^* + E_{q,p;C}\left(\frac{p_k}{p}\right)dk. \tag{16}$$

If the coefficient of dy^* in (14) is equal to zero, there is, of course, no systematic tendency for the location of households by income level to differ and, hence, no difference in the consumption of housing attributable to income differences at different distances from the CBD. But if dy^*'s coefficient is positive, one can solve (14) for dy^* in terms of dk. Substituting the resulting expression for dy^* in (16) and rearranging, one finds

$$\frac{\partial q^*}{\partial k} = -\left\{\left(\frac{p_{kk}}{p_k} - \frac{T_{kk}}{T_k}\right)E_{q,y;R}(1 - \rho_T E_{T,y}) + E_{T_k,y}E_{q:p;C}\left(\frac{p_k}{p}\right)\right\}$$

$$\div \{E_{q,y;R}(1 - \rho_T E_{T,y}) - E_{T_k,y}\}.$$

Since available data more readily permit comparing housing expenditures, rather than consumption, in different locations,

$$\frac{\partial(pq)^*}{\partial k} = \frac{\partial p^*}{\partial k} + \frac{\partial q^*}{\partial k},$$

or

$$\frac{\partial(pq)^*}{\partial k} = \left\{\left(\frac{p_k}{p} - \frac{p_{kk}}{p_k} + \frac{T_{kk}}{T_k}\right)E_{q,y;R}(1 - \rho_T E_{T,y})\right.$$

$$\left. - (1 + E_{q,p;C})E_{T_k,y}\left(\frac{p_k}{p}\right)\right\} \div \{E_{q,y;R}(1 - \rho_T E_{T,y}) - E_{T_k,y}\}.$$

$$\tag{17}$$

I will discuss equation (17) further in Chapter 4, below.

The relation of income to optimal location is important also for analyzing changes in the equilibrium housing price-distance function. Consider the effects of a general increase in the incomes of the residents of a particular city. The increase in incomes will lead to an increase in housing consumption on the part of all households. Provided that the effects of this increased housing consumption outweigh the effects of increased transport costs, the equilibrium distance from the CBD will increase for all households if their initial equilibrium was a uniquely determined one. Put differently, the demand for housing tends to increase at locations more distant from the CBD relative to that in the more central locations. Therefore, housing prices tend to rise in the more distant locations relative to those closer to the CBD and the rate of decrease in housing prices with distance, p_k, tends to decline numerically. Even if the initial equilibrium was a neutral one, equation (3) still implies that the price gradient must decline numerically if the rise in income increases housing expenditures relative to marginal transport costs. The implication, then, is that the price gradient tends to vary inversely with the income level of the city so long as the effect of income on housing consumption exceeds that on transport costs.

THE EFFECTS OF HOUSING PRICE AND TRANSPORTATION COST ON THE EQUILIBRIUM LOCATION

The equilibrium location for a household and the price gradient in my model are affected by the level of housing prices in the city and by transportation costs as well as by income. As discussed earlier, a change in either housing prices or transport costs may have an income effect on the quantity of housing consumed and on equilibrium location similar to the usual income effect as a price change, and a change in housing prices has a substitution effect as well. Finally, a change in the price gradient on the marginal costs of transport will affect the equilibrium location of the household and, hence, indirectly its consumption of housing. While it would be relatively easy to derive a relation showing the change in q resulting from a change in either p or T, for the purposes of this study the effects on equilibrium location and the price gradient are much more important. In this section, therefore, I shall concentrate on the latter effects.

Let us first consider the effects on the equilibrium household location which results from a rise in the level of housing prices. Many factors might affect the price per unit of housing services; among these the most important are construction costs, interest rates, and property taxes. An increase in any one of these will generally increase the relative price of housing services. To be more explicit, let me suppose that p_0 changes but that p_k is provisionally held constant everywhere. Equation (12) then implies that

$$-q p_{kk}\, dk \;-\; \left\{ \frac{\partial q}{\partial y}\,(-q\, dp_0) \;+\; \left(\frac{\partial q}{\partial p}\right)_c (dp_0 + p_k\, dk) \right\} \;-\; T_{kk}\, dk = 0.$$

Upon rearranging and converting to elasticity form, the assumption of a uniquely determined location implies

$$\frac{\partial k}{\partial p_0{}^*} = -\left(\frac{p_0}{p}\right)\{E_{q,p;C} - \rho_q E_{q,y;R}\} \div \left\{ E_{q,p;C}\left(\frac{p_k}{p}\right) + \left(\frac{p_{kk}}{p_k} - \frac{T_{kk}}{T_k}\right)\right\} \le 0,$$

(18)

where $\rho_q = pq/y$ is the proportion of income spent on housing.

Equation (18) implies that with a rise in the level of the price-distance function, holding its slope everywhere constant, the equilibrium distance of the consumer from the CBD declines. The reasons for this could be illustrated on a figure similar to Figure 2 (the reader can readily construct one for himself). The numerator of (18) is the usual elasticity of the demand for housing holding money income constant, which consists of a substitution effect, $E_{q,p;C}$, and an income effect, $\rho_q E_{q,y;R}$, of the price change. (If real income rather than money income is held constant, of course, the second term in the numerator vanishes.) This numerator gives the change in the household's consumption of housing that results from the price change at the old equilibrium location. Because of the decline in the consumption of housing, the savings on housing expenditure per unit change in distance curve, $-qp_k$, shifts downward and to the left. As in equation (15), the denominator of (18) gives the change in the difference of the ordinates of the $-qp_k$ and T_k curves, or the change in the net savings on housing and transport costs, per unit change in distance. Hence, their ratio gives the number of miles, say, by which location must change to make the net savings on housing and transport costs again equal to zero.

Up to this point I have been assuming that the slope of the price-distance function remains constant. But, of course, as with the effects of a change in income, the change in equilibrium locations which results from a change in the level of housing prices will tend to change the price gradient. As all households attempt to move closer to the CBD following a rise in level of housing prices, the demand for housing close to the CBD rises relative to that in more distant locations. Hence, housing prices tend to rise relatively more in the vicinity of the CBD as compared with the edges of the city, and the price gradient becomes numerically greater. I therefore conclude that price gradients in absolute terms will be directly related to the level of housing prices, and hence to construction costs, interest rates, and property taxes. In relative terms, however, the price gradient may increase, remain unchanged, or decrease depending upon whether the price elasticity of housing demand is algebraically less than, equal to, or greater than minus one. As equation (3') shows, the price gradient in relative terms varies inversely as expenditures on housing. The latter, in turn, will decline or increase with a price increase depending upon whether housing demand is elastic or inelastic.

The effects of changes in transport costs on the equilibrium location of households are similar to those of housing price changes. As with a price change, one must distinguish between level and slope effects or, more conveniently, changes in fixed components of transport costs on the one hand and changes in marginal transport costs on the other. First, consider the effects of a change in the fixed component of transport costs, T_0. A change in T_0 affects only Δ in equation (10) and its only effect on location is an income effect similar to that of a change in non-wage income. Thus,

$$\frac{\partial k}{\partial T_0^*} = \rho_{T_0} E_{q,y;R} \div \left\{ E_{q,p;C} \left(\frac{p_k}{p}\right) + \left(\frac{p_{kk}}{p} - \frac{T_{kk}}{T_k}\right) \right\} \leq 0, \qquad (19)$$

where ρ_{T_0} is the ratio of fixed transport costs to income. Thus, like an increase in the level of housing prices, an increase in the fixed costs of transport reduces the quantity of housing consumed at the old equilibrium location and, hence, induces a move toward the city center.

Contrast the above with an exogenous change in the marginal cost of transport. An increase in the marginal cost of transport increases the total cost incurred in living at any given location, Δ in equation (10), and thus has an income effect on housing consumption and location similar to a change in the fixed component of transport costs. However, a change in the marginal costs of transport also has a direct effect on location through its effect on the net savings on housing and transport costs. In terms of Figure 1*b*, an increase in T_k causes the $-qp_k$ curve to shift downward and to the left and the T_k curve to shift upward and to the right. Each of these shifts means that the new equilibrium location is closer to the city center. Now, the precise location change for any household depends upon the pattern of change in the marginal costs of transport at all distances up to its equilibrium location, as the presence of the term Δ in the above indicates. To carry the evaluation further, one must make some explicit assumption about this pattern of change. Since empirical evidence I will mention in Chapter 4 indicates that a constant marginal cost per unit distance is a good empirical approximation to the structure of transport costs, at least for auto transport, I will assume that $T = T_0 + kT_k$ or $\Delta = k \, dT_k$ (hence, $T_{kk} = 0$). Making these substitutions one finds

$$\frac{\partial k}{\partial T_k^*} = \{\rho_{T_k} E_{q,y;R} + 1\} \div \left\{ E_{q,p;C} \left(\frac{p_k}{p}\right) + \left(\frac{p_{kk}}{p_k}\right) \right\} \leq 0, \qquad (20)$$

where $\rho_{T_k} = kT_k/y$ is the relative importance of variable transport costs in the consumer's expenditures. Since I have already argued that the income elasticity of housing demand is of the order of 1 to 2 and the relative importance of transport costs is small, say of the order of 0.1, the direct effects on location are likely to be much more important than the income effects. (For the same reason, (20) is likely to be numerically large compared to (19).) In any event, an increase in either the fixed or the marginal costs of transport decreases the equilibrium distance from the CBD for any household, given the old price-distance function. The overall effects of an increase in transport costs are thus similar to those of a rise in the level of housing prices.

Some Modifications of the Initial Model

So far in my discussion I have stuck closely to the original assumptions detailed in the first section of this chapter. I now consider some modifications of these assumptions which are most appropriately considered under the heading of consumer behavior. These are the assumption of a fixed number of CBD trips per household, the effect of preferences for location, and the effects of uniformly distributed local employment. Other modifications of my initial assumptions will be considered where most appropriate to the subject matter of following chapters.

Since my analysis takes the location of employment centers as given, the assumption of a fixed number of CBD trips is probably not a bad one. Work trips are quantitatively by far the most important type of trip, and these are unlikely to vary within rather wide limits for CBD workers. Of course, the average number of days worked per week might conceivably decline with increasing incomes and an accompanying increase in the average age of entry into the labor force, decrease in retirement age, and decrease in average number of days worked per worker. While such changes might be important for comparing cities in 1900 with those today, or cities in the United States today with those in India, I would expect that differences in the number of work trips would generally be small over the range of income variation which is appropriate for most problems. The aggregate number of CBD work trips might also respond to changes in the cost per trip through a change in importance of the CBD relative to other employment centers, but I am generally ruling considerations such as the latter out of my analysis, and indeed, very little is known empirically about the strategic factors influencing the location of employment centers.

Non-work CBD trips are for the purchase of commodities, especially for goods and services such as specialized items of apparel or entertainment. The principal reason why such commodities are available only in the CBD is that they are infrequently purchased and, hence, need a large market area such as the whole city to support their production and sale. By their very nature, therefore, one would expect that such trips would be relatively few. Little is known empirically about the demand elasticities for non-work CBD trips. But since the demand for such trips is derived from the demand for commodities purchased in the CBD, some inferences might be drawn about the probable magnitudes of these elasticities on a priori grounds.[10]

Goods and services purchased in the CBD, whether Brooks Brothers clothing, meals at a French restaurant, or night club performances by

---

[10] See Walter Y. Oi and Paul W. Shuldiner, *An Analysis of Urban Travel Demands*, chap. 2, for a fuller discussion.

Alan Sherman, are predominantly what are usually considered luxury goods and have relatively high income elasticities of demand. The forces influencing the price elasticity of derived demand for a productive factor such as transport for the purchases of CBD goods and services were analyzed by Marshall with later elaboration by Hicks.[11] They are: the elasticity of demand for the final product, the elasticity of supply of other factors, the ease of substitution in production, and the relative importance of the factor. Since these goods and services are frequently unavailable elsewhere in the city they probably have few close substitutes, although to a very real extent ready-made clothing is a substitute for custom-made and the Johnny Carson show for an evening at the Hungry i. It is thus difficult to judge the price elasticity of demand for the final product on a priori grounds. The appropriate elasticity of substitution in production is probably large, since a single trip can be made for the purchase of any number of products. Since substitution in production is easy, the relatively small cost of transportation in relation to the price of the final product probably makes for an elastic demand for non-work CBD trips. On balance, then, the price elasticity of non-work CBD trip demand as well as the income elasticity may be fairly high. But since non-work CBD trips are relatively small, their demand elasticities probably do not contribute much to the total.

Interesting as such speculations are, the really important consideration is the effect that allowing the number of trips to vary has on the analytical convenience and predictive content of the model. If the number of trips, t, becomes a choice-variable, it must be introduced as an argument of the household's utility function; thus, the latter becomes $U = U(x, q, t)$. Likewise, instead of transport cost, the budget constraint, g, now contains a term which is the product of the number of trips and the cost per trip, $c = c(k, y)$, which depends upon distance traveled and income. Maximizing U subject to g yields the revised first-order conditions:

$$\frac{\partial L}{\partial x} = U_x - \lambda = 0 \tag{21}$$

$$\frac{\partial L}{\partial q} = U_q - \lambda p = 0$$

$$\frac{\partial L}{\partial t} = U_t - \lambda c = 0$$

$$\frac{\partial L}{\partial k} = -\lambda\{qp_k + tc_k\} = 0$$

$$\frac{\partial L}{\partial \lambda} = y - \{x + p(k)q + c(k, y)t\} = 0.$$

---

[11] Alfred Marshall, *Principles of Economics*, 8th. ed., pp. 382–87 and mathematical Appendix, note 15, p. 853, and John R. Hicks, *The Theory of Wages*, appendix, pp. 241–46.

The first two of these, of course, are identical with those established earlier, and the last two are only slightly different. The first three of (21) taken together imply

$$U_x = \frac{U_q}{p} = \frac{U_t}{c},$$

or again, that expenditures on housing, CBD transportation, and everything else are so adjusted by the consumer that the marginal utility per dollar spent is the same on all. The fourth of equations (21) requires still that the net savings on housing and transport expenditure, where both q and t are optimal for the particular location, be equal to zero or,

$$p_k = -\left(\frac{t}{q}\right)c_k < 0 \quad \text{for} \quad c_k > 0, \tag{22}$$

or

$$(pq)\left(-\frac{p_k}{p}\right) = tc_k.$$

Finally, by differentiating (22) one finds the following sufficient condition for stability of locational equilibrium

$$p_{kk} \geq -\frac{1}{q}\left\{p_k\left(\frac{\partial q}{\partial k}\right)_c + c_k\left(\frac{\partial t}{\partial k}\right)_c + tc_{kk}\right\}. \tag{23}$$

Provided only that the partial of housing consumption with respect to distance in (23) is positive and that of the number of trips is negative, (23) implies that $p_{kk} \geq 0$ as before. That these restrictions should hold seems reasonable if housing price declines and trip cost increases with distance. So far, therefore, permitting a variable number of trips makes little difference in the implications of the model or in my ability to handle it.

However, when one turns to considering the effects of changes in the assumed given conditions on the model's endogenous variables, the analysis becomes considerably more complex. This complexity can be readily illustrated by considering the effect of income differences on optimal household location. In addition to those features of the problem already considered earlier, with an increase in income the household's demand for CBD trips at the old equilibrium location probably increases because of a positive real income elasticity. This increase by itself would undoubtedly lead the household to seek out a location closer to the CBD. However, the rise in income, if due to an increase in wage rates, leads to an increase in the valuation of travel time and, hence, to an increase in trip costs; the latter by itself implies a reduction in number of trips and a new equilibrium location further from the CBD. These and other less obvious effects can be shown by deriving a relation similar to equation (15), though with even more false steps and tedious manipulation; it is

$$
\frac{\partial k}{\partial y^*} = -\{(E_{q,y;R} - E_{t,y;R})(1 - \rho_t E_{c,y})
$$

$$
+ (E_{q,c;C} - E_{t,c;C})\, E_{c,y} - E_{c_k,y}\}
$$

$$
\div \left\{ (E_{q,p;C} - E_{t,p;C})\left(\frac{p_k}{p}\right) + (E_{q,c;C} - E_{t,c;C})\left(\frac{c_k}{c}\right) \right.
$$

$$
\left. + \left(\frac{p_{kk}}{p_k} - \frac{c_{kk}}{c_k}\right)\right\}. \tag{24}
$$

In addition to the elasticities in (15), equation (24) contains the real income elasticity of CBD-trip demand, $E_{t,y;R}$, the compensated own price elasticity $E_{t,c;C}$, as well as the compensated cross-partial elasticities of trip demand in relation to housing price, $E_{t,p;C}$, and of housing consumption in relation to trip cost, or $E_{q,c;C}$. And, like (15), equation (24) implies that the equilibrium distance from the CBD may either increase, decrease, or remain unchanged depending upon the magnitudes of the relevant elasticities. Hence, dropping the assumption of a fixed number of CBD trips complicates the analysis considerably without changing its conclusions for my purposes.[12] Therefore, in what follows I shall return to my initial assumption of a fixed number of CBD trips per household unless specific notice is given to the contrary.

Matters become even worse when my assumption of no locational preferences is modified. When this assumption is dropped, the utility function of the household becomes $U = U(x, q, k)$. Since the budget constraint is the same as initially, only the third of equations (1) is changed, and it becomes

$$
\frac{\partial L}{\partial k} = U_k - \lambda(qp_k + T_k) = 0.
$$

The solution of these equations is

$$
U_x = \frac{U_q}{p} = \frac{U_k}{qp_k + T_k} \quad \text{and} \quad x + p(k)q + T(k, y) = y.
$$

---

[12] I realize, of course, that for other purposes, such as the study of transport demands, much of the problem is assumed away if one assumes a fixed number of CBD trips per household. As my subsequent empirical results demonstrate, however, the assumption that the average income level in different parts of the city on purely locational grounds is the same, would probably be a good one for studies of transport demand.

Thus, in effect, $(qp_k + T_k)$ becomes the price of locating a unit distance farther from the CBD. Alternatively, one could write

$$qp_k + T_k = \frac{U_k}{U_x} \gtreqless 0 \quad \text{as} \quad U_k \gtreqless 0,$$

or

$$p_k = -\frac{1}{q} T_k + \frac{U_k}{qU_x}. \tag{25}$$

Equation (25) implies that p_k could be positive, even though T_k is positive, if U_k is positive and the ratio (U_k/U_x) is sufficiently large. Introducing preferences for location as done above, therefore, renders the theory devoid of any empirical content.

Now, I do not mean to deny that consumer preferences might exert an influence on consumer locational choices. My point is that, if preference hypotheses are to be empirically meaningful, they must be related to observable variables. Many kinds of such relations could be mentioned. But rather than attempt to catalogue them here, I will discuss them at appropriate points throughout Part I. Since I am currently considering the effects of accessibility to work or shopping centers—more specifically the CBD—I will note a few factors related to accessibility. First, households may differ among each other according to their preferences for different items making up what I have called other consumption. Thus, some may be especially fond of imported woolens, the legitimate theater, or art galleries. Since items such as these are generally available close to the city center for reasons mentioned before, such households would make more non-work CBD trips than others. In the framework of my initial model, they have higher transport costs and thus live closer to the CBD. Other households may place especially high value on birdwalks or drives in the country. By locating close to the edge of the city they tend to reduce the transport costs especially relevant for them.

Other "preference" factors relating to work trips may also be readily fitted into my initial model through their effects on transport costs. Households with two or more CBD workers make more work trips and hence have higher transport costs than those with only one or no CBD workers. Those whose places of employment may vary frequently, such as domestic servants or salesmen who make calls at locations scattered throughout the whole city, may find locations close to the CBD attractive because of its maximum accessibility to the whole city. Finally, physicians whose practice requires frequent visits to a particular hospital or college professors who make frequent visits to lab, library, or seminar, may find locations close to their employment desirable because of their greater number of work trips.

The last of the modifications of my initial assumptions I wish to discuss is uniformly distributed local employment in addition to a concentration in the CBD. A little reflection suggests that throughout the city one can find both workers who commute to the CBD and those working locally in significant numbers.[13] In this study I take the locations of employment as given and generally do not try to explain them. But a possible reason for this widely scattered local employment is the nature of demands for certain goods and services which are generated by residential locations. Thus, wherever residencies exist there are demands for schools and groceries, and hence for teachers and grocery clerks. Since rates of demand per unit area are strongly relative to any economies of scale internal to the individual firm, and transport costs are relatively high because such goods are frequently purchased in relatively small amounts at any one time, these goods tend to be produced in widely scattered locations. Because relatively few workers are employed at any one of these scattered places of employment, accessibility to any particular local work place does not command an above-average price of housing. Local workers, then, can minimize their transport costs or maximize their real incomes by locating as close as possible to their place of work.

Now, if locally employed workers and CBD workers tend to intermingle throughout this city, as it would appear to me that they do, they must pay the same unit price for housing at any location. My initial model implies that housing prices are lower at more distant locations because of the extra transport costs incurred by CBD workers, so housing prices decline with distance for locally employed workers as well. Of course, transport costs for non-work CBD trips are greater for locally employed workers at greater distances from the CBD, but since the relative importance of such costs as compared with housing expenditures are certainly quite small, I shall neglect them in what follows. If, then, locational equilibrium is to prevail for locally employed workers, the wage rate received by any class of worker, defined in terms of the wage rate they receive in any given location, must decline with distance from the CBD. Otherwise, locally employed workers at greater distances from the CBD would be better off than those closer to the CBD.[14] Of course, if wage rates are lower at greater distances from the CBD, the prices of commodities other than housing which are purchased locally may decline as well. But for reasons discussed in the first section of Chapter 3 I would expect the decline in

---

[13] I will consider concentrations of employment outside the CBD in Chapter 4, below.

[14] After the first draft of this study was written, a paper by Leon N. Moses, "Towards a Theory of Intra-Urban Wage Differentials and Their Influence on Travel Patterns," appeared, which makes this same point.

wage rates to be small relative to the decline in housing prices. Hence, I shall continue to neglect changes in the prices of commodities other than housing with distance from the CBD.

The argument above can be made more explicit by considering the constrained maximization of utility by the households of locally employed workers. The utility function to be maximized is the same as for CBD worker households, $U = U(x, q)$. The budget constraint, however, is different, namely

$$g = x + p(k)q - w(k),$$

where $w(k)$ is the wage income of workers employed at a distance k miles from the CBD. As noted above, I am ignoring the non-work CBD trip costs of locally employed workers and the variation in the prices of commodities other than housing, since they are small compared to housing expenditures and prices. Also, I shall temporarily ignore differences in the non-wage incomes of locally employed workers, since there is no reason to suppose that for any particular worker such income depends upon his location choice. The first derivatives of L with respect to x, q, and λ are the same as for CBD worker households. That with respect to k, however, is

$$\frac{\partial L}{\partial k} = -\lambda(qp_k - w_k) = 0$$

or

$$w_k = qp_k \leq 0 \qquad \text{for} \qquad p_k \leq 0. \tag{26}$$

Some notion of the relative magnitude of wage rate decreases with distance can be formed by rewriting equation (26) above as

$$\left(\frac{w_k}{w}\right) = \left(\frac{pq}{w}\right)\left(\frac{p_k}{p}\right) \tag{26'}$$

Since housing expenditures are generally no more than one-fifth of income, and wage income is about three-quarters or more of total income, the wage gradient would be about one-quarter of the price gradient or less. The second-order condition on locational equilibrium can be developed as before; it is

$$-qp_{kk} - p_k\frac{\partial q}{\partial k} + w_{kk} \leq 0,$$

or

$$E_{q,p;C}\left(\frac{p_k}{p}\right) + \left(\frac{p_{kk}}{p_k} - \frac{w_{kk}}{w_k}\right) \leq 0 \tag{27}$$

This last condition, like (6), will be analyzed more fully in Chapter 4.

Several implications of equations (26) or (26′) deserve mention here. First, and perhaps foremost for my purposes, is the fact that the decline in money wage incomes of locally employed workers tends to offset the qualified tendency noted earlier for the money incomes of CBD workers to rise as the distance of their residence from the CBD increases. The greater the relative importance of local versus CBD employment the more important will this fact be in influencing reported money incomes by place of residence. Another implication of (26) is that, like CBD workers, local workers of any given class with stronger preferences for housing in relation to other consumption, x, will tend to locate at greater distances from the CBD where housing prices are lower. This is illustrated in Figure 3, where

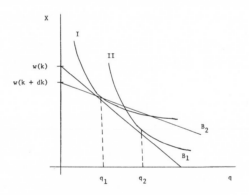

FIG. 3.—Differences in Tastes for Housing

I and II are the indifference curves of two different local workers at a given distance k, B_1 the common budget line, and q_1 and q_2 the quantities of housing consumed by the two households at k. If, now, k is the equilibrium location for household I, the budget line B_2 for a short move dk miles away from the CBD must intersect the point of tangency of B_1 and I. This means, however, that II can increase its real income by moving further from the CBD. Similarly, locally employed workers with higher non-wage incomes will tend to locate at greater distances from the CBD since they purchase more housing and save a greater amount on any given decline in housing prices. Last, if there are differences in skill and real incomes of different classes of workers, those with higher wage rates tend to consume more housing at any distance k. But since p_k must be the same for all residing at any k, w_k is numerically larger for the more highly paid workers. Assuming that the relative importance of non-wage income is the same for all, if the real income elasticity of housing demand were equal to one, pq/w would be the same for all classes of workers. Hence, (26') would imply that w_k/w is the same for all classes. However, a real income elasticity greater than one would imply that pq/w is greater and hence that w_k/w is numerically greater the more highly paid the class of worker.

3 The Equilibrium of Housing Producers

I now turn to a consideration of the behavior of producers, especially housing producers, at different locations within the city. In the first section of this chapter I shall consider the locational equilibrium of firms and the equilibrium of the urban land market. The second section develops the implications of the variation of housing prices with distance for the behavior of residential land rentals. Next, I explore the effects of variation of land rentals on the firm's relative use of land as compared with other productive factors and thus on the output of housing per square mile of land. The fourth section deals rather briefly with the effects on the supply side of allowing different kinds of housing, distinguished by differences in the relative importance of land, in the analysis. Finally, in the last section I turn to the analysis of differences other than locational ones among parcels of real estate and consider the difference between short- and long-run adjustments of housing prices, land rentals, and the intensity of residential land use.

THE EQUILIBRIUM OF FIRMS AND THE URBAN LAND MARKET

The determination of the location of economic activity is but a part of the problem of the determination of the prices of final products and of productive factors, including land rentals, and the amount of production of various kinds. There are four conditions for the equilibrium of firms in space: (1) equilibrium of firms at a given location, (2) locational equilibrium, (3) equilibrium in the market for land, and (4) equality of demand and supply for final products. I shall discuss each of these conditions in turn in the present section. In the sections which follow, the implications of these conditions for the behavior of residential land rentals and the intensity of residential land use are developed.

In the following discussion and in my initial analysis of residential land use I will concentrate my attention upon one very important characteristic of urban land—spatial uniqueness. Thus, I will treat urban land much as any other factor of production, that is, as perfectly homogeneous except for location and as perfectly divisible. Such a procedure will no doubt strike many readers as patently "unrealistic." To many persons the very essence of housing and urban problems is the very great importance of the heritage of the past because of the durability of buildings and other im- mobile improvements to urban land. However, I submit, and I believe that my analysis bears me out, that many of the features of city structure and urban land use can be explained without reference to the heritage of the past. To the extent that there is any distinction between land, especially urban land, and other factors of production, such a distinction would seem to arise chiefly from the fact of spatial uniqueness. Other commonly cited differences between urban land or real estate and other productive factors, such as durability and consequent inelasticity of supply, heterogeneity, and immobility (inasmuch as this means something different from spatial uniqueness), are clearly matters of degree rather than kind. In fact, spatial uniqueness is not as clearly a distinction in kind as one might initially suppose. If labor were not sometimes highly immobile, and hence spatially unique, there would probably be no depressed area or farm problems. And, the supply of land with certain spatial characteristics is sometimes in- creased by filling in areas along waterfronts and more frequently through investment in transport facilities.

There is another justification for beginning my analysis as I do, apart from analytic simplicity and convenience in exposition. If one is to under- stand the effects of factors such as durability and heterogeneity on urban land use, one must first determine what the world would be like without them. In a later part of this chapter I explore the effects of departures from my long-run equilibrium assumptions of homogeneity and divisibility by treating each parcel of urban land as unique in all respects. Such complete uniqueness might result, for example, from the existence of fixed capital improvements. I show there that complete uniqueness makes little difference in the pure theory of urban land use and value.

In discussing land rentals[1] or values, I shall make no distinction between agricultural and situation value, as does Marshall,[2] and I will use the terms land and site rental interchangeably. While Marshall's distinction may be helpful for expository purposes, it is not very useful analytically and may even be misleading. Thus, two urban sites may be perfectly identical in all characteristics which are relevant for urban value but of differential

---

[1] Throughout this study I have tried to use the term rental to refer to the returns to land in order to distinguish this return from economic rent. The latter, which may be a part of the return to any resource, refers to the excess of the expected return to a particular factor of production over the minimum necessary to induce that factor into a specific use.

[2] Alfred Marshall, *Principles of Economics*, bk. 5, chap. 11, p. 441. This chapter contains an excellent discussion of the determinants of urban land values.

fertility for agriculture. They would then have different situation values, even though they are perfectly identical in all features relevant to their actual use. Also, as I will show below, the next best alternative use for land containing a shopping center, say, might be housing or a manufacturing plant, in which case the site's value if used for agriculture would not be relevant for the analysis of any concrete problem. In addition, I shall not concern myself very much with the relation of rentals to value. Value, of course, is the capitalized value of expected future net rentals. But factors affecting expectations and capitalization rates are not very important for the kinds of problems I discuss below, least of all for the analysis of long-run equilibrium.[3] I find it convenient to consider rentals, primarily, rather than values in most of my discussion. Initially, when treating urban land as perfectly divisible and homogenous, the term rental refers to the price per unit of the services of land alone, which, while it may vary with location, is otherwise the same for all units of land. When discussing the complete uniqueness case, however, rental means the returns to a particular plot and to its capital improvements.

A few other assumptions should be explicitly noted before proceeding with the analysis. Throughout this study I assume that firms as well as households are competitive in both product and factor markets. Thus, while firms can affect the prices they pay or receive by their choice of location, they cannot do so by varying the amounts they buy or sell. As I noted in the previous chapter in connection with homeowners, I treat owner-occupiers as landlords who sell the services of their properties to themselves as tenants. Finally, throughout most of the analysis I assume that all firms producing a given commodity are identical, or have identical production functions. In the fourth section of this chapter, however, I drop this assumption and develop the implications of differences in production functions among different groups of housing producers.

The conditions for firm equilibrium at a given location are well known. Assume that firms purchase two classes of inputs, land, L, and non-land, N, at unit prices r and n, respectively.[4] Let π stand for the firm's profit or income, p and Q the price per unit received and output, respectively, and the subscript i for firms in the i-th industry. Then equations (2) are necessary conditions for a maximum of

$$\pi_i = p_i Q_i(L_i, N_i) - r_i L_i - n_i N_i:$$ (1)

$$\frac{\partial \pi_i}{\partial L_i} = p_i Q_{i,L} - r_i = 0, \quad \frac{\partial \pi_i}{\partial N_i} = p_i Q_{i,N} - n_i = 0.$$ (2)

---

[3] For a discussion of some of the more important determinants of the relation of rental to value see Ralph Turvey, *The Economics of Real Property*, pp. 6–7.

[4] So long as the relative prices of various non-land inputs vary within the city, the above procedure is not strictly correct. Put differently, if there is not a unique set of

The second equilibrium condition, which I choose to call the condition of locational equilibrium, is less familiar because for most problems it is not necessary to take account of spatial uniqueness. Spatial uniqueness, however, is the very essence of location theory, of which the theory of the city structure is but a special case. Locational equilibrium requires that firms choose their locations in such a way that their incomes cannot be increased by any move. Since I assume for now that all firms in any given industry have identical production functions, the condition of locational equilibrium requires that their profits are the same everywhere and are independent of their location. Differentiating equation (1)

$$d\pi_i = (Q_i \, dp_i - L_i \, dr_i - N_i \, dn_i) + (p_i \, dQ_i - r_i \, dL_i - n_i \, dN_i). \quad (3)$$

Assuming, however, that with any change in its location a firm readjusts its inputs of land and non-land factors so as to maintain the first-order conditions for equilibrium at a given location (2), the second parenthesis of (3) becomes

$$p_i(dQ_i - Q_{i,L} \, dL_i - Q_{i,N} \, dN_i) = 0,$$

because $dQ_i = Q_{i,L} \, dL_i + Q_{i,N} \, dN_i$ is the change in the firm's output that accompanies its change in location. If locational equilibrium is to prevail, for any small change in location the firm's profit must remain unchanged, so $d\pi_i = 0$ implies $dr_i = (Q_i/L_i) \, dp_i - (N_i/L_i) \, dn_i$, or

$$dr_i^* = \frac{1}{\rho_L} \, dp_i^* - \frac{\rho_N}{\rho_L} \, dn_i^*, \quad (4)$$

$\rho_L = r_i L_i / p_i Q_i$ is the relative importance of land in production or land's share in the revenues of the firm,[5] and $\rho_N = n_i N_i / p_i Q_i$. Equation (4) thus implies that the rental of land will be bid up by firms in locations where product price is especially high owing to favorable location vis-à-vis the local market or transport terminals for shipment to outside markets. In like manner, where non-land costs are low—near terminals in the case of raw materials, if land rentals are not higher than elsewhere, firms located there will earn higher profits than less favorably situated firms, and competition for favorable locations will bid up land rentals.

Equilibrium in the land market requires that any parcel of land be devoted to that use which pays the highest rental. For if not, landowners

---

relative prices for different non-land inputs, an index number problem exists. For analytic simplicity, however, I neglect this problem. My procedure is justified not by descriptive realism but by its convenience and the usefulness of the results it yields.

[5] Throughout this monograph whenever I use terms such as the relative importance of a factor or the share of a factor I shall mean only total payments to the factor relative to total value of output, never the physical quantity of the factor used relative to output in physical terms. As will become clear later, a factor's share may vary quite differently than the physical input of the factor relative to output.

can increase their incomes by changing the use to which their land is put. Figure 1 shows a hypothetical configuration of the natural logarithm of rental plotted against distance, k, from the CBD in one direction only. The curves r_1^* and r_2^* show the rental firms in two different industries, say retailing and housing, would offer for different locations. As the figure is drawn, land from the CBD, k_0, to k_1 and from k_2 to k_4 around a second

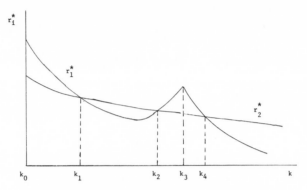

FIG. 1.—Rentals and the Allocation of Land

center k_3 would be used by firms in the first or retail industry. Note that, if around any center or nucleus, firms of the industry with the steeper sloped rental function or larger gradient are to produce at all, its rental function must lie above that of the second industry somewhere in the neighborhood of this center.[6] For, if r_2^* were everywhere above r_1^* in the neighborhood of the secondary center at k_3, despite the local peak in r_1^* at k_3 in retail, firms would use no land there. More generally, around any center or nucleus, firms in industries with the steepest rental gradient tend to be located nearest the center and those with the flattest locate farthest away if they produce in the vicinity of this center at all.

Equation (4) above suggests two reasons or forces responsible for differences in rental gradients. Rental gradients tend to be steeper for those industries in which land is of least importance as a productive factor or for whom land's share is smallest.[7] Second, the rental gradient at any point will be steeper the greater the relative change in the price of the product or in non-land costs per unit distance. Transport costs, of course, are a very important determinant of either at the point of production.

---

[6] If the two rent functions coincide, either kind of firm may locate on any particular plot of land.

[7] Note that land's share is a constant only in the case of a unitary elasticity of substitution in production. This point is discussed more fully below.

Consider now the last of the requirements for equilibrium of the urban economy, equality of demand and supply. In order to sustain the locational pattern of firms illustrated in Figure 1, there must be no unsatisfied buyers or sellers of any product. Changes in the demand for the output of one or more industries or changes in the conditions of supply will lead to a shift in rental functions and, hence, in the areas of location of firms.[8] Suppose, for example, that because of an increase in population or income of consumers located elsewhere in the city, the demand for retail services near the

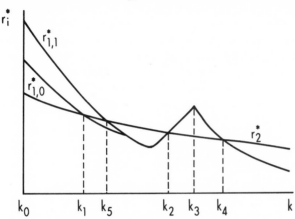

FIG. 2.—Effect of Changes in Rentals upon Land Uses

city center increases but the demand for housing in the direction shown in Figure 1 remains unchanged. The increase in demand increases the price of retail services and, hence, the rentals that retail firms are willing to offer for land near the center. The new rental function is shown as $r^*_{1,1}$ in Figure 2, the old one being denoted by $r^*_{1,0}$. The rental which retail firms will offer for land at the old boundary k_1 and immediately beyond it is now greater than that which firms producing housing will offer, and the area occupied by retail firms will tend to expand to k_5.

THE VARIATION OF RESIDENTIAL LAND RENTALS

If all firms producing housing are identical or have the same production functions, then all must earn equal incomes or profits if the existing locational pattern is to be an equilibrium one. As already shown in equation (4), equality of profits requires that rentals vary directly with prices received at the point of production and inversely with non-land costs. If, for example, housing firms were to pay the same prices for all productive

---

[8] For a more complete discussion of a special case of this see my "Economic Change and Rural-Urban Land Conversions."

factors at all locations but the price received for housing varied inversely with distance from the CBD, firms located close to the city center would earn greater incomes than those located farther away. It would then be in the interest of firms located at greater distances to offer more for land located close to the CBD than centrally located firms were currently paying. Land rentals would thus rise in the central locations and fall in the more distant ones, and this process would continue so long as firms in different locations earned different incomes.

My analysis in Chapter 2 also implies that, when uniformly distributed local employment is introduced into the analysis, wage rates tend to fall with distance from the CBD because housing prices do. This fall tends to counter the fall in land rentals which results directly from the decline in housing prices with distance. However, the effects of the fall in wages are likely to be quite small. Since I am provisionally assuming that housing prices, and hence wage rates, vary only with distance from the CBD, equation (4) can be rewritten as

$$\left(\frac{r_k}{r}\right) = \frac{1}{\rho_L}\left(\frac{p_k}{p}\right) - \frac{\rho_N}{\rho_L}\left(\frac{n_k}{n}\right). \tag{5}$$

As was indicated in the final section of Chapter 2, the wage gradient is likely to be less than approximately one-quarter of the price gradient. Since wage costs are generally about one-half of construction costs, the gradient of non-wage costs, $(m_{k/n})$, in equation (4) would be about one-eighth of the price gradient or less. Furthermore, the slight decline in wage cost with distance may tend to be offset by the increased cost of construction materials if the latter are shipped from the center of the city to the construction site. The rental gradient, therefore, would probably depend primarily upon the price gradient.[9]

Because land's relative importance in the production of housing services is quite small, equation (5) indicates that the rental gradient is large relative to the price gradient. Data gathered by the U.S. Housing and Home Finance Agency indicates that the proportion of site value to total property value for new FHA-insured single-family dwellings was 11.5 percent in 1946 and 16.6 percent in 1960.[10] Site value is defined to include street

---

[9] The Boeckh index of residential construction costs for brick structures in 1949 was about 3 percent below that for the central city in surburban Pittsburgh and 4 percent below the central city in suburban Philadelphia. Part of these differences might be accounted for by differences in the degree of unionization of construction workers. Unionization has been shown to be significantly related to wage levels in the skilled construction trades by Stephen P. Sobotka, "Union Influence on Wages: The Construction Industry."

[10] *Fourteenth Annual Report*, table III-35, p. 110.

improvements and utilities, rough grading, terracing, and retaining walls,[11] and the costs of these capital improvements might easily exceed the value of the unimproved land. Furthermore, interest plus tax costs are roughly three-fourths the cost of providing housing services.[12] The relative importance of land in providing housing services is thus of the order of 5 percent, or, as equation (4) indicates, the rental gradient is of the order of twenty times the price gradient and perhaps 200 times the gradient in non-land costs. Since the variation of non-land costs with distance is so small relative to the variation in rentals, in what follows I shall neglect the variation in non-land costs with distance from the CBD and assume they are the same everywhere.

My analysis of the residential rental gradient so far suggests that it is primarily influenced by the housing price gradient and large relative to the latter. But what might be said about variations in the rental gradient with distance from the CBD? Neglecting the second term of equation (4), differentiation yields

$$\frac{d}{dk}\left(\frac{r_k}{r}\right) = \frac{1}{\rho_L}\frac{d}{dk}\left(\frac{p_k}{p}\right) - \frac{1}{\rho_L{}^2}\left(\frac{p_k}{p}\right)\frac{d}{dk}\rho_L. \tag{6}$$

In Chapter 4, below, I will show that in general

$$\frac{d}{dk}\left(\frac{p_k}{p}\right) \geq 0$$

or that the slope of the log price-distance function tends to decline numerically with distance from the CBD. Hence, the first term of (6) by itself would tend to cause rentals to decrease at a decreasing rate with distance. But the contribution of the second term of (6) may be either positive or negative. As is well known, the relative importance of a factor or that factor's share in the expenditures of a firm either increases, decreases, or remains unchanged with a rise in its price per unit depending upon whether the elasticity of substitution of the factor vis-à-vis others in production is less than, greater than, or equal to unity.[13] Thus, the log rental-distance function may have either positive or negative curvature depending upon the curvature of the log price-distance function and the elasticity of substitution. I will return to this point in Chapter 4.

---

[11] *Ibid.*, p. 119.

[12] The remainder is depreciation and maintenance and repair expenditure, but these expenditures are not incurred on site values.

[13] This relationship holds in the absence of a non-neutral technological change, as is shown in my "The Derived Demand Curve for a Productive Factor and the Industry Supply Curve."

The Effect of Variation in Rentals on the Intensity of Residential Land Use

Equation (5), which relates land rentals to housing prices and non-land costs, was derived on the assumption that firms in various locations adjust their factor inputs so as to maximize incomes in response to variations in relative factor prices. I now consider explicitly the adjustment of factor proportions to differences in land rentals and the implications of this adjustment for the intensity of residential land use in different locations. I will then consider the reactions of housing producers to increases in demand, construction costs, and the supply of land for residential uses and how these reactions differ in different locations.

In what follows I will assume that the firm's payments to owners of land and other hired factors, including those owned by the firm itself, exactly exhaust its total receipts or that there are no entrepreneurial rents. Assuming that entrepreneurial rents are zero together with the assumption that firms are competitive in the factor markets implies that the marginal cost of the firm is constant and that, on the supply side, the size of any individual firm is indeterminate. I make this assumption partly because it enables me to simplify the following discussion considerably and partly because I suspect that limitation on the size of any given firm is not an important feature of the kinds of problems considered in this study.

Given that payments to hired productive factors exhaust the receipts of a firm producing housing I can write

$$pQ = rL + nN,$$

where the symbols are as defined in the first section. (The subscript i has been dropped since I am now considering only housing firms, all of whom are assumed to be identical.) Dividing both sides of the above equation by L and differentiating,

$$d\left(\frac{pQ}{L}\right) = dr + n\,d\left(\frac{N}{L}\right),$$

or

$$d\left(\frac{pQ}{L}\right)^* = \rho_L\,dr^* + \rho_N\,d\left(\frac{N}{L}\right)^*, \tag{7}$$

since I am here neglecting variation in non-land costs. Variation in the ratio of non-land to land inputs, in turn, depends upon the variation of land rentals. In fact, it follows directly from the definition of the elasticity of substitution, σ, that

$$d\left(\frac{N}{L}\right)^* = \sigma\,d\left(\frac{r}{n}\right)^*,$$

so upon substituting in (7) the total effect of variation in r is seen to be

$$d\left(\frac{pQ}{L}\right)^* = (\rho_L + \rho_N \sigma)\, dr^*. \tag{8}$$

Furthermore, using (4) I can substitute for dr^* in (8) and obtain

$$d\left(\frac{pQ}{L}\right)^* = \left(1 + \frac{\rho_N}{\rho_L}\sigma\right) dp^*. \tag{9}$$

In equation (9), (pQ/L) is the value of housing produced per unit of land and is a measure of the intensity of residential land use. The coefficient of dp^* is the elasticity of the value of housing produced per unit of land. (The latter, of course, is one plus the elasticity of housing output per unit of land. I concentrate on the value rather than the physical measure of land use intensity because the empirical data used in Part II are primarily in value terms.) The elasticity of the value of housing produced per unit of land varies inversely with the relative importance of land and directly with the elasticity of substitution. Since, as I have indicated above, the relative importance of land is of the order of 0.05, this elasticity is of the order of twenty, provided that the elasticity of substitution is close to one. The relative change in the value of housing produced per unit of land with distance from the CBD is simply (pQ/L)'s price elasticity multiplied by the price gradient, or

$$\frac{d}{dk}\left(\frac{pQ}{L}\right)^* = \left(1 + \frac{\rho_N}{\rho_L}\sigma\right)\left(\frac{p_k}{p}\right) < 0. \tag{10}$$

Thus, if the relative importance of land and the elasticity of substitution, and hence the elasticity of residential land use intensity with respect to price, were known, the price gradient could be determined from knowledge of the relative change in the intensity of residential land use with distance. And, as I indicated in the preceding chapter, knowing the price gradient and the per household expenditure on housing per unit time, the marginal costs of transport can be determined.

The variation of the intensity of residential land use described by equation (10) is illustrated in Figure 3. At a distance k_1 miles from the CBD the rental of land is r_1 and the ratio of land to non-land costs (r_1/n). The isoquant shown in Figure 3 is the locus of all combinations of N and L which will produce a given dollar's worth of housing. Different points along the isoquant can be interpreted as representing different kinds of housing. Proceeding along the isoquant in a southeasterly direction one passes from elevator to walk-up apartments, row houses, duplexes, and single-family detached houses, each type containing progressively more

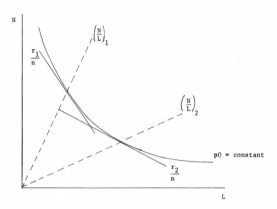

FIG. 3.—Substitution of Land for Non-Land Factors

land relative to structure than the last.[14] At a greater distance k_2 the rental of land r_2 is less than r_1, hence the factor price ratio is smaller than at k_1. The conditions of equilibrium for housing firms require that they use more land relative to non-land factors at k_2, the ratio $(N/L)_2$ rather than $(N/L)_1$. This might mean, for example, that duplexes rather than walk-up apartments are the predominant type of structure.

The difference between the intensity of residential land use at two different locations depends upon three things. First, the greater the difference in housing prices between k_1 and k_2 the greater the difference in land rentals and the further firms must move along an isoquant to equate its slope to the lower factor price ratio at the more distant location. Second, the smaller the relative importance of land the greater the difference in land rentals for any given difference in housing prices and hence the greater the difference in (N/L) between the two locations. Finally, for any given difference in land rentals the greater the elasticity of substitution, σ, the smaller is the curvature of the isoquant and the greater must be the angular separation between the rays whose slopes are equal to (N/L). Thus, as is also shown by equation (9), variations in the intensity of residential land uses are greater the greater the variation in the price of housing services and the elasticity of substitution of land for non-land factors and the smaller the relative importance of land in the production of housing services.

Let us now consider variations in the slope of the curve which relates the log of the value of housing per square mile to distance from the CBD.

---

[14] The size of the individual dwelling units depends upon conditions of demand, of course. An elevator apartment building can consist of 3-room or 8-room apartments, and single-family homes can be either small or large structures on small or large lots.

Differentiating equation (10) yields

$$\frac{d^2}{dk^2}\left(\frac{pQ}{L}\right)^* = \left(1 + \frac{\rho_N}{\rho_L}\,\sigma\right)\frac{d}{dk}\left(\frac{p_k}{p}\right) + \left(\frac{p_k}{p}\right)\frac{d}{dk}\left(1 + \frac{\rho_N}{\rho_L}\,\sigma\right). \quad (11)$$

As was noted in connection with equation (6) above,

$$\frac{d}{dk}\left(\frac{p_k}{p}\right) \geq 0,$$

so the decline in the price gradient with distance by itself causes the slope of (10) to become numerically smaller with increasing distance from the CBD. The variation in the elasticity of housing value per square mile can be positive or negative depending upon whether the elasticity of substitution is greater than or less than one and hence the ratio (ρ_N/ρ_L) decreases or increases with distance from the CBD. The variation in this elasticity with distance might be substantial if the substitution elasticity differs from one. Assuming that the elasticity of substitution is everywhere the same—mostly because I know of no reason why it should vary with location—the variation in the elasticity of the value of housing produced per square mile with distance is given by

$$d\left(1 + \frac{\rho_N}{\rho_L}\,\sigma\right) = \sigma\,d\left(\frac{n}{r}\right)\left(\frac{N}{L}\right) = \sigma(\sigma - 1)\,\frac{\rho_N}{\rho_L}\,dr^*$$

or

$$\frac{d}{dk}\left(1 + \frac{\rho_N}{\rho_L}\,\sigma\right) = \sigma(\sigma - 1)\,\frac{\rho_N}{\rho_L}\left(\frac{r_k}{r}\right). \quad (12)$$

If, for example, $\sigma = 0.75$ and $\rho_L = 0.05$, the coefficient of dr^* in (12) equals -3.6. As I shall argue later in Part II, it would appear that housing prices decline by about 1 percent per mile, so by (5) the relative change in residential land rents per mile is about -0.20. Hence, (12) approximately equals 0.7 per mile, and over a ten-mile range the elasticity of the value of housing produced per unit of land would vary by about one-half its average value.

Having considered variations in the intensity of residential land use by location at a given time, I now want to explore the response of housing output to changes in demand and hence housing prices. In so doing, I shall continue to assume that non-land costs remain constant. While this assumption seems quite reasonable for comparisons among different locations in a given city at the same time, it is perhaps less so at first glance for considering changes over time. In the long run, though, I would expect

that most non-land factors are highly mobile as among cities. If so, differential changes in the demand for non-land factors would not affect
intercity differentials in non-land costs. And in an earlier study I failed to
find evidence that construction costs vary with changes in the rate of construction of new housing at the national level.[15] Thus, on empirical grounds
I believe the assumption of constancy of non-land costs is a good one.
Furthermore, if it is assumed that in the long-run the entry of new firms
eliminates any entrepreneurial rents generated in the short-run by the
change in demand, then the rental of land in any location must rise in
accordance with equation (4). If such is the case, equation (9), above,
gives the change in the value of housing produced per unit of land on land
used to produce housing. (Of course, with an increase in the demand for
housing, land might be shifted from the production of other commodities
to residential uses, but I will delay consideration of such shifts until the
following chapter.) The elasticity of value of housing produced per unit of
land tends to be large because the relative importance of land is small, so
with an increase in housing demand the increase in intensity of residential
land use would be large relative to the increase in the price of housing
services. In addition, the argument in connection with equation (12) suggests that the variation in the elasticity of the value of housing produced
per square mile with distance from the CBD can be of substantial practical
importance. With an elasticity of substitution which is less than unity and,
therefore, an increasing price elasticity with distance, an increase in housing
demand will lead to a greater relative increase in housing produced, and
hence in population, in the more distant parts of the city. Thus, the
greater the demand for housing in the city the slower would be the rate of
decline in the value of housing produced per unit land with distance from
the CBD.

   Finally, I would like to consider the effects of exogenous changes in non-
land costs, n, and in the supply of land to the housing industry on the intensity of residential land use and variations in the latter throughout the
city. Such changes are more difficult to analyze than those investigated
earlier in this section. With an increase in construction costs, for example,
the consequent reduction of housing supply raises housing prices. Without
knowing the extent to which housing prices increase, equation (4) cannot
be used to determine the change in land rentals, and the method of
analysis previously used in this section breaks down. Under the assumptions made earlier in this section, however, I can write the following system
of equations describing displacements from the equilibrium of the industry
housing services at any particular location of the residential part of the

---

[15] "The Demand for Non-Farm Housing," pp. 42–46.

city:

$$dQ^* - \eta\, dp^* \qquad\qquad = 0 \qquad\qquad (13)$$

$$dQ^* - \rho_N\, dN^* - \rho_L\, dL^* \qquad = 0$$

$$\sigma\, dp^* - \rho_L\, dN^* + \rho_L\, dL^* \qquad = \sigma\, dn^*$$

$$\sigma\, dp^* + \rho_N\, dN^* - \rho_N\, dL^* - \sigma\, dr^* = 0$$

$$dL^* - e_L\, dr^* = dL_0^*$$

The first of these is the equation of a given consumer demand curve for housing in logarithmic differential form, with η the price elasticity of the demand for housing services, while the second expresses the relative change in industry output as a function of the relative change in inputs used by the industry. The third and fourth of the equations (13) are the usual conditions that factor inputs are paid the value of their marginal product. In the third the relative change in non-land costs, dn^*, is taken as exogenously determined. The last of equations (13) is the supply curve of land to the housing industry; e_L is the elasticity of land supply and dL_0^* an exogenous shift parameter. Shifts in the land supply function could result from shifts in the demand for land for non-residential uses or from differences in topography and hence in the total supply of land for all uses. The above system can be solved most conveniently by first eliminating dr^* and then dQ^* and dp^*; after solving for dN^* and dL^*, dQ^* can be obtained from the second, dp^* from the first, and dr^* from the last of equations (13).[16]

From the solution to the above system one readily obtains

$$\frac{\partial}{\partial n^*}\left(\frac{pQ}{L}\right)^* = \frac{\rho_N\{(1+\eta)\sigma + (1-\sigma)e_L\}}{(\rho_N\sigma - \rho_L\eta + e_L)} \qquad (14)$$

$$\frac{\partial}{\partial L_0^*}\left(\frac{pQ}{L}\right)^* = -\frac{(\rho_N\sigma + \rho_L)}{(\rho_N\sigma - \rho_L\eta + e_L)} \qquad (15)$$

Clearly, an increase in the supply of residential land will reduce the intensity of residential land use, but the effects of an increase in construction costs may go either way depending upon the relative size of the demand, substitution, and supply elasticities. In the following chapter I argue that $\eta = -1$ and $\sigma \le 1$; if so, an exogenous increase in non-land costs will increase or leave unchanged the intensity of residential land use.

Perhaps even more interesting for my purposes is the effect of changes in conditions of factor supply on the relative decline in the value of housing

---

[16] For a fuller discussion of this system and its properties see my "The Derived Demand Curve for a Productive Factor and the Industry Supply Curve." The following partial derivatives can readily be derived from the reduced-form equations given in the appendix to the above paper by letting the elasticity of supply of non-land factors go to infinity. In fact, the coefficient of dp^* in equation (9) above can be derived in the same way by also letting the demand elasticity go to minus infinity.

produced per square mile with distance. There is little reason to expect variation in the demand or substitution elasticities for housing with distance. But, as indicated several times earlier, if $\sigma \neq 1$, the relative importance of land and non-land expenditures by firms will vary along with land rentals with distance from the CBD. In addition, the analysis of variations in the supply of land to the housing industry in the following chapter suggests that, if anything, the elasticity of supply of residential land will increase with distance from the center of the city. Differentiating equations (14) and (15) above with respect to ρ_N yields

$$\frac{\partial^2 \left(\frac{pQ}{L}\right)^*}{\partial \rho_N \, \partial n^*} = \frac{(-\eta + e_L)\{(1 + \eta)\sigma + (1 - \sigma)e_L\}}{(\rho_N \sigma - \rho_L \eta + e_L)^2}; \tag{16}$$

$$\frac{\partial^2 \left(\frac{pQ}{L}\right)^*}{\partial \rho_N \, \partial L_0^*} = \frac{\{(1 + \eta)\sigma + (1 - \sigma)e_L\}}{(\rho_N \sigma - \rho_L \eta + e_L)^2}. \tag{17}$$

The value of both of these cross partial derivatives depends upon the same quantity as the partial of $(pQ/L)^*$ with respect to n^*, and hence I would expect both to be non-negative. Thus, as a result of an increase in construction costs or in the supply of residential land I would expect the relative decline in land use intensity with distance to become smaller. Similarly, differentiating with respect to e_L one finds

$$\frac{\partial^2 \left(\frac{pQ}{L}\right)^*}{\partial e_L \, \partial n^*} = -\frac{\rho_N(\rho_L + \rho_N \sigma)(\sigma + \eta)}{(\rho_N \sigma - \rho_L \eta + e_L)^2}; \tag{18}$$

$$\frac{\partial^2 \left(\frac{pQ}{L}\right)^*}{\partial e_L \, \partial L_0^*} = \frac{(\rho_N \sigma + \rho_L)}{(\rho_N \sigma - \rho_L \eta + e_L)^2}. \tag{19}$$

The second of these is strictly positive, while (18) is so if the demand elasticity is numerically larger than the substitution elasticity. Thus, I would expect that any tendency for the elasticity of residential land supply to increase with distance would also cause the rate of decline in residential land use intensity to become numerically smaller with an increase in construction costs or in the supply of land to the housing industry.

THE EFFECTS OF DIFFERENT HOUSING TYPES

Up to this point I have been assuming that all firms producing housing have the same production functions. This assumption does not mean, however, that all housing is built the same way. As I have shown in the preceding section, at greater distances more land is used relative to other factors of production in producing housing because land is relatively cheaper. The fact that single-family units tend to predominate in the outer parts of a city and apartments near the center, therefore, may be interpreted as resulting from factor substitution in response to differences in relative factor prices. In this section I shall indicate how similar implications for type of housing in various parts of the city are implicit in the assumption of differences in production functions among firms. I shall also explore other implications of differences in production functions among firms producing housing. Differences among firms could conceivably arise from two separate sources, differences in housing types, say houses versus apartments, and differences in firm's abilities to use land as compared with other productive factors.

Let us begin by supposing that there are two kinds of firms distinguished by the type of housing they produce, say apartments and single-family houses. Under such conditions, each group of producers may be considered a separate industry, and each industry will have its own rental-distance function such as equation (5). The industry for which land is a relatively more important productive factor or for which p_L is greater, the single-family house industry in this example, will tend to have a flatter rental-gradient at any given distance from the market. It was shown in the first section that if both industries are to use land in positive quantities, the industry with the steeper rental-gradient at any given location must be located closer to the center of activity from which the function is drawn, since those firms for whom land is a relatively unimportant factor have a comparative advantage in locating where land is expensive. Thus, under the assumptions I have made here, firms producing housing in the form of apartments will locate in the first annulus around the CBD and those producing single-family housing will tend to locate in the outer part of the city.

Now, of course, everything said above about rental-gradients and the value of housing produced per square mile in the residential annulus applies within the single-family and apartment annuli in the two-industry case. Rentals per unit of land and the value of housing produced per square mile will both tend to decline with distance from the CBD in each of the two annular regions because the price consumers are willing to offer for housing services does. Within either annulus, the log rental and value of housing per square mile functions tend to have positive curvatures because of positive curvature in the log housing-price function. But, if the elasticity of substitution of land for non-land factors is less than unity, the decline in the relative importance of land with distance will tend to offset this tendency since the latter tends to produce a negative curvature. At any given distance from the CBD both the rental and value of housing per square mile gradients would tend to be steeper for apartment than for single-family house firms because of the greater relative importance of land for the latter. If locational equilibrium is to prevail, of course, both housing types will be found only at the boundary separating the areas of location of the two industries. Thus, there will be a break in the slopes or abrupt decline of the rental and value of housing per square mile functions at the boundary separating the areas of location of the two types of firms.

The size of the annuli occupied by the apartment and single-family houses industries, of course, will depend upon the relative demand for the two types of housing. The point is illustrated in Figure 4, where $r^*_{1,1}$ is the log of the rental offered for land at any given distance by apartment firms prior to a change in demand, and $r^*_{1,2}$ that after the change. Similarly, $r^*_{2,1}$ is the log rental-distance function for single-family house firms before and $r^*_{2,2}$ after a change in demand, while k_1 is the initial boundary separating the areas of location of the two industries. Suppose, now, that an increase in the relative demand for single-family houses takes place. The initial effect of such a change will be for housing prices to rise in the single-family annulus relative to those in the apartment annulus. Because of these price changes, the rental of land will rise in the single-family relative to that in the apartment annulus. At the old boundary, land now receives a higher return when devoted to single-family housing rather than apartments. The single-family house annulus thus expands toward the CBD and the apartment annulus contracts as old dwellings are replaced by new ones. As the relative supply of single-family housing increases, of course, the relative price of housing and land rentals in the single-family area tend to decline as compared with those in the apartment area, but such changes cannot wipe out the initial relative increase. In the new long-run equilibrium, the log rental-distance functions, taking account of the secondary changes mentioned in the above sentence, are $r^*_{2,2}$ and $r^*_{1,2}$ for the single-family and apartment industries, and the new boundary separating them is k_2.[17]

So far in this section I have been assuming that there are only two types of housing, apartments and single-family houses. When one takes account of many different types, such as elevator and walk-up apartments of various kinds as well as row houses, duplexes and various kinds of one-unit detached houses, the analysis is essentially the same. For each house type there is a log rental-distance function such as equation (5), and the rental gradient varies inversely with the relative importance of land. Thus, the areas of location of the different house types tend to be annular surround-

---

[17] The case in which households regard houses and apartments as different commodities but where these merely reflect different factor proportions on the same production function is the limiting case of the above for which the slopes of the rental function on either side of k_1 and k_2 become the same.

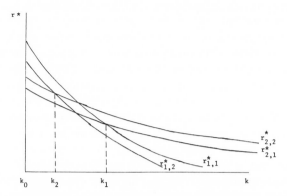

FIG. 4.—Changes in the Areas of Location of Different House Types

ing the CBD, with the intensity of land use declining and the relative importance of land increasing by type of housing with distance from the CBD. At the boundaries separating one kind of house type from another, there is a discontinuous decline in the rental and value of housing per square mile gradients. With many such breaks, however, the existence of any one of them would be difficult to detect. Rather, the log rental and log value of housing per square mile versus distance functions would give the appearance of positive curvature.

The Effects of Heterogeneity and Indivisibility of Urban Land

Up to this point I have been concentrating my attention on one aspect of urban land, namely spatial uniqueness. I believe I have demonstrated that many features of urban land use can be readily explained by treating urban land as if it were perfectly divisible and homogeneous except for differences in location. However, for many purposes it is desirable to take other characteristics of land into account. This is especially true for considering short-run responses of the urban land market. In this section, then, I will first modify my previous analysis to take account of differences among parcels of urban land other than locational ones. I shall also explore the difference between certain short-run and long-run effects of differential changes in demand for housing at different locations.

Heterogeneity and indivisibility of urban land results primarily from the existence of fixed capital improvements in the form of structures, streets and utility facilities. Indivisibility also results from the fact of diverse ownership of contiguous parcels of land and structures.[18] When fixed

---

[18] The effects of diversity of ownership of contiguous parcels and the consequent difficulty of land assembly for redevelopment will be discussed in Chapters 5 and 6, below.

capital improvements on land exist, the relevant factor of production is no longer urban land but real estate. Also, rentals now refer to the returns to land plus existing capital improvements together, for indeed, there is no unique way to separate out the returns attributable to various parts of the fixed factor when their proportions are given.[19] The presence of existing improvements on separate parcels of land affects the marginal returns to non-land factors applied to any particular parcel in the production of some commodity such as housing. In general, the more durable the improvements or the shorter the calendar time allowed for adjustment, the more elastic or steeper the schedule of marginal productivity of non-land factors applied to any given site. The existence of fixed improvements also means that otherwise similar plots of land may differ in the schedule of marginal productivity of non-land factors applied to them and means that certain parcels may be adapted more readily to changing conditions than others.

The simplest way to proceed in the analysis of what I have called complete uniqueness is to allow the production possibilities of firms in any given industry on each particular parcel to differ. I continue to assume that firms in any given industry have the same production possibilities and treat firms with different production possibilities as belonging to different industries. Thus, in my discussion below I shall let $Q_{ij}(N_{ij})$ refer to the output firms in the i-th industry would obtain from the j-th parcel of real estate if the amount of non-land factors used is N_{ij}. Also let p_{ij} and n_{ij} respectively be the unit price received by firms in the i-th industry for the product they produce and unit price paid for the non-land factors used if they use the j-th parcel of real estate in production. I still assume that firms are competitive in product and factor markets, and so the p_{ij} and n_{ij} are treated as given by them. Finally, for simplicity, I shall continue to assume that entrepreneurial rents are zero so that the maximum rental, r_{ij}, offered by firms of industry i for parcel j is simply the largest excess of receipts over non-land expenditures that can be produced. The necessary and sufficient conditions that

$$r_{ij} = p_{ij}Q_{ij}(N_{ij}) - n_{ij}N_{ij} \tag{20}$$

be a maximum are

$$p_{ij}Q'_{ij}(N_{ij}) - n_{ij} = 0, \tag{21}$$

and

$$p_{ij}Q''_{ij}(N_{ij}) < 0.$$

[19] See Ralph Turvey, *Economics of Real Property*, pp. 21–24, for a discussion of this point in the particular case of sites with existing structures.

The first of (21) is merely the usual condition that the use of a variable factor be carried to the point where the value of the marginal product is equal to the price per unit of the factor, while the second states that at the optimal point the marginal physical product must be declining.

Consider, now, the effects on r_{ij} which result from differences in prices or non-land costs. Differentiating (20) with respect to p_{ij} gives

$$\frac{\partial r_{ij}}{\partial p_{ij}} = \{p_{ij}Q'_{ij}(N_{ij})\} + \{p_{ij}Q_{ij}(N_{ij}) - n_{ij}\}\frac{\partial N_{ij}}{\partial p_{ij}} > 0,$$

or

$$\frac{\partial r^{*}_{i\,j}}{\partial p^{*}_{i\,j}} = \frac{p_{ij}Q_{ij}(N_{ij})}{r_{ij}} = \frac{1}{\rho_L}. \tag{22}$$

In like manner,

$$\frac{\partial r_{ij}}{\partial n_{ij}} = \{p_{ij}Q'_{ij}(N_{ij}) - n_{ij}\}\frac{\partial N_{ij}}{\partial n_{ij}} - N_{ij} < 0,$$

or

$$\frac{\partial r^{*}_{i\,j}}{\partial n^{*}_{i\,j}} = -\frac{n_{ij}N_{ij}}{r_{ij}} = -\frac{\rho_N}{\rho_L}. \tag{23}$$

Combining (22) and (23),

$$dr^{*}_{i\,j} = \frac{1}{\rho_L}dp^{*}_{i\,j} - \frac{\rho_N}{\rho_L}dn^{*}_{i\,j}, \tag{24}$$

which is identical in form with (4), the latter having been derived on the assumptions of perfect divisibility and homogeneity except for location. Under complete uniqueness, therefore, rentals to existing parcels of real estate vary with prices and non-land costs as in the earlier analysis. However, the relative importance of land plus existing structures is likely to be greater than the rentals of land alone, and so the relative variations of rentals to existing parcels of real estate are likely to be smaller for any given relative change in prices or non-land costs. In addition, rentals may now vary for many other reasons as well which may be summarized under the heading of physical differences among parcels or in their surroundings.

The variations in the value of output per parcel of real estate under complete uniqueness are also quite similar to those described in section two. Differentiating the value of output from a parcel with respect to price

$$\frac{\partial(p_{ij}Q_{ij})}{\partial p_{ij}} = Q_{ij} + p_{ij}Q'_{ij}(N_{ij})\frac{\partial N_{ij}}{\partial p_{ij}},$$

while by differentiating the necessary condition for firm equilibrium, one finds

$$Q'_{ij}(N_{ij}) + p_{ij}Q''_{ij}(N_{ij}) \frac{\partial N_{ij}}{\partial p_{ij}} = 0,$$

or

$$\frac{\partial N_{ij}}{\partial p_{ij}} = -\frac{Q'_{ij}(N_{ij})}{p_{ij}Q''_{ij}(N_{ij})} \geq 0.$$

Substituting then yields

$$\frac{\partial (p_{ij}Q_{ij})}{\partial p_{ij}} = Q_{ij}\left[1 - \frac{Q'_{ij}(N_{ij})^2}{Q_{ij}Q''_{ij}(N_{ij})}\right] > 0,$$

or

$$d(p_{ij}Q_{ij})^* = \left(1 - \frac{\rho_N}{E_{Q_N,N}}\right) dp^*_{ij}, \tag{25}$$

where

$$E_{Q_N,N}$$

is the elasticity of the marginal physical product of N with respect to its rate of use. The latter plays a role analogous to that of the elasticity of substitution in my earlier discussion. In fact, since

$$\sigma = \frac{-\rho_L}{E_{Q_N,N}},$$

equation (9) can be cast into exactly the same form as (25). The value of housing output per parcel of real estate in the complete uniqueness case thus tends to behave in much the same way as the value of output per unit land in my earlier discussion, declining with distance from the CBD if housing prices do. Also, if the relative importance of non-land factors tends to increase with distance, as still seems likely, and Q_N is less elastic or flatter, the coefficient of

$$dp^*_{ij}$$

in (25) will become numerically larger with distance, and an increase in demand will lead to a greater relative increase in value produced in the more distant locations. However, once one admits of physical differences in parcels of real estate there are many reasons other than location why prices of housing services will vary among parcels of real estate. If households prefer new to old dwellings, the price of housing services of new dwellings will be higher than for old dwellings. Or, if some buildings are surrounded by more attractive buildings or better streets with more parking

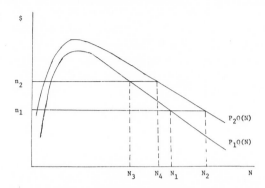

FIG. 5.—Determination of Rentals, Complete Uniqueness of Land

spaces than others, the price of housing services and hence rentals will be higher in them.

The variations of rentals and output with prices and non-land costs are illustrated in Figure 5. Suppose that value of output as a function of non-land factors applied to a particular parcel of real estate is that given by the curve $p_1 Q(N)$ and that non-land costs are n_1. So long as $p_1 Q(N)$ is above n_1 the excess of receipts over non-land costs can be increased by using more non-land factors in production. Rental is maximized when N_1 units are used and is the area under the $p_1 Q(N)$ curve up to N_1 less n_1 multiplied by N_1. An increase in price increases the optimal N to N_2, so that output and the rental imputable to the property increase. An increase in n from n_1 to n_2 with price fixed at p_1, however, leads to a decline in the amount of non-land factors used from N_1 to N_3, with a consequent decline in output and rental value.

Under complete uniqueness, equilibrium in the land or real estate market still requires that each parcel be devoted to that use which yields the highest rental. Thus, with an increase in, say, the demand for retail or office space, structures originally designed for residential purposes may be converted to other uses. The returns to a parcel of real estate must be greater in the new than in the old use by an amount at least sufficient to cover the necessary annual return to funds invested in conversion. But since the existence of fixed improvements means that the schedule of marginal productivity of non-land factors is more elastic at any given non-land cost than otherwise, the returns to the parcel will generally rise relatively less than they would if it were clear of such improvements.

I would now like to consider the relation of the short-run to the long-run response to a change in demand for a product such as housing. Suppose, for example, that because of a fall in transport costs, the demand for housing in areas close to the CBD falls, while housing demand in more distant locations rises. Such a change is illustrated in Figures 6a and 6b, which show demand and supply schedules for housing in central and distant locations. The curves D_1 are the demand curves prior to the change in demand, and p_1 is the price per unit of housing. The curves D_2 are those which result from the change in transport costs and are drawn on the assumption that price in the other location is p_2. The curves S_I are the initial stock of housing or the instantaneous housing supply schedules,

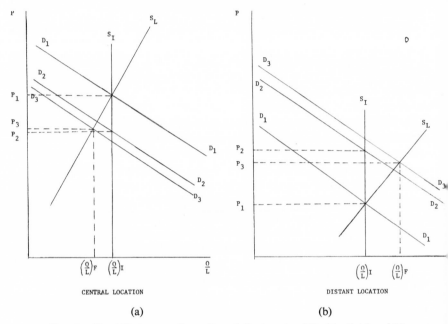

CENTRAL LOCATION   DISTANT LOCATION

(a)   (b)

FIG. 6.—Short-Run versus Long-Run Adjustments of Residential Land Use

while the curves S_L are longer-run supply schedules. (My remarks earlier in this chapter suggest that in the longest of all long runs these schedules are highly elastic.) The initial impact of the change in demand is wholly on price and causes price to fall (rise) at the central (distant) location from p_1 to p_2. At the central location the fall in price reduces the returns to existing properties and, hence, the incentive for owners to maintain them. One might thus expect properties to depreciate more rapidly in the central area where demand has fallen. The reverse is true, of course, in the more distant locations where housing prices rise.

As time for adjustment increases, the housing supply schedule becomes more elastic, reflecting conversions of existing dwellings and the wearing out of old buildings and their replacement by new ones. At the central (distant) location, price tends to rise (fall) along the demand curve D_2. However, with the fall (rise) in price at the distant (central) location, the demand schedule at the central (distant) location shifts downward (upward) to D_3, reflecting the change in price of the substitute commodity. Of course, the intersection of D_3 and S_L at the central (distant) location cannot be at a price lower (higher) than p_2, since this is inconsistent with the assumed shift of the other curve. This analysis, then, suggests that the immediate change in the price differential between central and distant locations is greater than the longer-run change.

Also, consider changes in the total value of housing produced at the two locations. Since the quantities of housing services produced remain initially unchanged, the fall (rise) in price from p_1 to p_2 at the central (distant) location implies a fall (rise) in value produced per square mile. The change in value which results from a movement along D_2, of course, depends upon the elasticity of demand. It would appear that the demand elasticity for all housing is no more than -1.[20] But since there are more substitutes for housing in any given location than for all housing, demand in each of the locations is probably elastic. If so, the movement along D_2 further reduces (increases) the value of housing produced per square mile in the central (distant) location. Finally, the shift of the demand curve from D_2 to D_3 in Figure 6 has the same effect. Thus, I conclude that the change in value of housing per square mile tends to be greater the greater the length of time allowed for adjustment. Of course, this is true also of the output of housing, since the schedule S_L is more elastic the longer the time allowed for adjustment. And, given the per capita consumption of housing, total population will rise (fall) in the distant (central) location by a greater amount the greater the time for adjustment.

---

[20] See my "The Demand for Non-Farm Housing," p. 72, and Margaret G. Reid, *Housing and Income*, p. 381.

4

The Distribution of Population and Housing Output within Cities

Having considered forces influencing the behavior of consumers and producers of housing separately in the preceding two chapters, I now wish to consider them jointly and show the implications of my analysis for the distribution of population within cities. While it may seem unusual for an economic analysis to be concerned with population distribution, the variation of housing prices and land rentals within the city affects the distribution of population through their effect on the consumption and production of housing. Letting D stand for population density, P for population, and H for households, it can be seen readily that

$$D = \frac{P}{L} = \left(\frac{P}{H}\right)\left(\frac{pQ}{L}\right) \div \left(\frac{pQ}{H}\right),$$

or

$$\frac{dD^*}{dk} = \frac{d}{dk}\left(\frac{P}{H}\right)^* - \frac{d}{dk}\left(\frac{pQ}{H}\right)^* + \frac{d}{dk}\left(\frac{pQ}{L}\right)^*, \tag{1}$$

where asterisks stand for natural logarithms. Thus, population density varies directly with the average size of households, (P/H), and the value of housing produced per unit of land, (pQ/L), and inversely with housing expenditures per household, (pQ/H). I have already discussed the behavior of the last two in some detail. While economic analysis has some implications for variation in the average size of household, I will show in Part II that such variations are quite small relative to those in the other two components of population density.

An empirical fact of great interest is the tendency, noted by Colin Clark over ten years ago,[1] for population densities to decline negatively exponentially with distance from the center of the city. In the first section of this chapter I shall discuss a highly simplified model, one of whose

---

[1] "Urban Population Densities."

implications is a negative exponential population density function.[2] In succeeding sections I shall then discuss various complications. This will be continued in the following chapter where I discuss the impact of factors such as the age of dwelling units, tastes and preferences, and other factors traditionally emphasized in writings on real estate.

A Simplified Model of Intracity Population Distribution

In beginning the analysis of this chapter I shall revert to most of the assumptions made in Chapters 2 and 3. I assume, in particular, that residential land is perfectly divisible and homogeneous except for location, that households have no preferences for different types of housing or for location and that the CBD is the only center of economic activity accessibility to which has value. All workers are employed either in the CBD or in widely scattered employment centers outside it. Similarly, goods and services at retail are purchased only in the CBD or locally, in the latter case there being no advantage of any one site over any other. With regard to transportation, each household makes a fixed number of CBD trips per unit of time, and transport costs are the same in all directions from the city center.

In addition, partly for convenience in exposition and partly to show the relationship of this analysis to my earlier paper on this subject, I will make four special assumptions in this section, all of which will soon be relaxed. First, all households are identical in that all are the same size and have the same tastes and preferences and the same opportunities. This means that their real incomes net of transport costs must be the same in equilibrium. The latter, in turn, implies that the money incomes of workers employed in the CBD must be the same, regardless of the location of their residences, and that the money incomes of locally employed workers must decline with distance from the CBD. Second, consumers have log-linear demand functions for housing. Since I am assuming that tastes and preferences and real incomes are the same for all households, the logarithm of the quantity of housing consumed per household depends only upon the relative price of housing services and is linearily related to the log of relative price. In my earlier study of housing demand I found that either a linear or a log-linear demand function for housing was a good approximation. Third, I assume that all producers of housing have the same logarithmically linear or Cobb-Douglas production functions in land and non-land inputs and that these exhibit constant returns to scale. Since the log-linear production function has been widely used in mathematical models and in empirical

---

[2] These results were first presented in my "The Spatial Structure of the Housing Market." As I noted there, this simplified model was developed prior to my learning of Clark's paper.

research in economics, it would seem to be the natural one with which to begin. Rather shortly, however, I will show that this third assumption is unsatisfactory for this particular purpose. Finally, I initially assume that the proportion of land which is used for residential purposes is constant throughout the residential annulus of the city. Thus, I need not distinguish between gross density, or population divided by all land, and net density, which is population divided by land used for residential purposes, since the latter is a constant multiple of the former. The proportion of land used for residential purposes, of course, depends upon the relative demands for land in residential and other uses, and I shall consider the latter problem in the third section of this chapter.

If all households have the same tastes for housing and the same real incomes, the locational equilibrium of CBD workers must be a neutral one, and it follows from equation (2.6)[3] that

$$\frac{p_{kk}}{p_k} + E_{q,p;C}\left(\frac{p_k}{p}\right) = \frac{T_{kk}}{T_k}. \tag{1}$$

Now as indicated in the preceding chapter, empirical studies by Margaret Reid and by me indicate that the real income constant elasticity of housing demand is about equal to -1, though it may be even more elastic. Furthermore, using data from the Washington, D.C., area, William Pendleton found that distance from the CBD accounted for 84 to 94 percent of the variation of measures of driving time to the CBD and job accessibility and that driving time was more closely related to simple mileage than to its logarithm.[4] Since the variable elements in transport costs are more or less inversely proportional to driving time on city streets, Pendleton's result would suggest that the marginal costs of transport are constant rather than decreasing with distance. The values $E_{q,p;C} = -1$ and $T_{kk} = 0$ when substituted into (1) above imply $(p_{kk}/p_k) = (p_k/p)$. Since

$$\frac{d}{dk}\left(\frac{p_k}{p}\right) = \left(\frac{p_k}{p}\right)\left(\frac{p_{kk}}{p_k} - \frac{p_k}{p}\right), \tag{2}$$

these values imply that the price-distance function must be negative exponential or that

$$p(k) = p_0 e^{-gk}, \tag{3}$$

where $g = (-p_k/p)$ is the price gradient.

---

[3] I.e. chap. 2 of this monograph, equation (6). This method of designating equations, tables, and figures appearing in other chapters is used throughout.

[4] William C. Pendleton, "The Value of Highway Accessibility," pp. 22–25. He also found a statistically significant but small sector effect.

The equilibrium for locally employed workers must also be a neutral one under the conditions assumed in this section. Hence (2.27) implies

$$\frac{w_{kk}}{w_k} = \left(\frac{p_{kk}}{p_k}\right) + E_{q,p;C}\left(\frac{p_k}{p}\right), \tag{4}$$

from which it follows that $w_{kk} = 0$. In the case discussed here, then, the money incomes of locally employed workers must decline by a constant absolute amount per unit distance.

Consider, now, variations in the per household consumption of housing with distance from the CBD. Since tastes for housing, real income and the prices of other items of consumption are the same everywhere by assumption and since empirically its appears that the real income constant demand elasticity is -1, the per household consumption of housing is

$$\left(\frac{Q}{H}\right) = q = A_0 p(k)^{-1} = A_0 p_0^{-1} e^{gk}, \tag{5}$$

when equation (3) is substituted. Thus, the per household consumption of housing increases exponetially with distance at a relative rate equal to the price gradient. Per household expenditures on housing, however,

$$\left(\frac{pQ}{H}\right) = pq = A_0, \tag{6}$$

are constant and invariant with distance from the CBD.

Knowing the form of the price-distance function and the production function of housing, the value of housing output per square mile of land can be derived. Where the production function for housing is given by

$$Q = a_0 L^{a_1} N^{1-a_1},$$

it is well known that $\sigma = 1$ and $\rho_L = a_1$, $\rho_N = 1 - a_1$, regardless of the relative quantities of L and N used in production and, hence, the location of production. Substitution of these values into equation (3.11) yields

$$\frac{d}{dk}\left(\frac{pQ}{L}\right)^* = \left(1 + \frac{1 - a_1}{a_1}\right)\left(\frac{p_k}{p}\right) = -\frac{1}{a_1}g. \tag{7}$$

Under the conditions assumed here, the slope of the log-value of housing per square mile function is invariant with distance. It follows from equation (1) that the variation in the log of population density with distance is identical with that of the log of the value of housing produced per unit of land in (7). The value of the price gradient, in turn, was shown in equation (2.3′) to be directly proportional to marginal transport costs and inversely proportional to the per household expenditure on housing.

If population densities decline negative exponentially with distance from the CBD at the same rate in all directions, it is a relatively simple matter to derive expressions for the level of population density when extrapolated to the city center, D_0, and for the total population residing within a distance not more than k miles from the center, $P(k)$. The latter is simply the definite integral of population density times the incremental land area at a given distance from the center taken over the residential annulus up to a distance of k miles. As shown above, population density at any point in the residential sector is

$$D(k) = D_0 e^{-D_1 k}. \tag{8}$$

I have already made the assumption that a constant proportion of the total land area is used for residential purposes throughout the residential annulus. Assuming for simplicity that the area of the CBD is zero—it is certainly small relative to the area of the city—in the residential annulus the total amount of land up to any given distance from the CBD is

$$L(k) = \frac{\xi k^2}{2}, \tag{9}$$

where $(\xi/2\pi)$ is the fraction of total area used for residential purposes. Therefore,

$$P(k) = \int_0^k D(v)L'(v)\,dv \tag{10}$$

$$= \xi D_0 \int_0^k v e^{-D_1 v}\,dv$$

$$= \frac{\xi D_0}{D_1^2} \times f(D_1, k),$$

where

$$f(D_1, k) = 1 - (1 + D_1 k)e^{-D_1 k}.$$

Equation (10) is illustrated in Figure 1. It is easy to show by differentiating (10) twice with respect to k that up to a distance $k = D_1^{-1}$, population residing within a distance k of the center increases at an increasing rate. The latter is true because the relative decline in population per unit area is offset by the increase in incremental land area. Beyond this point, however, $P(k)$ increases but at a decreasing rate. Assuming that the radius of the urbanized area is k_2 miles, the total population of the urbanized area, P, is equal to $P(k_2)$. Hence, it follows that

$$D_0 = \frac{PD_1^2}{\xi f(D_1, k_2)}. \tag{11}$$

The level of population densities, as described by the parameter D_0 or density extrapolated to the center of the city,[5] depends, then, upon the total population of the urbanized area, the proportion of land devoted to residential uses, the density gradient, and the radius of the urbanized area.

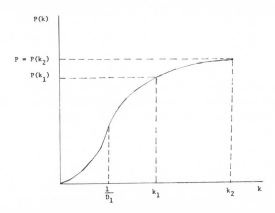

FIG. 1.—Population Residing within a Given Distance from the CBD

I shall comment upon k_2 in the following paragraph. The proportion of land used for residential purposes in the city depends upon the relative strengths of the derived demands for land to produce housing as compared with other non-agricultural commodities. I shall discuss this question in the third section of this chapter.

Finally, from the relationships in the above paragraphs it is relatively easy to derive expressions for the central city population and the land area occupied by the urbanized area. If one supposes that the central city of the

---

[5] By equations (9) and (10), the average population density up to a distance k miles from the CBD is

$$\frac{P(k)}{A(k)} = D_0 f(D_1, k) \bigg/ \frac{(D_1 k)^2}{2}.$$

Since, using Taylor's series with remainder,

$$e^{D_1 k} = 1 + D_1 k + \frac{(D_1 k)^2}{2} e^{\theta D_1 k}, \qquad 0 \leq \theta \leq 1,$$

$$\frac{P(k)}{A(k)} = D_0 e^{-(1-\theta)D_1 k}, \qquad 0 \leq 1 - \theta \leq 1,$$

$$\lim_{k \to 0} \frac{P(k)}{A(k)} = D_0.$$

Hence, D_0 is also the limiting value of average density as distance goes to zero.

urbanized area occupies a circular area of radius k_1 surrounding the CBD, by (10) its population, P_1, is

$$P_1 = \frac{\xi D_0}{D_1{}^2} f(D_1, k_1),$$

which becomes, upon substituting (11),

$$P_1 = \frac{Pf(D_1, k_1)}{f(D_1, k_2)}. \tag{12}$$

Thus, the central city's share of the total population of the urbanized area depends only upon the density gradient and the radius of the central city and of the urbanized area in the model formulated here. The radius of the central city depends mainly upon the vagaries of the political process and, apart from matters relating to municipal finance, has little economic significance. Elsewhere I have shown how the radius of the urbanized area, which also affects central density D_0, is determined by the relative strengths of the demand for land for housing and other urban uses, on the one hand, and for local agriculture, on the other.[6] As a practical matter, however, an urbanized area is defined by the Bureau of the Census as essentially all the land surrounding the CBD for which population densities exceed a certain minimum amount, D_m. Substituting D_m and k_2 into (8),

$$k_2 = \frac{(D_0^* - D_m^*)}{D_1} \tag{13}$$

defines k_2 if P is taken to be the urbanized area population as defined by the Census Bureau. If (13) is substituted into (9), the total land area occupied by the urbanized area, L, is thus determined. L is then seen to depend upon precisely the same factors as central density, D_0.

For interpreting the empirical comparisons of differences among cities in central city population and urbanized area land area to be presented in Part II, it is useful to derive log-linear approximations to the equations describing P_1 and L from which k_2 has been eliminated. Differentiation of (13) yields

$$dk_2^* = \frac{dD_0^*}{D_1 k_2} - dD_1^*, \tag{14}$$

while from (11),

$$dD_0^* = dP^* + \left(2 - \frac{\partial f_2^*}{\partial D_1^*}\right) dD_1^* - d\xi^* - \frac{\partial f_2^*}{\partial k_2^*} dk_2^*, \tag{15}$$

---

[6] "Economic Change and Rural-Urban Land Conversions."

where

$$\frac{\partial f_2^*}{\partial D_1^*} = \frac{\partial f_2^*}{\partial k_2^*} = \frac{(D_1 k_2)^2 e^{-D_1 k_2}}{f(D_1, k_2)}.$$

Substituting for dD_0^* in (15) and solving for dk_2^*,

$$dk_2^* = \alpha \, dP^* - (1 - 2\alpha) \, dD_1^* - \alpha \, d\xi^*, \tag{16}$$

where

$$\alpha = \frac{f(D_1, k_2)}{D_1 k_2 (1 - e^{-D_1 k_2})}.$$

Since from (9),

$$dL^* = d\xi^* + 2 \, dk_2^*,$$
$$dL^* = \beta \, dP^* - 2(1 - \beta) \, dD_1^* + (1 - \beta) \, d\xi^*, \tag{17}$$

where $\beta = 2\alpha$. Similarly, from (12),

$$dP_1^* = dP^* + \left\{ \frac{\partial f_1^*}{\partial D_1^*} - \frac{\partial f_2^*}{\partial D_1^*} \right\} dD_1^* + \frac{\partial f_1^*}{\partial k_1^*} dk_1^* - \frac{\partial f_2^*}{\partial k_2^*} dk_2^*, \tag{18}$$

$\partial f_1^* / \partial D_1^*$ being defined analogously with $\partial f_2^* / \partial D_1^*$ in (15). Substituting (16) for dk_2^* in (18),

$$dP_1^* = (1 - \gamma) \, dP^* + 2(\delta - \gamma) \, dD_1^* + 2\delta \, dk_1^* + \gamma \, d\xi^*, \tag{19}$$

where

$$\gamma = \frac{D_1 k_2}{(e^{D_1 k_2} - 1)} \quad \text{and} \quad \delta = \frac{1}{2} \frac{\partial f_1^*}{\partial D_1^*}.$$

The coefficients of dP^* and dD_1^* in (17) and (19), when evaluated using information on D_1, k_1, and k_2 and compared with estimated regression coefficients, will provide a useful check upon the consistency of the model developed in this section with real world behavior.

Effects of Differences among Households on Population Distribution

Perhaps the greatest shortcoming of the simplified model discussed in the preceding section is its assumption that the real incomes of all households are the same. Clearly, great differences exist in the real world, and, as I have shown in Chapter 2, one might expect to find systematic differences in the location and consumption of housing of households with different incomes. I will consider the needed modifications to the analysis that arise from income differences as well as from differences in tastes and in transport costs in this section. I will also discuss the effects of departures from my assumption that all producers have the same logarithmically linear production functions here.

Let us begin by considering the effects of income differences arising from differences in wage rates received by workers employed in the CBD. As was shown in Chapter 2, the effects of wage income differences on the location of CBD worker households depends upon the relative effects of higher incomes on housing consumption and on the marginal costs of transport. In Chapter 2, I argued on empirical grounds that, if anything, the former is likely to outweigh the latter and lead the higher wage income CBD workers to locate at greater distances from the CBD. Suppose first, for the sake of argument, that the two effects exactly balance. If so, the analysis of the preceding section need not be modified because there are no systematic tendencies on locational grounds for higher-paid CBD workers to live at greater distances. Rather, the locational equilibrium for all classes of CBD workers is still a neutral one. In terms of Figure 2.1b, the $-qp_k$ and T_k curves coincide for any class of worker, but the curves for the higher paid workers are above those for the lower paid workers.

If, as seems more reasonable to me, the effect of higher money-wage incomes in housing consumption outweighs the increased valuation of travel time, the higher-paid workers must then live at greater distances from the CBD. Suppose, first, that there are only two classes of CBD workers as defined by the wage incomes they receive. The two classes of CBD worker households then reside in annular areas around the CBD, with the higher-paid workers in the outer area. Within each of the two annuli the locational equilibrium is a neutral one, and so the price gradient is constant. Per household expenditures on housing are unaffected by price differences within or between the two areas if the real income constant demand elasticity is -1, but they are greater in the outer annulus because of the higher real incomes of households residing there. Since I am assuming that the marginal costs of transport are the same at different distances, the price gradient must then be smaller in the outer annulus by equation (2.3'). More generally, if there are n discrete classes of CBD workers there will be n concentric annuli of workers around the CBD, with the money and real income of CBD worker households increasing as one progresses from the innermost to the outermost annulus. Within each annulus the price gradient and the per household expenditure on housing by CBD worker households are constant. But the price gradient is smaller and per household expenditure greater the more distant the annulus from the CBD. The log price-distance function is thus a piecewise linear one which, overall, exhibits positive curvature.

Suppose, now, that the wage incomes of CBD workers vary continuously. The inequality in (2.6) must then hold, so for $E_{q,p;C} = -1$ and $T_{kk} = 0$, equation (1) becomes

$$\frac{p_{kk}}{p_k} - \frac{p_k}{p} < 0, \tag{20}$$

which, according to equation (2), implies that the price gradient must decline with distance from the CBD or the log price-distance function has positive curvature. And as was indicated in Chapter 3, positive curvature of the log price-distance function induces a positive curvature in the log rental-distance and log value of housing per square mile-distance functions. Positive curvature of the latter, in turn, tends to make population densities decline less rapidly with distance from the CBD than the negative exponential function would imply. Also, the per household expenditure on housing is no longer constant as implied by (6). Rather, substituting $E_{q,p;C} = -1$ and $T_{kk} = 0$ into equation (2.17) gives the variation in housing expenditures by CBD worker households with distance as

$$\frac{\partial(pq)^*}{\partial k} = -\left(\frac{p_{kk}}{p_k} - \frac{p_k}{p}\right)E_{q,y;R}(1 - \rho_T E_{T,y})$$

$$\div \{E_{q,y;R}(1 - \rho_T E_{T,y}) - E_{T_k,y}\} > 0, \tag{21}$$

or

$$= -\left(\frac{p_{kk}}{p_k} - \frac{p_k}{p}\right) \div \left\{1 - \frac{E_{T_k,y}}{E_{q,y;R}(1 - \rho_T E_{T,y})}\right\}.$$

If the elasticity of the marginal costs of transport with respect to income is, say, three-fourths of the relative increase in housing consumption which results from the income effect alone, then the relative increase in the value of housing consumption per household per mile would be four times the relative change in the slope of the log price-distance function.

The situation is somewhat different for locally employed workers. As argued in Chapter 2, workers employed at widely scattered, non-concentrated employment places outside the CBD can maximize their real incomes by locating as close to their places of work as possible. Hence, the location of local workers of different relative wage classes is determined by the distribution of their work places. Assuming that local workers all have the same preferences for housing, their locational equilibrium is still a neutral one, and equation (4) must still hold. Hence,

$$\frac{w_{kk}}{w_k} = \frac{p_{kk}}{p_k} - \frac{p_k}{p} < 0,$$

and since $w_k < 0$, $w_{kk} > 0$, or wage rates decline at a decreasing numerical rate with distance from the city center. Since locally employed workers of a given wage class are in neutral equilibrium with respect to location, the real incomes of any class of locally employed workers are everywhere the same, and thus their per household expenditures are still invariant with location. Like the distribution of local workers by income, then, housing expenditures of local workers depends upon the distribution of their work places. I am unable to think of any very convincing reasons why these should vary systematically with distance from the CBD.

Now consider the effects of differences in tastes for housing as compared with other consumption and in non-wage income as among households. In Chapter 2 I demonstrated that CBD worker households with stronger preferences for housing or higher non-wage incomes would tend to choose residences at greater distances from the CBD. Suppose that preferences for housing and non-wage incomes of CBD worker households vary continuously. Then, in order for their locational equilibrium to be a determinate one it is also sufficient that the price gradient decline with distance from the CBD. Either on account of higher non-wage incomes or stronger preferences for housing the CBD workers residing at greater distances are on higher indifference curves or, in effect, have larger real income. Since the effect of variation in the price of housing with distance is such as to leave housing expenditures unchanged, the higher real incomes of CBD workers at greater distances imply that housing expenditures tend to increase with distance from the CBD. Likewise, locally employed workers with stronger preferences for housing or higher non-wage incomes will tend to live and work at greater distances from the CBD and spend more on housing on account of their higher real incomes. But the locational equilibrium of local workers must be unique under these conditions, so that equation (2.27) implies

$$\frac{w_{kk}}{w_k} > \frac{p_{kk}}{p_k} - \frac{p_k}{p},$$

and it is no longer possible to predict the sign of w_{kk}.

Finally, consider for a moment the effects of differences among CBD worker households in transport costs. In the framework of my analysis, transport costs of a particular household would be greater than average if it had an above-average valuation of travel time, number of CBD workers, or preferences for commodities available only in the CBD. Whatever the reason, for any given money-income level,[7] households with above-average transport costs have lower real incomes and spend less for housing on this account. Above-average transport costs also cause the household to live closer to the CBD than average, but because the real-income con-

---

[7] The effects of money-income differences have already been taken into account.

stant-demand elasticity for housing appears to be unity, relative price effects have no influence upon expenditures for housing. Hence, also because of differences in transport costs, the per household expenditure on housing tends to vary directly with distance from the CBD. And, if differences in transport costs are to lead to stable locational equilibrium for different households, it is sufficient that the price gradient decline with distance from the CBD.

In summary, then, differences in money wage incomes or in transport costs of CBD worker households and differences in non-wage incomes or in tastes and preferences for housing versus other consumption have qualitatively similar effects in my model. First, any of the above would tend to result in an increase in the per household expenditure on housing with increasing distance from the CBD. The density gradient, therefore, reflects this variation in addition to the variation in the value of housing produced per unit of land at varying distances. And second, once differences among households are recognized, each household's locational equilibrium is unique. Given the values $E_{q,p;C} = -1$ and $T_{kk} = 0$, it is sufficient for a unique equilibrium that the price gradient decline with distance from the CBD. As was shown in Chapter 3, the effect of a declining price gradient is to make the rental and the value of housing per unit of land gradients numerically smaller at greater distances from the CBD. The latter, in turn, would tend to impart a positive curvature to the log density-distance function.

At this point it is convenient to consider the effects of departures from my assumption that all firms producing housing have identical, logarithmically-linear production functions. As was noted in Chapter 3, data published by the Housing and Home Finance Agency indicate that from 1946 to 1960 the ratio of site value to total property value on new FHA-insured single-family houses rose from 11.5 to 16.6 percent. During the same period, the HHFA reports that the values of equivalent sites rose more than 1.8 times.[8] Construction costs, however, as measured by the residential construction component of the implicit GNP deflator rose only about 77 percent.[9] This behavior is inconsistent with a single Cobb-Douglas production function for producers of housing assumed earlier, unless a non-neutral technological change increased a_1, the exponent of land, and hence land's share. Rather, it must be explained by an elasticity of substitution less than unity for the housing production function common

---

[8] *Fourteenth Annual Report*, p. 109.

[9] Computed from data in U.S. Department of Commerce, *U.S. Income and Output* (Washington: U.S. Government Printing Office, 1958), table 1, pp. 118–19, and "National Income and Product in 1962," *Survey of Current Business* 43 (July, 1963), tables 6, 14.

to all firms or by differences in production functions for different house types with an increase in the relative importance of house types for which land is relatively more important and for which the exponent a_1 tends to be larger.

Consider the implications of the first explanation. Assuming that all firms producing housing have the same production function, an increase in land's share can accompany an increase in the ratio of prices of land to non-land factors only if the elasticity of substitution is less than unity.[10] In fact, I have shown elsewhere that the above values imply an elasticity of substitution about equal to 0.75.[11] An elasticity of substitution which is less than unity by itself imparts a negative curvature to the log rental-distance and log value of housing produced per unit of land-distance functions, as was demonstrated in Chapter 3. This negative curvature tends to offset the positive curvature imparted to these functions by the positive curvature of the log price-distance function. Hence, the rental and land-use intensity gradients, as well as the density gradient, may be approximately constant, even though the price gradient declines with distance from the CBD. Equation (3.12) also implies in the case of an elasticity of substitution less than unity that the elasticity of value of housing produced per square mile increases with distance from the CBD. If such is the case, then with an increase in demand for housing, holding the price gradient constant, the output of housing, and hence population, would tend to grow relatively more rapidly in the outer parts of the city.

The increase in site value relative to total property value which accompanied the increase in land values relative to construction costs might also have arisen because of an increase in the relative importance of those house types for which land's relative importance is greater. Suppose that producers of each house type have logarithmically linear production functions which differ among house types in the magnitude of a_1, land's exponent in the production function and its relative importance. Then, as shown in the third section of Chapter 3, those producers of housing for whom land is relatively more important will tend to locate at greater distances from the CBD. As a consequence, the increased relative importance of land in house-type annuli at greater distances from the CBD will tend to impart a positive curvature to the log rental-distance function, as shown by equation (3.6). Since the decrease in the price gradient does so as well, the rental gradient would then clearly decline with distance from the CBD. Likewise, both the decrease in the price gradient and the increase in land's share with

---

[10] Unless a non-neutral technological change occurs. See my "The Derived Demand Curve for a Productive Factor and the Industry Supply Curve."
[11] *Ibid.*, p. 13.

distance would impose a positive curvature on the log value of housing produced per square mile-distance function, equation (3.11), so that population densities would decline less rapidly than negative exponentially with distance from the city center. In addition, the elasticity of the value of housing per unit land in equation (3.9) would become smaller at increasing distances from the CBD because of the increasing relative importance of land, and an increase in housing demand with a given price gradient would lead to a greater relative growth in housing output and population in the central parts of the city. The implications of the different production function hypothesis are thus quite different from those of the single function, less than unit elasticity of substitution hypothesis. Empirical evidence bearing on these two hypotheses will be presented and discussed in Part II.

The Proportion of Land Area Used for Residential Purposes

Thus far I have made no distinction between gross and net population densities and housing output intensities. Gross and net magnitudes differ in that the latter is obtained by deducting non-residential land area from the denominator. If, as I have been assuming, the proportion of land area used for residential purposes is invariant with distance, then gross and net magnitudes are everywhere proportional to each other, and the distinction between them is trivial. If this proportion is a random variable with constant mean, its variation introduces random variation of gross densities around their means. Finally, if this proportion varies systematically with distance from the CBD, it introduces a systematic difference between net and gross magnitudes.

Irrespective of the proportion of land used for residential purposes, the proceeding analysis applies in full to the value of housing produced per unit of land used for residential purposes and to net population densities. As I have argued above, the logarithms of these magnitudes tend to decline at a constant or numerically decreasing rate with distance from the CBD. What happens to gross densities depends upon the behavior of the proportion of land used for residential purposes as distance varies. More specifically, letting D_g and D_n stand for gross and net population densities and L_q the land area used to produce housing,

$$D_g^* = \left(\frac{P}{L}\right)^* = \left(\frac{P}{L_q}\right)^* + \left(\frac{L_q}{L}\right)^* = D_n^* + \xi^* - (2\pi)^*, \tag{22}$$

where, as noted earlier, $(\xi/2\pi)$ is the proportion of land used for residential purposes. Differentiating (22) twice with respect to distance:

$$\frac{dD_g^*}{dk} = \frac{dD_n^*}{dk} + \frac{d\xi^*}{dk}, \tag{23}$$

and

$$\frac{d^2 D_g^*}{dk^2} = \frac{d^2 D_n^*}{dk^2} + \frac{d^2 \xi^*}{dk^2}.$$

Perhaps the most likely alternative to constancy of the proportion of land used for housing, as argued below, is that the proportion increases with distance from the CBD. If so, the gross density gradient would tend to be smaller than the net density gradient and would reflect variations in ξ in addition to forces influencing the price gradient of housing and the elasticity of housing supply. Since it is bounded from above by unity, it seems quite unlikely that ξ could increase at a constant or increasing relative rate throughout the city. I would therefore expect variation in ξ to impart a negative curvature to the gross density and also the gross housing-intensity functions after some point.

The proportion of land area used for residential purposes, of course, depends upon the demand for land as derived from the demand for housing and upon the supply of land to the housing industry. But since the total supply of land for all uses in any given location is fixed, the supply of land to the housing industry is simply this fixed amount less the demand for land in all other uses. Furthermore, the amount of land devoted to residential purposes depends both on the position and elasticities of the demands for land in housing and all other uses. For, with equiproportional increases in the demand for land in all uses, the proportion of land area devoted to a particular use will vary inversely with its elasticity of demand relative to elasticities for other uses of land.

The best available explanation for the spatial pattern of retail and service industries is that provided by central place theory.[12] The latter suggests that shopping centers tend to form a more or less regular, hierarchical pattern with the CBD at the hub as the highest order center. If such a pattern exists, there is little reason to expect any marked variation in the concentration of retail and service business and its demand for land at different distances from the CBD. In regard to manufacturing and other processors, these firms tend to seek out locations close to harbors, rail lines, and highways because of the savings of terminal and other transport costs these locations afford. Now, of course, to the extent that railroads and streets move radially from the center of the city, the land they use and the amount of land adjoining them to any given depth is constant in absolute amount and so a decreasing proportion of the total land area as

[12] Central place theory is developed most completely by August Lösch, *The Economics of Location*, esp. pp. 103–37. An excellent short summary of Lösch's ideas is given in Stefan Valavanis, "Lösch on Location."

For a discussion of the spatial pattern of retail firms within a city see Brian J. L. Berry, *Commercial Structure and Commercial Blight*, esp. pp. 19–24 and 106–16.

distance from the CBD increases. In addition, some retail and service business tends to be oriented along major streets rather than areally, and the land along radial streets is a declining proportion of total area with increasing distance. For these reasons, one might expect the proportion of land used for residential purposes to increase at a decreasing rate with distance from the CBD.

The forces influencing the elasticity of demand for a productive factor such as land, which were mentioned earlier, in Chapter 2, are the elasticity of demand for the final product, the elasticity of supply of other factors, the ease of substitution in production, and the relative importance of the factor. Marshall argued that the greater any one of these the greater the elasticity of derived factor demand. Now, as my analysis in the first section of Chapter 3 suggests, there is a presumption that users for whom land is a relatively unimportant factor will tend to locate near the center of the city. In the language of international trade theory, these users have a comparative advantage in locating where land is relatively expensive, even though firms in all industries might find an absolute advantage in central locations. But, as Hicks showed, the elasticity of derived demand varies directly with the relative importance of the factor only if the elasticity of demand for the final product exceeds the elasticity of substitution in production. To the extent that firms in a given local industry sell only a small part of the output in a national or even worldwide market, the local industry demand curve is highly elastic and the Hicks condition would probably hold. If, however, the local industry is the sole supplier of a regional or even city-wide market, there is no presumption that the industry demand elasticity would exceed the elasticity of substitution. Thus, if anything, I would expect that because of the varying relative importance of land at greater distances from the CBD, the demand elasticity of land for non-residential, and hence the supply elasticity of residential, land would tend to be greater at greater distances from the CBD.

There would seem to be no grounds based on either the second or third of Marshall's factors for the demand elasticity of non-residential land to vary systematically throughout the city. It is quite difficult to infer anything about differences in the elasticity of substitution of land for non-land factors in production among different users of land. And, to the extent that non-land productive factors are highly mobile within a city, at least in the long run, one might expect a very high elasticity of supply of non-land factors to all users at all distances from the city center. As concerns differences in demand elasticities, there are two grounds for expecting a systematic difference. Firms whose market area is the whole of the city tend to locate near the center in order to maximize accessibility to their market. For this reason the output of firms near the city center would tend to have lower demand elasticities due to the existence of fewer substitute commodities than firms located near the edges. And second, at the edge of the city the major competitor with housing for land is agriculture. Since local agricultural firms generally account for only a small fraction of output sold nationally, I would expect their demand elasticity to be very great. The elasticity of land supply to the housing industry, therefore, may be relatively high near the edge of the city. And, since the demand for farm products has grown less historically than for most others, the supply of land to the housing industry has probably grown most rapidly at the edges of the city.[13]

In summary, both on account of the relative importance of land and final product demand elasticity, the supply elasticity of land to the housing industry if anything is likely to be greater in the outer parts of the city than in areas near the center. Consequently, as among cities of different sizes at any given time or as cities grow over time, differences in the demand elasticities for land in housing and other uses would have an effect on the spatial distribution of population and housing output. One might expect the proportion of land devoted to housing to increase more rapidly with distance from the CBD in the larger cities. And, if the elasticity of land supply to the housing industry is greater at greater distances from the CBD, gross population densities would tend to decline less rapidly with distance in the large cities.

SOME FURTHER MODIFICATIONS

Until now I have been assuming that a single concentration of employment and shopping exists in what is known as the CBD and that transport costs are the same in all directions from the CBD. I now wish to modify these assumptions. I shall first consider the effects on my model of introducing other centers of employment or purchase of commodities. Then I shall consider the effects of rapid transit facilities or express highways, which make transport costs dependent upon direction as well as distance from the CBD. In the chapter following this one I shall consider other factors, principally tastes and preferences and demographic ones, which influence the prices people will pay for housing and their effects on the spatial pattern of urban land use.

Suppose that a second concentration of employment exists along a certain radial from the CBD at a distance of k_2 miles from it, as illustrated

---

[13] One further point deserves notice. Farm or vacant land is probably converted to other uses more rapidly than other kinds of land because of lower conversion costs and smaller quasi-rents to capital improvements per unit of land. This factor would have only short-run significance, however.

in Figure 2*a*. By a concentration I mean a volume of employment great enough that all workers cannot live adjacent to their workplaces, so that accessibility to this common workplace has value. Figure 2*a* shows the variation of housing prices with distance from the CBD along the radial. As before, housing prices decline with distance from the CBD because

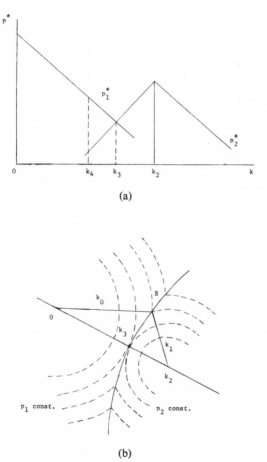

(a)

(b)

FIG. 2.—Effect of a Second Concentration of Employment upon Residential Land Use

transport costs increase, as shown by the segment of the curve labeled p_1^*. For exactly the same reasons, housing prices paid by workers employed at the second center decline from k_2, as shown by the segment p_2^*, both toward the CBD and away from it. Thus, in the neighborhood of k_2, land rentals, the wages of locally employed workers, and the value of housing produced per unit of land all decline with distance from the second center in the same manner as they decline with distance from the CBD. At any point along the horizontal axis of Figure 2a the price of housing that prevails is the greater of p_1 and p_2. Thus, at k_4, workers employed in the CBD would offer more for housing than workers employed in the second center, so the price of housing is that given by p_1^*. A worker employed in the second center would not live at k_4, since he could reduce both his transport costs and the price paid per unit of housing by moving toward k_2. Hence, k_3, where $p_1 = p_2$, is the boundary separating the residential areas of workers employed in the two centers.

The boundary at k_3 in Figure 2a is defined by the condition that workers living there are indifferent between employment in the CBD or in the secondary center. Since the price of housing at k_3 is the same for workers employed at either center, workers employed in the two centers who reside in the vicinity of the boundary will be on the same level of utility only if their money incomes net of transport costs are the same. Letting the subscripts 0 and 1 stand for the CBD and the second center respectively, y_i the money income of the worker if employed in the i-th center, and letting $T(k_i, y_i) = T_{0,i} + T_k k_i$, where $T_{0,i}$ represents the level of transport costs appropriate to income level y_i and T_k is assumed to be the same in the vicinity of each of the two centers, this condition becomes

$$y_0 - T_{0,0} - T_k k_0 = y_1 - T_{0,1} - T_k k_1,$$

or

$$(k_0 - k_1) = \frac{(y_0 - T_{0,0}) - (y_1 - T_{0,1})}{T_k}. \tag{24}$$

Equation (24) defines the difference in distance from the two centers at which the residential area boundary occurs. The difference is greater the greater the difference in money incomes of workers less the fixed and time costs of transport at the two centers and smaller the greater the marginal costs of transport. Since the locus of all points B, the difference of whose distances from two fixed points is constant, is a hyperbola, in two dimensions, as in Figure 2b, the boundary is one branch of the hyperbola defined by equation (24).[14] Figure 2b also shows contours of constant housing

---

[14] The specific functional form of the boundary depends critically upon the conditions assumed above. If, instead, money incomes net of the fixed transport costs were the same for workers employed in the two centers but the marginal costs of transport were higher about k_1, then the boundary around k_1 would be a circle whose center was to the right of k_1 on the line joining k_0 and k_1. If both money incomes net of transport costs and marginal transport costs differ about the two centers, the functional form of the boundary is more complicated. Where marginal transport costs differ, the rate of decline of housing prices also differs about the two centers, but the analysis is similar in other respects to that presented above.

prices as dashed lines; these are circles or segments of circles with centers at the CBD and the second center. As one moves outward along the residential area boundary away from the line joining the CBD and the second center, housing prices, of course, decline.

The location of the boundary in Figures 2a and 2b depends upon money-wage rates in the two centers and, hence, upon the relative demands for labor in the two centers. Let some employers move their workplaces from the CBD to the second center, so that the demand for labor declines in the CBD and rises in the second center, and for simplicity suppose that all households are identical in the sense of the first section of this chapter. With the fall in money-wage incomes of CBD workers and a rise in those of workers employed at the secondary center, workers in the vicinity of the boundary who previously worked in the CBD will find it advantageous to shift their place of employment to the secondary center. Likewise, in the new equilibrium workers who previously worked at the secondary center must pay higher prices for housing than before the change, while workers who continue to be employed in the CBD must pay lower prices for housing. Since I am assuming that all households are identical, CBD and secondary center workers must have the same real incomes both before and after the change in the relative demand for labor in the two centers. Furthermore, if, as seems reasonable, the total quantity of labor supplied to the two centers together depends only upon the real wage income received per worker, the change in the distribution of a given total employment among the two centers will leave real incomes unchanged. But money-wage incomes paid to CBD workers have fallen, and those paid to secondary center workers have increased. If housing prices were to remain unchanged everywhere, the real incomes of CBD workers would be lower than before the change and those of secondary center workers higher. Thus, in the new equilibrium the function p_1^* in Figure 2a must be lower than before, the function p_2^* higher, and the boundary separating the two areas closer to the CBD. Therefore, land rents, the value of housing produced per square mile, and population densities are higher than before in the secondary-center worker residential area and lower in the CBD worker area.[15]

Where many secondary employment centers exist, the analysis is quite similar to the two-center case. In the vicinity of each employment concentration, housing prices and thus land rents, the value of housing produced and population densities decline with distance from the center. Workers employed in the various centers live in non-overlapping residential areas. The boundaries between any pair of areas are branches of hyperbolas

---

[15] Since the shift in workplace alone will not change the real incomes of workers under the conditions assumed here, the per household expenditures on housing and the price gradient in either area are the same as before the change.

determined by equations such as (24). The overall boundary for the residential area of workers employed in any given center is made up of segments of these various hyperbolas and thus may be irregular in shape. The number of workers employed in the various centers and the size of their various residential areas depend upon the relative demand for labor in these centers, which I take as given in this analysis.

When secondary employment centers exist, housing prices and hence land rents, land use intensity and population densities no longer decline everywhere with distance from the CBD. Rather, local peaks surrounding these secondary centers exist. As can be seen from Figure 2a, a straight line fitted to the log price-distance function so as to minimize the sum of squared deviations about it would have a flatter slope than either p_1^* or p_2^*. And, indeed, a quadratic fitted to this function might provide a closer fit, even though the log of price declined linearly with distance from either employment center. The greater the employment in the secondary centers the higher the local peaks in housing prices relative to those about the CBD and the less rapidly would a least-squares fitted line tend to decline with distance. Now it has been shown above that the patterns of decline in land rents, land use intensities, and population densities generally tend to follow that of housing prices. Thus, I would expect that, overall, the rate of decline of population densities with distance from the CBD would be greater the greater the relative importance of employment in the CBD relative to that in secondary centers.

I now wish to relax the assumption that no residential site differs from another in terms of accessibility to goods and services purchased outside the CBD. As I have suggested earlier, shopping centers tend to be located in a more or less regular, hierarchical pattern with the CBD as the highest-order center. Under these conditions, consumers who are otherwise similar but with differential accessibility to a given shopping center would have different real incomes if they paid the same prices for housing. If locational equilibrium is to prevail, housing price differentials must reflect differential accessibility to these non-CBD shopping centers. Hence, in the vicinity of these centers, I would expect land rents, the value of housing produced per square mile, and population densities to decline with distance from them in much the same way as about the secondary employment centers.

Finally, I wish to consider the effects upon spatial patterns of land use that result from the fact that transport costs may differ with direction as well as distance from the CBD. For concreteness, suppose as in Figure 3, that an expressway or rapid transit line, L, extends eastward from the CBD, the point O. For travel along this route the marginal costs of transport are only a fraction, a, as great per unit distance as they are for any other direction of travel. Consider the travel path of a CBD worker residing at the point P, whose coordinates are (X_1, Y).[16] If the worker follows a circuitous route, traveling from his residence at (X_1, Y) to the line L at $(X_0, 0)$ and then on L to the CBD, his transport costs are a function of effective distance traveled, k_e, where

$$k_e = aX_0 + [Y^2 + (X_1 - X_0)^2]^{1/2}. \tag{25}$$

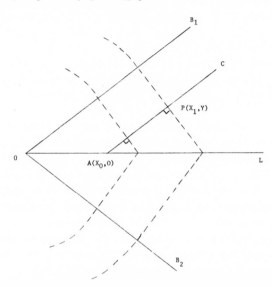

FIG. 3.—Effect of Rapid-Transit Route on Residential Land Use

The minimum effective distance and transport costs are obtained by differentiating (25) with respect to X_0, equating this to zero and solving for X_0:

$$\frac{dk_e}{dX_0} = a - \frac{(X_1 - X_0)}{[Y^2 + (X_1 - X_0)^2]^{1/2}} = 0, \tag{26}$$

or

$$X_0 = X_1 - \left\{\frac{a}{(1 - a^2)^{1/2}}\right\} |Y| \quad \text{or} \quad 0,$$

whichever is the larger. Thus, all CBD workers residing within the sector B_1OB_2, or for whom

$$|Y| \leq \frac{(1 - a^2)^{1/2}}{a} X_1,$$

---

[16] The analysis here depends heavily on Herbert Mohring, "Land Values and the Measurement of Highway Benefits," pp. 240–41.

will find that their transport costs are minimized by following a circuitous route, first along the line C in Figure 3 to X_0 as defined by (26) and then to the CBD on L, while all others will travel directly to the CBD.[17]

With the existence of rapid travel routes, distance to the CBD is no longer a satisfactory metric because contours of constant transport costs are no longer circles. Rather, within the sector B_1OB_2 the minimum effective distance or transport cost for any CBD worker is found by substituting (26) into (25); doing so one obtains

$$k_e = aX_1 + (1 - a^2)^{1/2}|Y|, \tag{27}$$

or

$$Y = \pm \left[\frac{k_e}{(1 - a^2)^{1/2}} - \frac{a}{(1 - a^2)^{1/2}} X_1 \right]$$

Equation (27) states that the contours of constant transport cost in the sector B_1OB_2 are composed of straight line segments which are orthogonal to the travel paths such as C. These are shown as straight lines in Figure 3. The value of k_e, and hence of transport costs, for any such contour is given by the distance at which it intersects the lines B_1 and B_2 from the CBD at O. Elsewhere, of course, the contours of constant costs are segments of circles centered on the CBD. Not surprisingly, the smaller is the constant a the steeper are the travel paths C, the flatter are the contours of constant transport cost in the sector B_1OB_2 and the greater is the residential area of workers using L for travel to the CBD.

When a low transport cost route such as L exists, of course, housing prices are now constant along the contours of constant transport costs rather than along circles centered on the CBD. But otherwise the previous analysis needs little modification. Like housing prices, land rentals, the value of housing produced per unit of land, and population densities are constant along contours of constant transport cost and all decline as one moves from lower to higher cost contours. Thus, along any straight line to the CBD in the sector B_1OB_2 all tend to be higher at any given distance from the CBD and tend to decline less rapidly with distance from the CBD.

The existence of several low transport cost routes requires only trivial amplification on the above. For each such route there will be a sector similar to B_1OB_2 in Figure 3, which delineates the residences of CBD workers who use it. Contours of constant transport cost will be composed

---

[17] Because of congestion phenomena, or perhaps for other reasons, relative transport costs along L may differ with the time of day. Thus, there may be one zone of expressway use for work trips or during rush-hours and another for off-peak travel. Such phenomena change the details of the analysis but not its substance for my purposes.

of linear segments within these sectors and segments of circles between them.[18] Otherwise, the preceding analysis applies in full. Summarizing, if I substitute the term effective distance or accessibility to the CBD for distance, the analysis developed earlier applies in full. But when differences in transport cost with direction from the CBD exist, empirical measurement or testing of the above analysis becomes much more complicated.

---

[18] Of course, in some cases the sectors of low transport cost routes may be adjacent to each other. If so, there will be no intervening circular segment to the contours of constant transport costs and no zone of direct travel to the CBD.

5   *Other Determinants of Residential Land Use*

Thus far I have focused upon accessibility and its effects upon spatial patterns of residential land use. I have done so partly because I believe accessibility to be of great importance empirically and partly because the effects of accessibility on the kinds and intensity of residential land development have never been very thoroughly analyzed. In my earlier analysis I have emphasized long-run, static equilibrium conditions and have neglected preferences of households for housing of different types. In this chapter I wish to consider the effects of some additional factors. First, I shall examine the effects of the age of a neighborhood and its dwelling units upon the intensity of residential development and the households who locate there. Next I will consider briefly a variety of hypotheses about tastes and preferences for housing and their effects on residential location. In the third section I will inquire into the subject of residential segregation and discrimination. Finally, I shall reexamine the question of residential location choice when households do not regard housing of various types as equivalent.

THE AGE OF BUILDINGS AND NEIGHBORHOODS

Most textbooks and other writings on real estate and land economics have stressed the importance of the legacy of the past on the pattern of land use in cities. Many have emphasized that the relatively great durability of buildings means that, once initially developed, the pattern of land use in a neighborhood is fixed for relatively long periods of time. The durability of buildings is generally considered to be of such importance that the effects of current conditions are completely overwhelmed by the heritage of the past. Ralph Turvey[1] expressed this view most clearly and succinctly:

...It is impossible to present a comparative statics analysis which will explain the layout of towns and the pattern of buildings; the determining background

---

[1] *The Economics of Real Property*, pp. 47–48.

conditions are insufficiently stationary in relation to the durability of buildings. In other words, each town must be examined separately and historically. The features of London, for example, can be fully understood only by investigating its past; it is as it is because it was as it was.

I believe this view is largely incorrect. Of course, if the phrase "fully understood" is taken literally, the statement is tautologically correct but uninteresting. If Turvey's remarks are understood as a judgment about the relative worth of comparative static analysis versus historical analysis, however, this monograph, I believe, demonstrates that, far being overwhelmed, long-run comparative static analysis is a highly fruitful source of propositions which stand up quite well to empirical testing. Yet I would be the last to deny that the heritage of the past may have important implications for the spatial pattern of residential land use in cities. In this section I wish to consider some of the effects of the time of development upon the subsequent pattern of land-use intensity and upon the kinds of households which locate in a particular area.

The pattern of land use in a particular area within a city is undoubtedly influenced greatly by the levels of transport costs prevailing at the time of its initial urban development. Of course, expected future changes affect decisions currently made through their effect upon land values. However, it is probably fair to say that few persons anticipated the great impact of the development of the automobile prior to its introduction. Transport costs, especially time costs, were much greater per unit distance prior to the auto. Because of these greater transport costs I would expect that a greater premium would have been paid for accessibility to the city center, to other concentrations of employment and the purchase of goods and services, and to rail and other routes providing rapid transport to these centers. In addition, greater transport costs would imply that housing prices have fallen off more rapidly with distance from these centers and transit routes. This is illustrated in Figure 1, where the price of housing is shown in one direction from the city center at the origin and where for simplicity it is supposed that accessibility to the center is the only determinant of the pattern of housing prices. The log price-distance function prior to the automobile is p_1^*, while the long-run equilibrium pattern appropriate to the era of automobile transport is that designated p_2^*. Up to a certain distance, k_1 in Figure 1, the long-run equilibrium price of housing falls with the introduction of automobile travel, while beyond that point the long-run equilibrium housing price is greater than previously.

As argued at length in Chapter 3, the spatial pattern of land rentals in the residential ring and the output of housing per unit of land is similar to that of housing prices. In particular, the greater the price of housing and hence residential land rentals, the greater the intensity of residential land use. Thus, areas to the left of k_1 which were developed prior to the automobile era would tend to have greater outputs of housing per square mile than appropriate to the new long-run equilibrium price-distance function. This might mean, for example, that lot sizes were smaller, buildings occupied a higher proportion of these lots, and that more multi-unit structures were built than would be the case if the area had been developed later. On the other hand, the reverse would be true in areas more distant from the center, or to the right of k_1 in Figure 1.

Given sufficient time, of course, the older areas would tend to be rebuilt in accordance with the changed transport cost and housing price relationships. But there are several factors which might tend to inhibit this redevelopment. When a few scattered buildings in the older areas wear out or when previously vacant lots or sections are built upon, the newer buildings might tend to conform to the earlier established pattern of the neighborhood. If streets and utilities have already been put in and lot sizes already established, there may be severe physical limitations upon the kinds of structures it is profitable to build.[2] Also, the demand for newly built structures of various kinds in an area may be greatly affected by the nature of the surrounding neighborhood. It seems quite likely that households would offer less for single-family detached housing in the older areas where multi-unit structures predominate than in comparably located areas of newer, single-family houses. On the other hand, new apartments might command higher rentals in a previously single-family unit area because of its desirable neighborhood characteristics than in an older, multi-unit area, so that the more intensive redevelopment in the areas more distant from the city center may be hastened on this account.

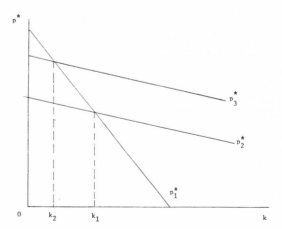

FIG. 1.—Effect of the Automobile on Residential Land Use

[2] On this point see Hoover and Vernon, *Anatomy of a Metropolis*, pp. 132–33.

Another factor which may under some conditions inhibit redevelopment is zoning restrictions.[3] Even if a private developer of one or a few lots were to find it profitable to erect structures which differ from the majority of those in the area, he might be prohibited or at least delayed from doing so by such restrictions. Since zoning restrictions frequently set only an upper limit on the intensity of land use, they may be more likely to delay redevelopment in previously single-family unit areas where housing prices are now higher than previously. This is likely to be especially so in the case of so-called "fiscal zoning" in municipalities outside the central city—the alleged use of zoning controls to prevent the greater school and other municipal expenditures which would result from more intensive development and the consequent greater property tax burdens on existing residents. However, I would expect that, with the passage of time, more and more residents of the area would desire to redevelop their properties to newer uses, so that zoning restrictions would be modified or variances granted.[4]

When existing buildings cease to earn quasi-rents in excess of site rentals when redeveloped to their current best uses less interest on demolition costs, they will be ready for replacement. If the structures in a neighborhood were erected at about the same time, they will tend to be ready for replacement at about the same time. The relatively great durability of structures implies that their redevelopment may be long delayed. This factor is likely to be more important in areas which call for less intensive land use when redeveloped, since, after any given time from their initial development, site values are likely to be greater relative to quasi-rents accruing to existing structures than in the less intensively developed more distant areas. Also, redevelopment may be hampered by the fact that it requires assembly of many plots under fragmented ownership. Not only can such site assembly be costly and time consuming, but any single owner may learn of the developer's plans and hold out for a higher price for his property than he might otherwise try to obtain. If so, redevelopment is made more costly and may be delayed.

While the durability of buildings and the other factors discussed above may delay adjustments to changed conditions, it should not be supposed that no adjustments to these changes are possible. Durability affects primarily the exteriors of buildings. Conversions of interiors to a smaller number of larger apartment units in areas where housing prices have fallen, and the reverse where they have risen, are still possible. And, with

---

[3] *Ibid.*

[4] For an analysis of the conditions under which modification of zoning restrictions would appeal to a sufficient number of voters to be undertaken, see Otto A. Davis, "Economic Elements in Municipal Zoning Decisions."

the fall in housing prices in the older, more intensively developed areas, smaller-sized households may occupy quarters of any given size so that population densities fall on this account.

Finally, the effects on housing prices of a decline in the marginal costs of transport, such as that brought about by the automobile, may be offset by a growth in population. With a growth in population housing prices will tend to rise at all distances from the center because of the relative inelasticity of the supply of urban land. Thus, in Figure 1 the resultant of a decline in transport costs and population growth might be that that log price-distance function shifts from p_1^* to p_3^*. Despite the fall in transport costs, areas developed prior to the change in the range k_2 to k_1 in Figure 1 will experience an increase rather than a decline in housing prices, and more rather than less intensive redevelopment will be called for there. Population growth may also increase the demand for the output of CBD firms proper as well as those manufacturing and wholesaling firms around the CBD's edges. Such a growth in demand tends to offset the decline in demand for residential and other uses of land in the vicinity of the center resulting from the lower marginal costs of automobile and truck transportation. When this happens, previously residential land near the center will be converted to other uses and old housing demolished. The effects of population growth may thus partly offset those of declining transport costs in the more central parts of the city.

In addition to its influence on the intensity of residential development, the age of a neighborhood may also have an important effect on the kinds of households that locate in it. As will be demonstrated in Part II, there is a strong tendency for higher-income groups to live in newer housing. There are several possible reasons for this. What first comes to mind is that buildings and neighborhoods necessarily deteriorate over time, both because of physical wear and tear and because of obsolescence. After a point such buildings no longer provide a sufficient quantity of housing for the residents they once housed, and the latter are replaced by lower-income households, which find the smaller quantity of housing more suited to their circumstances. The decline in quantity of housing as it ages may, too, be largely relative. Over time, as the incomes of all households tend to increase, the relatively higher-income groups might find that the quantity of housing they wish to consume has increased and move into newer, larger, and better quality dwellings than they previously inhabited. The next income class in relative terms finds the housing previously inhabited by the highest relative income group now suitable for itself, and so forth. Considerations such as these seem to form the basis for the notion of "filtering," which is so frequently belabored in the real-estate literature. Finally, newer housing may be inhabited by the higher-income groups because they have stronger preferences for, or are willing to pay a greater premium for, new housing than the lower-income groups. If this last is the case, then the quality of housing of any given age might be adapted to the income level of the inhabitants who choose to live in it, rather than the reverse, as implied by the first of the hypotheses mentioned above.

Whatever the reason for the negative association between the age of buildings and the income level of its inhabitants, one would expect to find that the per household consumption of housing is larger in the newer than in the older neighborhoods. This follows from the positive income-elasticity of demand for housing. The effect of age on the output of housing per unit of land is a bit more complicated. If, over time, the cost of transport has fallen, in areas close to the city center one would expect to find a greater output of housing per unit of land in the older than in newer areas, but the reverse would be true in the outer parts of the area. In the central areas, both because of greater output of housing per unit land and smaller per household consumption of housing, population densities would tend to be higher in the older areas. In neighborhoods in the outer parts of the city, however, these two effects of age on population density work in opposite directions, and their net effect cannot be determined on a priori grounds.

OTHER FACTORS AFFECTING THE DEMAND FOR HOUSING OF DIFFERENT TYPES

Many factors might conceivably affect the relative demand for housing of different types and thus indirectly the pattern of urban residential land use. Among these are housing-type preferences associated with the level of a household's income, those related to its life-cycle stage, the relative cost of housing of different types, and various neighborhood effects. I shall discuss each of the above and their effects in this section.

Studies by Margaret G. Reid,[5] by John R. Malone,[6] and by me[7] all suggest that the consumption of housing is strongly related to income and rises at least in proportion to it. The increase in expenditure for housing that accompanies rising incomes can take a variety of forms, two of which are of particular interest for my purposes. In explaining the tendency for population densities to decline with distance from the center of the New York Metropolitan Region, Hoover argues that "higher income people use their superior purchasing power to buy lower density" and that "rising incomes and leisure are the basis for a demand for newer houses as such,

---

[5] *Housing and Income.*
[6] "A Statistical Comparison of Recent New and Used Home Buyers."
[7] "The Demand for Non-Farm Housing."

and in general for more spaciously sited homes."[8] I have already argued that housing which uses a relatively high proportion of land to other productive factors tends to be built at greater distances from the city center, since land rents are lower relative to construction costs there. Thus, if higher-income persons prefer housing made up of more land relative to structures than lower-income persons, one would expect to find income level and the per household consumption of housing rising with distance from the city center and population densities falling on this account. In addition, as incomes grow over time, one would expect the demand for housing at greater distances from the city center to rise relative to that in areas near the center and the price and density gradients to fall.

It might also be argued that higher-income persons or those of higher occupational status have stronger preferences for home ownership or for single-family dwellings. Data on the housing status of non-farm families gathered for various years by the Survey of Consumer Finances indicates a strong tendency for the proportion of households who are home owners and live in single-family dwellings to increase with income.[9] There are several possible explanations for this tendency. First, if there are economies of scale in construction, the relative cost of single-family detached houses as compared with apartments of comparable size might decline with increasing dwelling size. Higher-income persons might also have stronger preferences for the privacy and prestige that home ownership affords. They may also tend to move less frequently so that the costs of home ownership are smaller for them. Finally, the federal income tax advantage to home ownership, to be discussed in greater detail below, increases with increasing income. Since single-family, detached houses tend to be more land-intensive than apartments, an increase in the relative demand for them with increasing income would mean both that at any given time higher-income persons tend to live at greater distances from the city center and that with a general rise in incomes the demand for housing more distant from the city center tends to increase.

The Survey of Consumer Finances data cited also show a marked tendency for home ownership to increase with age of the head of the household, at least up to ages thirty-five to forty-five. This tendency no doubt results partly from the desire for more space which accompanies increasing numbers of children. In addition, younger households probably move about more frequently than do older ones. But perhaps most important is that younger households typically have accumulated less non-human capital

---

[8] Hoover and Vernon, *Anatomy of a Metropolis*, p. 169 and p. 222.
[9] See, for example, "1958 Survey of Consumer Finances, Purchases of Durable Goods," *Federal Reserve Bulletin* 44 (July, 1958): 773.

than older ones. For this reason borrowing costs are probably greater, and hence the costs of home ownership greater relative to renting, than for households whose heads are in their middle or later years. If the relative demand for single-family, owner-occupied homes depends upon the age distribution of the population, the demand for housing in different parts of the city will tend to be affected as well. In this regard, the increase in both absolute and relative terms of apartment building in recent years is generally attributed to the fact that, in the sixties, households in the younger age-groups will increase most rapidly. Thus, in the sixties, the relative decline in population of the older, more central parts of cities may tend to be reversed.

While available data suggest that the proportion of households that are home owners increases with the age of the head until middle age, they show little or no tendency for the proportion to decline among still older households. In addition, the housing expenditures of older households tend to be greater, especially at lower current income levels, than the expenditures of younger households. These tendencies may result partly from the fact that moving costs, especially the non-monetary costs of giving up accustomed associations, are greater for older households, which have shorter expected life-times over which to amortize them. Also important is the fact that the relevant income variable for analyzing housing decisions is not current annual income level but rather permanent income, or income expectations averaged over a period considerably longer than a year. Because the proportion of households that are home owners shows little decline after middle age, there would seem to be little reason to expect that an aging population would bring a back-to-the-city movement, as some anticipate.

The relative demand for single-family houses is also affected by the relative prices of housing of different types. Two factors which have been quite important in affecting the relative prices of single-family housing during the past thirty years are the FHA mortgage-insurance and VA mortgage-guarantee programs and the federal income-tax treatment of income from owner-occupied housing. The federal mortgage programs reduce interest costs for single-family, owner-occupied housing, especially for households with little accumulated non-human wealth.[10] The annual costs of the services of a $10,000 house, for example, would be about $1,200. With a 90 percent FHA loan at $5\frac{1}{2}$ percent per year plus the $\frac{1}{2}$ percent insurance charge, the interest costs of borrowed funds would be $540 per year. An alternative to federally assisted financing would be a

---

[10] See my "Interest Rates, Contract Terms, and the Allocation of Mortgage Funds," esp. pp. 67 and 79.

conventional loan, which until quite recently was limited to 70 percent of the value of the mortgaged house, plus a second mortgage for the balance. Assuming a 6 percent rate of interest on a $7,000 loan plus a 12 percent rate on the $2,000 second mortgage (interest rates on second mortgages are typically around twice those on first mortgage loans[11]), the total annual interest cost would be $660 per year. Use of an FHA-insured loan by a home-owner with few funds of his own to invest in his home, therefore, would result in a saving on interest costs of about $120 per year on a $10,000 house or about 10 percent of its annual service cost. Because the federal mortgage programs reduce the cost of housing from owner-occupied housing to borrowers with little accumulated non-human wealth, they tend to increase the relative demand for single-family, owner-occupied housing.

Under the federal personal-income tax, income (net of depreciation) from owner-occupied housing is tax exempt, since owners are not required to report the rental value of their dwellings as income but can deduct mortgage interest and state and local property taxes.[12] Of course, the tax exemption applies regardless of house type, and, indeed, the growth of cooperative apartments since the middle thirties is probably due in large part to favorable tax treatment. But the cooperative apartment has not yet achieved widespread importance.[13] I suspect that this fact is in large part due to difficulty of resale resulting from the fact that the market for cooperatives is thin and approval of a sale by other members of the cooperative is required. Ownership of a cooperative apartment unit is also more risky than ownership of a house, since each member of the cooperative is liable for the mortgage indebtedbess of the other members.[14] Hence, the principal effect of the increased magnitude of the tax saving on owner-occupied housing resulting from the increase in federal personal income taxes since the middle thirties has been to stimulate the demand for single-family houses. Favorable income-tax treatment is also, no doubt, an important reason why home ownership tends to increase with income level. This results from the fact that at higher income levels more is spent on housing, and hence greater tax savings result from owner occupancy.

---

[11] See Saul B. Klaman, *The Postwar Residential Mortgage Market*, pp. 236–37.

[12] For a fuller discussion see Richard Goode, "Imputed Rent of Owner-Occupied Dwellings under the Income Tax."

[13] Louis Winnick, "Rental Housing: Problems for Private Investment," in *Conference on Savings and Residential Financing*, 1963 Proceedings, ed. Leon T. Kendall and Marshall D. Ketchum, p. 112, estimates that even in New York City, where cooperatives are more important than in other cities, they account for less than 5 percent of the apartment inventory.

[14] The development of the condominium may be viewed as an attempt to overcome these difficulties.

Now, it might be argued that so-called accelerated depreciation—the federal income-tax provisions which allow greater deductions for depreciation from taxable income from housing than the decline in value actually experienced—tends to offset or even eliminate the effects of tax exemption of income from owner-occupied housing. Accelerated depreciation does tend to reduce the effective tax rate on income from rental housing and, hence, the latter's relative price. But a little reflection readily shows that accelerated depreciation cannot wholly eliminate the effects of a positive tax rate. Let N be the net income after taxes from a parcel of residential property, G be income gross of federal income taxes but net of property taxes and expenses, i be the federal income-tax rate, D be depreciation allowable for federal income-tax purposes, and V be the value of the parcel for tax purposes. Then

$$N = G - i(G - D) = (1 - i)G + iD.$$

Under the 1954 tax code, as an alternative to straight-line depreciation for a period of T years, a taxpayer could deduct a fraction $2 \times (1/T) = \tau$ of the undepreciated balance of the original cost of the property from his taxable income. Use of this so-called double declining balance method, of course, is more favorable to the taxpayer than straight-line depreciation. Under the double declining balance method $D = \tau V$ or $dV/dt = -\tau V$, so $D = \tau V_0 e^{-\tau t}$ and

$$V_0 = \int_0^\infty N(t)e^{-\delta t}\,dt = (1 - i) \int_0^\infty G(t)e^{-\delta t}\,dt + \frac{i\tau V_0}{(\delta + \tau)}, \qquad (1)$$

where V_0 is the original value of the property and δ is the rate at which the taxpayer discounts future income. Letting R be the ratio of the present value of future gross income as defined earlier to the original value of the property, equation (1) can be rewritten as

$$R = \frac{1}{(\delta + \tau)} \left\{ \frac{\delta}{(1 - i)} + \tau \right\}. \qquad (2)$$

Note that this formulation assumes that any excess of depreciation over gross income can be offset against other income. The actual provisions of the tax laws are less favorable to the taxpayer, so that V_0 is somewhat overstated by (1), and R is understated by (2).[15]

---

[15] Of course, if $i \geq 0$, for a given V_0 and any $t \geq 0$ accelerated depreciation means that the value of a building to its original owner is less, and declines more rapidly over time, than would have been the case at time t had the rate of depreciation for tax purposes been equal to the true depreciation rate. Once the discrepancy in these two values has become as large as the costs of selling the building, the original owner will sell out to someone else. The new owner will then deduct a greater amount for depreciation than the original owner would have done and will receive a larger net return from the building. The original owner, however, by reinvesting the proceeds of the sale, net of selling costs, at the prevailing market rate of return, will receive

For home owners, $i = 0$, therefore $R = 1$, but it can be readily seen that for $i \geq 0$, no matter how large τ is, $R \geq 1$. Indeed for an interset rate of 6 percent per year and a "true" rate of depreciation of 2 percent per year, $\tau = 0.05$ (corresponding to $T = 40$ for multifamily structures allowed by the tax guidelines) converts a marginal income-tax rate of 50 percent into one of about 42 percent. Alternatively, substituting the values $\delta = 0.06$, $\tau = 0.05$ and $i = 0.5$ into (2), $R = 1.54$ approximately. Thus, if for home owners the ratio of the average annual gross rental to original value is about 0.08, for landlords this last ratio would be about 0.123. Adding in allowance for property taxes (0.025) and maintenance and repair expenditures (0.015), the ratio of price per unit of services to original value is around 0.12 for home owners and 0.16 for renters.[16] Since in the long run the original values of the two kinds of property are approximately fixed by highly elastic supply schedules, the overall effect of the federal income-tax system is to reduce the price of housing services from home ownership as compared with renting by about 25 percent.

By reducing the price of housing to home owners and thus increasing their consumption of housing, by (2.3) the price gradient must be smaller at the home owner's new equilibrium location. As argued earlier, this will be at greater distances from the CBD. In addition, relative housing demand may increase in the outer part of the city because single-family housing is relatively cheaper there. For these reasons, federal mortgage programs and income-tax treatment of owner-occupied housing would tend to increase the demand for housing at more distant locations and hence cause population to grow relatively more rapidly in the outer parts of cities. Indeed, it is possible that federal mortgage subsidies and tax treatment, which together reduce the cost of housing by as much as 35 percent for home owners, may have contributed substantially to the massive post-World War II redistribution of population toward suburban areas. With rising income levels, this effect will probably become even stronger. Elimination of mortgage subsidies and favorable tax treatment—such subsidies are hard to justify on any grounds—might well stimulate again the demand for housing in apartments, and so in areas closer to the city center.[17]

---

exactly the same return he would have received by retaining ownership of the building. For this reason, no modification of (2) is required because of the incentive for change of ownership of assets which accelerated depreciation provides.

[16] Note that the above gross rates of return on housing correspond quite closely with the ratios of property value to gross monthly rental commonly used by real estate appraisers, namely 100 and 72 for single-family houses and apartments, respectively.

[17] The proposal advanced by the Kennedy administration in early 1963 to limit deductions for federal income-tax purposes would substantially eliminate this favorable tax treatment for many middle-income home owners, since a major part of their deductions are for mortgage interest paid and for state and local real property taxes.

Finally, the relative demand for housing in various locations may be influenced by a whole host of features external to the individual structure commonly termed "neighborhood effects." Earlier I argued that housing in the proximity of local employment or shopping centers would tend to be higher priced than other housing a comparable distance from the city center because transport costs would be lower for households locating there. On the other hand, because of unsightly appearance, noise, unpleasant odors, or traffic congestion such locations may be undesirable. If so, lower housing prices on their account may tend to offset higher prices due to superior accessibility. Other features of the city such as a university or other cultural centers or a park in the neighborhood may make location in the vicinity more desirable and cause housing prices to be greater than they otherwise would be.

As observed by Homer Hoyt and others, areas of higher-priced housing are not scattered uniformly throughout the city; rather, they tend to cluster together, frequently proceeding out from the center of the city along certain radials.[18] Such sectoring might result from the presence along these radials of physical features, such as the lake front in Chicago, the mountains in Los Angeles, or a major street such as Park Avenue in New York, or from the absence of undesirable ones, such as rail lines or commercial streets, which, respectively, attract or repel higher-income households. The clustering of neighborhoods of higher-priced housing also might result from the fact that households prefer to live among others of similar economic and social characteristics. Once districts of higher-income residents are established, housing of any given quality of structure may tend to be more expensive than elsewhere because of the more attractive surroundings in these districts.

The effects of neighborhood characteristics, such as those mentioned above, on land rentals, on the output of housing per unit of land, and on population densities are quite similar to those of accessibility. As with nearness to the city center, external features which increase housing prices lead to a bidding up of residential land rentals if firms producing housing are to earn the same incomes regardless of their locations. Higher land rentals, in turn, lead to a greater output of housing per unit of land. The latter effect, by itself, would tend to make population densities higher in attractive neighborhoods. But if higher income households tend to locate in these neighborhoods, the per household consumption of housing is greater and population densities smaller on this score.

---

[18] *The Structure of Residential Neighborhoods in American Cities*, pp. 72–78.

RACIAL SEGREGATION AND DISCRIMINATION

Most of the readers of this book are familiar enough with racial segregation, or separation, in housing that they will not require any documentation of its existence. For those few skeptics, Karl E. Taeuber has demonstrated that in most large cities in the United States around 90 percent of the Negro population would have to move to new residences in order for them to be spatially distributed in the same way as the native white population. He has also shown that little of the Negro segregation vis-à-vis the native white population can be attributed to income and occupational differences.[19] Of course, the residential clustering of certain groups is not limited to Negroes. Many neighborhoods in American cities are noted as the residential locations of various ethnic groups; others are justly characterized as workingmen's neighborhoods, suburbs of younger, middle-income groups with large families, and so forth. However, the residential segregation of Negroes is of great current interest because of the Negro drive for racial equality, and it is frequently alleged to have important effects on the intensity of residential land use and the quality of urban housing. This section, therefore, will be concerned primarily with the residential segregation of Negroes.

It is commonly believed that residential segregation results from the refusal of landlords to rent to Negroes in white areas and of real-estate agents in these areas to deal with potential Negro buyers. Indeed, so-called "open occupancy" legislation would seem to be designed with this hypothesis in mind. While landlords and real-estate agents probably behave as alleged above, it is important to inquire into the reasons for their behavior. One explanation, which I call the seller's preference hypothesis, is that renters or sellers of housing have a unique aversion to dealing with Negroes not shared by the community at large and thus refuse to do so. I find this explanation quite unsatisfying. In the first place, segregation occurs in many other forms where landlords and real-estate agents are not involved. While it might be argued that the failure to serve Negroes in some restaurants and to hire Negroes in some establishments may be due to the aversion of their owners to deal with Negroes, segregation also occurs in churches and country clubs as well as in many fraternal organizations where there is no handy villain to be found. In addition, members of many ethnic groups tend to congregate in cities without apparent coercion. Finally, and most important, if landlords refuse to rent to Negroes because of their own aversion to doing so, they will tend to have a greater number

---

[19] "Negro Residential Segregation, 1940–60: Changing Trends in the Large Cities of the United States." Conclusions similar to Taeuber's were reached by Anthony H. Pascal, "The Economics of Housing Segregation."

of vacancies in their buildings on the average and earn lower incomes from these buildings than they otherwise would. Similarly, if real-estate agents fail to deal with potential Negro buyers because of their own preferences, they will make fewer sales and earn lower incomes. It would thus be in the interest of renters or sellers of real estate to sell out to others without an aversion to dealing with Negroes; by so doing they could increase their incomes, since potential buyers without these aversions would offer more than the capitalized value of the business to the landlords or real-estate agents who are averse to dealing with Negroes.

An even less satisfying explanation for the residential segregation of Negroes is what might be termed the collusion hypothesis. According to the latter, some landlords and real-estate agents, perhaps in concert with other persons, actively collude to limit the range of residences open to Negroes in order to profit from higher Negro housing prices. To a great extent the collusion hypothesis suffers from the same shortcomings as the seller's preference hypothesis. For it is difficult to account for segregation in non-profit organizations or for the segregation of various other social and ethnic groups on the basis of such a hypothesis. More important, however, is the fact that such collusive agreements, which would necessarily involve literally hundreds of participants in large cities, would be impossibly difficult to administer and enforce without active governmental support. It is almost inconceivable that such a large number of participants could agree upon or carry out a plan for dividing the gains from collusion. Any party to the collusive agreement would stand to benefit by breaking it so long as the other members of conspiracy were to follow the agreement. Furthermore, if somehow the conspiracy were organized and succeeded for a time in raising housing prices to Negroes, it would be profitable for non-members of the agreement to sell occupancy rights to their properties to Negroes. Thus, such a conspiracy would probably break down quickly.

A much more reasonable explanation for residential segregation is that whites have a greater aversion to living among Negroes than do other Negroes.[20] If so, whites would offer more for housing in predominantly white neighborhoods than would Negroes, and separation of the residential areas of the two groups would result. To see why this is so, consider the residential configuration schematized in Figure 2, where the symbol *W* stands for a white resident and *N* for a Negro resident. Suppose that whites are willing to pay more for housing to the right of the line *B* than are Negroes. Negroes may either be willing to pay more for residences to the left of *B* or to the right; in the latter case it is only necessary that they be

[20] See Gary S. Becker, *The Economics of Discrimination*, p. 59.

willing to pay less for these residences than white buyers. Under such conditions white buyers will tend to move to the right of line *B* since they are willing to offer more for occupancy rights to such housing than the Negroes currently living there, and the converse will apply to Negroes. The two groups will thus tend to gravitate into separate residential areas. Note also that the price of housing along the line *B* will differ from that in the interior of the same area. If whites have an aversion to living in proximity to Negroes, they will inhabit residences along the right of the boundary between the white and Negro areas only at a lower price for housing than in the interior of the white area. If, as seems likely, some Negroes are willing to pay more for housing in proximity to whites, or have an aversion to segregation, the price of housing immediately to the left of the line *B* will tend to be greater than in the interior of the Negro area.

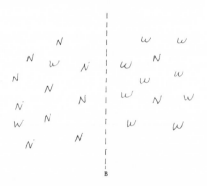

FIG. 2.—Race and Residential Location

This alternative explanation for residential segregation suffers none of the shortcomings of the seller's preference of collusion hypotheses enumerated above. Segregation in stores, eating places, and the like, and in employment may similarly be explained in terms of preferences of customers or employees,[21] as can segregation in religious and fraternal organizations and the residential separation of ethnic groups. The failure of landlords to rent to or real-estate agents to deal with Negroes is also readily understandable in terms of this explanation. The landlord's refusal may be interpreted as based upon a desire to avoid the loss of white tenants, the real-estate agent's, similarly, on the desire to avoid the loss of future business—even if the white seller for whom he is acting as agent has no aversion to selling to a Negro buyer. Under these conditions, no other person would be willing to offer more for the landlord's building or the

---

[21] *Ibid.*, pp. 47–58.

agent's business and to deal with Negroes, since he would be subject to the same restrictions. Now, it might be argued that landlords and agents act as they do in the mistaken belief that their customers have an aversion to living near Negroes. But this suggestion is subject to the same short-comings as the seller's preference hypothesis.

If the customer preference hypothesis is correct, then enforced open-occupancy legislation would have little effect on the residential segregation of Negroes. Such legislation might force some landlords who otherwise would not rent to Negroes to do so. But, if their white tenants have an aversion to living among Negroes and comparable housing is available to them elsewhere at the same price, they will tend to move out of the inte-grated buildings and neighborhoods, and the area will come to be inhabited wholly by Negroes. The enforced open-occupancy legislation would tend primarily to penalize landlords and real-estate agents for catering to the preferences of their customers.[22] Such legislation, however, might tend to make the area inhabited by Negroes grow more rapidly over time by making it easier for them to obtain housing outside existing Negro areas. The effects of other measures to break down the residential segregation of Negroes, such as President Kennedy's famous "stroke of the pen" for-bidding refusal to sell federally-assisted housing to Negroes, are likely to have similar effects so long as whites are willing to pay higher prices for housing in proximity to other whites than are Negroes.

As ably pointed out by Becker, the fact of residential segregation need not imply discrimination, or higher prices for housing of comparable quality in the Negro than in the white area.[23] While Negroes and whites may tend to live in separate areas and Negroes may be unable to obtain housing in the interior of the white area at any given time, the relative prices of housing in the two areas depend upon the size and rate of growth of the Negro area in relation to the Negro demand for housing. In fact, if the customer preference hypothesis described above is correct, then under certain circumstances housing prices in the Negro area might even be lower than in the white area. Returning to Figure 2, suppose initially that prices in the interior of the Negro area were the same as in the interior of the white area. Assuming that Negroes prefer integration and whites segregation, prices would then be higher than in the interior on the Negro side of the boundary and lower on the white side.

Thus, at the boundary separating the two areas, housing prices in Negro occupancy would be higher, owners of occupancy rights on the white side

---

[22] Cf. Milton Friedman's remarks on so-called fair employment practice legislation in *Capitalism and Freedom*.
[23] *The Economics of Discrimination*, p. 59.

of the boundary would have the incentive to sell them to Negroes, and the boundary would tend to shift toward the white area. If there are no external forces to prevent this movement and if the Negro and white demands for housing are changing at the same rate, then as the boundary shifts and the supply of housing to Negroes grows relative to the white supply, housing prices to Negroes will fall relative to those paid by whites. Under such conditions, the only possible equilibrium position is one in which prices are equal on the Negro and white sides of the boundary. Such a situation implies, of course, that housing prices in the interior of the Negro area would be lower than in the interior of the white area.[24]

Of course, in many large cities the Negro population is growing relative to the white population. Under these conditions the Negro demand for housing would grow relative to the white demand for housing, and it could do so at a great enough rate relative to the increase in the size of the Negro area so that any initial price differential for housing in the interior of the two areas would tend to be maintained or even increased over time.[25]

The analysis of the three preceding paragraphs readily suggests why so-called "block-busters" may make money by purchasing occupancy rights to residences on the white side of the boundary and selling these rights to Negroes. Even if housing prices in the interiors of the Negro and white areas were the same, a greater aversion on the part of whites to living among Negroes would imply that at the boundary separating the two areas the Negro price would exceed the white price. Block-busters profit by buying in the lower-price market and selling in the higher-price one. The returns to block-busting may be increased by the refusal of established real-estate agents to handle transactions in racially changing neighborhoods. Their refusal, coupled with a fall-off in demand by white buyers and a lack of knowledge about potential Negro buyers on the part of white sellers, would enable block-busters to purchase occupancy rights from white sellers at a lower price than they otherwise would. There is little reason to expect that block-busters are enabled to sell at an above-normal price to Negro buyers, however, since the alternative opportunities of the latter are in no way restricted by the conditions described in the previous sentence. The refusal of established real-estate agents to take part in transactions in changing neighborhoods would also tend to slow down the expansion of the Negro residential area in the face of a relative growth in Negro demand. For this reason, prices in the Negro area are probably higher than they would otherwise be.

---

[24] Cf. Martin J. Bailey, "Note of the Economics of Residential Zoning and Urban Renewal," upon whose penetrating analysis I have drawn heavily here.

[25] Becker, *The Economics of Discrimination*, pp. 60–62, suggests this hypothesis to explain the differential he believed to exist.

Evidence on housing prices by race is difficult to obtain. Consumer expenditure surveys and census data on average contract rents generally show that Negroes make greater expenditures on housing than do whites at any given income level. Such evidence is frequently taken to mean that housing prices are higher to Negroes than to whites, but this evidence is faulty for several reasons. Data from consumer expenditure studies are frequently distorted by various eligibility requirements for inclusion as well as by the fact that such studies often include repayment of mortgage principal and exclude interest on the owner's equity for those in owner-occupied housing. Census data on average contract rents include, in addition to space rent, any payments for rental of furnishings and for utilities furnished the tenant, and these may differ systematically among various groups. In addition, Negroes tend to have more persons per room, mostly because of their lower incomes, than do whites. Rentals they pay may be larger on this account because of greater costs for utilities and depreciation. But most important is the fact that the effect of price differences on expenditure differences depends critically upon the elasticity of demand for housing. Evidence cited earlier suggests, in fact, that the price elasticity of the demand for housing is at least equal to unity and perhaps even numerically larger. Thus, if housing prices for Negroes were higher than for whites, Negroes would tend to spend the same or less for housing on this account, not more. Even when using census data, it is quite difficult to eliminate the effects of size, condition, and other factors making for differences in quantity purchased as well as such factors as accessibility and neighborhood effects which, apart from race, affect housing prices.

The only convincing previous evidence on the relation of housing prices to race of which I am aware is that provided in a recent study by Martin J. Bailey.[26] Bailey analyzed the selling prices, as measured by the amount of federal real-estate transfer tax stamps affixed to the deed, of single-family houses in the Hyde Park–Kenwood area of Chicago. In addition to a large number of variables describing the physical characteristics of dwellings and their locations, Bailey included the percentage of the non-white population in the block in which the property was located and also that in the surrounding ring of blocks.[27] For sets of transactions in both the periods 1948–51 and 1954–57 his results imply that in the interior of the non-white residential area selling prices were *below* those of comparable properties in the interior of the white area, as these terms are used above. His findings are also consistent with the hypothesis that whites have an aversion to, but

---

[26] "Effects of Race and Other Demographic Factors on the Values of Single-Family Houses."

[27] His blocks were defined as all the dwellings on either side of a given north-south street between adjacent east-west streets.

non-whites prefer, residential integration. For they imply that on the non-white side of the boundary separating the two residential areas prices are higher than those of comparable properties in the interior of the non-white area, while on the white side of the boundary they are lower than prices in the interior of the white area.

If Negroes really pay more for housing of comparable quality than do whites, one would expect to find effects as between white and Negro areas which are similar to those of differences in accessibility. Indeed, evidence of such effects would be far more convincing to me than comparisons of housing expenditures, for the reasons two paragraphs above. Higher housing prices for Negroes would lead to a greater output of housing per square mile and a smaller per household consumption of housing, so that population densities would tend to be greater in Negro areas than in similar white areas. Even in the short run, owners of dwellings changing to Negro occupancy could convert their properties to a larger number of smaller units. In addition, if housing prices were higher for them, Negroes would tend to double-up, and dwellings of a given size would be occupied by a large number of persons in Negro areas. Of course, such short-run responses to a Negro-white housing price differential would probably result in less of a differential in population densities as between Negro and white areas than the long-run response, since possibilities for substitution either in consumption or in production tend to be greater the greater the time period for adjustment. As discussed in more detail in the following chapter, if Negroes pay higher prices for housing, one would expect to find a higher proportion of Negro households living in substandard dwellings at any given income level. Finally, most of the difficulties in inferring something about the Negro-white price differential for housing from census data can be avoided by comparing rents and values in a given area before and after part of the area changes from white to Negro occupancy. I shall present evidence on the race differential in housing prices of the kind suggested here in Part II, below.

THE EFFECTS OF PREFERENCES FOR DIFFERENT HOUSE TYPES ON
RESIDENTIAL LOCATION CHOICE

The present chapter has discussed many reasons why households might consider different kinds of housing as qualitatively different. In my earlier discussion of residential location choice, however, I tentatively assumed that consumers regarded all housing as identical. I now wish to relax this assumption and inquire briefly into how preferences for different types of housing affect both the locational choice of the consumer and the spatial pattern of residential land use in cities.

It is simplest and also sufficient for this purpose to suppose that housing can be divided into a finite number of house types. Housing of various kinds might be characterized by, say, houses and apartments, new and old housing, and housing in white and Negro neighborhoods. Within each of these types the assumptions of Chapter 2 are assumed to hold, in particular, that households regard all housing in any given type category as identical, that the price of housing of any given type varies with distance to the city center, and that transport costs increase at a non-increasing rate with distance from the center.[28]

Each household, then, determines in the manner already discussed in Chapter 2 its optimal location and amount of housing consumption for each of the house-type categories. Its global utility maximization, and hence the location and amount of housing consumed that it actually selects, is then determined by selecting from among these local utility maximums the one which yields the greatest utility. Thus, for the house type actually selected all the properties of the optimal location and housing consumption choice developed in Chapter 2 must hold. This means in particular that for any given house type the price of that type of housing must decline at a decreasing rate with distance from the city center. Of course, to say that higher-income households have stronger preferences for single-family housing means that a higher proportion of them than of lower-income households find that their global utility maximum entails choosing single-family housing.

With a change in one of the model's exogenous variables, the local utility maximization within each house-type category is affected precisely as described in Chapter 2. If, say, the marginal costs of transport fall with everything else remaining the same, the household's optimal distance from the city center for each house type increases. This would result in an increase in the relative demand for housing of each type in the more distant parts of the city. But the analysis is complicated by the fact that the optimal house type may change. This is especially the case with an increase in income. As before, the effect upon optimal household location for any given house type depends upon the relative strength of the increased income on housing consumption and on the marginal costs of transport. In addition, because of the increase in the tax saving on owner-occupied housing and other factors discussed above, a larger number of households would find that their grand utility maximization is found by choosing single-family housing. Since this type of housing tends to be produced in

---

[28] The reader can easily supply the modifications necessary where more than one employment or shopping concentration exists or where transport costs vary with direction as well as distance from the various centers.

the outer part of the city, the equilibrium distance from the center would increase for this reason for some households. Finally, the equilibrium location for a household might change independently of the factors discussed earlier if, for example, the head of the household ages or the number of children in the household increases, because the optimal house-type changes.

6 *The Determinants of Dwelling-Unit Condition*

Despite the widespread concern over poor-quality housing or slums, the many pages written on the subject, and the large sums of money and resources devoted to improving housing quality by federal and local governments, surprisingly little attention has been given to the causes of poor-quality housing. Books on slums and urban renewal typically devote only a few pages to examining the causes of slums before turning to ways of dealing with the problem. This is probably the case because slums seem so obviously bad that the need for taking action against them is clearly established. And yet, without proper diagnosis, any proposed treatment may be largely ineffective. In my study of the slum problem I have become convinced that this is the case. Most arguments commonly given are defective for one or more of a variety of reasons and ignore the basic cause of poor housing quality, which is the poverty or low incomes of its inhabitants. With the possible exception of public housing, most suggested remedies for slums do little or nothing to remove or reduce poverty and they may even tend to increase it. Hence, they are likely to be ineffective in the long run.

Certain arguments for the existence of slums are obviously incomplete and of little value. Thus, it is very often said that slums result from the greed of landlords and their neglect to maintain their properties in good condition. But one might justifiably argue that all landlords desire to earn as large incomes as they can from the properties they own or manage. The relevant question to be asked, and most fail to ask it, is why some landlords find it profitable to maintain their properties in good condition while others do not. Likewise, it is frequently asserted that slums result from the failure of cities to enforce building, occupancy, and similar codes.[1] But this second assertion quite obviously begs the question of why the need for enforcement exists.

---

[1] This point is heavily stressed by the Subcommittee on Urban Redevelopment of the President's Advisory Committee on Government Housing Policies and Programs, *A Report to the President of the United States* (Washington: Government Printing Office, 1953) pp. 108–9.

While many other arguments for the existence of slums are logically complete, they are inconsistent with at least one of three fairly simple empirical facts. I will discuss these arguments in the first section of this chapter, and the facts upon which they founder in the second. In the third section I will outline a theory which is consistent with these basic facts. Finally, in the last section I discuss spatial aspects of poor housing quality and the effects of housing quality on the spatial pattern of land-use intensity.

THE AGE AND NEGLECT AND OTHER TRADITIONAL THEORIES OF SLUMS

Many frequently cited theories of slum formation are based upon a decline in the demand for housing in what were once good neighborhoods. While the reasons for the assumed decline in demand are varied, its effects are quite similar in all these theories. I shall discuss these theories first. Next, I shall discuss several closely related theories whose emphasis is on factors inhibiting investment in housing or new assets generally and which lead to much poor-quality housing. In the following section I discuss three important facts with which these theories are in conflict.

Perhaps the most commonly advanced reason for the decline in demand for housing in once good-quality neighborhoods which is believed to initiate slum formation is age and obsolescence. It is frequently argued or implied that physical deterioration and obsolescence by itself inevitably makes the housing in older areas progressively less desirable for places of residence.[2] This might be the case if the cost of maintaining structures in good repair increased over time, so that maintenance expenditures on any given building or its neighbors would decline with age.[3] Or, it might be argued that, even if maintained in good condition, old housing becomes progressively less desirable over time as new types of dwellings and more attractive neighborhood patterns are developed. Other forces which affect the demand for residences might be closely associated with the age of a neighborhood and its buildings. In discussing the origin of cheap residential areas in Chicago, Hoyt observes that:

Workingmen's cottages tended to grow up in all sections of the city between the belts of fashionable land and the industries and factories along the Chicago River.... The tracts they occupied were close to the noise and dust of factories

---

[2] See, for example, Thomas F. Johnson, James R. Morris, and Joseph G. Butts, *Renewing America's Cities* (Washington: The Institute for Social Science Research, 1962) pp. 3–5; Richard U. Ratcliff, *Urban Land Economics*, p. 402; and *Slums, Large Scale Housing, and Decentralization*, Report of President's Conference on Home Building and Home Ownership, ed. John M. Gries and James Ford, p. 2.

[3] Ratcliff, *Urban Land Economics*, p. 402.

but not directly contiguous to water or rail transportation. Such sites were poorly provided with street improvements and surface car transportation.[4]

While such dwellings may have provided satisfactory accommodation to their original inhabitants, because of rising incomes or for other reasons the demand for housing in these areas has fallen over time. Many writers also stress the neglect by municipal governments of older residential areas as a cause of the decline in the demand for housing. Failure to plan effectively and to enforce zoning laws as well as the lack of parks and other recreational facilities and inattention to street maintenance and lighting are mentioned as specific instances of this neglect.[5]

While the reasons given for the decline in the demand for housing in older neighborhoods are varied, the effects of this decline noted by those who consider explicitly the process of slum formation are quite similar.[6] The decline in demand reduces the price of housing in old neighborhoods. With the fall in housing prices, investment in existing dwellings declines because of the fall in returns to such investment, and the quality of housing deteriorates. If quality deterioration itself caused the initial decline in demand, the latter accelerates the deterioration of the neighborhoods. With the fall in demand and quality deterioration, older residents move to newer neighborhoods where the available housing is more suited to their tastes and circumstances. Their places are taken by lower-income households, who have less aversion for poorer-quality housing than higher-income groups, and dwellings may be converted to smaller units more suitable to the size quarters these lower-income groups wish to occupy. The relative, and in some cases absolute, decline in population in the older, more central parts of cities is often attributed to the decline in housing demand due to age and/or related factors.

Another frequently cited cause of the decline in demand for housing in the older, more central parts of cities is the fall in transport costs brought about by the automobile.[7] I have already argued in Chapter 5 that the fall in the marginal costs of transport which accompanied the automobile reduced the relative rate of decline of housing prices with distance from the city center. As illustrated in Figure 5.1, the effect of this decline in the price gradient will be a fall in housing prices in residential areas near the city center and an increase in the outer parts of the city. The fall in prices near the center reduces the returns to investment in housing, and for this

---

[4] *One Hundred Years of Land Values in Chicago,* p. 311.

[5] Subcommittee on Urban Redevelopment, *Report to the President,* pp. 108–9.

[6] These effects are best described by Ratcliff, *Urban Land Economics,* pp. 402–3.

[7] This is emphasized by Gries and Ford, *Slums,* p. 2 and Hoover, *The Location of Economic Activity,* pp. 208–11, and hinted at by Mabel L. Walker, *Urban Blight and Slums,* p. 17.

reason expenditures for maintenance and repair are reduced, and housing deteriorates. The effects of the deterioration in quality are much the same as in the age and neglect theory discussed above: housing prices fall further, higher-income groups move out of the older areas, and lower-income households move in.[8]

Of course, one might ask why the older areas closest to the city center are not converted to other uses if returns to residential uses have declined. Apart from factors peculiar to real property which inhibit redevelopment generally, two classes of reasons might be given.[9] First, if anything, it would seem that land in the CBD has become more intensively used. It is sometimes argued that factors such as improved construction methods and the development of better elevators have reduced the relative costs of taller buildings. (Such changes, however, may merely reflect that taller buildings have become relatively more profitable for other reasons.) In addition, while the introduction of the automobile and truck may have reduced the marginal cost of transport outside the CBD, the increased traffic congestion in the center may have actually increased marginal transport costs there. Second, with the auto era the central parts of the city no longer have as great a comparative advantage as they once did for many non-residential activities. With residential populations more widely dispersed in the city and circumferential travel relatively less costly than radial movement, the advantage of the CBD as a place for retail and service business has probably declined. As another example, wholesaling and some types of manufacturing may no longer find locations close to rail freight terminals near the center as desirable as they did prior to truck transportation. For reasons such as these, in many instances conversion of the deteriorated residential areas to other uses is not profitable.

A third set of reasons sometimes advanced for the decline in the demand for housing in the older, more central parts of cities can be classified under the heading of external effects. Several kinds of such effects can be distinguished. An expansion of manufacturing firms out of a neighboring industrial district or retail and service firms beyond their original locations along major streets may make housing in surrounding areas less desirable because of increased dirt, noise, or for many other reasons.[10] Or the owner of a parcel in a neighborhood of, say, single-family residences, may find it profitable to him to convert it to a grocery store, filling station, or a rooming house. However, by so doing he may reduce the desirability of

---

[8] Gries and Ford, *Slums*, p. 2, and Walker, *Urban Blight*, p. 17.
[9] These are best discussed in Edgar M. Hoover, *The Location of Economic Activity*, pp. 209–11.
[10] Gries and Ford, *Slums*, p. 2.

surrounding residences, with the already familiar effects of declining housing demand.[11]

Closely related to the decline in demand theories discussed above are external factors which are said to operate so as to limit the amount of investment in housing generally and, hence, to increase the supply of poor-quality housing. As many of the above arguments imply, the demand for the housing provided by any particular type of structure depends upon the nature of the surrounding structures as well as the quality of structure actually inhabited. This means that the owner of any particular residential parcel in making an investment produces benefits not only for himself in the form of the increased rental value of his property but also for the owners of surrounding properties by making their housing more desirable and thus increasing its rental value. If individual owners carry investment in their properties only to the point where the marginal returns to them equal marginal cost, too little investment will be made from the social point of view since the marginal social returns exceed marginal social cost by the marginal increase in the rental value of surrounding properties.[12] This argument, of course, applies to all types of neighborhoods, regardless of their age, location, and quality. In fact, if, as seems not unlikely, higher-income and other households inhabiting better-quality housing are more influenced by the external character of the neighborhood in which they live, it would apply with special force to better neighborhoods. However, by limiting investment in housing generally, such external effects would result in a large number, both absolutely and relatively, of dwellings being below any given level of quality, and hence more slum housing.

Now there are several reasons why the effects noted in the preceding paragraph might not occur. In the first place, it would be in the interest of a single owner to acquire a group of contiguous properties. Under the conditions assumed by the argument, a group of contiguous properties would be worth more under common than under fragmented ownership. The principal obstacle to so internalizing these external effects would seem to be the difficulties of land assembly; I have mentioned some of these already in Chapter 5. Another obvious method of dealing with the problem of external effects is cooperation among owners of contiguous parcels. However, cooperation is likely to break down since any individual owner has the incentive to avoid making the extra expenditure on his property and to reap the benefits of the extra expenditure of others. Finally, collective action in the form of zoning or other municipal land-use controls

---

[11] Clarence Arthur Perry, *The Rebuilding of Blighted Areas: A Study of the Neighborhood Unit in Replanning and Plot Assemblage*, p. 8.

[12] For a fuller discussion see Otto A. Davis and Andrew B. Whinston, "The Economics of Urban Renewal."

might be mutually beneficial. But such controls may be expensive to enforce, and, indeed, it is frequently asserted that existing controls are inadequate and poorly enforced.

Several other forces might also increase the supply of poor-quality housing. It is sometimes argued, for example, that dwellings in certain parts of a city may be poorly maintained because of capital market imperfections which raise interest rates or make loans unavailable to property owners in these areas. I have never seen a convincing explanation of why such capital market imperfections exist, and, indeed, there is good reason to believe that interest rates would be high or loans unavailable for investment in changing or slum neighborhoods. In either kind of neighborhood there is likely to be more risk attached to investment than in neighborhoods of better housing quality—in slums because of the risk of loss of income due to code enforcement and in changing neighborhoods because of uncertainty about the future of the area. Furthermore, if otherwise socially desirable and privately profitable investment in housing is not made because of capital market imperfections which affect the availability of funds to certain property owners, others—perhaps insurance companies—not affected by these imperfections would find it profitable to buy up the properties and make the investment themselves. The failure of such purchases to be made might result, however, from difficulties in land assembly.

Certain features of the tax system are sometimes cited as contributing to slums. It is argued that slum properties are taxed at lower effective rates than others, perhaps because assessments are based primarily on outward appearance rather than the income the property produces or perhaps because of differential underassessment by some related factor such as age. Or it may be argued that taxation of site and improvements rather than site value only results in too little investment on sites generally, and hence too much poor-quality housing. Finally, depreciation provisions in the federal income-tax structure are sometimes mentioned as a cause of poor-quality housing. As I noted in Chapter 5, for federal income-tax purposes allowable deductions for depreciation exceed the true rates at which properties depreciate. For this reason, it is argued by some, dwellings are retained in the housing stock longer than they otherwise would, or the housing stock is older than would otherwise be the case. (This argument, of course, applies equally to physical assets other than dwellings.) More poor-quality housing than otherwise will result, however, only if there is a tendency for dwellings to be of poor quality purely for reasons associated with age.

The effects of depreciation provisions in the federal tax structure are similar to several other arguments which are often mentioned as inhibiting socially desirable redevelopment and causing slums.[13] The crudest of these is the assertion that owners place unrealistically high values on their properties and refuse to sell for redevelopment at "reasonable" prices.[14] As with most such glib explanations of economic phenomena, further examination in the third section suggests good reasons why seemingly unrealistic values may, in fact, be quite consistent with market conditions. Or Hoyt argues that once a neighborhood acquires the reputation as a poor-quality one, builders prefer to invest in other sections.[15] But this merely says either that demand for new housing in the area is not strong enough to make redevelopment privately profitable or that other factors inhibit redevelopment on a small enough scale to be undertaken privately. One of these inhibiting factors is the possibility that redevelopment, to be privately profitable and socially desirable, must include a new street system or new schools, parks, and other services commonly provided by municipal governments. Other obstacles to large-scale private development of an area under fragmented ownership have already been discussed in Chapter 5. Especially important is the fact that the assembly of large tracts of contiguous properties under diverse ownership may be too expensive and time-consuming to undertake except where, as in urban renewal projects, properties may be acquired using the power of eminent domain. Factors such as these, like the external economies, capital market imperfection, and tax-related arguments, tend to increase the supply of poor-quality housing and prevent private individuals from undertaking socially desirable redevelopment.

Shortcomings in the Traditional Theories of Slums

The theories of slums discussed in the first section are, or can be made, logically complete, and some—the declining transport-cost argument in particular—have a certain a priori plausibility. My empirical analysis in Part II will suggest that some of the forces stressed by these theories might have some empirical relevance, But, almost without exception, the traditional theories are deficient in that they are inconsistent with, or at best fail to provide an explanation for, three simple but important empirical facts. These are: first, that slum housing seems to be expensive in relation to its quality; second, that urban renewal projects lose money; and, third, that contrary to widespread opinion, housing quality seems to have improved markedly over the decade of the fifties. I wish to discuss these facts in relation to the theories discussed previously in more detail in the present section.

---

[13] These are given special emphasis by Ratcliff, *Urban Land Economics*, pp. 427–31.
[14] *Ibid.*, p. 430, and especially Walker, *Urban Blight*, p. 17.
[15] *One Hundred Years of Land Values in Chicago*, p. 311.

The theories of slums discussed in the preceding section all imply that the increase in the relative quantity of slum housing which the theory attempts to explain, results from an increase in the supply of slums relative to that of good-quality housing in the city as a whole. The age and neglect, decline in transport cost, and encroachment of hostile land-uses theories assert that this occurs because of a fall in the demand for housing generally in some particular area or areas of the city. Because of the decline in demand, the returns to investment in structures in the affected areas fall, and housing is allowed to deteriorate. With this deterioration, the fraction of the whole city's housing stock which is poor quality tends to increase. The external economies, capital market imperfection, tax, and barriers to redevelopment arguments, however, all stress factors which increase the supply of poor-quality housing directly. In either case, with an increase in the relative supply of poor-quality housing such as any of the above-noted forces may produce, the price per unit of housing service[16] of poor-quality housing will fall relative to that of good-quality housing, provided that the relative demand for the two types of housing is not perfectly elastic.

The traditional theories thus imply that with the increase in the relative quantity of slum or poor-quality housing, the rental values of slum housing would decline. This decline results primarily from the fall in the price per unit of housing service for properties used to produce poor-quality housing prior to the change. For properties converted to slum use, rental values will also decline because the converted dwellings now contain fewer units of housing services than prior to their conversion. With the fall in the price of the services of slum housing, the returns to properties used to produce slum housing before the change would fall. These properties would thus become less profitable to their owners when evaluated at property prices which prevailed prior to the change or at their estimated reproduction cost less depreciation. Hence, the prices of properties used to produce slum housing prior to the change would fall. The same is true for properties converted to poor-quality use because of the changed conditions, except perhaps for certain of the tax arguments cited earlier, even though these properties tend to be worth more when converted than if they were to remain in the good-quality use.

The implications of the traditional theories developed in the two preceding paragraphs would seem to be at variance with common popular beliefs that slum housing is expensive in relation to its quality and highly

---

[16] I stress the qualification "per unit of housing service." Since poor-quality dwellings provide fewer units of housing services per unit of time than good-quality ones, expenditure on or rental value of poor-quality dwellings per unit of time would be smaller than for good-quality dwellings if the prices per unit of housing service of the two types were the same.

profitable to its owners. Slum housing provides fewer units of housing services per unit of time and can have a high rental value in relation to its quality only if the price per unit of housing service for slum housing is greater than that for good-quality housing. But, as can be seen from the above, the traditional theories fail to provide any reason why this last should be the case.[17] These theories also imply that the profitability of slum housing, evaluated at previously existing property values or at estimated reproduction cost less depreciation, would have declined with the increase in the relative quantity of the slums. For the profitability of slum housing to be greater than average, in the sense described above, and at the same time to have fallen, it must have been higher still prior to the increase in the relative quantity of slum housing. But none of the theories described in the first section give any indication why this should be so.

Now, of course, since there is almost no good empirical evidence on the price per unit of housing services and on rental and property values in slum versus other areas, the profitability of slum housing may be more apparent than real. Direct evidence on housing prices in relation to quality is quite difficult to obtain. The difficulties are largely the same as those discussed in the preceding chapter in regard to evidence on housing prices in relation to race. In addition, it is quite possible that rentals may be higher in relation to housing quality in slums than in better neighborhoods because of greater operating and/or depreciation costs, a more rapid turnover of tenants, or because of higher rental collection costs and/or delinquencies.[18] Furthermore, even if rentals net of the costs listed above were higher in slums after taking account of quality differences, slum operation would not necessarily be especially profitable. The higher rentals might merely reflect the greater risks inherent in slum properties, such as the possible losses of income from sporadic occupancy and building code enforcement. In the last section of this chapter I shall discuss some indirect kinds of evidence which can be brought to bear on housing prices and the profitability of slums.

Another fact which is inconsistent with many of the theories discussed earlier is that urban renewal projects almost universally lose money or

---

[17] Of the writers cited earlier, Walker, *Urban Blight*, p. 17, is one of the few to recognize this difficulty. She observes that in some slum areas properties may yield good returns "because of the sheer density of population forced by necessity to live in the most undesirable surroundings." In discussing barriers to redevelopment, Ratcliff, *Urban Land Economics*, p. 429 argues that property owners may earn good returns by overcrowding or by deferring maintenance expenditures. Gries and Ford, *Slums*, p. 2, also note that "In some cases a slum has become economically profitable because of the high rents that can be obtained for improper use..." Neither of the latter two works indicates why the apparently high returns can be earned.

[18] Hoyt, *One Hundred Years of Land Values in Chicago*, p. 314, asserts this is the case.

require a governmental subsidy. By this I mean that the expenditures for acquiring properties plus costs of planning, demolition, and improving the site exceed the receipts from the resale of the cleared site to private re-developers. Indeed, acquisition costs alone generally exceed the resale value of the cleared site by a wide margin.[19] Now if the decline in demand for housing which is alleged to have caused the deterioration of an area came about because of obsolescence, because of encroachment or intro-duction of hostile land uses, or because the area was originally poorly planned or poorly supplied with municipal services, then a renewal program which corrected these deficiencies should certainly result in an excess of receipts from resale of the redeveloped site over acquisition costs. And, if external effects, capital market imperfections, or various barriers to private redevelopment prevent socially desirable redevelopment, then governmental renewal projects employing powers of eminent domain should result in a surplus, or at least not in a subsidy.[20] To reconcile the existence of a governmental subsidy to renewal projects with these tra-ditional arguments for slum formation, one would have to argue that renewal has been premature or poorly planned and executed, that slum properties are taxed at rates which are too low, or that condemnation awards for properties acquired for the programs are too high.[21]

The third major fact with which most traditional theories of slum for-mation are inconsistent is that in recent years the quality of the housing stock in cities appears to have improved markedly. Data on the quality of the housing stock which permit comparisons over time are quite limited, partly because data on housing condition were first obtained by the census in 1940 and partly because for each succeeding decennial census there has been a change in the definition of housing condition. Furthermore, com-parison of data from the 1950 Census of Housing and the 1956 National Housing Inventory, which employed identical definitions of housing con-dition, is made difficult by the non-reporting of quality for some dwellings and by the fact that the classification of individual dwellings by condition

---

[19] For example, in those parts of the Hyde Park–Kenwood program in Chicago known as Hyde Park A and B, acquisition costs were of the order of $10 million and receipts from resale of the cleared site $1 million. For information on the costs of federally supported urban projects in the nation as a whole see Martin Anderson, *The Federal Bulldozer*, pp. 19–23 and table A.1.

[20] Note that such factors as enumerated may result in too much poor-quality housing even though renewal is not justified because of conversion costs.

[21] Also note that the existence of a governmental subsidy need not mean that urban renewal projects are socially undesirable. Such projects may yield external benefits in the form of increases in the value of surrounding properties, a reduction in the cost of municipal services, or, perhaps, a reduction in crime and disease. These social benefits would not be reflected in the offers of private redevelopers for the cleared sites.

is not wholly reliable. Nevertheless, estimates made by Beverly Duncan and Philip M. Hauser[22] using these data point to a great quality improvement from 1950 to 1956. Of the six Standard Metropolitan Areas they studied, only in New York does it appear that the number of substandard dwelling units—units which are dilapidated or lack private bath—have increased. In the five other SMA's—Boston, Chicago, Detroit, Los Angeles and Philadelphia—and in the cities of Chicago and Philadelphia, the number of substandard dwellings declined on the order of one-third from 1950 to 1956.[23] About 90 percent of this reduction was due to improvement in the quality of given units and only about 10 percent to demolitions, mergers, and other changes.[24]

It is quite difficult, if not impossible, to account for this great improvement in quality on the basis of the hypotheses discussed in the first section. In fact, on the basis of some of these arguments one would expect an increase in the proportion of dwellings that are substandard. Most neighborhoods and dwellings aged six years during the period of quality improvement; the buildings of express highways and other improvements in transportation would have further reduced marginal transport costs, and property tax rates increased in many cities.

Thus, the traditional theories of slums seem to be seriously deficient. Some of these theories, however, may have some empirical relevance and I will subject them to further tests in Part II of this study. If age of dwellings or factors related to it were responsible for the existence of slums, one would expect the proportion of substandard dwellings to vary with age, both among census tracts in a given city and among cities. Likewise, if slums and blight have resulted from a decline in transport costs, one would expect the proportion of substandard dwellings in a census tract to be inversely related to the tract's distance from the CBD. This is because the extent of the decline in housing prices that resulted from a fall in marginal transport costs would be greater in relative terms the smaller the distance to the CBD, as illustrated in Figure 5.1. And, if the encroachment or mixture of hostile land uses is an important determinant of the condition of residential structures, one would expect to find a higher proportion of substandard dwellings in tracts close to manufacturing or retail centers.

---

[22] *Housing a Metropolis—Chicago*, pp. 56–58.
[23] Data such as these which point to housing quality improvement are frequently discounted as being unreliable. The evaluation of the U.S. Bureau of the Census, however, suggests that census data provide an accurate estimate of the decline in the number of occupied substandard dwellings from 1950 to 1960. It also concludes that census tract data on substandard housing provide a ranking of tracts according to housing condition which is relatively free from error. See "Quality of Housing: An Appraisal of Census Statistics and Methods," pp. III-8 to III-10.
[24] Duncan and Hauser, *Housing a Metropolis*, pp. 63–68.

Finally, to the extent that these theories offer any explanation at all for the association between the condition of dwellings and the incomes of their inhabitants, it is that dwelling-unit condition is an important determinant of the locational choice of households. This hypothesis, too, will be examined empirically in Part II.

AN ALTERNATIVE THEORY OF SLUMS

In order to account for the apparently high price and profitability of slums one must consider factors which tend to increase the demand for poor-quality housing or limit its supply. I now turn to the consideration of such factors and will attempt to show how they are consistent with those three facts with which theories discussed earlier are not.

As I have already mentioned several times, recent evidence indicates that housing demand increases at least in proportion to income. The increase in housing consumption which follows an increase in income may take various forms: more rooms per dwelling, larger rooms, better-quality materials, more attractive and frequent interior decoration, larger lot sizes, and so forth. Indeed, casual observation would suggest that higher-income households would typically consume more housing in most or all of these ways. It would certainly not seem strange, therefore, if the lower-income households tended to occupy poor-quality housing and to use smaller amounts of space per person. In fact, the strong association between poor-quality housing and crowding may be mostly due to the fact that these are merely different aspects of a small per household consumption of housing.[25]

Now there is nothing very novel in an economist's suggesting that poor-quality housing is purchased by low-income households, or, indeed, that poor-quality housing results from poverty rather than the reverse. What is surprising, however, is that in popular or even in scholarly discussions of slums, this fact is so rarely mentioned. Walker is one of the few writers discussed in the first section who mention poverty as a cause of slums, and she argues that poverty and blight need not be closely related.[26] Furthermore, these writers have generally argued that poor-quality housing exists primarily for other reasons and that low-income households have less of

---

[25] Viewing, say, space and quality as inputs into the production of satisfactions called housing, they will tend to vary directly so long as they reflect variations in the quantity of housing demanded. However, under certain circumstances, space and quality may vary inversely if their relative prices as inputs into the production of housing vary. Thus, near the centers of cities where space is relatively expensive, rooms may be small though of high quality. Conversely, in older areas houses with large or many rooms may be relatively cheap but of below-average quality for their size.

[26] *Urban Blight*, p. 23.

an aversion to living in it than do higher-income ones. An alternative hypothesis, which I will evaluate in the latter part of this study, is that the location of lower-income households is determined primarily by other forces and that the quality of the housing stock in the neighborhoods low-income households choose to inhabit is adapted to their circumstances. This would be done primarily through conversions of existing structures to a larger number of smaller units and allowing these units to deteriorate by deferring maintenance and repairs.

While previous research has clearly established that income is one of the most important determinants of housing consumption, other variables have an important effect on the quantity of housing a household consumes. One of these is the relative price of housing. Just as a decline in income, so an increase in the relative price of housing could be expected to lead to poorer-quality housing. Since I have argued earlier that housing prices tend to decline with distance from the CBD, one might expect to find that the proportion of dwelling units which are substandard declines for this reason. Also, one would expect to find that in cities where construction costs are relatively high, the price per unit of housing service would also be relatively high, and thus the proportion of substandard units would be higher than average. Along these lines, if housing prices paid by Negroes are higher than those paid by whites for comparable quarters, I would expect that at any given level of income a higher proportion of Negroes inhabit poor-quality housing and less space per person than whites. Indeed, it is frequently said that a higher proportion of Negroes live in poor housing because of residential discrimination.[27] In discussions of this question, however, the fact that Negroes' incomes are, on the average, lower than those of whites is frequently overlooked.

It is not difficult to account for a strong and rising demand for poor-quality housing in the central cities of our metropolitan areas on the hypothesis that it is but an aspect of a low per household consumption of housing. During the first half of this century the per capita stock of non-farm housing showed relatively little increase in the United States. I would attribute this primarily to the fact that the relative price of housing has risen greatly during this period.[28] Low-income migrants to this country have tended to congregate in cities. While the flow of migration from abroad was greatly reduced following 1920, large-scale migration of lower-income persons from the rural South—many of them Negroes—has taken

---

[27] For example, see Subcommittee on Urban Redevelopment, *Report to the President*, p. 109.

[28] For a more complete discussion see my "The Demand for Non-Farm Housing," pp. 73–74.

place. This migration was especially heavy during the 1940's. In addition, the natural rates of population growth of Negroes and perhaps of other lower-income groups have tended to be higher than for others. During the same time, higher-income households have tended to move away from central cities to their suburbs. Thus, while on the average the per capita consumption of housing showed but little increase, the central cities of our metropolitan areas came to be increasingly inhabited by persons of lower than average income and housing consumption.

The relative price of slum housing and the proportion of dwelling units which are poor-quality also depend upon conditions of supply. If the supply of poor-quality relative to good-quality housing were perfectly elastic, an increase in demand would increase the proportion of poor-quality dwellings but, after adjustment to the new equilibrium position, would not raise the price of such dwellings relative to that of better ones. There is good reason to think, however, that the relative supply of slum housing is less than perfectly elastic. Slum housing in American cities today is rarely newly constructed as such; rather, it tends to be produced primarily through the conversion of existing dwellings to smaller ones and, by deferring maintenance and repair, allowing them to deteriorate in quality. But surely dwellings differ in the ease and cost with which they can be converted or, stated differently, they differ in the relative amounts they can earn as good- versus poor-quality housing.[29] I would expect, for example, that single-family dwellings on large lots and newer dwellings generally would be more costly to convert than would apartment buildings and older dwellings. In addition, enforcement of building and occupancy codes by local governments tends to limit the conversion of existing dwellings to smaller or poorer-quality ones, and these codes may be enforced more strictly in certain areas of cities than others. Under these conditions a growth in demand will tend to raise the relative price of slum housing as well as the proportion of poor-quality dwellings. And, under these conditions, the ownership of slum dwellings will tend to become more profitable with an increase in demand for slum as opposed to good-quality housing. If this analysis is correct, then it is easy to see why urban renewal programs lose money. In effect, they shift sites from a high to a low price market.

But, one might ask, if the above is correct, how can one account for the marked improvement in housing quality that took place during the early fifties? I suspect this was due mainly to a decline in the demand for poor-quality housing. Unlike what happened in the first half of this century, a substantial increase in housing consumption took place during the early fifties. Data from the 1956 National Housing Inventory suggest that the

---

[29] The implications of this point will be more fully discussed in the following section.

number of occupied dwelling units in the United States increased by 16.5 percent from 1950 to 1956, while population increased by only 12 percent.[30] The increase in average quality per unit was much greater during this same period. The median value of one-unit, owner-occupied non-farm dwellings increased by 54 percent and the median contract rent of tenant-occupied non-farm units by 47 percent, as compared with an increase in construction costs of only 27 percent.[31] Raymond W. Goldsmith's [32] estimates of the stock of private, non-farm housekeeping units (including land) in 1947–49 prices point to a similar conclusion, increasing by about 23 percent from the end of 1949 to the end of 1955. Migration from the rural South slowed down noticeably during the 1950's. In addition, even the incomes of the lower-income groups rose rapidly during the forties and early fifties. But, because of rent controls, many lower-income households may have been prevented from acquiring better accommodations or preferred to remain in dwellings with low, controlled rentals before 1950. While the area inhabited by the lowest fifth, say, of a city's households by income level no doubt expanded in the early fifties, and some housing may have deteriorated in the process, with rising incomes and per household consumption of housing the absolute level of housing quality of the lowest relative income group would tend to improve. Hence, the number of dwellings substandard, or below a given absolute level of quality, would decline.

The existence of rent controls during the forties may also have tended to increase the relative supply of poorly maintained housing. To the extent that rent controls are successful in preventing increases in nominal rentals during periods of rising prices, real rentals decline as does the profitability of maintaining properties. With the removal of controls and the subsequent increase in rentals, the profitability of maintenance is increased. In this regard it is interesting to note that of the six SMA's examined in the study by Duncan and Hauser cited above, New York, the only one where rent controls were still in existence, is the only one to show an increase in the number of substandard units. Other factors which may have reduced the supply of poor-quality housing during the early fifties are more vigorous enforcement of building and occupancy codes resulting from greater concern over housing quality, demolitions for expressways, renewal programs, and other purposes. These latter could not have been very

---

[30] Data on number of units, median value and median contract rent cited here are from U.S. Bureau of the Census, 1956 *National Housing Inventory*, vol. 3, part 1 (Washington: U.S. Government Printing Office, 1959).

[31] As measured by the Boeckh index of residential construction costs, brick. Because of the removal of rent controls prior to 1950, the above increase may overestimate the quality improvement of tenant-occupied dwellings.

[32] *The National Wealth of the United States in the Postwar Period* (Princeton: Princeton University Press, 1962), table B-12, p. 235.

important, however, since Duncan and Hauser's results indicate that most of the reduction in the number of substandard dwellings took place because of an improvement in quality of given dwellings.

In sum, while considerations such as those discussed above do not necessarily constitute an "airtight" case for the hypothesis that slums are merely an indicator of low housing consumption, they clearly indicate that this alternative hypothesis can more easily explain the apparent high price and profitability of slum housing and the recent improvement in housing quality than can the traditional explanations for slums cited earlier.

IMPLICATIONS OF SLUM HOUSING FOR THE SPATIAL PATTERN OF LAND USE

Another important fact about poor-quality housing is that it tends to be spatially concentrated, frequently in areas close to the center of the city. I wish to discuss the reasons for this concentration here. I will also consider some of the implications of slum housing for the spatial pattern of land use in cities and some implications of the hypothesis that slum housing is highly priced in relation to its quality—a hypothesis that will later be empirically tested.

The reasons for the spatial concentration of poor-quality housing, not surprisingly, depend partly upon the reasons for the existence of this poor-quality housing. If slums result from a decline in demand for housing in older areas of the city, concentration of slums in the more central parts of today's cities could readily be explained by the fact that the central parts of today's cities are generally the oldest. If slums result because of a decline in transport costs, as described earlier, then the areas hardest hit would be those closest to the city center. Or, if slums result from the encroachment of hostile land uses, they would tend to be located near areas of concentration of these uses. Such areas are frequently in the older, more central parts of the city. Finally, if, contrary to the above, slums are the result of the low incomes of their inhabitants, the location of slums will be governed by the locational determinants of low-income households as well as those of dwellings which are cheapest to convert. I have already suggested several reasons why low-income households would tend to locate nearest the city center, and I will argue below that, if anything, those dwellings most easily converted to poor-quality ones will tend to be those nearest the center.

Quite apart from these factors discussed above, there is good reason to expect that the poor-quality dwellings will tend to be spatially concentrated and that an increase in the number of poor-quality units will tend to take place at the edges of existing concentrations rather than develop in new areas. The best explanation for the spatial concentration of poor-quality housing is quite similar to the customer preference explanation for the residential segregation of Negroes discussed in Chapter 5. For reasons quite apart from race, although the fact that many low-income persons in American cities are Negroes may tend to enhance this effect, it is quite reasonable to suppose that higher-income persons have more of an aversion to living in the vicinity of slum dwellers than do other slum dwellers. Some reasons for such preferences might be that: people prefer to live among those of similar circumstances and backgrounds, pleasant surroundings may well be a good with a relatively high income elasticity, the kinds and qualities of goods and services purchased by the higher-income groups are probably more readily available locally in higher-income neighborhoods than in slum areas,[33] and the public schools in higher-income neighborhoods may be more strongly preferred by higher-income persons. If so, higher- and lower-income households will tend to live in spatially separate areas for the same reasons as were given for the residential segregation of Negroes. In fact, if one substitutes the phrases higher- and lower-income households or good- and poor-quality housing for white and Negro in the argument presented in connection with Figure 5.2, little further modification is needed.[34] The one major difference between segregation by race and by income or housing quality is that conversion costs are likely to be much more important in the latter instance. Thus, properties will be converted from low- to high-income occupancy by private owners only if the gain from so doing exceeds the costs of conversion. Furthermore, conversion costs might differ among properties. If a single high conversion-cost property is surrounded by properties which are converted, the neighborhood effects are likely to be powerful enough to cause it to be converted as well, despite the high costs of doing so. But if several blocks of contiguous properties with relatively high conversion costs exist, they may remain in, say, good-quality use, even if all surrounding properties are converted to poor-quality use. In the latter case, however, external effects are likely to cause a decline in value of the good-quality properties.

Since higher-income persons may be presumed to have an aversion to living among slum dwellers, housing prices on the good-quality side of the boundary separating areas of different quality will tend to be lower than in the interior of the good-quality area. In addition, if anything it seems likely that lower-income persons will pay more for housing in proximity to areas

---

[33] For evidence on this point, see Berry, *Commercial Structure and Commercial Blight*, pp. 60–61.

[34] Although, for simplicity, I suppose throughout that there are only two income groups and quality types of housing, the analysis could readily be generalized to a larger number.

of better quality, so that prices along the boundary of the slum area will tend to be higher than in its interior. This point is illustrated in Figure 1.[35] Here it is assumed that the slum area is to the left of D street and the non-slum area to the right, that the price of housing services in the slum and non-slum areas net of operating costs and an allowance for risk are p_x and p_y respectively, and that within one block of the boundary differentials d_x and d_y between housing service prices in the interior exist. Thus, with the

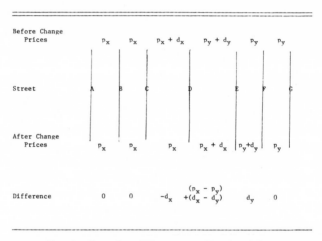

FIG. 1.—Boundary Effects upon Housing Prices

boundary at D street prices between C and D streets are $p_x + d_x$, while to the left of C street they are p_x, etc. Now, if prices on the slum side of the boundary exceed those on the non-slum side by interest on the costs of conversion, c, or more, the boundary will tend to shift toward E street if different properties are held by separate owners. In symbols, the boundary will tend to shift toward E street provided that:

$$(p_x + d_x) - (p_y + d_y) \geq c, \tag{1}$$

or

$$(p_x - p_y) \geq -(d_x - d_y) + c.$$

The term $(d_x - d_y)$ tends to be positive on the assumptions made above, so that the price per unit of poor-quality housing may be either greater or less than that of good-quality housing while the slums are expanding, depending upon the relative size of the differentials d_x and d_y and the cost of

---

[35] The argument given here was developed by Martin J. Bailey, "Note on the Economics of Residential Zoning and Urban Renewal." The following analysis depends heavily upon Bailey's.

conversion. Thus, the fact that properties are being converted from good- to poor-quality use does not necessarily imply that poor-quality housing service prices, adjusted for differences in operating costs and risk, exceed those of good-quality housing in the interiors of the respective areas. Furthermore, because of external effects, owners of properties in the interior of the poor-quality area might not undertake conversion to good-quality housing individually, even though it might be mutually profitable if a relatively large number did do simultaneously.

Under the conditions outlined above the only possible equilibrium position is one in which equality in (1) holds. So long as prices on the slum side of the boundary exceed those on the non-slum side by more than conversion costs, individual property owners on the non-slum side will have an incentive to convert. However, if the demand for poor-quality housing grows rapidly enough relative to the demand for good-quality housing, the rate of conversion and expansion of the poor-quality housing area might not be rapid enough to reduce the profitability of conversion at the boundary. In addition, enforcement of building and occupancy codes might tend to limit the rate of conversion over time and, hence, make p_x higher in comparison with p_y than it would have been otherwise; alternatively, one could interpret code enforcement as raising the costs of conversion. On the other hand, factors stressed by the age and neglect and similar theories may be interpreted as reducing the costs of conversion With a fall in conversion costs at the margin, given conditions of demand, the slum area will tend to expand, p_x will decline relative to p_y, and the profitability of slum property in the interior of the slum area will tend to be reduced.

As the slum area expands, either because conditions of demand have raised p_x relative to p_y or because costs of conversion have fallen, the location of the external effects of slums changes but on balance they tend to cancel out. Thus, if in Figure 1 the boundary shifts from D to E street, housing service prices fall between C and D and between E and F streets. But, the price of housing services tends to rise and to offset these changes in the conversion area between D and E streets. What is relevant for appraising the efficiency of resource use is $(p_x - p_y)$ in relation to c. One implication of this analysis is that an increase in the values of properties adjoining an urban renewal project is not necessarily a net social benefit since these increases will tend to be offset by declines elsewhere. However, if, as the slum area expands, its circumference increases, then the external effects on the non-slum side of the boundary will tend to exceed their offsets in the conversion area. Also, if properties along the boundary differ in their cost of conversion to slum uses, or if the relative earnings of poor- and good-quality uses differ, then owners of high conversion-cost properties may suffer losses even though the majority of those who convert gain. In fact, conversion costs for some properties may be so high that they remain in good-quality use even though the majority of properties in the area are converted.

It is not unreasonable to expect that the costs of converting good- to poor-quality housing rise as the slum area expands from the center of the city. If anything, I would expect that newer dwellings and single-family houses on larger lots would be more costly to convert to slum uses. Such dwellings are relatively more numerous the greater the distance from the city center. In addition, the stringency with which building and occupancy codes are enforced might well depend upon the wishes of a majority of the property owners in the area.[36] As the properties which are more costly to convert become relatively more numerous, code enforcement may prevent the expansion of slums even though, in the aggregate, the increase in property values in the area would exceed the costs of conversion. This consideration may explain the frequent existence of neighborhood improvement groups, composed mostly of single-family home owners and small businessmen who sell to them, who strive to prevent the expansion of slums even though slums are seemingly profitable. It may also explain the widespread feeling that absentee ownership is conducive to slum formation. In any event, if the costs of conversion to slum uses rise at the boundary as the slum area expands, the relative supply of slums is, in effect, less than perfectly elastic. An increase in the demand for poor- as compared with good-quality dwellings will then tend to increase p_x relative to p_y, and the profitability of slums in the interior of the slum area, even in the long run.

The argument in this section so far suggests that housing prices in the interior of poor- and good-quality areas may differ for many reasons. The relative level of housing prices in the two areas affects the relative intensity of residential land use in the two areas. Indeed, the relative land use intensities in slum and good-quality areas is one of the most convincing pieces of evidence on the relation of housing service prices in the interiors of the two areas. Only if prices net of additional operating costs and an allowance for risk are higher in the slum area will sites, or sites plus existing structures, be priced higher there. If price differentials are offset by cost differentials, net incomes of firms producing housing in the two areas will be the same, and the condition of locational equilibrium of firms will not require higher values for existing real properties in the slum area. If housing service price differentials are not offset by cost differentials, existing real properties will

---

[36] For an analysis of a similar problem, the enforcement of zoning regulations, see Otto A. Davis, "Economic Elements in Municipal Zoning Decisions."

be valued more highly and, consequently, firm equilibrium requires that they be more intensively used in the higher housing-service price area. Fixed structures, street layout, and the like, may limit substitution possibilities in the short run and, hence, the incremental output resulting from the housing price differential, But through expenditures for interior conversions to more units with more cooking and toilet facilities, the output of housing per unit land can increase even in the short run. In addition, more people may inhabit a given amount of space in the higher-priced area because the effect of higher prices is to reduce the per household or per capita consumption of housing services. Thus, a given family may occupy smaller quarters in the higher-priced area than it otherwise would, older relatives or younger adults may forgo separate quarters, families may take in roomers, and so forth. For these reason, if prices net of higher costs are greater in slum areas, I would expect that the output of housing per unit of land, crowding, and population densities would be greater in slum areas than in non-slum areas of comparable location and other characteristics which affect these magnitudes.

PART II

Empirical Findings

7 The Spatial Pattern of Population Densities in the United States

In Part II, I present an empirical analysis of spatial patterns of population densities, the output of housing per unit of land, and the per household consumption of housing in cities in the United States. The present chapter presents measures of the relative rate of decline of population densities with distance from the CBD in forty-six cities for 1950. It also relates these relative rates of decline to factors discussed in Part I and examines the distribution of population between the central city and suburbs of an urbanized area and the land area occupied by the latter. Chapter 8 considers the behavior of components of population density and analyzes them in relation to the age of dwellings and the income of their residents as well as distance from the city center. Chapters 9 and 10 present a more detailed investigation of residential land use on the south side of Chicago, where, in addition to the variables considered earlier, measures of land use intensity are related to the particular pattern of employment and shopping centers and transport facilities which characterize Chicago's south side. Chapter 9 is concerned primarily with measures of housing output and consumption, and Chapter 10 deals mainly with condition of the dwelling units of a census tract and the income level of its inhabitants. In the last chapter of Part II, I present a comparison of changes in rents and values in an area of Chicago's south side which changed from white to Negro occupancy during the fifties, in order to provide further evidence on the matter of housing prices and race. Part III of the study will be concerned primarily with summarizing the theoretical and empirical analyses presented and pointing out those factors which would seem to be of greatest empirical importance in determining the spatial structure of urban housing markets.

In the present chapter primary attention is paid to population densities for several reasons. First of all, the spatial pattern of population densities is of great interest for its own sake, and it has important implications for many problems such as the intensity of demand for municipal services in various parts of the city and the design of transport systems. Second, as I have pointed out earlier, population density is simply the output of housing per unit of land divided by the per capita consumption of housing. Thus, anything affecting either the output or the consumption of housing in different parts of the city will be reflected in population density. Finally, population data are not subject to the many vexing measurement problems that are inherent in using census housing data. (These problems are described in the following chapter.)

My analysis in Part I suggests that population densities will decline with distance from the CBD and that under certain simple but rather restrictive conditions the relative rate of decline will be constant. The previous analysis has also suggested many factors which might complicate this pattern. One of the aims of this chapter is to determine how well the negative exponential function fits real-world data on population densities. It would indeed be fortunate if so simple a function in only two parameters would give an adequate fit to the population density data, since the analysis of many problems would be considerably simplified. Shortcomings in the fit of the negative exponential function might, however, suggest modifications which would improve our understanding of the forces influencing the spatial distribution of population in urban areas. The first section of this chapter presents evidence on the goodness of fit of the negative exponential density function to population data for forty-six American cities in 1950. In addition to its goodness of fit, the usefulness of the negative exponential approximation to the spatial pattern of population densities depends upon the predictability of the relative rate of decline of population density with distance from the CBD. Therefore, in the second section the estimated density gradients for various cities will be related to variables suggested by the analysis of Part I, in an attempt to determine which are of strategic importance.[1] The third section of this chapter examines the consistency of the negative exponential density function with average densities of central cities. The final two sections continue the examination of differences in density gradients and explore the relationship of such differences to differences in the central city's share of total population and the total land area occupied by the urbanized area.

---

[1] The estimated density functions as well as part of the analysis of differences in density gradients among cities were presented in my earlier paper "The Spatial Structure of Housing Market." The remainder of the material on density gradient differences and the 1950 central city population and urbanized area land area comparisons were presented in my "The Distribution of Population with Urban Areas," in *Determinants of Investment Behavior*, ed. Robert Ferber (New York: National Bureau of Economic Research, 1967), pp. 271–99.

EVALUATION OF THE NEGATIVE EXPONENTIAL DENSITY FUNCTION

This section describes the techniques I used in fitting the negative exponential function to 1950 population density data and presents and evaluates the resulting estimates. Previous estimates of the pattern of urban residential densities are deficient for my purposes in at least two important respects. First, estimates have been made for only relatively few American cities, although we are fortunate to have data for several different years in some cases.[2] But, more important, the basic data for most estimates are average densities in concentric annuli at progressively greater distances from the city center. Such measures hide virtually all the variation about the regression line and are too few in number to test for deviations of the observed pattern of decline from that expected to prevail.

For these reasons I have used data on average gross density for census tracts, more specifically for a random sample of twenty-five census tracts in each city.[3] All told, I used data for forty-six American cities in 1950. Starting with the list of all tracted cities in the continental United States, I had to eliminate those for which the central business district tracts could not be identified.[4] I also eliminated three urbanized areas with more than one central city of fifty thousand or more—New York, Minneapolis–St. Paul, and San Francisco–Oakland—because it would have been quite difficult to determine to which of the central city CBD's the population density for a particular tract should be related. The forty-six cities studied have urbanized area populations ranging from about a hundred thousand to almost five million.

Population data for the tracts included in the several samples were obtained from the census tract statistics of the 1950 population census.[5] To obtain densities, the population figures were divided by the areas of the census tracts in square miles; in most cases these areas were measured with a polar planimeter using the census tract maps given in the tract statistics

---

[2] See Clark, "Urban Population Densities"; Halliman H. Winsborough, "A Comparative Study of Urban Residential Densities"; and Calvin F. Schmid and Vincent A. Miller, *Population Trends and Educational Change in the State of Washington*.

[3] In each case I omitted tracts in the central business district and any tract with fewer than 100 residents from the population of tracts sampled, on the grounds that, in these, land is devoted almost entirely to other than residential uses. Likewise, for uniformity the population sampled included only tracts in the central city, since the outlying parts of metropolitan areas are not tracted in all cases, and, where tracted, the outlying tracts are larger and less homogeneous internally than central city tracts.

[4] Central business-district census tracts are listed in U.S. Bureau of the Census, *1954 Census of Business, Central Business District Statistics, Summary Report* (Washington, D.C.: U.S. Government Printing Office, 1958), pp. APP1–6.

[5] U.S. Bureau of the Census, *1950 Census of Population*, vol. 3 (Washington, D.C.: U.S. Government Printing Office, 1952), table 1.

TABLE 1

SUMMARY OF DENSITY-DISTANCE REGRESSIONS, 46 U.S. CITIES, 1950

City	$D_0 \times 10^{-3}$	D_1	r^2	Linearity Fa	Curvature
Akron, Ohio	38	0.84	0.72	1.0	
Atlanta, Ga.	22	0.48	0.43	0.13	
Baltimore, Md.	69	0.52	0.53	0.19	
Birmingham, Ala.	9.4	0.20	0.35	0.23	
Boston, Mass.	78	0.30	0.35	0.66	
Buffalo, N.Y.	29	0.19*	0.16	3.6†	+
Chicago, Ill.	60	0.18	0.47	0.12	
Cincinnati, Ohio	120	0.69	0.67	4.2†	+
Cleveland, Ohio	22	0.13***	0.048	5.2††	−
Columbus, Ohio	10	0.19	0.43	0.50	
Dallas, Tex.	26	0.48	0.47	4.5††	−
Dayton, Ohio	18	0.32	0.22	0.67	
Denver, Colo.	17	0.33	0.41	0.094	
Detroit, Mich.	19	0.098	0.30	4.7††	−
Flint, Mich.	26	0.73	0.42	0.14	
Fort Worth, Tex.	17	0.42	0.73	0.14	
Houston, Tex.	14	0.28	0.58	8.7†††	−
Indianapolis, Ind.	9.2	0.18	0.30	0.47	
Kansas City, Mo.	13	0.26	0.33	0.059	
Los Angeles, Calif.	14	0.078*	0.20	2.6	
Louisville, Ky.	29	0.47	0.30	1.2	
Memphis, Tenn.	14	0.22	0.46	0.52	
Miami, Fla.	14	0.24	0.22	7.2††	+
Milwaukee, Wis.	61	0.44	0.70	0.044	
Nashville, Tenn.	9.3	0.071***	0.022	3.0†	−
New Haven, Conn.	46	0.99	0.74	0.35	
New Orleans, La.	35	0.41	0.69	1.3	
Oklahoma City, Okla.	16	0.43	0.64	0.21	
Omaha, Nebr.	18	0.38	0.46	3.0†	+
Philadelphia, Pa.	86	0.40	0.50	0.38	
Pittsburgh, Pa.	17	0.091***	0.022	2.0	
Portland, Ore.	11	0.16*	0.18	0.48	
Providence, R.I.	14	0.41	0.50	1.5	
Richmond, Va.	41	0.82	0.49	0.078	
Rochester, N.Y.	43	0.64	0.54	9.5†††	−
Sacramento, Calif.	15	0.36	0.38	0.010	
St. Louis, Mo.	47	0.28	0.27	2.7	
San Diego, Calif.	18	0.39	0.62	17†††	−
San Jose, Calif.	21	0.46	0.24	1.0	
Seattle, Wash.	25	0.31	0.57	0.61	
Spokane, Wash.	5.9	0.34	0.31	0.45	
Syracuse, N.Y.	48	0.92	0.45	0.026	
Toledo, Ohio	6.1	0.20	0.42	0.17	
Utica, N.Y.	51	1.2	0.46	2.1	
Washington, D.C.	20	0.27	0.43	0.49	
Wichita, Kansas	19	0.53	0.36	12†††	−

a With 1 and 22 degrees of freedom.
* Not significantly greater than zero at the 0.01 level.
*** Not significantly greater than zero at the 0.10 level.
† Significant at the 0.10 level.
†† Significant at the 0.05 level.
††† Significant at the 0.01 level.

reports.[6] The line-of-sight distance from the geometric center of the CBD to the geometric center of the census tract in miles was measured with a ruler; the locations of the centers were estimated by eye. Repeated measurements made on the same characteristic suggest to me that measurement errors in the distance variable are small relative to those inherent in the area measurements and, hence, the density variable.

For each city two least-squares regressions were computed with the natural log of density as dependent variable, one linear and one quadratic in distance. The results of these are summarized in Table 1. The first three columns show central density, D_0, the density gradient, D_1, and the coefficient of determination as estimated from the linear regression. The fourth column shows the F-ratio for testing the significance of the second-degree term in the quadratic regression, and the fifth the sign of the second-degree term where it is significant.

In all but six of the forty-six cities the density gradient shown in Table 1 is significantly greater than zero at the 0.01 level, and in all but three at the 0.10 level. The coefficients of determination, r^2, ranged from about 0.02 in Nashville and Pittsburgh to 0.74 in New Haven, the median being about 0.45. Thus, on the average, distance alone explains a little less than one-half the density differences among census tracts. There is no significant tendency for the goodness of fit of the linear regressions to vary with city size or region of the country. Spearman's rho for r^2 and urbanized area

TABLE 2

MEAN RANK OF r^2 BY REGION

Region	No. of Cities	Mean Rank
Northeast	11	21.2
North Central	11	23.2
South	12	20.7
West	12	28.8
Total	46	23.5

$H = 2.70$; Probability $\cong 0.5$

---

[6] *Ibid.* For two cities, Los Angeles and Cleveland, measurements were taken from larger tract maps obtained through the census tract key persons in those cities. In all cases, three measurements of area were made and averaged. If one of the three differed from the average of the other two by as much as one-third it was discarded and another measurement made. For three cities already available area measurements were used. For Boston these were taken from unpublished measurements supplied by the Research Division, United Community Services; for Chicago from Chicago Community Inventory, "Gross Land Area and Gross Population Density of Census Tracts and Community Areas for the City of Chicago, 1950" (unpublished, November, 1952); for Philadelphia from Philadelphia City Planning Commission, "Population Densities in 1940 and 1950 by Census Tracts—Philadelphia" (unpublished, August, 1954).

population is -0.099. The Kruskal-Wallis H for testing the significance of regional differences, computed from the ranks of the r^2's, is significant only at about the 0.50 level.

Turning now to the quadratic regressions, in twelve of the forty-six cities an F-ratio significant at the 0.10 or smaller level was observed, indicating too much deviation from linearity to attribute to chance variation alone in those samples. Now one would, of course, expect some significant results purely by chance in forty-six samples. Table 3 indicates, however, that over all too many deviations from linearity were observed to attribute to sampling variation. But there is no tendency for departures from linearity to be associated with city size or region. Spearman's rho for F and urbanized area population is $+0.15$, significant at about the 0.40 level, while the H statistic for testing the significance of regional difference in the F's was significant only at the 0.98 level.

TABLE 3

DISTRIBUTION OF F-RATIOS, OBSERVED AND
EXPECTED ON THE HYPOTHESIS OF LINEARITY

F	Probability	Observed	Expected
< 1.00	> 0.5	25	23.0
1.00–2.94	0.5–0.1	9	18.4
> 2.94	< 0.1	12	4.6
Total	. . .	46	46.0

$X^2(2) = 16.9$; Probability < 0.001

TABLE 4

MEAN RANK OF F BY REGION

Region	No. of Cities	Mean Rank
Northeast	11	23.1
North Central	11	25.3
South	12	23.0
West	12	22.8
Total	46	23.5

$H = 0.256$; Probability $\cong 0.98$

Also, among the regressions summarized in Table 1 there is no significant tendency for departures from linearity to result in predominantly positive or negative curvature in the relationship between log-density and distance. Nor is there any tendency for the sign of curvature to be associated with city size or region. Of the twelve samples with significant F's curvature was negative in eight cases; on the null hypothesis of equally probable positive and negative departures, the probability of a divergence from expectation as great or greater than observed is about 0.40. Likewise, for all forty-six samples curvature was positive in twenty-eight cases, but this is significant only at the 0.20 level. Table 5 indicates almost identical

TABLE 5

RELATION OF CITY SIZE TO DIRECTION OF
CURVATURE

CITY SIZE (RANK)	CURVATURE	
	Positive	Negative
650 thousand (1–16)	10	6
365–650 thousand (17–31)	9	6
365 thousand (32–46)	9	6
Total	28	18

$X^2(2) \cong 0$; Probability $\cong 1$

distributions of curvature for large, medium, and small cities. While the distribution of curvature differs among regions, these differences are significant only at about 0.30 level, as shown in Table 6.

TABLE 6

RELATION OF REGION TO DIRECTION OF
CURVATURE

REGION	CURVATURE	
	Positive	Negative
Northeast	9	2
North Central	5	6
South	6	6
West	8	4
Total	28	18

$X^2(3) = 3.9$; Probability $\cong 0.3$

In summary, in forty of the forty-six cities there was a significant tendency for population densities to decline with distance from the CBD at the 0.01 level. The linear regression in distance alone explains slightly less than half of the variation in population density among census tracts, and there is no apparent tendency for the goodness of fit of the negative exponential function to vary with city size or region of the country. Too many significant deviations from linearity were observed to attribute to sampling variability, but the deviations were not predominantly positive or negative, nor were they associated with city size or region of the country.

DIFFERENCES IN DENSITY GRADIENTS AMONG CITIES

One of the most striking features of the estimates presented in Table 1 is the great variation in the estimated 1950 density gradients among cities. While most of the estimated density gradients fall between 0.2 and 0.5 per mile, they vary all the way from 0.07 in Nashville to 1.2 in Utica.[7] In this section I will attempt to relate these differences to factors suggested by the analysis of Part I. These include factors affecting the locational equilibrium of CBD worker households, the spatial distribution of employment and shopping centers, and factors associated with tastes and preferences for housing in various parts of the city.

Data Used: Factors affecting the locational equilibrium of CBD worker households are summarized in the condition for locational equilibrium [equation (2.3′)]:

$$-\left(\frac{p_k}{p}\right) = \frac{T_k}{pq}. \tag{1}$$

Any factor which increases the marginal cost of transport tends to increase the price and thus the density gradient, while anything which increases per household expenditures on housing will tend to reduce these gradients. Transport costs, however, are quite difficult to measure directly. About the best one can do is to use some surrogates for this variable.

From unpublished data which the American Transit Association has kindly furnished me I have computed miles of line of local transit systems per square mile of urbanized area, MILINE, vehicle miles operated per mile of line, VEHMIL, and passengers carried per vehicle mile operated, PASCAR.[8,9] The first of these related to coverage of the city by public transit routes, while VEHMIL is a measure of the frequency of service on these routes. PASCAR is probably a measure of size of vehicle used, and

---

[7] Since the D_1's in Table 1 are but sample estimates of the true values, part of the variation among them is due to sampling variability. However, examination of the estimated variances of the gradient estimates suggest that sampling variability accounts for about 10 percent of the variance of the estimated gradients among cities.

[8] Throughout the empirical part of this study I shall designate variables by six-letter code names rather than by more conventional symbols. While doing so entails some sacrifice of brevity, I have found it much easier to remember the definition and meaning of the variables when designated in this way and hope it will spare the reader some confusion as well. A glossary at the end of this book identifies all the code names used throughout Part II.

[9] These measures cover only those local transit companies and public authorities which reported to the Association on their operations for 1950 (1960), and are available for only 37 (30) of the 46 cities for which I computed density gradients. These were sent to me in papers titled "Transit Operating Reports—1950," part 1 (New York: American Transit Association, 1951) and "Transit Operating Reports —1960," part 1 (New York: American Transit Association, 1961). Miles of line were divided by the area in square miles of the urbanized area obtained from U.S. Bureau of the Census, *1950 Census of Population*, vol. I, part 1, table 17.

large values of this variable would most likely reflect a higher percentage of rail than of street transportation. Because data on passengers carried was not available for four of the cities for which I had measures of the other variables, it was omitted from most of the comparisons made.

Two characteristics of the city which might be related to transport costs were also included in the analyses of density gradients. The first of these is what has been called the age of the SMA, AGESMA, which is the number of decades since it first attained a population of 50,000.[10] One might suspect that the older the city the less adaptable would its street system be for motor vehicles and the greater the time and other costs of traveling a given distance. A closely related measure is the proportion of the SMA's growth that took place since 1920, GROPOP, or 1950 less 1920 population divided by 1950 population.[11] I would expect that in cities which have grown up mostly after the introduction of the automobile, of which Los Angeles is a prime example, streets would be wider and better suited to auto transport, parking facilities would be more readily available, and so forth. Also, it might be argued that in cities which have grown more rapidly since 1920 the pattern of population densities would be less affected by the heritage of the past and more nearly adjusted to the equilibrium pattern for the auto era. For both of these reasons I would expect GROPOP to be negatively related to the estimated density gradient. A final surrogate for transport costs is car registrations per capita in principal SMA counties, CAREGS.[12] I would expect that where the costs of private automobile transport are low, especially if income is held constant, relatively more people would own autos, and hence I would expect CAREGS to be negatively related to the estimated density gradient.

The most important variable affecting the average per household expenditure on housing in a city is income. As I have argued earlier, however,

---

[10] From Donald J. Bogue and Dorothy L. Harris, *Comparative Population and Urban Research via Multiple Regression and Covariance Analysis*, app. table 1, p. 73.

[11] Inclusion of this variable was suggested by Wingo, *Transportation and Urban Land*, pp. 23–25. The population data used are from Donald J. Bogue, *Metropolitan Growth and the Conversion of Land to Nonagricultural Uses*, app. table 2, pp. 28–32. For 1960, GROPOP was defined analogously. The 1920 population data from Bogue, with minor adjustment for comparability, was compared with the 1960 SMA population data from U.S. Bureau of the Census, *U.S. Census of Population: 1960*, Final Report PC(1)–1C (Washington, D.C.: U.S. Government Printing Office, 1962), table 141.

[12] Car registrations data were obtained from Automobile Manufacturers Association, *Automobile Facts and Figures*, 31st ed. (Detroit: Automobile Manufacturers Association, 1951), pp. 24–25, and Automobile Manufacturers Association, *Automobile Facts and Figures, 1961 edition* (Detroit: Automobile Manufacturers Association, 1961), pp. 22–23; the population data are from U.S. Bureau of the Census, *1950 Census of Population*, vol. 2, tables 4 and 5, and U.S. Bureau of the Census, *U.S. Census of Population: 1960*, vol. 1, table 13.

to the extent that differences in income of CBD worker households result from wage-income differences, higher-income households would value travel time more highly and hence marginal transport costs would be higher for them. Higher incomes, therefore, would tend to increase both the numerator and denominator of (1). But, as discussed more fully in Chapter 2, on balance I would expect the price gradient to be smaller the higher is income. It would seem likely that the income elasticity of marginal transport costs would be less than equal to unity, while the income elasticity of housing demand is probably at least equal to unity and perhaps as high as two. The analysis of Chapter 5 also suggested several other reasons why the demand for housing might grow more rapidly in the outer parts of cities as income increases. If higher-income households have stronger preferences for newer housing, an increase in the average income level of the city would increase the relative demand for new housing, and the latter is typically located in the outer part of the city. Or, if preferences for good-as opposed to poor-quality housing increase with the income level of a household, the concentration of poor-quality housing in the central parts of the city would mean a relative decline in the demand for housing there with an increase in income. Finally, for various reasons higher-income households may have stronger preferences for space versus other characteristics of housing, or for single-family housing. Since space is relatively cheaper in the outlying parts of the city, population and housing output might, for this last reason, increase more rapidly near the edges of the city with a growth in income. The income measure included in the comparisons below is the median income of families and unrelated individuals (families) in 1949 (1959) in dollars per year in the urbanized area, URBINC.[13]

Another important determinant of housing consumption, and thus the price gradient, is the price of housing services. But the impact of differences in housing prices on the price gradient depends critically upon the price elasticity of housing demand. If the latter is -1, as the previous research cited earlier would suggest, then expenditures for housing, which is price times quantity purchased, would be the same irrespective of the level of housing prices. The most likely alternative to a unit elasticity of housing demand is an elastic one, in which case expenditures on housing would vary inversely and the price gradient would vary directly with the level of housing prices. I showed in Chapter 2 that variation in the per household expenditure on housing with distance depends upon the price gradient. The greater this gradient the greater the incentive for higher-income CBD worker households or households with stronger preferences

---

[13] From *1950 Census of Population*, vol. 2, part 1, table 93, and *U.S. Census of Population: 1960*, Final Report PC(1)–1C, table 152.

for housing to locate at greater distances from the city center, and so the greater the increase in the per household consumption of housing with distance.

The size of the price gradient also affects the rate of decline in the value of housing produced per square mile of land with distance. If housing prices were to increase, for example, because of an increase in property-tax rates, the effect upon variations in the intensity of residential land use with distance would depend upon the effect on the price gradient only. But if housing prices vary because of an increase in non-land costs or in the supply of land to the housing industry, the effect on the rate of decline in residential land use intensity depends upon the effects of factor cost changes on the optimal way to produce housing in the different parts of the city. Because it would appear that the relative importance of land declines as land rents do with distance from the CBD and, if anything, the elasticity of land supply to the housing industry is likely to increase, I argued in Chapter 3 that an increase in either non-land costs or in the supply of land to the housing industry would reduce the rate of decline in the value of housing output per square mile with distance from the CBD.

Housing prices depend upon construction costs and the level of land rentals as well as upon interest and property-tax rates. There is virtually no data available on intercity variation in the latter three factors. However, in cities which are built on the edge of a lake or an ocean, such as Chicago or Miami, the total supply of land up to any given distance from the CBD is only about half of that in other cities, so that one might expect land rentals would be greater in waterfront cities than in others of comparable size. To take account of such conditions I have used a dummy variable 180CIT which makes the value 1 for waterfront cities and 0 for others.[14] One might also expect that land rentals and thus housing prices would be greater in larger cities, and the size variable discussed below might be expected to reflect this possibility. I have also used a measure of residential

---

[14] This is admittedly a very crude procedure. For example, Seattle, which is mostly built on a narrow corridor of land between Puget Sound and Lake Washington, obviously has less land surrounding the CBD than other waterfront cities. On the other hand, Boston is built on a sector of approximately 270 degrees surrounding Massachusetts Bay. More land surrounds Boston's CBD than Chicago's, but still more surrounds the CBD of cities such as Indianapolis. There is also the problem of how to treat cities such as St. Louis whose CBD's are separated from much of the surrounding land area by major rivers. But, because land costs are but a small fraction of the price of housing, it didn't seem worthwhile to attempt to construct a more sophisticated land availability variable unless preliminary investigation suggested that this factor might be of decided importance. Cities treated as waterfront cities and assigned the value 1 for the 180CIT variable are: Buffalo, Chicago, Cleveland, Detroit (because of the national boundary), Miami, Milwaukee, San Diego, and Seattle.

construction costs for 1949, CONCST, to account for some of the possible variation among cities in housing prices.[15] But since the latter was available for only twenty-eight of the forty-six cities studied here, it was omitted from most of the comparisons made.

Another group of factors affecting density gradients is the spatial pattern of employment and shopping centers within the city. It was argued in Chapter 4 that the existence of concentrations of employment outside the CBD would lead to a less rapid apparent decline in population densities with distance from the CBD. To the extent that the spatial distribution of retail centers as shopping rather than employment places affects the distribution of population, one would expect the dispersion of shopping centers to have effects similar to those of employment centers. Thus, I will include in my comparisons the proportion of SMA manufacturing employment located inside the central city in 1947 (1958), MANCIT, and the proportion of SMA retail sales within the CBD in 1954 (1958), RETCBD.[16] If anything, I would expect both of these variables to be positively associated with the density gradient.

In addition to the considerations already discussed, it might be argued that the prices consumers will pay for housing in different parts of the city are influenced by tastes and preferences proper. If, say, a relatively high proportion of the dwelling units in the central city are substandard and consumers have an aversion to living near such residences, the premiums they would offer for living close to the CBD would be smaller than they would otherwise be. Hence, housing prices would decline less rapidly with distance, and the density gradient would be smaller than otherwise. This factor and closely related ones are frequently stressed in popular as well as some scholarly discussions as being of great importance in affecting the demand for housing in different parts of the city, and I have discussed them previously, in Chapter 6, in relation to the slum problem. In my

---

[15] This is the Boeckh index for brick structures, 1926–29 U.S. average = 100, and I wish to thank its compiler, Mr. E. H. Boeckh of Washington, D.C., for making these unpublished data available to me. I found the Boeckh index to be significantly associated with housing consumption both over time and among different cities in 1950 in my "The Demand for Non-Farm Housing."

[16] MANCIT for 1950 was computed from data in Evelyn M. Kitagawa and Donald J. Bogue, *Suburbanization of Manufacturing Activity within Standard Metropolitan Areas*, app. table A-1, pp. 132–38. For 1960, MANCIT was derived from data in U.S. Bureau of the Census, *United States Census of Manufacturers: 1958*, vol. 3 (Washington, D.C.: U.S. Government Printing Office, 1961), table 3. The RETCBD variable was obtained from *1954 Census of Business, Central Business District Statistics, Summary Report*, table 4, and U.S. Bureau of the Census, *1958 Census of Business*, vol. 7 (Washington, D.C.: U.S. Government Printing Office, 1961), table 5. Data on SMA retail sales in 1954 were not available for one of the 37 cities for which I have data relating to local transit systems.

earlier paper I included the following taste variables in the analysis: SUBSTD, the proportion of central city dwelling units which are substandard (dilapidated and/or without private bath); MFGEMP, the proportion of urbanized area manufacturing employment (male) in manufacturing; and DENCIT, the average population density of the central city in persons per square mile, all for 1950.[17] In addition, AGESMA might be interpreted as a taste variable, in which case its relationship to the estimated density gradient should be negative rather than positive, which would be the case if it were reflective of high transport costs.

As is discussed more fully below, my initial results showed a significant negative relation between SUBSTD and the estimated density gradients. To test the possibility that it is not dwelling unit condition itself but rather some variable or variables closely related to it that accounts for this association, several other taste variables were introduced into the comparisons later. These additional taste variables relate to characteristics of the inhabitants of poor-quality dwellings rather than to dwelling-unit condition as such. They are: the proportion of central city dwelling units with more than one person per room in 1950, PEROOM, which is another measure of crowding; the median income of families and unrelated individuals in 1949 in dollars per year for the central city, CITINC; and the proportion of the central city population that was Negro in 1950, POPNEG.[18] With respect to the last of these, it is frequently argued that the expansion of Negro and other minority groups in the older parts of cities has led the former residents of these areas to seek out new neighborhoods and has thus promoted a rise in property values in the outer parts of the city.[19] Likewise, in many discussions of so-called suburban sprawl it is asserted that the immigration of Negroes and other minorities into the central city is partly responsible for the movement of whites to the suburbs. In these later experiments I also included the proportion of the central city's dwelling units which were built prior to 1920, AGEDUS, to test the

[17] The 1950 data on these variables were obtained from *1950 Census of Population*, vol. 3, table 3; vol. 2, table 2; and vol. 1, table 17. For the 1960 comparisons only the first and last were used; they are from U.S. Bureau of the Census, *1960 Census of Housing*, vol. 1, part 1 (Washington, D.C.: U.S. Government Printing Office, 1963), table 15, and U.S. Bureau of the Census, *U.S. Census of Population: 1960*, Final Report PC1–1A, (Washington, D.C.: U.S. Government Printing Office, 1961), table 22, respectively.

[18] Data on persons per room were obtained from the U.S. Bureau of the Census, *Census of Housing: 1950*, vol. I, part 1 (Washington, D.C.: U.S. Government Printing Office, 1953), table 29. The other variables were obtained from *1950 Census of Population*, vol. II, part 1, table 92, and vol. 2, table 34. Only the last two were used for the 1960 comparisons. Data on CITINC are from *U.S. Census of Population: 1960*, Final Report PC1–1C, table 154, and POPNEG from *U.S. Census of Population: 1960*, vol. I, table 21.

[19] See, in particular, Hoyt, *One Hundred Years of Land Values in Chicago*, p. 317.

hypothesis that households have an aversion to living in the central city because of the age of its dwelling units.[20]

The last of the variables included in the comparisons is a measure of size, the natural log of the urbanized area population, URBPOP.[21] Casual inspection of Table 1 suggests a rather marked negative relationship between size and D_1, but size is rather strongly intercorrelated with several of the other variables—URBINC for example. I initially included size as a test for the omission of some important variable, for I could not think of any very convincing reasons why the density gradients should be negatively related to size itself. Indeed, to the extent that traffic congestion increases with city size when other measures of transport cost are held constant, one might expect marginal transport costs and hence the density gradient to increase with size. Also, as mentioned above, one would expect land rentals to increase with city size. If the relative price elasticity of demand for housing services is less than -1, higher land rentals and consequently higher housing prices would reduce per household expenditure on housing. For this reason, too, density gradients would tend to be larger in larger cities.

The negative association between size and the estimated density gradient is partly to be explained, I believe, by the less than unit elasticity of substitution of land for other factors in producing housing. As was argued in Chapters 3 and 4, the elasticity of housing supply is inversely related to the relative importance of land. With a less than unit elasticity of substitution in production, the relative importance of land declines with distance from the CBD as land rentals do, and consequently the elasticity of housing supply per unit of land increases. With an increase in total population and the resulting rise in housing prices in all parts of the city, the output of housing and residential population increases relatively more rapidly in the outer parts of the city. Therefore, even though the price gradient might increase with city size, the relatively greater response in housing output in the outer parts of the city could more than offset this and result in a decline in the density gradient. In this regard, an increase in the average income level of a city's households, like an increase in population, leads to an increase in housing demand. With an increasing price elasticity of housing output with distance from the center, an increase in income too would lead to a greater relative growth of housing output and population in the outer parts of cities.

---

[20] Data on age of dwelling units were obtained from *Census of Housing: 1950*, vol. I, part 1, table 30.

[21] Use of logs with this variable resulted in a more nearly linear scatter. The population data are from *1950 Census of Population*, vol. 1, part 1, table 17, and *U.S. Census of Population: 1960*, Final Report PC1–1A, table 22.

In all the comparisons reported below I used the natural logarithm of the estimated density gradient, DENGRA, as the dependent variable. Logs were used for two reasons. First, scatter diagrams indicated that the simple regressions between D_1 and the variables described above are on the whole more nearly linear if the logs of the D_1's are used. And, second, the standard errors of the estimated density gradients in Table 1 tended to vary directly with the gradient. For this reason, the scatter about the regression lines appears to be more nearly homoscedastic when using the logs of the D_1's.

Empirical Findings: My regression analyses of intercity differences in DENGRA are summarized in Tables 7 through 10. In all these, the regression coefficients of the explanatory variables listed in the stub are given on the same line in the body of the table, and the standard errors of these coefficients are shown beneath them in parentheses. The constant terms in the regression equations are omitted. Unless otherwise noted, all the coefficients shown are estimated by conventional least-squares regression methods. Finally, with the exception of those in Table 9, the regressions are based upon the thirty-six cities for which all the necessary data are available.

The regressions initially run and reported in my earlier paper are summarized in Table 7. Of the indicators of transport cost, the sign of VEHMIL is consistently negative, but the coefficient itself is never very much larger than its standard error. The coefficient of GROPOP in the first three regressions probably reflects its intercorrelation with URBPOP, since the coefficient is numerically small and has the wrong sign in (5). The coefficient of CAREGS is negative in all four equations and more than twice its standard error in the last two; it is the only indicator of transport cost that is statistically significant in equation (5). While the coefficient of URBINC is negative throughout, it is statistically significant only in (4), and here it probably reflects the positive correlation between income and size for urbanized areas, for when URBPOP is added in (5) the coefficient of URBINC declines to less than half its value in equation (4).

The coefficients of the indicators of the spatial distribution of employment and shopping centers are quite interesting. Except for the size variable, none of the variables in Table 7 is more strongly and consistently related to DENGRA than MANCIT. The central city retail sales variable, RETCBD, on the other hand, while exhibiting a simple correlation coefficient with DENGRA (not shown) which is larger than that for any variable except URBPOP, has the wrong sign in equations (3) and (5) and is numerically quite small in (3) and (4). These results indicate that the spatial distribution of manufacturing employment is closely associated

TABLE 7

Iɴɪᴛɪᴀʟ Rᴇɢʀᴇssɪoɴ Rᴇsᴜʟᴛs, DENGRA, 1950

Exᴘʟᴀɴᴀᴛoʀʏ Vᴀʀɪᴀʙʟᴇ	Eǫᴜᴀᴛɪoɴ			
	(2)	(3)	(4)	(5)
MILINE	.072	.078	.065	.037
	(.057)	(.051)	(.049)	(.044)
VEHMIL × 10⁻⁶	−.82	−5.2	−5.6	−4.8
	(5.6)	(5.5)	(5.2)	(4.7)
AGESMA	−.096	−.046	−.034	.081
	(.062)	(.058)	(.064)	(.070)
GROPOP	−1.5*	−1.6*	−1.3*	.024
	(.82)	(.76)	(.85)	(.89)
CAREGS	−2.2	−3.8	−6.9*	−7.0*
	(3.5)	(3.3)	(3.4)	(3.0)
URBINC × 10⁻³	−.39	−.36	−.93*	−.40
	(.41)	(.37)	(.59)	(.55)
MANCIT	· · ·	2.0*	2.0*	1.5*
		(.77)	(.75)	(.69)
RETCBD	· · ·	−.14	.21	−2.3
		(1.7)	(1.7)	(1.8)
SUBSTD	· · ·	· · ·	−3.8*	−2.8*
			(1.6)	(1.5)
MFGEMP	· · ·	· · ·	1.8	1.4
			(1.1)	(.99)
DENCIT × 10⁻³	· · ·	· · ·	−.024	−.020
			(.052)	(.046)
URBPOP	· · ·	· · ·	· · ·	−.62†
				(.22)
R^2	.28	.47	.59	.69

* Significant at the 1-tail 0.10 level.
† Significant at the 2-tail 0.10 level.

with that of population in cities. But, in accord with central place theory, the spatial distribution of retail sales appears to be a result rather than a cause of urban population distribution. Of the three taste variables shown in Table 7, only the coefficient of SUBSTD is negative and larger than its standard error. The sign of URBPOP suggests that this variable reflects primarily the greater elasticity of housing supply in the outer parts of cities.

The results of the initial analysis of intercity differences in density gradients seemed clearly to be encouraging. Four of the variables in equation (5) have regression coefficients which are numerically too large to attribute to chance variation in sampling and almost seven-tenths of the inter-city variation in density gradients is explained by the regression equation. The analysis would seem to verify the hypothesis that density gradients vary directly with the level of marginal transport costs, since the coefficient of CAREGS is clearly significant whereas those of VEHMIL and AGESMA have the predicted signs and are about equal in magnitude to their standard errors in equation (5). The analysis, however, offers only slight support for the hypothesis that density gradients tend to decline as income increases.

There are three further questions which cause some uncertainty in interpreting these results shown in Table 7 and merit further investigation. First, does the apparently significant coefficient of SUBSTD in Table 7 reflect the effect of dwelling-unit condition itself or does it result from the intercorrelation of condition and some other variable? Second, are the coefficients biased by the omission of variables which were unavailable for all thirty-six cities, especially by the omission of CONCST, since this variable tends to be positively correlated with income and city size? Finally, I have interpreted the coefficients in Table 7 as reflecting the effect of these variables on density gradients. But, as discussed more fully below, do some of them, in fact, reflect the effect of differences in the gradients themselves on variables mistakenly taken as predetermined in the least-squares regression analysis? I will consider the first two of these questions in the remainder of this section and return to the third question in the fourth section of this chapter.

To explore the first question, the four additional taste variables described earlier were first introduced into the regression equation with the results shown in Table 8, equation (10). Introducing these additional taste variables drastically alters the coefficients of URBINC and SUBSTD and increases their standard errors, especially for the former variable. Of the

TABLE 8

Inclusion of Additional Taste Variables, DENGRA, 1950

Explanatory Variable[a]	Equation				
	(6)	(7)	(8)	(9)	(10)
$\vdots$ URBINC $\times\ 10^{-3}$	$-.45$	$.78$	$-.30$	$-.35$	1.5
$\vdots$	$(.56)$	(1.4)	$(.55)$	$(.58)$	(1.5)
SUBSTD	-2.0	$-3.0*$	-2.0	$-2.9*$	$-.87$
$\vdots$	(1.9)	(1.5)	(1.6)	(1.5)	(2.1)
PEROOM	-1.9	$\cdots$	$\cdots$	$\cdots$	-2.1
	(2.8)				(2.8)
CITINC $\times\ 10^{-3}$	$\cdots$	-1.2	$\cdots$	$\cdots$	-1.9
		(1.3)			(1.4)
POPNEG	$\cdots$	$\cdots$	-1.9	$\cdots$	$-2.9*$
			(1.6)		(1.8)
AGEDUS	$\cdots$	$\cdots$	$\cdots$	$.71$	-1.2
				(2.2)	(2.3)
R^2	$.70$	$.70$	$.71$	$.69$	$.74$

a In addition to the explanatory variables shown explicitly above, all the variables included in equation (5), Table 7, were included in each of the equations shown here as well. Their coefficients generally differed very little from their values in equation (5) and so were not repeated here.

* Significant at the 1-tail 0.10 level.

variables added, the coefficient of POPNEG appears to be significant at about the one-tail 5 percent level, and the coefficients of PEROOM and AGEDUS have the proper signs for taste variables but are numerically smaller than their standard errors. When the additional taste variables are added one at a time, as in equations (6) through (9), it appears that introducing either PEROOM or POPNEG reduces the coefficient of SUBSTD but that it is the former which increases the standard error of SUBSTD's coefficient. Not surprisingly, it is the introduction of CITINC that affects the coefficient of URBINC, since the simple correlation coefficient between them is quite high—0.94, but CITINC has the wrong sign in (7) as in (10) for a taste variable.

Of the four added variables, POPNEG is the only one whose coefficient is larger than its standard error in equations (6) through (9), and in (8) its t ratio is about the same as that of SUBSTD. These results suggest to me that the coefficient of SUBSTD in the earlier regressions may be partly reflecting the effects of the racial composition of the central city's population and that POPNEG ought to be included in further analysis. This probably results from the fact, discussed more fully in Chapter 10, that Negroes have lower incomes than whites and, consequently, a higher proportion of Negroes inhabit poor-quality dwellings. The results also suggest, if anything, that while CITINC does not operate as a taste variable, it may be a better income variable than URBINC. On practical grounds, however, there is little distinction between the two because they are so highly correlated. Since I prefer URBINC on a priori grounds, I decided to retain it in my further analysis. But, as the analysis in the fourth section demonstrates, the two income variables play quite different roles when one considers the determinants of the central city's share in the urbanized area population.

The other question I wish to examine in this section is the possibility of bias due to omission of important variables, especially variables which affect the price of and hence expenditures on housing. So far I have omitted PASCAR, a measure of availability of public transportation, because data was not available for four of the thirty-six cities for which other variables were available. These four cities were thus dropped, and conventional least-squares regressions were run both excluding and including PASCAR. The results are shown in the first two columns of Table 9. In equation (12) the coefficient of PASCAR has the wrong sign (if increasing values of PASCAR were indicative of lower marginal transport costs it should have a negative sign), its coefficient is numerically small relative to its standard error, and none of the other coefficients is affected in any important way when PASCAR is added. Clearly, these results suggest that no damage has been done by earlier omission of this variable.

The other variables omitted earlier are measures of variables affecting housing prices. This was done because CONCST was available for only twenty-eight cities, and for four of these VEHMIL was unavailable. For this reason, VEHMIL was dropped from the regression equation and CONCST and 180CIT were added to the other variables included in computing the regressions for the twenty-eight cities. The results are shown in equations (13) and (14), Table 9. The principal difference between

TABLE 9

Tests for the Omission of Variables, DENGRA, 1950

Explanatory Variable	Equation			
	(11)[a]	(12)[a]	(13)[b]	(14)[b]
VEHMIL × 10^{-6}	−2.7	−3.9	...	...
	(4.5)	(5.4)		
CAREGS	−10*	−10*	−7.8*	−9.6*
	(2.9)	(3.0)	(2.3)	(2.7)
URBINC × 10^{-3}	−.22	−.24	−.88*	−.33
	(.34)	(.35)	(.39)	(.54)
MANCIT	1.1*	1.1*	1.4*	1.5*
	(.61)	(.62)	(.58)	(.58)
SUBSTD	−2.8*	−2.8*	−2.1*	−2.5*
	(1.5)	(1.5)	(1.5)	(1.5)
URBPOP	−.49†	−.49†	−.39†	−.28†
	(.15)	(.16)	(.13)	(.15)
POPNEG	−2.2*	−2.1*	−2.5*	−3.4*
	(1.2)	(1.3)	(1.2)	(1.4)
PASCAR	...	.035	...	...
		(.087)		
CONCST	...	...	...	−.018
				(.016)
180CIT	...	...	...	−.42
				(.28)
R^2	.65	.65	.65	.69

[a] 32 cities only.
[b] 28 cities only.
* Significant at the 1-tail 0.10 level.
† Significant at the 2-tail 0.10 level.

equations (13) and (14) is the much larger (by one standard deviation) income coefficient in the former, which is due mostly to the difference in the cities included rather than to dropping VEHMIL from the regression equation. When CONCST and 180CIT are added in equation (14), however, the coefficient of URBINC falls back to about its former level, while most of the other coefficients change by small amounts relative to their standard errors. The change in the coefficient of URBINC takes place mostly when 180CIT is added, but adding the latter to the thirty-six cities used earlier has but a small effect on the coefficients of URBINC and the other variables as well.

The coefficient of CONCST is rather small as compared with its standard error in equation (14), but this coefficient has a negative sign as I would expect. With a housing demand elasticity equal to unity, the increase in housing prices that would follow from an increase in construction costs would leave the per household expenditure on housing, the price gradient, and thus the variation in the per household expenditure on housing with distance unchanged. But I argued in Chapter 3 that an increase in non-land costs would increase the value of housing produced per unit of land by greater amounts at greater distances from the CBD. On the other hand, I would expect the smaller supply of land to the housing industry in water-front cities to result in a greater rate of decline in housing output and hence population densities with distance. Because the partial correlation of CONCST with the density gradient is small for the twenty cities examined, I have deleted CONCST in subsequent comparisons. However, because I wanted to include 180CIT in the land area comparisons in the fourth section, I decided to retain it in other comparisons as well.

CONSISTENCY OF THE NEGATIVE EXPONENTIAL WITH MEAN DENSITIES

Previously in this chapter I have concentrated my attention on the fit of the negative exponential density function and variations in the slope of this function among cities for 1950. I would like now briefly to examine one other aspect of urban population distribution, the level of population densities or simply mean densities. The consistency of actual 1950 mean densities with those predicted by the measured 1950 density gradient provides an additional test of the usefulness of this characterization of the pattern of urban population distribution.

In Chapter 4, equation (4.11), I showed that the intercept of the negative exponential population density function, D_0, is equal to

$$D_0 = \frac{PD_1{}^2}{\xi f(D_1, k_2)}, \tag{15}$$

where

$$f(D_1, k_2) = 1 - (1 + D_1 k_2)e^{-D_1 k_2},$$

k_2 is the radius of the urbanized area or the circular approximation to it, $(\xi/2\pi)$ is the fraction of the total area surrounding the CBD which is used for urban (residential) purposes when densities are interpreted as gross (net), and P is the population of the urbanized area. The intercept or level parameter is therefore determined by many of the same forces which determine the density gradient. The only additional ones are the constant of proportionality ξ, which depends upon the topography of the area as well as upon the strength of the demand for land in residential versus other uses when densities are interpreted as net, and the urbanized area radius k_2, which itself depends upon the relative strength of urban and agricultural demands for land. Here I seek to determine how well the level of population densities in the various cities in 1950 agree with predicted levels based upon equation (15).

In doing so I shall work with what I shall call adjusted mean densities rather than with the D_0's in Table 1. Adjusted mean densities are essentially the average gross densities, $\bar{D}$, from the samples used in calculating the gradients shown in Table 1 divided by the urbanized area population, P. Average densities, or average density at the mean distance of tracts from the CBD, $\bar{k}$, rather than D_0 were used for comparison with predicted values for two reasons. First, in random sampling from a bivariate distribution of population densities and distances from the CBD by census tract, $\bar{D}$ and D_1 as estimated from a least-square regression are uncorrelated but D_0 and D_1 are positively correlated. Therefore, a comparison of the estimated D_0's with an increasing function of estimated D_1 would tend to show a positive correlation because of common sampling errors in the two terms alone. The true $\bar{D}$'s, however, will not vary exactly as the true D_0's because of differences in D_1 and $\bar{k}$, since $\bar{D} = D_0 - D_1\bar{k}$. For this reason, the comparisons made here will tend to show a less close association between actual and predicted density levels than in fact exists. Second, mean densities were divided by urbanized area population to gain a better idea of differences in density levels among cities which result from differences in the spread of cities alone rather than from differences in spread plus size. Virtually any theory of population distribution and the residential housing market would predict that average population densities would be directly proportional to size, so that a much sharper test of my analysis is obtained by adjusting observed density levels for differences in size. A final adjustment was made to divide mean densities of those cities designated waterfront cities above by two, since such cities have only about one-half the land area up to any given distance from the CBD that other cities have.

The logs of adjusted mean densities as defined in the paragraph above are compared with $\log\{D_1^2/f(D_1, k_2)\}$, which is the predicted value apart from a constant, in Figure 1. Values of D_1 used are shown in Table 1, while the radius of the urbanized area in miles was obtained from measurements made from the urbanized area maps in *1950 Census of Population*.[22]

---

[22] Vol. 2. For each urbanized area at most eight measurements separated by 45 degrees of the line-of-sight distance from the edge of the area to the CBD were made and averaged. The location of the CBD in these maps was determined with the aid of census tract maps of the central city of the area. The direction of the first measurement was selected at random from among 0 to 40 degrees by 5-degree intervals. Measurements were made only in those directions from the CBD in which the urbanized area extended.

The scatter of points obtained has a slope of about one as judged by eye and shows a strong tendency for adjusted mean density to vary directly with the predicted value, Spearman's coefficient of rank correlation rho being equal to $+0.816$. Thus, it would appear that, despite using $\bar{D}$ rather than D_0 as a measure of the level of population densities and neglecting some possible differences among cities in the proportion of land used for residential purposes, differences in the levels of population densities among cities seem to be consistent with those predicted by equation (15).

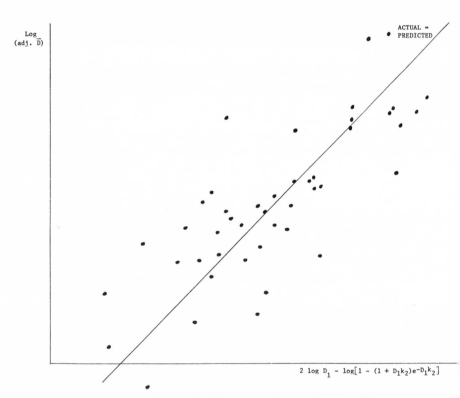

FIG. 1.—Actual and Predicted Adjusted Mean Densities

THE DISTRIBUTION OF POPULATION BETWEEN THE CENTRAL CITY AND ITS SUBURBS AND THE LAND AREA OCCUPIED BY THE CITY

One of the most important possible shortcomings of the analysis of the 1950 density gradients discussed earlier is the bias which might result from treating certain of DENGRA's explanatory variables as independent in conventional least-squares regressions when, in fact, they are jointly-determined. In this section I will examine this question by estimating equations similar to those shown in Tables 7–9 using the method of two-stage least-squares. In addition, I will present conventional and two-stage least-squares estimates of equations (4.17) and (4.19), which are log-linear approximations to the equations determining the land area occupied by the urbanized area and the central city's share of its population, respectively, using first the determinants of DENGRA and then DENGRA itself as explanatory variables. The distribution of population between the central city and its suburbs and the land area used for urban purposes both provide additional tests of my analysis of factors influencing the spread of population within urbanized areas and are of great interest for their own sakes. All the tables in this section and the discussion pertaining thereto refer to 1950 data, as did the material presented previously in this chapter. In the fifth section, some comparisons using 1960 data are presented.

Of the explanatory variables included in the regressions equations summarized in Table 7, one might argue that CAREGS, MANCIT, and SUBSTD should be treated as jointly dependent with DENGRA. Where cities tend to be more spread out or have smaller density gradients for reasons other than lower marginal transport costs, one would expect the demand for automobile transport and thus car ownership to be greater, other things being the same. The negative regression coefficient observed earlier might be due partly, or even wholly, to the effect of DENGRA on CAREGS rather than the reverse. Similarly, it might be argued that the distribution of population exerts a strong influence on the distribution of employment places because employers seek to reduce labor costs by locating close to the residences of their workers. It is hard to analyze the validity of such a contention because relatively little is known empirically about the relative importance of the determinants of location of employment places in cities. I am rather inclined to dismiss it, however, because I suspect that factors such as transport costs on material inputs and final products and land costs for assembly-line type plants are likely to be much more important empirically than intracity differences in wage costs, but I have no good evidence to back up these suspicions. Finally, as was pointed out in Chapter 6, it is frequently argued that slums result from the decline in demand for land near the city center which has accompanied improvements in transport costs. If so, and if the other measures of transport costs included fail to remove all the variation in DENGRA on this score, then the coefficient of SUBSTD may partly reflect the effects of lower transport costs.

To test possibilities such as these, the regression coefficients of the more important variables discussed thus far were estimated using the method of two-stage least-squares. In this method of estimation, conventional least-squares regressions for each of the variables on the righthand side of a particular regression equation which are treated as endogenous are run on all the predetermined variables in the equation system. The calculated values of each of the endogenous variables are obtained from these regressions. In the second stage, a conventional least-squares regression using the observed values of the variable on the left-hand side of the equation is run on the values of the other endogenous variables calculated from the first-stage regressions and on the observed values of the predetermined variables appearing in the particular equation. The coefficients obtained in the usual way from this second stage calculation are consistent estimators of the unknown true regression coefficients if the equation is correctly specified, have large sample variances no larger than any other consistent method of estimation which utilizes the same information, and are normally distributed in large samples. The estimated large sample approximation to the variances of the two-stage least-squares estimators are readily obtained from the second-stage calculations.[23] When using simultaneous equations methods of estimation, the relevant goodness-of-fit statistic is the R^2 in the reduced-form regression for the dependent variable in question. For this reason, I shall not show R^2 measures for the two-stage least-squares equations in the tables that follow but will call attention to the appropriate reduced-form R^2 in the text.

In applying the method of two-stage least-squares one must specify and use data on the predetermined variables which appear in other equations of the model. From other work discussed in Chapter 10, below, it would appear that SUBSTD depends upon the following variables discussed earlier: AGESMA, GROPOP, URBPOP, and CITINC. In addition, it would appear that SUBSTD is related to the proportion of the population one year old and over in 1950 who resided in the same dwelling unit in 1949 and 1950, designated as SAMHOU.[24]

Conventional least-squares regressions using CAREGS as the dependent variable indicated that in addition to DENGRA and SUBSTD, the coefficients of VEHMIL, URBINC, RETCBD and DENCIT had meaningful signs and were large relative to their standard errors. These results, not shown here, suggested using these last four variables as predetermined variables in the two-stage least-squares analysis. While it would have been

[23] For a fuller discussion of the method of two-stage least-squares see J. Johnston, *Econometric Methods* (New York: McGraw-Hill Book Company, 1963), pp. 258–64 and references cited there.

[24] Data were obtained from *Census of Population: 1950*, vol. 2, part 1, table 86. This variable, which is negatively associated with SUBSTD, probably reflects the higher rents control authorities allowed with a change in tenant. Its effect was negligible in 1960. For consistency with the 1950 comparisons, however, I included it in the 1960 ones, using data from *U.S. Census of Population: 1960*, vol. 1, table 72.

desirable to treat MANCIT as endogenously determined as well, I did not do so because so little is known about the locational determinants of manufacturing plants within cities.[25]

In addition to the variables already noted, three other predetermined variables were used in the analysis. These are: the natural log of manufacturing production worker employment in the Standard Metropolitan Area, SMAMFG;[26] a dummy variable which takes the value 1 for urbanized areas in the South (of Washington, D.C.) and West (of St. Louis, Mo.) and 0 for others, REGION; and the average distance in miles from the CBD to the boundary of the central city, k_1 of Chapter 4, here designated as RADCEN.[27] The reasons for including these last three variables will be described below. In calculating the two-stage least-squares regression estimates shown in the remainder of this chapter it was assumed that DENGRA, CAREGS, SUBSTD, CNTPOP, and LNAREA (the last two are defined below) are jointly determined by a system of five simultaneous equations. Examination of the system, and the estimates presented below, suggested that the rank condition for identifiability of the DENGRA, CNTPOP, and LNAREA equations is probably satisfied.

The resulting two-stage least-squares estimates of DENGRA's determinants are shown in equation (16), Table 10, and compared with conventional estimates in (17). Although the coefficients of CAREGS and MANCIT in (16) are both a little smaller numerically than the corresponding conventional least-squares estimates shown in equation (17), the greatest difference is in SUBSTD's coefficient. In equation (16) this coefficient is only about six-tenths as large numerically as in (17), and in the former it is decidedly smaller than its standard error. Thus, there is considerable doubt on statistical grounds whether locational preferences and, hence, the relative decline in population densities in cities are affected at all by the condition of the central city's housing stock. SUBSTD's coefficient in (16) is still large enough numerically to be of some practical importance, however, as explained more fully later. Figure 2 shows the actual values of DENGRA as compared with the ones calculated from

---

[25] Kitagawa and Bogue, *Suburbanization of Manufacturing*, pp. 49–60, using a set of economic and demographic variables similar to those used here were able to explain only about one-fifth of the variation among SMA's in the proportion of manufacturing employment outside the central city in 1947, and none of the explanatory variables taken separately showed a very strong association with the dependent variable.

[26] The data are from *ibid.* for 1950. For 1960 they are from *United States Census of Manufacturers: 1958*, vol. 3, table 3.

[27] As measured from the census tract maps in U.S. Bureau of the Census, *1950 Census of Population*, vol. 3. Measurements were made in a manner analogous to that described for measurement of k_2 in the preceding section.

equation (16); this figure gives little indication of non-linearity or hetero-scadisticity. The R^2 in the reduced-form equation for DENGRA is 0.65.

I now wish to consider the determinants of the central city's share in the urbanized area's population and the land area occupied by the latter. Equations (4.19) and (4.17), which relate central city population and the land area occupied by the urbanized area to the urbanized area population and the density gradient, were derived on the assumption that the same log-linear pattern of population density decline holds for the central city and its suburbs. There are several reasons why these equations might not prove to be very satisfactory, however. The pattern of population densities might tend to differ systematically from the negative exponential. While

TABLE 10

TWO-STAGE AND CONVENTIONAL LEAST-SQUARES
ESTIMATES OF DETERMINANTS OF DENGRA, 1950

EXPLANATORY VARIABLE	METHOD OF ESTIMATION (EQUATION)	
	Two-Stage (16)	Conventional (17)
VEHMIL × 10^{-6}	4.2	2.2
	(5.5)	(4.8)
CAREGS[a]	−6.3*	−9.3*
	(3.9)	(2.5)
URBINC × 10^{-3}	−.21	−.19
	(.34)	(.32)
MANCIT	.78	1.0
	(.66)	(.57)
SUBSTD[a]	−1.5	−2.4*
	(1.8)	(1.3)
URBPOP	−.47†	−.47†
	(.13)	(.13)
POPNEG	−2.6*	−2.8*
	(1.3)	(1.1)
180CIT	−.43	−.39
	(.31)	(.29)
R^2	...	.67

a Treated as simultaneously determined in (16).
* Significant at the one-tail 0.10 level.
† Significant at the two-tail 0.10 level.

these differences might not be strong enough to show up for the central city tract data in samples of the size I have used for the estimates shown in Table 1, the deviations might tend to be much greater in the suburban parts of the urbanized area. If the true population density function showed a negative curvature on a semi-log plot, for example, that is, if the relative rate of decline in density tended to increase numerically with distance from the CBD, the central city population would tend to be systematically

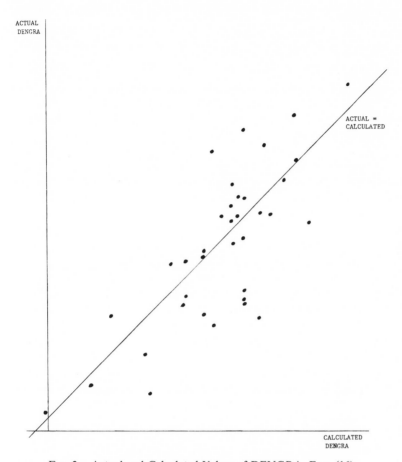

Fig. 2.—Actual and Calculated Values of DENGRA, Eqn. (16)

greater and the land area occupied by the urbanized area smaller than expected on the basis of the rate of density decline within the central city only.

More important, probably, certain factors influencing population distribution might operate with greater force as between the central city and its suburbs than within either separately. Among these are the advantages to home ownership afforded by federal income-tax treatment of income from owner-occupied housing and by federal mortgage programs, possible differences in property tax rates relative to municipal services provided, differences in the proportion of land used for residential and other purposes between central cities and their suburbs, and possible disequilibrium in population distribution between central cities and suburbs in 1950. As was argued in Chapter 5, federal income-tax treatment of income from owner-occupied housing and federal mortgage programs tend to reduce the relative price of housing to the owner-occupant and hence increase the demand for housing in owner-occupied dwellings substantially. Since such housing is located in the outer part of the city for reasons discussed in Chapter 3, the impact of these programs is to increase the output of housing and population in the suburban areas relative to that in the central city. Differential property-tax rates might have similar effects. Taxes to support welfare, educational, and other income redistributive expenditures for the lower-income groups concentrated in the central city tend to be levied mostly on central city residents. Liability for such taxes can frequently be escaped by living in the suburbs, and the relatively greater is the tax burden on higher-income groups in the central city the greater the incentive to live in the suburbs.[28]

On the other hand, differences in the proportion of land used for residential purposes and disequilibrium in population distribution are likely to result in a larger central city population and smaller land area than anticipated. While there might tend to be relatively more land in central cities used for commercial and industrial purposes and for streets and parks, I suspect this would be more than offset by higher proportions of land currently held vacant for future development in suburban areas. If so, gross but not net population densities would tend to be lower in suburban areas than in central cities after removing the effects of distance from the CBD, and thus actual suburbanization would tend to be less than that predicted by (4.19). Also, one might argue that the adjustment of population distribution toward the suburbs in response to changed conditions such as automobile transportation and federal tax treatment of income from owner-occupied housing and federal mortgage programs were delayed by the depression of the 1930's, World War II, and the readjustments of the late 1940's. If this were so, equation (4.19) would then tend to underestimate the central city population, and for the same reasons (4.17) would overestimate the urbanized area land area.

My initial regression equations with CNTPOP, the natural log of the central city population, and LNAREA, the natural log of the urbanized land area in square miles,[29] were very unsatisfactory. The difficulties encountered are illustrated by equations (18) and (19), Table 11. In general, most of the coefficients of variables I would interpret as affecting the density gradient have the wrong sign or are small relative to their standard

---

[28] I wish to thank Martin J. Bailey for pointing this out to me.

[29] The data used are from *1950 Census of Population*, vol. 1, part 1, table 17, and *U.S. Census of Population: 1960*, Final Report PC(1)–1A, table 22.

errors. The coefficients of VEHMIL, URBINC, and SUBSTD are all positive in the CNTPOP regression, equation (18), where I would have anticipated negative signs, and vice versa in the LNAREA regression. In addition, while the sign of the coefficient of CAREGS in (18) is negative as I would anticipate, this coefficient is only one-fifth as large as its standard error and much smaller than I would anticipate (see below), and MANCIT apparently has the wrong sign in (19). Finally, the explanatory power of equations (18) and (19) is rather small when judged by the statistic R_Δ^2 shown at the foot of the table. The latter is the fraction of the variance in the dependent variable unexplained by URBPOP alone which is accounted for by all of the other explanatory variables. Since the size of the urbanized area population would affect the central city population and urbanized area land area on virtually any hypothesis, naïve or otherwise, the additional explanatory power of the other variables used is the relevant consideration in judging the success of my analysis.

TABLE 11

INITIAL COMPARISONS OF CNTPOP

AND LNAREA, 1950

EXPLANATORY VARIABLE	DEPENDENT VARIABLE (EQUATION)	
	CNTPOP (18)	LNAREA (19)
VEHMIL × 10^{-6}	2.5	−4.5
	(1.1)	(2.7)
CAREGS	−.15	2.7*
	(.74)	(1.4)
URBINC × 10^{-3}	.016	−.53
	(.093)	(.18)
MANCIT	.46*	.40
	(.17)	(.32)
SUBSTD	.11	−.043
	(.45)	(.74)
URBPOP	.79*	1.0*
	(.049)	(.072)
POPNEG	.066	.94*
	(.37)	(.63)
180CIT	· · ·	.17
		(.17)
RADCEN	.22*	· · ·
	(.10)	
R_Δ^2 a	.61	.42

a See text for definition.
* Significant at the one-tail 0.10 level.

Partly because of the disappointing results illustrated by the equations shown in Table 11, I decided to treat the CNTPOP and LNAREA equations as part of the simultaneous system described earlier and to add several additional variables to the regression equations. In Table 12, the two-stage estimates of the revised equation (4.19), using the determinants of DENGRA rather than this variable itself, are shown in the second column. The coefficients of URBINC, MANCIT, and URBPOP are all significant by the usual standards of evaluation. The last, however, is not significantly different from unity, which is a more appropriate null hypothesis. Of even greater interest to me is the consistency of the estimated coefficients with my equation (4.19), which in effect assumes that suburban population is determined by extrapolating the behavior of population densities within the central city out to the suburbs, and the coefficients shown in equation (16), Table 10. The predicted values shown in the first column were derived from the coefficients in equation (16), Table 10, together with evaluations of γ and δ shown in equation (4.19). The latter were made using my estimated density gradients, the k_1 or RADCEN measurements, and the measurements made of k_2 described earlier. The

TABLE 12

TWO-STAGE AND CONVENTIONAL LEAST-SQUARES ESTIMATES OF THE DETERMINANTS OF CNTPOP, USING DETERMINANTS OF DENGRA, 1950

EXPLANATORY VARIABLE	PREDICTED COEFFICIENTS[b]	ACTUAL COEFFICIENTS (EQUATION)	
		Two-Stage (20)	Conventional (21)
VEHMIL $\times$ 10^{-6}	2.2	.45 (1.6)	1.1 (1.3)
CAREGS[a]	-3.3	-1.5 (1.5)	$-.50$ (.72)
URBINC $\times$ 10^{-3}	$-.11$	$-1.1*$ (.43)	$-1.1*$ (.36)
MANCIT	.41	.39* (.18)	.34* (.15)
SUBSTD[a]	$-.78$	$-.88$ (.78)	$-.49$ (.42)
URBPOP	.46	.92* (.063)	.90* (.052)
POPNEG	-1.4	.50 (.50)	.47 (.36)
180CIT	$-.43$	$-.023$ (.083)	.0096 (.078)
RADCEN	1.1	$-.024$ (.16)	.047 (.11)
CITINC $\times$ 10^{-3}	...	1.2* (.37)	1.1* (.31)
REGION	...	$-.0081$ (.11)	$-.055$ (.084)
$R_\Delta^{2\,c}$	...	...	.75

[a] Treated as simultaneously determined in (20).
[b] Calculated from (4.19), the coefficients of (16), and $\gamma = 0.30$, $\delta = 0.56$.
[c] See text for definition.
* Significant at the 1-tail 0.10 level.

average values of these parameters for the forty-six cities for which I have estimated density gradients are $\gamma = 0.30$ and $\delta = 0.56$. Now, equation (4.19) suggests that the regression coefficients vary with the γ and δ values for a city or, alternatively, that the γ and δ values should be used to weight the explanatory variables. I have not done so, however, because I have only sample estimates of γ and δ for each city, and these may be subject to considerable error because of sampling errors in DENGRA. It seemed to me that the specification error of not weighting is likely to be much less serious than the problem of measurement errors—and correlated ones, at that—in all the explanatory variables.[30]

Comparing the predicted coefficient column of Table 12 with the two-stage estimates, the coefficients of MANCIT and SUBSTD agree quite closely, while those of CAREGS disagree by about one standard error of the actual coefficient. The actual coefficients of URBINC and URBPOP, however, are much larger numerically than the predicted values. That of URBPOP indicates that the central city population increases more rapidly as the urbanized area population grows than I would expect from the variation of population density within the central city. The coefficient of URBINC suggests that, as income grows, the suburban population grows more rapidly than one would expect from extrapolating the greater relative growth of the outer parts of the central city. One possible explanation for this latter discrepancy is the inducements to home ownership provided by the federal income-tax advantage and federal mortgage programs. Such inducements would tend to increase the relative demand for housing in the outer parts of urban areas because single-family housing is relatively cheaper there. Their impact would be strongest in the suburban areas in the short run because vacant and agricultural land is more readily converted to new residential uses. The magnitude of URBINC's coefficient may also be influenced by the considerations relating to local taxation described in the following paragraph. Many other explanations could be offered, of course. Finally, the coefficient of POPNEG is positive, though not much larger than its standard error, while I would anticipate a negative one. This last suggests that, while an increase in the proportion of the central city population which is Negro may stimulate the demand for housing in the outer parts of the central city, it has no effect per se upon the distribution of population between the central city and its suburbs.

One other coefficient in equation (20), that of CITINC, is statistically significant by anyone's standards and, as explained more fully later on, of substantial practical importance. As noted earlier, in initial regressions using CNTPOP as the dependent variable I found a weak but positive

---

[30] Similar remarks apply to the LNAREA equations shown later.

coefficient for URBINC. Since the latter is contrary to what I would anticipate I included CITINC in the regression as well to see if its omission was responsible for the positive coefficient of URBINC. One explanation for the positive coefficients of CITINC is that higher-income households have an aversion to living among lower-income ones within the central city. There are two difficulties with this interpretation, however. I would expect an aversion to certain kinds of neighbors to be related to more visible phenomena such as housing quality or race. But, more importantly, in equation (7) CITINC's coefficient was rather strongly negative; if the presence of low-income households in the central city increases the demand for housing in the suburban parts of the urbanized area, I would expect it to do so in the other parts of the central city as well.

A better explanation can be found, I believe, in considering the effect of low-income households on taxes paid by higher-income central city residents noted earlier. If the incomes of, say, the lower third of central city households were to fall, taxes collected from them directly or indirectly through property taxes would fall. At the same time, central city expenditures for health and welfare purposes, which are financed in substantial part by taxes collected within the central city, would probably rise. The net effect would be an increase in taxes for higher-income central city households and business firms. Such a tax increase would have no differential effect on housing demand within the central city but would reduce the attractiveness of central city relative to suburban locations.

In Table 13 an alternative form of equation (20), in which DENGRA itself rather than its determinants is included among CNTPOP's explanatory variables, is shown. Like equation (20), (22) indicates that with an increase in URBINC the demand for suburban housing increases relatively more than would be anticipated from the increased housing demand in the outer parts of the central city. If URBINC's influence as between the central city and its suburbs was the same as within the central city, its total effect would be reflected in the coefficient of DENGRA, and its coefficient would be zero. In addition, with DENGRA and URBPOP held constant, an increase in the fraction of the central city population which is Negro leads to an increase in the central city population, again suggesting that, while the racial composition of the central city may affect the relative demand for housing within the central city, it does so to a lesser extent as between the central city and its suburbs. The coefficient of CITINC is again strongly significant in (22) and virtually the same as in (20). Finally, the coefficient of URBPOP is much larger than I would anticipate on the basis of equation (4.19) and that of DENGRA is much smaller. Together these comparisons suggests that the factors making for an outward movement of population away from the CBD operate in the same direction but with less force between the central city and its suburbs than within the central city. This finding is directly contradictory to most popular and scholarly explanation of so-called "suburban sprawl." One possible explanation for this last finding is that, because of the effects of the depression of the thirties and World War II on the volume of residential construction, a long-run disequilibrium existed in 1950 as between the central city and suburban populations.

TABLE 13

Two-Stage and Conventional Least-Squares Estimates of the Determinants of CNTPOP, Using DENGRA, 1950

Explanatory Variable	Predicted Coefficients[b]	Actual Coefficients (Equation)	
		Two-Stage (22)	Conventional (23)
URBPOP	.70	.96*	.91*
		(.061)	(.044)
DENGRA[a]	.52	.22*	.079*
		(.099)	(.042)
RADCEN	1.1	.17*	.15*
		(.11)	(.095)
180CIT	−.21	.080	.064
		(.078)	(.065)
URBINC × 10^{-3}	⋯	−1.1*	−1.2*
		(.38)	(.31)
POPNEG	⋯	.78	.66
		(.30)	(.24)
CITINC	⋯	1.3*	1.3*
		(.33)	(.27)
REGION	⋯	.0092	−.070
		(.10)	(.077)
R_Δ^{2} [c]	⋯	⋯	.68

[a] Treated as simultaneously determined in (22).
[b] Calculated from (4.19), the coefficients of (16), and $\gamma = 0.30$, $\delta = 0.56$.
[c] See text for definition.
* Significant at the 1-tail 0.10 level.

The actual values of CNTPOP are plotted against those calculated from equation (20) in Figure 3. The scatter of points exhibits about as much linearity and homoscedasticity as one might hope for. The fit is also extremely tight, but for reasons noted earlier this is misleading. The R_Δ^{2} statistic calculated from CNTPOP's reduced-form equation is 0.79; the latter indicates that all the other predetermined variables of the model's five equations account for about four-fifths of the variance of (the log of) CNTPOP which is unaccounted for by URBPOP alone. I also note that there are several important instances in which the conventional least-squares coefficients differ from the two-stage estimates. In Table 12, the conventional least-squares coefficients of CAREGS and SUBSTD are both much smaller numerically than the two-stage estimates. This is also true for the coefficients of DENGRA in Table 13. In all three cases the two-stage estimates correspond more closely with my a priori expectation.

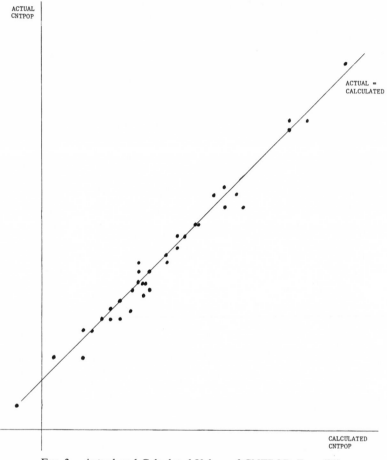

FIG. 3.—Actual and Calculated Values of CNTPOP, Eqn. (20)

I would now like to consider the determinants of the land occupied by the urbanized area, LNAREA, summarized in Tables 14 and 15. In the former the determinants of DENGRA are included, while DENGRA itself is used in the latter. In each of the tables I show both the actual two-stage least-squares estimates and the value of the coefficients predicted by equation (4.17), the coefficients of equation (16), and an average value for β of 0.65.[31] As was the case in the CNTPOP regressions, the actual coefficient of CAREGS would seem to be quite consistent with the predicted

---

[31] β was evaluated in a way analogous to that described earlier for γ and δ.

value, but in (24) the coefficients of both URBINC and POPNEG agree fairly well with their predicted values. The coefficient of URBPOP is somewhat low but differs less drastically from its predicted value than in the CNTPOP regressions. The major disagreements now seem to be the coefficients of MANCIT, which is too large, and SUBSTD, which is too small. The latter indicates here that, while the condition of the central city housing stock may influence the relative demand for housing in the outer

TABLE 14

TWO-STAGE AND CONVENTIONAL LEAST-SQUARES ESTIMATES OF THE DETERMINANTS OF LNAREA, USING DETERMINANTS OF DENGRA, 1950

EXPLANATORY VARIABLE	PREDICTED COEFFICIENTS[b]	ACTUAL COEFFICIENTS (EQUATION)	
		Two-Stage (24)	Conventional (25)
VEHMIL $\times 10^{-6}$	-2.9	$-.44$ (3.3)	-2.1 (2.5)
CAREGS[a]	4.4	5.2* (3.1)	.44 (1.3)
URBINC $\times 10^{-3}$	.15	.38 (.88)	.87* (.67)
MANCIT	$-.55$	.20 (.43)	.49 (.32)
SUBSTD[a]	1.0	$-.089$ (1.2)	$-.079$ (.69)
URBPOP	.98	.81* (.13)	.79* (.10)
POPNEG	1.8	1.4* (.97)	.46 (.63)
180CIT	.05	.036 (.18)	.075 (.14)
CITINC $\times 10^{-3}$	$\cdots$	$-.74$ (.72)	$-.87*$ (.58)
REGION	$\cdots$	.37* (.24)	.60* (.16)
SMAMFG	$\cdots$	.11 (.11)	.10 (.086)
R_Δ^{2} [c]	$\cdots$	$\cdots$	.63

[a] Treated as simultaneously determined in (24).
[b] Calculated from (4.17), the coefficients of (16), and $\beta = 0.65$.
[c] See text for definition.
* Significant at the 1-tail 0.10 level.

relative to the inner parts of the central city, it has no effect upon the demand for suburban versus central city housing. The coefficient of MANCIT might be explained by a smaller degree of substitutability of land for other productive factors in manufacturing than in the production of housing or a smaller variation in land rentals for industrial than for residential land. In either case, a shift of manufacturing plants from suburbs to the central city coupled with a reverse shift of residences would

tend to increase the urbanized area demand for land, since the reduction
in manufacturing demand would be numerically smaller than the increased residential demand.

TABLE 15

Two-Stage and Conventional Least-Squares Estimates of the
Determinants of LNAREA, Using DENGRA, 1950

Explanatory Variable	Predicted Coefficients[b]	Actual Coefficients (Equation)	
		Two-Stage (26)	Conventional (27)
URBPOP	.65	.49*	.83*
		(.25)	(.088)
DENGRA[a]	−.70	−.61*	−.046
		(.37)	(.087)
180CIT	−.24	−.18	−.046
		(.20)	(.12)
MANCIT	· · ·	1.1	.31
		(.69)	(.30)
SUBSTD	· · ·	−2.0	−.22
		(1.5)	(.60)
CITINC × 10^{-3}	· · ·	−.78*	−.11
		(.51)	(.19)
REGION	· · ·	.22	.48*
		(.24)	(.11)
SMAMFG	· · ·	.21*	.068
		(.15)	(.080)
R_Δ^{2} [c]	· · ·	· · ·	.57

a Treated as simultaneously determined in (26).
b Calculated from (4.17), the coefficients of (16), and $\beta = 0.65$.
c See text for definition.
* Significant at the 1-tail 0.10 level.

Also included among the explanatory variables in Tables 14 and 15 are
three which I would not expect to reflect differences in the relative rate of
population density decline within the central city. I included CITINC for
essentially the same reason here as in the CNTPOP regressions; initial
results, equation (19), indicated that increasing values of URBINC are
associated with decreasing amounts of urbanized land area. The LNAREA
coefficients of CITINC seem to be consistent both in magnitude and sign
within the CNTPOP regressions. REGION was included because the
earlier regression exhibited predominantly positive residuals for urban
areas in the South and West. The positive coefficient might result from a
lower agricultural demand for land and hence lower land rentals for urban
users in areas outside of the Northeast. SMAMFG was included because
I thought that the positive coefficient for MANCIT observed in earlier
regressions resulted from its inter-correlation with the former. Adding
SMAMFG did indeed make MANCIT's coefficient smaller, though in (24)

it remains larger than predicted by equation (4.17). The positive co-efficient of SMAMFG may reflect the fact that manufacturing is more land intensive than other nonresidential uses of land, so that the greater the employment in manufacturing given population size the greater the demand for urban land.

In Table 15 the coefficients of URBPOP and DENGRA both indicate a smaller response of total land use by the urbanized area than I would anticipate on the basis of the spread of population within the central city. The result here is similar to that observed in equation (22), though in (26) the differences between actual two-stage and predicted coefficients are only about one standard error of the former. The other variables included in equation (26) would seem to be consistent with the interpretation I gave for their coefficients in (24). Figure 4 shows the actual values of LNAREA plotted against the values calculated from (24). Here, as in Figures 2 and 3, there is evident little departure from linearity and homoscedasticity. The R_A^2 statistic for the two-stage LNAREA equations is 0.83, so the five equation model's other predetermined variables account for five-sixths of the variance unaccounted for by URBPOP alone. Finally, note that the differences between the two-stage and conventional least-squares estimates are even greater for LNAREA than they were in the CNTPOP comparisons. The differences are especially striking in the case of the coefficients of CAREGS and POPNEG in Table 14 and those of DENGRA, MANCIT and CITINC in Table 15. Where different, the two-stage estimates again are generally closer to the predicted values than the conventional least-squares estimates.

Further Tests of the CNTPOP and LNAREA Equations

Because of the experimentation I did with the 1950 data before arriving at what I felt were relatively satisfactory results, I reestimated equations (20) and (24) using 1960 data.[32] Exactly the same set of predetermined and, except for DENGRA, which was not needed for the comparisons made, jointly-dependent variables were used for 1960 as for 1950. Limitations on the availability of data for calculating VEHMIL made it necessary to restrict the 1960 analysis to thirty cities. The final 1950 results were re-peated exactly with no further inclusion or exclusion of variables or other experimentation.

---

[32] The analysis of density gradients was not repeated using 1960 data for two reasons. First, measurement of the land area of census tracts to obtain their popula-tion densities and estimating the density gradients for the necessary number of cities would be very laborious and time consuming. And, second, practically none of the calculations made using the 1950 data were suggested by the data themselves. For this latter reason, there seemed to be much less need of an independent check on the DENGRA comparisons.

The 1960 results are summarized in Table 16. By and large the results are very similar to the corresponding comparisons for 1950. In the CNTPOP comparison, equation (28), the coefficient of CAREGS is again negative but small relative to its standard error, and that of MANCIT is positive though even larger than previously. The coefficients of URBINC

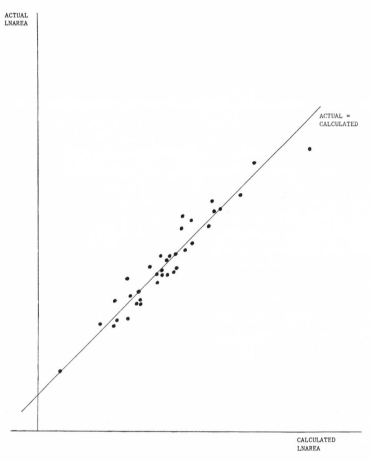

FIG. 4.—Actual and Calculated Values of LNAREA, Eqn. (24)

and CITINC are about equal numerically and opposite in sign, as in 1950, though much smaller numerically. In the LNAREA equation, (29), the coefficient of CAREGS is strongly positive and about the same as in 1950. The 1960 coefficients of SUBSTD and POPNEG are now consistent with each other. Both in (28) and (29) the coefficients of SUBSTD, though small relative to their standard errors, suggest that the lower the quality of the central city's housing stock the greater the demand for housing in the outer parts of the urbanized area. Both of the coefficients of POPNEG suggest, moreover, that the greater the proportion of the central city's population which is Negro the greater the housing demand in the central parts of the urbanized area. The R_Δ^2 statistics are also quite similar to their 1950 values, being 0.85 in (28) and 0.76 in (29).

TABLE 16

TWO-STAGE LEAST-SQUARES ESTIMATES OF THE
DETERMINANTS OF CNTPOP AND LNAREA,
USING DETERMINANTS OF DENGRA, 1960[a]

EXPLANATORY VARIABLE	DEPENDENT VARIABLE (EQUATION)	
	CNTPOP (28)	LNAREA (29)
VEHMIL × 10^{-6}	.082	1.9
	(2.1)	(3.9)
CAREGS[b]	−.72	4.7*
	(1.3)	(2.5)
URBINC × 10^{-3}	−.40*	−.19
	(.16)	(.31)
MANCIT	.73*	.47
	(.20)	(.40)
SUBSTD[b]	−.13	1.2
	(1.4)	(2.0)
URBPOP	.87*	1.2*
	(.086)	(.24)
POPNEG	.90	−.88
	(.43)	(.96)
180CIT	.079	−.081
	(.10)	(.20)
RADCEN	.10	· · ·
	(.15)	
REGION	−.019	.11
	(.093)	(.22)
CITINC × 10^{-3}	.45*	−.045
	(.16)	(.32)
SMAMFG	· · ·	−.078
		(.18)

[a] Using data for 30 cities only.
[b] Treated as simultaneously determined.
* Significant at the 1-tail 0.10 level.

Of greatest new substantive interest are the coefficients of URBPOP shown in Table 16. In Tables 12 and 13 I found much larger coefficients for URBPOP in the CNTPOP comparisons than I would anticipate on the hypothesis that the same pattern of population densities prevails in the suburbs as in their central city. I suggested that the apparent too little suburbanization of population in 1950 might have resulted from a long-run disequilibrium of the 1950 population. In equation (28), however, URBPOP's coefficient is almost the same as in (20), about a standard error smaller but still far greater than the predicted value shown in Table 12.

In the LNAREA equation for 1960 URBPOP's coefficient now is about a standard error larger than unity, as compared with the 1950 coefficient, which is about one and one-half standard errors less than unity. The latter comparison offers some slight support for the disequilibrium hypothesis. The difference in the relation of the estimated coefficients of URBPOP in the CNTPOP and LNAREA equations to their predicted values might be explained by the existence of scattered parcels of land in the suburbs which are being held for more extensive future development. But the finding of a smaller suburban population than anticipated remains a puzzle.

One further test to which I subjected the main results of this chapter was the comparison of residuals from different equations. This test turns out less favorably than the comparison just made of 1950 and 1960 co-efficients. In examining the residuals from the various regressions here and elsewhere in this study, I have limited myself to comparing their signs. In drawing formal inferences about the relationship among residuals I have used chi-square tests applied to the numbers of residuals with plus and minus signs. (In the present instance, however, such tests are hardly necessary.) These tests, of course, are quick and easy to perform, and they are virtually distribution free. But they are less powerful than tests based upon the magnitudes of the residuals as well. And, since the computed residuals from a given regression equation are correlated with each other in small samples, even though the unknown true residuals may be in-dependent, the tests are strictly valid only for large samples.

As one sees from Table 17 there is a strong negative association between the residuals from the CNTPOP and LNAREA equations. In 1950, the residuals were of opposite sign for twenty-five of the thirty-six cities, while in 1960 they had opposite signs for twenty of the thirty cities included in the regressions. It appears, then, that there are factors influencing the dis-persion of population in urbanized areas which I have failed to take into account in my comparisons. Furthermore, it would appear that these factors persist over time. For, when the residuals from a corresponding regression equation for 1950 and 1960 are compared, as in Table 18, one sees even stronger but positive association of the residuals. Interestingly enough, however, there is practically no association between either CNTPOP or LNAREA residuals for 1950 with the DENGRA residuals for that year. These last comparisons are shown in Table 19. I would conclude, therefore, that whatever the factors may be which have been omitted from the CNTPOP and LNAREA comparisons, they are not factors which influence the relative rate of decline of population density within the central city. Rather, the omitted factors would appear to be peculiar to the distribution of population between the central city and its suburbs.

TABLE 17a
CNTPOP VERSUS LNAREA RESIDUALS, 1950

SIGN, CNTPOP (20)	SIGN, LNAREA (24)		
	+	−	Total
+	6	14	20
−	11	5	16
Total	17	19	36

$X^2(1) = 5.34$; Probability $\cong 0.02$

TABLE 17b
CNTPOP VERSUS LNAREA RESIDUALS, 1960

SIGN, CNTPOP (28)	SIGN, LNAREA (29)		
	+	−	Total
+	5	11	16
−	9	5	14
Total	14	16	30

$X^2(1) = 3.29$; Probability < 0.10

TABLE 18a
CNTPOP RESIDUALS, 1950 VERSUS 1960

SIGN, 1950 (20)	SIGN, 1960 (28)		
	+	−	Total
+	11	3	14
−	4	9	13
Total	15	12	27

$X^2(1) = 6.23$; Probability < 0.02

TABLE 18b
LNAREA RESIDUALS, 1950 VERSUS 1960

SIGN, 1950 (24)	SIGN, 1960 (29)		
	+	−	Total
+	10	2	12
−	4	11	15
Total	14	13	27

$X^2(1) = 8.59$; Probability < 0.01

TABLE 19a
DENGRA VERSUS CNTPOP RESIDUALS, 1950

SIGN, DENGRA (16)	SIGN, CNTPOP (20)		
	+	−	Total
+	12	9	21
−	8	7	15
Total	20	16	36

$X^2(1) = 0.05$; Probability $\cong 0.80$

TABLE 19b
DENGRA VERSUS LNAREA RESIDUALS, 1950

SIGN, DENGRA (16)	SIGN, LNAREA (24)		
	+	−	Total
+	11	10	21
−	6	9	15
Total	17	19	36

$X^2(1) = 0.54$; Probability $\cong 0.50$

In concluding, I would like to comment briefly upon the quantitative effect of some of the more important variables influencing the distribution of population in cities. The urbanized area's population, of course, is an important determinant of its central city's total population and the total land area it occupies. But the estimates presented earlier suggest that neither the central city's share in the urbanized area population nor land area per capita is very responsive to the total population of the urbanized area. The latter, however, is more strongly correlated with the relative rate of decline of population in the central city than any of the other variables examined. Because of the great variation in size among different cities at a given time, size is also the quantitatively most important determinant of differences in DENGRA cross-sectionally. The elasticity of DENGRA with respect to URBPOP shown by Table 10 is about −0.5, so that with a doubling of size DENGRA would tend to decline by about 50 percent, or from 0.30, which is roughly the median of the estimates shown in Table 1, to about 0.15. The quantitative effects of increases in the urbanized area population over time are also substantial, but less striking. Over the decade of the fifties, URBPOP increased by about 30 percent on the average for the cities studied here. Such an increase would tend to reduce the density gradient by about 15 percent, or from about 0.30 to 0.25.

Of the other determinants of the distribution of population in cities, car registrations per capita, which I have interpreted as a proxy for the costs of automobile transport, is probably the most important. The coefficient of CAREGS exceeded its standard error substantially in most of the DENGRA and LNAREA comparisons. While not significantly different from zero statistically in the CNTPOP regressions, neither was it significantly different from the value I anticipated on a priori grounds. More importantly, though, CAREGS increased from about 0.26 to 0.35 during the 1950's in the cities studied here. Such an increase, according to equation (16), would be sufficient to reduce the relative rate of decline of population densities within the central city by about 57 percent, or from 0.30 to 0.13. According to the coefficients of equations (24) and (29), it would increase the urbanized area land area by about 45 percent. Even if CAREGS's coefficient is as low as shown by equations (28) and (20), the increase occurring during the fifties would be accompanied by a reduction in central city population by 7 to 14 percent. Hence, the effects of the improvements in automobile transportation reflected in the increase in CAREGS during the 1950's are dramatic indeed.

The quantitative effects of some of the other determinants of urban population distribution that I have examined, while less striking than those already discussed, are still potentially large enough to be of some practical importance. The average value of MANCIT for the cities included in the 1950 comparisons was about 0.70; for several cities, however, MANCIT was 0.90 or more, while in quite a few others it was 0.50 or less. Differences of this magnitude would, according to the estimated coefficients of $+0.8$ to $+1.0$, be associated with differences in density gradients of as much as ± 20 percent of the average, or from 0.24 to 0.36. During the fifties the average fraction of SMA manufacturing employment in the central city fell to a little over 0.60. Such a decline would reduce the density gradient by about 7 percent and the central city population by around 4 percent. A growth of incomes of about 3 percent per year would, in a decade, raise the 1950 average both for URBINC and CITINC of $3,000 by about $1,000. The latter, in turn, would reduce the density gradient by almost 20 percent. Thus, even though URBINC's coefficient is of doubtful statistical significance in the DENGRA equation, the effect of income growth during the 1950's could have been quantitatively greater than that of population growth. Finally, it should be noted that the effects estimated here from cross-section data agree well with the observed average changes in CNTPOP and LNAREA during the decade of the fifties. The changes in URBPOP, CAREGS, and MANCIT just discussed imply an increase in CNTPOP of 9 percent, which was the actual average increase from 1950 to 1960 for the thirty-six cities used for the 1950 estimates. For the same cities and time period LNAREA increased by about 82 percent; changes in CAREGS and URBPOP during the fifties would imply increases of from

71 to 83 percent in LNAREA, depending upon whether URBPOP's co-efficient in (24) or (29) is used.

On the basis of the results presented in this chapter, it is hard to make much of a case for the proposition that the physical characteristics of the central city have much influence on the distribution of population in urbanized areas. With but one exception, the coefficients of all the variables which might be interpreted as representing the effects of physical condition —AGESMA, SUBSTD, MFGEMP, DENCIT, and AGEDUS—were either small relative to their standard errors or had the wrong sign when included in the DENGRA comparisons. The one exception is SUBSTD, whose coefficient was negative, as would be expected, and about twice its standard error in equation (5). Introducing POPNEG, however, reduced the coefficient of SUBSTD by about one-third so that it was no longer clearly too large numerically to attribute to chance variation. In the two-stage least-squares equation, (16), this coefficient was smaller still. The coefficient of SUBSTD is still large enough in (16), though, so that an increase of 10 percentage points in the central city's dwelling units which are substandard would reduce the density gradient from about 0.30 to 0.25. On the other hand, during the fifties the proportion of the central-city dwellings which are substandard fell by about half, or from about 0.20 to 0.11. Thus, it is hard to sustain the widespread view that the decentralization of population observed during the fifties was associated with changes in the quality of the central-city housing stock.

A somewhat stronger case can be made for the proposition than an increase in the fraction of the central city's population which is Negro increases housing demand in the outer parts of cities relative to their inner zones. In equation (16) the coefficient of POPNEG is twice its standard error; it implies, for example, that with an increase of 10 percentage points in POPNEG, density gradient would decline from 0.30 to about 0.22. Both in 1950 and 1960, however, POPNEG was positively associated with CNTPOP, while in 1960 it was negatively associated with LNAREA. Therefore it would not seem that the increases in POPNEG observed during the fifties in most of the cities studied here can account for the observed fall in the central city's share in the urbanized area population nor in the increase in the land area occupied by the latter. Now, some may be inclined to attribute the positive association of POPNEG and CNTPOP to the exclusion in some sense, of Negroes from the suburbs. In view of the analysis in Chapter 5, however, I would not place much confidence in such an explanation. For if significant numbers of Negroes felt suburban residence desirable, I would expect Negro residential areas to be established outside the central city. Indeed, many cities have such enclaves of Negroes in their suburban areas. With increasing relative numbers of Negro residents who desired a suburban as opposed to central city residence, I would expect these suburban Negro residential areas to grow relative to such areas in the central city.

It would appear to me that the distribution of population between the central city and its suburbs and the land used by the urbanized area are largely governed by the same forces influencing population distribution within the central city. But several qualifications must be made to this statement. From my CNTPOP and 1960 LNAREA regressions, an influx of lower-income persons into the central city would tend to increase the proportion of the urbanized area's population that is suburban and also its total land area. The best explanation for this effect, I believe, is the increase in the tax burden on higher-income central-city households and upon business firms which the in-migration of low-income persons would imply. Secondly, my results imply that the central-city population tends to respond less than I would anticipate to factors which reduce the relative rate of population-density decline within the central city. Such a result cannot be attributed to a long-run disequilibrium in 1950 in urbanized area population distribution, for the 1960 CNTPOP regressions produced much the same results as the 1950 ones. If anything, the apparent attenuation in the suburbs of forces making for population decentralization is inconsistent with the statements one frequently hears that urban decentralization has been carried too far. Finally, examination of the estimated residuals from the various regression equations suggest the existence of certain persistent, unknown forces which tend both to reduce CNTPOP and to increase LNAREA or vice versa. Such forces, however, would not appear to be related to the relative rate of population-density decline within the central city.

8 Components of Population Density in Cities in the United States

In the preceding chapter it was found that the negative exponential function in distance from the CBD alone fits population density data for American cities in 1950 rather well. About half the intertract variance in population density was explained, and the fit of this function is about the same for cities of different size and in different parts of the country. Departures from the pattern of negative exponential density decline do not seem to tend predominantly toward positive or negative curvature, nor do they appear to be associated with city size or region of the country. More importantly, perhaps, via repression analysis it was possible to explain a substantial fraction of the variation in density gradients among cities in terms of variables suggested by the analysis of Part I. And, finally, it would appear that variations in the level of population densities among central cities, central city's share of population in different urbanized areas and the land area these occupy are all consistent with variation among them in their density gradients.

But while the preceding empirical results are certainly encouraging, it is not surprising that they leave several important questions unanswered. First, how important is the variation in the various components of population density with distance from the CBD and how well can their variation be accounted for by the analysis of Part I? Second, one of the greatest shortcomings of the negative exponential density function is that too many instances of significant curvature were observed to explain by sampling variability. What is the source of this curvature and how might it be accounted for? Also, many variables but especially the age of dwelling units and the incomes of their inhabitants vary systematically with distance from the CBD. How much of the observed variation of densities with distance is accounted for by intercorrelation with these other variables and by how much is the explanation of population densities improved by using age of dwellings and income as additional explanatory variables? Finally, whereas a weak tendency was found for density gradients to vary inversely with income among cities, what might account for this variation? In particular, can it be attributed to the tendency for the optimal location in terms of distance for CBD worker households to increase with income?

In an attempt to provide answers to these questions this chapter does two things. First, for sixteen of the forty-six American cities studied in the previous chapter the variation of population per household, the value of housing consumption per household, and the value of housing output per square of mile of land in relation to distance from the CBD are examined. Second, for six of the forty-six cities, variation in these components of population density and related measures are compared with age of dwellings and incomes of their inhabitants in addition to distance from the CBD. This investigation is continued in Chapters 9 and 10 in much more detail for the south side of the city of Chicago.

THE RELATION OF COMPONENTS OF POPULATION DENSITY TO DISTANCE

In Chapter 4 it was pointed out that population density consists of three components: population per household, the value of housing consumed per household, and the value of housing output per square mile of land. Thus, the variation of population density with distance can be expressed as

$$\frac{d}{dk} D^* = \frac{d}{dk}\left(\frac{P}{H}\right)^* - \frac{d}{dk}\left(\frac{pQ}{H}\right)^* + \frac{d}{dk}\left(\frac{pQ}{L}\right)^*. \tag{1}$$

The analysis of Part I paid little attention to the first of these. Indeed, little can be said about variation in the average size of household with distance. One might expect families with larger numbers of children to have stronger preferences for space as compared with other aspects of housing and, perhaps, for housing rather than other items of consumption expenditure. They might also have stronger preferences for the more pleasant surroundings and better schools to be found in outlying areas. For reasons such as these one might expect population per household to increase with distance from the CBD. On the other hand, if housing prices are higher near the CBD, one way to reduce the consumption of housing per family is by sharing accommodations with relatives, who might otherwise inhabit separate dwellings, or with roomers. The latter might be found especially where lower-income households have moved into neighborhoods whose dwellings were originally built for higher-income groups and consequently contain more housing per dwelling than typically consumed by the newer residents. The effect of this, of course, would be a reduction in the population per household with distance from the CBD.

Variation in the per household expenditures on housing depends upon variation in housing prices and income. If the relative price elasticity of

housing demand were unity, then the relative increase in quantity purchased would just be offset by the relative decline in price with distance,
and expenditures on housing would be invariant with respect to price
changes. As I have argued before, the most likely alternative to a unitary
housing demand elasticity is an elastic one, in which case the per household
expenditures on housing would increase with distance from the CBD. An
increase in the average income level of households would also lead to increasing per household expenditures with distance. Various reasons were
given in Part I why higher-income households might tend to locate at
greater distances from the CBD. With increasing incomes it would appear
that housing expenditures are likely to rise more rapidly than the marginal
costs of transport for CBD worker households, so that their equilibrium
location is to be found at a greater distance from the CBD. Second, higher-
income households might have stronger preferences for newer and better-
quality housing, and the latter tends to be located in the outer parts of
the city. Finally, higher-income households might have stronger preferences
for land or space relative to other features of housing, of for single-family
dwellings, and hence tend to locate in the outer parts of the city where such
housing, being relatively land intensive, is cheaper.

The value of housing output per square mile of land tends to decline
with distance from the CBD as land is substituted for other factors in producing housing in response to declining land rentals. If all firms producing
housing have the same production functions with less than unitary
elasticity of substitution of land for non-land factors, the relative importance of land will decline with distance. This is because the relative increase in land used in producing a given quantity of housing is smaller
than the relative decline in the rental per unit of land. The effect of the
decline in the relative importance of land is to increase the elasticity of the
value of housing per unit of land and hence to increase the relative decline
in the value of housing with distance. However, this last would tend to be
offset by a decline in the relative rate of decrease of housing prices with
distance from the CBD, which by itself would tend to reduce the relative
decline in the value of housing output. Alternatively, if the producers of
different housing types have different production functions, those for
which land has the greatest relative importance will tend to locate in the
outer part of the city where land is the cheapest. In this case the relative
importance of land will tend to increase with distance from the city center
and the elasticity of the value of housing produced per square mile will
tend to decrease. Both for this reason and because of the decrease in the
price gradient, the slope of the log value of housing output per square mile-
distance function would tend to become numerically smaller at greater
distances from the city center or exhibit positive curvature. Finally,

variation in the proportion of land used for residential purposes will affect the value of housing produced per square mile of land in different parts of the city. The most likely alternative to a constant fraction of land used for residential purposes is one which increases at a decreasing relative rate. In the latter case, the value of housing output per square mile of total land area would tend to decrease at a decreasing rate with distance.

Data Used: As should be apparent from the above paragraph, contrary to many instances in economics the curvature as well as the slope of the components of population density are of some substantive interest. For this reason I wished to examine components of population density for cities whose estimated population density functions exhibited different kinds of curvature. Four of the cities listed in Table 7.1 had functions which exhibited a significant positive curvature and eight exhibited a significant negative curvature. I decided to examine density components for all of the former and for a random selection of four of the latter. In addition, partly for comparative purposes, I selected at random four cities whose density functions showed a non-significant positive curvature and four with a non-significant negative curvature, resulting in a total of sixteen cities whose density components were examined.

To measure population per household I used the total population in households divided by the number of households in the tract, PERHOU.[1] Population in households differs from total population in that the institutional population is omitted and seemed a better measure than total population for my purposes. While the population data are relatively free from error, this is not the case with census value of housing data. In the census block statistics, data on the average contract rent of tenant-occupied dwellings and the average value of owner-occupied, one-dwelling-unit structures are given. The data on average contract rent include, in addition to what might be called space rental, payment for any furnishings and utilities included in the rental agreed on by the landlord and the tenant. They thus overestimate the amount of expenditures for housing proper. In addition, the lingering effects of rent control in 1950 may have distorted the pattern of space rentals that would have prevailed in a free market and held rentals in some areas below levels they would otherwise have reached. Data on values of owner-occupied units are given only for single-family units, and to make this data comparable with the data for tenant-occupied units values must be converted to equivalent rentals. It is commonly believed by real estate appraisers that the monthly rental of single-family houses is about 1/100th of the value of the house.[2] This is equivalent to an

---

[1] Data are from *1950 Census of Population*, vol. 3, table 1.
[2] For a discussion of the relation of rental to value see Leo Grebler, David M.

annual gross rate of return on housing of about 12 percent per year, which seems to be of the right order of magnitude.[3] Another difficulty with the census value data is that the number of one-unit dwellings reporting values is frequently much smaller than the total number of owner-occupied units in the tract.

Using this census data the total value of housing produced and consumed in dollars per month in a census tract was estimated by the sum of the number of units reporting contract rents multiplied by average contract rent and the number of units reporting values multiplied by 1/100 of the average value of one-unit, owner-occupied dwellings.[4] To obtain a measure of the average value of housing consumed in dollars per household per month, VALHOU, the total value of housing as defined above was divided by the sum of the units reporting contract rentals and values of one-unit, owner-occupied dwellings. The inclusion of furnishings and utilities in contract rentals means that VALHOU tends to overestimate housing consumption, while the effects of rent control may be to cause an underestimation. More importantly, if the proportion of units with furnishings and utilities included in contract rent declines with distance and/or if the income elasticity of the demand for furnishings and utilities is less than that for space, my measure of VALHOU is likely to underestimate the true increase in per household expenditures with distance. This underestimation will tend to be offset for 1950, however, if the effects of rent control tend to decline with distance, as seems likely for several reasons. The effects of exclusion of non-reporting owner-occupied units are difficult to determine. As a measure of the value of housing produced in dollars per square mile of land per month, VALAND, I used the total value of housing per tract divided by the square mile land area measure described in Chapter 7. The measure of the total value of housing produced almost certainly underestimates the true value because of the omission of non-reporting units. But the latter's effect on the slope of the log value of housing produced per square mile-distance function is less certain. Finally, the measures of distance to the CBD used are the same ones described in Chapter 7.

Empirical Results: The results of my analysis of the three components of population density in relation to distance from the CBD are summarized in Tables 1 through 3. As with population densities themselves in Table 7.1,

Blank, and Louis Winnick, *Capital Formation in Residential Real Estate: Trends and Prospects*, app. 1.

[3] It would appear that mortgage interest rates are around 6 percent per year, depreciation 2 percent, property taxes 2 to 3 percent, and maintenance and repair expenditures a little over 1 percent per year.

[4] All the data are from U.S. Bureau of the Census, *United States Census of Housing: 1950*, vol. 5 (Washington: U.S. Government Printing Office, 1952), table 2.

two regressions were run using the natural log of the density component as the dependent variable, one linear and one quadratic in distance. For each component and city the slope or gradient, the r^2 for the linear regression, the F-ratio for testing the significance of the quadratic term, and the direction of curvature where it is significant are shown. The gradients and curvatures shown are expressed in terms of their contributions to the behavior of the density gradient, D_1, defined so as to be positive. Thus, the negative gradient for Buffalo in Table 3 means that VALAND tended to increase with distance from the CBD and hence to cause population densities to increase with distance and make the density gradient for Buffalo negative; likewise, the plus sign in the fourth column for Buffalo in Table 3 means that the curvature in VALAND tended to impart a positive curvature to the log density-distance regression or to make the density gradient decline numerically with distance.

TABLE 1

SUMMARY OF PERHOU-DISTANCE REGRESSIONS, 16 U.S. CITIES, 1950

City	Gradient	r^2	Linearity F	Curvature
Density functions with significant positive curvature				
Buffalo, N.Y.	.0091	.0024	3.5†	—
Cincinnati, Ohio	−.028†	.24	.28	
Miami, Florida	.010	.012	.85	
Omaha, Nebr.	−.034†	.22	.21	
Density functions with non-significant positive curvature				
Atlanta, Ga.	−.0032	.00056	1.5	
Baltimore, Md.	.0020	.00039	.039	
Louisville, Ky.	−.030	.092	.42	
Philadelphia, Pa.	−.014†	.12	.023	
Density functions with non-significant negative curvature				
Birmingham, Ala.	−.0077	.021	1.5	
Flint, Mich.	−.070†	.45	1.2	
Fort Worth, Texas	−.018†	.16	2.3	
St. Louis, Mo.	−.0061	.0076	.096	
Density functions with significant negative curvature				
Cleveland, Ohio	.017	.10	4.6†	+
Dallas, Texas	−.019†	.12	.011	
Houston, Texas	−.015	.072	1.0	
Nashville, Tenn.	−.057†	.17	1.4	

† Significantly different from zero at the 0.10 level.

Table 1 reveals a distinct tendency for the average size of household to increase with distance from the CBD. Twelve of the cities have negative gradients, and seven of these are significantly different from zero at the 0.10 level. However, the correlation between PERHOU and distance is less than 0.2 in thirteen of the sixteen cases, suggesting that in general the association is quite weak. Furthermore, PERHOU's gradient in all cases is quite small relative to the gradients of the other two components of density. The largest gradient in Table 1, for Flint, is only 0.07. And, in only two cases is there a significant degree of curvature in the log PERHOU-distance regression; in both of these the curvature is in the opposite direction to that of the curvature of the log density-distance function. It would thus appear that the density-distance relationship is affected very little by the variation in the average size of household with distance.

TABLE 2

SUMMARY OF VALHOU-DISTANCE REGRESSIONS, 16 U.S. CITIES, 1950

City	Gradient	r^2	Linearity F	Curvature
Density functions with significant positive curvatures				
Buffalo, N.Y.	.29*	.71	2.5	
Cincinnati, Ohio	.30†	.56	28†	+
Miami, Florida	.088	.062	6.9†	+
Omaha, Nebr.	.13*	.13	.032	
Density functions with non-significant positive curvature				
Atlanta, Ga.	.52*	.73	.000	
Baltimore, Md.	.20*	.57	2.8	
Louisville, Ky.	.22*	.21	.64	
Philadelphia, Pa.	.095*	.27	1.4	
Density functions with non-significant negative curvature				
Birmingham, Ala.	.14*	.24	.24	
Flint, Mich.	−.15	.14	.55	
Fort Worth, Texas	.063*	.13	1.8	
St. Louis, Mo.	.28*	.65	3.6†	+
Density functions with significant negative curvature				
Cleveland, Ohio	.23*	.87	2.5	
Dallas, Texas	.067*	.11	2.3	
Houston, Texas	.022	.012	.34	
Nashville, Tenn.	.44*	.50	.84	

* Significantly greater than zero at the 0.10 level.
† Significantly different from zero at the 0.10 level.

On the other hand, the results summarized in Table 2 suggest that the variation in the value of housing consumed per household makes an important contribution indeed to the variation of density with distance. As shown in the first column, the VALHOU gradient is significantly greater than zero in thirteen out of the sixteen cities. In eight of these cases VALHOU increases by 20 percent or more per mile. I find this variation far too great to account for by variation of housing prices with distance. Even for a relative price elasticity of housing demand of −2, which seems a plausible lower limit, the gradients in Table 2 would imply that price declines by 20 percent per mile or more on the average. So great a variation seems quite implausible on the basis of casual observation and since it would imply by equation (2.3′) that marginal transport costs per mile are one-fifth of housing expenditures. I suspect, therefore, that the variations in VALHOU in Table 2 result mostly from variations in income with distance from the CBD. The simple correlations in Table 2 tend to be much higher than for either of the other two components of density, being 0.5 or more in seven of the sixteen cases. Finally, three cases of significant curvature—all positive—are observed; for Cincinnati and Miami the curvature in VALHOU would seem to account for the positive curvature in the log density-distance regressions.

TABLE 3

Summary of VALAND-Distance Regressions, 16 U.S. Cities, 1950

City	Gradient	r^2	Linearity F	Curvature
Density functions with significant positive curvature				
Buffalo, N.Y.	−.12	.043	5.3†	+
Cincinnati, Ohio	.42*	.44	.000	
Miami, Fla.	.11*	.13	.046	
Omaha, Nebr.	.26*	.18	1.2	
Density functions with non-significant positive curvature				
Atlanta, Ga.	−.067	.0086	.025	
Baltimore, Md.	.37*	.31	.44	
Louisville, Ky.	.27*	.12	.34	
Philadelphia, Pa.	.31*	.24	.26	
Density functions with non-significant negative curvature				
Birmingham, Ala.	.070	.029	.001	
Flint, Mich.	.94*	.52	.64	
Fort Worth, Texas	.40*	.62	2.3	
St. Louis, Mo.	−.075	.015	6.8†	−
Density functions with significant negative curvature				
Cleveland, Ohio	−.13	.046	7.3†	−
Dallas, Texas	.42*	.42	9.8†	−
Houston, Texas	.28*	.36	6.4†	−
Nashville, Tenn.	−.42	.20	2.6	

* Significantly greater than zero at the 0.10 level.
† Significantly different from zero at the 0.10 level.

While the association between VALAND and distance is not as strong as between the latter and VALHOU—in only two cases is r^2 equal to 0.5 or more—it is consistent with the earlier analysis in that the VALAND gradient in Table 3 is significantly positive in ten out of sixteen cases and it is large and negative in only one. But, if anything, VALAND's contribution to the population density gradient is quantitatively slightly more important than that of VALHOU. In ten of the sixteen cities the gradient in Table 3 is numerically larger than VALHOU's in Table 2. In addition, the size of the gradients of VALAND seem to be of a reasonable order of magnitude. The median of the gradients in Table 3, 0.26 to 0.27, when divided by the estimate of the elasticity of value of housing produced per square mile suggested in Chapter 3, around 15, yields an estimate of the price gradient of a little under 2 percent per mile. Turning to the curvature of the log VALAND-distance functions one finds a significant curvature in five cities, four of which are negative. It would appear in particular that negative curvature in the log density-distance functions in Table 7.1 results from that in VALAND. As I have suggested earlier in this section, the negative curvature might be accounted for by the decreasing relative importance of land with distance from the CBD because of a less than unit elasticity of substitution of land for other factors in producing housing or by an increase at a decreasing rate in the proportion of all land which is used for residential purposes. There is only one instance of a positive curvature of VALAND in Table 3, so that little support is found for the different production functions for different housing types hypothesis. Finally, note that in only one city, St. Louis, is a significant curvature in one density component offset by that in the other to produce a non-significant log density-distance function.

THE RELATION OF POPULATION DENSITY AND ITS COMPONENTS TO AGE OF DWELLINGS AND INCOMES OF THEIR INHABITANTS

The major purpose of this section is to determine the extent to which the association between population density and its components with distance results from the intercorrelation of the latter with the age of dwelling units and the incomes of their inhabitants. The theoretical analysis of Part I emphasized primarily the relation of distance to costs of transport. However, in Chapter 5 it was pointed out that age and income may affect the intensity of residential land use as well and that these factors might vary systematically with distance from the CBD. Those parts of the city first developed for residential uses are those located near the CBD. As argued previously, since transport costs were probably greater at the time of their initial development, they were more intensively built up than they would have been if developed later. For this reason one might expect that the output of housing per square mile of land would be greater in these older areas than in comparably located areas of newer buildings. In addition, age of dwellings may be related to the kinds of households that inhabit them. If higher-income households have stronger preferences for newer housing or if older dwellings are more cheaply converted to lower-income housing, older buildings would tend to house the lower-income households whose housing consumption is smaller. And, as discussed in Chapter 6, for one of many reasons the demand for housing in these older areas might have fallen and the buildings deteriorated as a consequence

If lower-income households have less of an aversion to living in poor-quality housing, they will be attracted to these areas, and for this reason, too, the per household consumption of housing will be smaller in the areas of older buildings and population densities greater.[5]

Income of the residents of an area might tend to affect population density for reasons other than its association with age and condition of buildings. One of the most important of these is that higher-income households may have stronger preferences for space relative to other aspects of housing. If so, they would tend to live in the outlying parts of the city where space is relatively cheap. Or, if other factors are of more importance in determining their location, one would expect to find higher-income households occupying relatively more space wherever they live. In addition it might be argued that higher-income households have stronger preferences for home ownership and for single-family versus multifamily dwellings. The tendency for higher-income households to live in single-family dwellings might also be due in part to the fact that the federal income-tax incentive for home ownership is stronger the greater the household's income and its consumption of housing. For any of these reasons one might expect higher-income households to live in areas of lower population densities.

Data Used: To test hypotheses such as these, multiple regressions using gross population densities, GRODEN, and its two major components, VALHOU and VALAND, in addition to certain related measures to be described below, as dependent variables were run for six of the cities for which density functions were estimated in Chapter 7. Measures of density and its two major components used are those described earlier. The forty-six cities listed in Table 7.1 were divided into three approximately equal groups on the basis of urbanized area population, and two cities were chosen at random from each of these groups. The cities chosen from the largest third by urbanized area population were Houston and Milwaukee; Memphis and San Diego were selected from the middle third and Dayton and Syracuse from the smallest third by size. In each case but one, the same twenty-five randomly selected census tracts previously used in estimating population density functions were used for the multiple regressions.[6]

---

[5] Older areas in the outlying parts of the city might have been less intensively developed initially than what would have been called for by current conditions. But since the comparisons presented here are restricted to central city census tracts, relatively few older areas which are underdeveloped will be included.

[6] For one of the Syracuse tracts most of the population was institutional, and so this tract was eliminated from comparisons. Hence, for Syracuse the comparisons are based on twenty-four tracts only, instead of twenty-five as for the other five cities.

In each of the regressions distance to the CBD in miles, DISCBD, as described earlier was used as an independent variable. In a second regression, the proportion of dwelling units reporting age which were built prior to 1920, AGEDUS, was included as a measure of age of dwellings and neighborhood, and the median income of families and unrelated individuals for the tract, in dollars per year, INCOME, was the income measure used.[7] From scatter diagrams plotted for each of the cities, the various simple relationships appeared to be roughly linear and homoscedastic if all the variables mentioned above except DISCBD and AGEDUS were transformed to natural logarithms; the latter two were used in natural form.

In addition to the above variables, three others were used in the analysis. For comparison of the value measure of housing consumption, two physical measures reported by the census were used. These are the proportion of dwelling units reporting condition that were substandard (dilapidated and/or without private bath), SUBSTD, and the proportion of dwelling units reporting persons per room with more than one person per room, PEROOM, a measure of crowding. Natural logarithms of both of these variables were used. Certainly, the average consumption of housing per household will vary inversely with these variables. But since substandard condition or crowding as defined above is at best indicative only of an amount of housing consumption less than a certain level, the relation between quantity of housing consumed per household and either SUBSTD or PEROOM need not be a strictly linear one. In addition, both of these measures refer strictly to consumption of structural features of housing rather than land, since it is conceptually possible, though empirically unlikely, for households living in substandard housing and/or under crowded conditions to occupy relatively large amounts of land. The condition of dwelling units also reflects the incentive of owners to maintain their properties, and thus it may be influenced by variables not directly related to the per household consumption of housing. The third additional variable, the proportion of dwelling units which were in single-family structures, ONEFAM, was used as a measure of the physical output of housing per unit of land.[8] Since one-unit structures generally use more land per structure than other housing types, the physical intensity of residential land use most probably varies inversely with ONEFAM; but, of course, the relation here need not be

---

[7] Data for these are from *1950 Census of Population*, vol. 3, tables 3 and 1, respectively.

[8] More exactly, the proportion of dwelling units in one-unit detached (including trailers), one-unit attached and one- and two-unit semi-detached structures, from *ibid.*, table 3.

a strictly linear one either. The natural rather than logarithmic form of this variable seemed the better form of this variable on purely statistical grounds.

TABLE 4

SIMPLE AND PARTIAL CORRELATION COEFFICIENTS OF GRODEN WITH DISTANCE, AGE, AND INCOME

CITY	EXPLANATORY VARIABLES			R^2
	DISCBD	AGEDUS	INCOME	
Large cities				
Houston, Texas	−.76*	. . .	. . .	.58
	−.76*	−.35	−.18	.63
Milwaukee, Wis.	−.84*	. . .	. . .	.70
	−.47*	.49*	−.021	.78
Medium cities				
Memphis, Tenn.	−.68*	. . .	. . .	.46
	−.31*	.20	−.0072	.48
San Diego, Cal.	−.78*	. . .	. . .	.62
	−.74*	−.17	.12	.66
Small cities				
Dayton, Ohio	−.47*	. . .	. . .	.22
	.11	.48*	.10	.42
Syracuse, N.Y.	−.71*	. . .	. . .	.50
	−.27	.22	−.30*	.59

* Significant at the 1-tail 0.10 level.

Empirical Findings: Simple correlation coefficients between GRODEN and DISCBD and partial correlation coefficients between GRODEN and DISCBD, AGEDUS and INCOME are shown in Table 4. (Since closeness of association is my principal concern here, these rather than regression coefficients and their standard errors are reported for most of the relationships investigated. Where the regression coefficients themselves or elasticities are of interest, they are shown separately.) In all six of the cities gross population densities show a significant tendency to decline with distance from the CBD, and the simple correlation coefficient is about equal numerically to 0.7 or more in five of these. When AGEDUS and INCOME are added, as shown in the second line for each city, the partial correlation coefficients are distinctly smaller for all of the cities except Houston and San Diego but still significantly less than zero in four cities and almost so for Syracuse. Only in the case of Dayton, moreover, is a substantially larger fraction of the variance among tracts explained by adding AGEDUS and INCOME, as shown by the R^2's in the last column of Table 1. The partial correlation of AGEDUS is positive in four cases, significantly so in two, while the partial correlation coefficients of INCOME are generally quite small and significantly negative only for Syracuse. Thus, it would appear that the simple association between distance and

GRODEN is indeed partly the result of the interrelationship of DISCBD and AGEDUS. But even when age and income are held constant, there remains a strong negative relationship between GRODEN and DISCBD. It would appear, indeed, that among comparably located tracts, densities tend to be positively associated with age of dwellings but that the association between GRODEN and AGEDUS is not as strong as between density and distance. Finally, the partial association between density and income is quite weak, and the one significant negative relationship observed could easily result from sampling variability.[9]

TABLE 5

SIMPLE AND PARTIAL CORRELATION COEFFICIENTS OF VALHOU AND
DISCBD, AGEDUS, AND INCOME

CITY	EXPLANATORY VARIABLES			R^2
	DISCBD	AGEDUS	INCOME	
Large cities				
Houston, Texas	.11	. . .	. . .	.012
	−.60†	−.17	.85*	.82
Milwaukee, Wis.	.83†	. . .	. . .	.69
	.43†	−.61*	−.12	.80
Medium cities				
Memphis, Tenn.	.30	. . .	. . .	.091
	−.21	−.25	.85*	.79
San Diego, Cal.	.000	. . .	. . .	.000
	−.40	.079	.61*	.50
Small cities				
Dayton, Ohio	.56†	. . .	. . .	.32
	.18	−.22	.76*	.80
Syracuse, N.Y.	.67†	. . .	. . .	.44
	−.28	−.50*	.77*	.84

* Significant at the 1-tail 0.10 level.
† Significant at the 2-tail 0.10 level.

Turning now to variations in the value of housing consumed per household, Table 5 shows a distinct tendency for VALHOU to increase with DISCBD, the partial correlation coefficient being significantly different from zero at the 0.10 level in three cases and positive in two others. As suggested in the first section, however, this is due mostly to the increase in income with distance. For, when AGEDUS and INCOME are added, the

[9] The probability of obtaining one or more significant results at the 0.10 level from six independent samples purely by chance is about 0.47. The probability of two more such results, however, is only about 0.11, while four or more such results would occur in only about one out of a thousand cases. Thus, I would deem two or more significant results too unlikely to ascribe to chance variation and four or more to be highly significant. Considering only the signs of the coefficients, the probability of obtaining four or more plus signs if there is no relationship, that is, if plus and minus signs have the same probability of occurrence, is about 0.34, while the probability of five or more plus signs is only about 0.11. Hence, four agreements in sign is not especially convincing evidence for a particular hypothesis, but five or more is.

partial correlation of VALHOU with DISCBD is significantly positive only for Milwaukee and negative in all other cases. The partial correlation coefficients of income, however, are quite high for all cities except Milwaukee, and, except for San Diego, about 80 percent of the variation among tracts in the per household consumption of housing is accounted for. For five of the cities, AGEDUS is negatively associated with VALHOU, and this association is significant in two cases. The last result suggests that less housing per dwelling unit is contained in older buildings, since with a housing demand elasticity of -1 lower prices per unit for older dwellings would not affect the per household expenditure on housing. A smaller quantity per unit, in turn, might reflect depreciation or the fact that older units were designed and built for the lower incomes of their original inhabitants. In either case, households that have weaker preferences for housing and purchase less of it at any given level of income may tend to locate in areas of older housing with smaller quantities per dwelling unit.

TABLE 6

SIMPLE AND PARTIAL CORRELATION COEFFICIENTS OF SUBSTD AND
DISCBD, AGEDUS, AND INCOME

CITY	EXPLANATORY VARIABLES			R^2
	DISCBD	AGEDUS	INCOME	
Large cities				
Houston, Texas	.000	...	...	.000
	.77	.35*	$-.88*$	.86
Milwaukee, Wis.	$-.84*$	...	...	.70
	$-.46*$	.48*	$-.064$	.77
Medium cities				
Memphis, Tenn.	$-.24$	...	...	.056
	.092	.066	$-.76*$	.63
San Diego, Calif.	$-.48*$	...	...	.23
	.23	.24	$-.62*$	.74
Small cities				
Dayton, Ohio	$-.57*$	...	...	.32
	.19	.63*	$-.67*$	.84
Syracuse, N.Y.	$-.75*$	...	...	.57
	$-.092$	.73*	$-.64*$	.88

* Significant at the 1-tail 0.10 level.

Tables 6 and 7 indicate that the results are quite similar when SUBSTD and PEROOM are used as measures of the per household consumption of housing. SUBSTD shows a significant negative association with distance in four cases and PEROOM in three, but when income is added the partial association disappears for all cities except Milwaukee. Again, for all cities but Milwaukee there is a strong negative partial correlation with income, and the R^2's tend to be quite high, especially for SUBSTD, despite obvious shortcomings in the data used.

TABLE 7

SIMPLE AND PARTIAL CORRELATION COEFFICIENTS OF PEROOM AND
DISCBD, AGEDUS, AND INCOME

CITY	EXPLANATORY VARIABLES			R^2
	DISCBD	AGEDUS	INCOME	
Large cities				
Houston, Texas	.046	· · ·	· · ·	.022
	.72	.18	−.85*	.81
Milwaukee, Wis.	−.53*	· · ·	· · ·	.28
	−.46*	−.17	.050	.31
Medium cities				
Memphis, Tenn.	−.24	· · ·	· · ·	.056
	−.046	−.078	−.71*	.54
San Diego, Calif.	.26	· · ·	· · ·	.067
	.54	.039	−.48*	.44
Small cities				
Dayton, Ohio	−.45*	· · ·	· · ·	.20
	.022	.24	−.70*	.72
Syracuse, N.Y.	−.62*	· · ·	· · ·	.39
	.25	.15	−.75*	.77

* Significant at the 1-tail 0.10 level.

The major difference between the results in Tables 6 and 7 is that
AGEDUS is significantly related to SUBSTD in four cities and positive in
the other two, while the partial association between PEROOM and
AGEDUS is quite weak. This last result suggests that the smaller quantity of
housing per dwelling in older buildings may take the form of poorer quality
but not less space. The association of age and condition with income held
constant lends some support to those theories of slum formation discussed
in Chapter 6 which attribute poor-housing quality to the decline in demand
for housing in older neighborhoods. The lack of any substantial negative
association between SUBSTD and DISCBD when age and income are
included, however, casts doubt on the hypothesis that the decline in demand
for housing in older parts of the city which accompanied the lowering of
marginal transport costs by the automobile has led to slum formation.
For if this were the case, the decline in demand, and hence in housing
prices, and the incentive to maintain housing in good condition, would
have been relatively greater the nearer the CBD. However, if in response
to such declining demands some old housing had already been replaced
by 1950, the age variable might partly reflect the effects of automobile
induced slum formation.

Since SUBSTD and PEROOM are physical rather than value measures
of housing consumption, one might expect a negative partial association
between them and DISCBD if housing prices decline with distance from
the CBD. There are two reasons, however, why this effect might not show
up. First, as noted above, both variables are strictly measures of the

consumption of structural features only and not of land. If housing prices and hence land rentals tend to decline with distance, the former leads to more consumption of structural features—which are related to non-land factor inputs—but the decline in land rentals tends to reduce the consumption of structural features. The strength of the former effect depends upon the price elasticity of housing demand and that of the latter upon the elasticity of substitution in production. The values suggested earlier are about −1 and 0.75, respectively, and so these two effects may tend roughly to cancel out. And second, especially in view of the above, SUBSTD and PEROOM may be too crude as physical measures of housing consumption to capture the effects of declining housing prices at the rate of less than 2 percent per mile, the rate suggested in the first section.

TABLE 8

PARTIAL INCOME ELASTICITIES OF MEASURES OF HOUSING
CONSUMPTION PER HOUSEHOLD

CITY	DEPENDENT VARIABLE		
	VALHOU	SUBSTD	PEROOM
Large cities			
Houston, Texas	1.15	−3.74	−2.76
Milwaukee, Wis.	−.056[a]	−.18[a]	.10[a]
Medium cities			
Memphis, Tenn.	1.18	−1.89	−1.51
San Diego, Calif.	1.71	−3.76	−2.77
Small cities			
Dayton, Ohio	1.16	−2.94	−2.35
Syracuse, N.Y.	.99	−1.77	−2.23

[a] Not significant at the 1-tail 0.10 level.

The partial income elasticities of the various measures of housing consumption for the six cities are shown in Table 8. The elasticities of VALHOU tend to cluster around a value just slightly greater than +1. This value is consistent with my earlier finding using time-series data for the nation as a whole,[10] but is somewhat smaller than those found by Margaret Reid for a variety of comparisons.[11] The VALHOU elasticities in Table 8 may tend to be somewhat too low because of the inclusion of furnishings and utilities in contract rent, though rent control effects may tend to offset this, and because part of the intertract variation in income is of a transitory rather than a permanent nature. However, the agreement

---

[10] "The Demand for Non-Farm Housing."
[11] *Housing and Income.* Reid found elasticities of owner-occupied housing value only with respect to income, using income as independent, for census tracts, carefully selected so as to remove most of the differences in household type to which value and income data refer, which averaged about +1.5 for seven large cities (pp. 176–81).

of the elasticities in the first column of Table 8 with previous estimates is quite encouraging in view of the obvious crudeness in VALHOU as a measure of average expenditures on housing. The partial elasticities of SUBSTD and PEROOM with respect to income shown in the second and third columns of Table 8 are substantially larger numerically than those of VALHOU, averaging about −2.5. The estimated elasticities of PEROOM agree quite closely with those found by Reid using data for different metropolitan areas.[12] In view of the fact that both SUBSTD and PEROOM refer to housing of the poorest quality, elasticities of this magnitude are not surprising. The fact that the estimated income elasticities of SUBSTD and PEROOM are so nearly the same bears out the suggestion I made ir Chapter 6 that condition and crowding are but closely related aspects of housing consumption and respond in a similar fashion to its determinants.

TABLE 9

SIMPLE AND PARTIAL CORRELATION COEFFICIENTS OF INCOME,
DISCBD, AGEDUS, AND SUBSTD

CITY	EXPLANATORY VARIABLES			R^2
	DISCBD	AGEDUS	SUBSTD	
Large cities				
Houston, Texas	.47*	・・・	・・・	.22
	.10	−.55*	・・・	.45
	.71*	.066	−.088*	.87
Milwaukee, Wis.	.48*	・・・	・・・	.23
	.22	−.12	・・・	.24
	.16	−.072	−.064	.25
Medium cities				
Memphis, Tenn.	.35*	・・・	・・・	.12
	−.069	−.32*	・・・	.21
	.024	−.16	−.76*	.66
San Diego, Calif.	.62*	・・・	・・・	.38
	−.071	−.70*	・・・	.68
	.091	−.37*	−.62*	.80
Small cities				
Dayton, Ohio	.39*	・・・	・・・	.15
	−.22	−.55*	・・・	.41
	−.031	.10	−.67*	.67
Syracuse, N.Y.	.80*	・・・	・・・	.63
	.66*	−.34*	・・・	.68
	.44*	.29	−.64*	.81

* Significant at the 1-tail 0.10 level.

Having seen that the principal source of variation in the consumption of housing is in income, it is of interest to examine the factors associated with variation in income within cities. As shown in the first column of Table 9, the simple correlation coefficient between income and distance is significantly positive in all six cities, although in only one of these does

---

[12] *Ibid.*, esp. pp. 326–27.

distance explain more than two-fifths of the intracity variance of income. But when AGEDUS is added to the regressions, as shown in the second line for each city, the partial correlation between INCOME and DISCBD is negative in three cities and significantly positive only for Syracuse. The partial correlation coefficient between INCOME and AGEDUS is negative for all six cities, significantly so in five of them. This result suggests that it is the intercorrelation of DISCBD and AGEDUS rather than distance itself which accounts for the increase in income, and hence the per household consumption of housing with distance from the CBD. However, as was seen in Table 6, above, AGEDUS tends to be associated with SUBSTD, and one wonders whether it is age itself or the poorer average quality of old buildings that causes higher-income households to avoid them. A partial answer to the latter question can be found when SUBSTD is added to the regressions, as in the third line for each city. Here, INCOME and AGEDUS are negatively associated in only three of the cities, significantly so only in San Diego. Interestingly enough, when SUBSTD is added the partial correlation coefficients of INCOME and DISCBD become positive in five cities and significantly greater than zero in two.

TABLE 10

REGRESSION COEFFICIENTS OF INCOME ON DISCBD

City	Simple	Partial, Including AGEDUS and SUBSTD
Large cities		
Houston, Texas	.081*	.087*
Milwaukee, Wis.	.10*	.060
Medium cities		
Memphis, Tenn.	.056*	.0042
San Diego, Calif.	.065*	.0070
Small cities		
Dayton, Ohio	.083*	−.0067
Syracuse, N.Y.	.38*	.16*

* Significantly greater than zero at the 0.10 level.

From the above results it appears clear that most of the tendency for the median incomes of families and unrelated individuals to increase with distance from the CBD is due to factors interrelated with distance rather than to the fact that, with increasing incomes, housing consumption increases more rapidly than the marginal costs of transport. This can also be seen by examining the regression coefficients of log income on distance in Table 10. While the simple regression coefficients in column one indicate that income increases from between 5 to 10 percent per mile in five of the six cities and by almost 40 percent in the other, the partial coefficients with AGEDUS and SUBSTD held constant are negligible for three of the cities. In two others the partial is only about half as large as the simple coefficient. It would appear, however, that there is still a slight tendency for higher-income households to locate at greater distances from the CBD even holding AGEDUS and SUBSTD constant. There is considerable doubt whether it is age of buildings or their condition which accounts for most of the tendency for income to increase with distance, since it is uncertain whether the strong partial correlation between INCOME and SUBSTD reflects the effect of income on condition or vice versa. I shall return to a consideration of this question in more detail in Chapter 10, where the relationship between income and dwelling-unit condition will be examined in much more detail.

I now wish to consider the other major component of population density, the value of housing output per square mile of land. Simple and partial correlation coefficients for VALAND are shown in Table 11. The simple correlation of DISCBD is significantly negative in five of the six cities, and, when AGEDUS and INCOME are added, the partial correlation coefficients for these five cities remain so. But, rather surprisingly, the association between AGEDUS and VALAND appears to be quite weak. Although five of the partial correlation coefficients in the second column of Table 11 are positive, only that for Dayton is significantly so. Even more surprising is the fact that all of the partial correlation coefficients of INCOME and VALAND are positive and three are greater than 0.5. This last result suggests that, if anything, the intensity of housing output per unit of land is greater in higher-income neighborhoods, rather than the reverse as has been frequently suggested, if the effects of differences in location are removed.

Some insight into the reasons for these unexpected results can be found by examining the proportion of dwellings in one-unit structures, ONEFAM, which I would interpret as a physical rather than a value measure of housing output per unit of land. Table 12 shows that the simple correlation coefficients of ONEFAM with DISCBD are significantly positive in all six cities, while the partials are in four, indicating again a decline in the output of housing per square mile with distance from the city center. As contrasted with the results for VALAND in Table 11, the partials of ONEFAM and AGEDUS in Table 12 are all negative—significantly so for four of the cities—indicating a greater physical output of housing per unit of land in older neighborhoods apart from differences in location. Also quite different from the results of Table 11 are the partials of ONEFAM and INCOME in the third column of Table 12. There is little association between land use intensity and income, for, while four of the partials are positive, only one is significant.

Taken together, the partials of AGEDUS in Tables 11 and 12 would seem to imply that, in line with the decline in demand theories of slum formation discussed in Chapter 6, the price per unit of housing in older neighborhoods is lower than in newer ones. The positive association in Table 12 suggests that the physical output of housing per unit land is indeed greater in older neighborhoods of comparable location, but the weak association in Table 11 indicates that price times quantity per unit land is but little different as between the two kinds of areas. Alternatively, the

TABLE 11

SIMPLE AND PARTIAL CORRELATION COEFFICIENTS OF VALAND AND
DISCBD, AGEDUS, AND INCOME

| CITY | EXPLANATORY VARIABLES | | | R^2 |
	DISCBD	AGEDUS	INCOME	
Large cities				
Houston, Texas	− .60*	. . .	. . .	.36
	− .84*	− .42	.55	.73
Milwaukee, Wis.	− .65*	. . .	. . .	.42
	− .28*	.25	.046	.45
Medium cities				
Memphis, Tenn.	− .41*	. . .	. . .	.17
	− .32*	.095	.54	.41
San Diego, Calif.	− .66*	. . .	. . .	.44
	− .72*	.0096	.37	.61
Small cities				
Dayton, Ohio	− .22	. . .	. . .	.050
	.25	.54*	.51	.36
Syracuse, N.Y.	− .54*	. . .	. . .	.29
	− .32*	.097	.0052	.30

* Significant at the 1-tail 0.10 level.

TABLE 12

SIMPLE AND PARTIAL CORRELATION COEFFICIENTS OF ONEFAM AND
DISCBD, AGEDUS, AND INCOME

| CITY | EXPLANATORY VARIABLES | | | R^2 |
	DISCBD	AGEDUS	INCOME	
Large cities				
Houston, Texas	.69*	. . .	. . .	.47
	.69*	− .076	− .37	.56
Milwaukee, Wis.	.56*	. . .	. . .	.31
	− .12	− .59*	.001	.55
Medium cities				
Memphis, Tenn.	.66*	. . .	. . .	.44
	.28*	− .32*	− .34	.53
San Diego, Calif.	.31*	. . .	. . .	.094
	− .29	− .40*	.10	.40
Small cities				
Dayton, Ohio	.79*	. . .	. . .	.62
	.57*	− .035	.21	.65
Syracuse, N.Y.	.81*	. . .	. . .	.66
	.35*	− .73*	.60*	.90

* Significant at the 1-tail 0.10 level.

effects of depreciation, which is associated with age, may be to reduce the number of units of housing of given quality per dwelling and thus the value of output per unit of land. ONEFAM, however, relates to original intensity of output rather than to this intensity currently. Either of these interpretations is consistent with the higher proportion of substandard dwellings in older neighborhoods noted in Table 6. Another interpretation of the conflicting results might be that a larger fraction of total land area in census tracts in older areas of the city is used for non-residential purposes. If so, the value of housing output per square mile of total land area would be reduced, but ONEFAM would not be so affected since it more nearly approximates output per unit of land actually used for residential purposes. Still another possibility is that older areas were more strongly affected by rent controls, and hence the value of housing output was more greatly underestimated in these areas.

On the other hand, the partials of INCOME in Tables 11 and 12 may indicate that the price per unit of comparable housing, and hence land rentals, is higher in higher-income neighborhoods because of favorable "neighborhood effects." If higher-income households had stronger preferences for space versus structural features of housing, they would tend to live in areas of lower output of housing per unit land on this account. But higher land rents resulting from more desirable surroundings would work in the opposite direction. Then if the output of housing per unit of land were about the same in higher- and lower-income neighborhoods but price per unit of housing were higher in the former, the value of housing output per unit of land would be greater in the higher-income neighborhoods.

Differences in the effects of rent control and the fraction of total land area used for residential purposes might also help account for these results. It is possible that rent controls had less impact on higher-income neighborhoods, so that the market equilibrium value of housing output is less underestimated in these areas. Or persons whose incomes had risen during the period of rent control and who might normally have moved to single-family dwellings because of this increase might have chosen to remain in multifamily units because of their low, controlled rentals. It is also possible that higher-income households have an aversion to living in areas of mixed land uses and so locate in areas remote from commercial and industrial uses. If this were the case, the fraction of land for residential purposes, and hence the total value of housing, would be greater per square mile of total land area in the higher-income neighborhoods, but ONEFAM would not be. I shall return to these various explanations of the effect of age of dwellings and incomes of their inhabitants on the output of housing per unit land in the following chapter, where I hope to be able to test some of these alternative explanations.

Whatever the reasons for the associations of AGEDUS and INCOME with VALAND and ONEFAM, it appears quite clear from Tables 11 and 12 that variations in the output of housing per unit of land with distance from the city center are not primarily the result of factors correlated with distance. When AGEDUS and INCOME are introduced the partial correlation coefficients generally remain statistically significant and of correct sign, and the regression coefficients of VALAND on DISCBD (not shown) give little evidence of decline on the average for the six cities examined. This is quite different from the case of VALHOU, where most of the variation with distance was accounted for by AGEDUS and INCOME. Thus, whereas in the first section of this chapter it was seen that the increase in VALHOU was almost as large in relative terms as the decline in VALAND, this is no longer the case where age of dwellings and the incomes of their inhabitants are held constant. As the partial regression coefficients of DISCBD in Table 13 show, in only two cities does VALHOU tend to increase with distance itself, and only in Milwaukee is this relative increase fairly large numerically as compared with VALAND's coefficient.

TABLE 13

PARTIAL REGRESSION COEFFICIENTS OF DISCBD HOLDING
AGEDUS AND INCOME CONSTANT

CITY	DEPENDENT VARIABLE	
	VALHOU	VALAND
Large cities		
Houston, Texas	−.085†	−.48*
Milwaukee, Wis.	.074†	−.17*
Medium cities		
Memphis, Tenn.	−.042	−.19*
San Diego, Calif.	−.094†	−.66*
Small cities		
Dayton, Ohio	.053	.30
Syracuse, N.Y.	−.11	−.54*

* Significant at the 1-tail 0.10 level.
† Significant at the 2-tail 0.10 level.

Whatever effect age and income together have on population density operates mostly through their effects on housing consumption rather than output. If anything it would appear that average household expenditures on housing are lower in older areas, and population densities therefore higher, since the value of housing output per unit of land appears to be about the same in older areas as in newer ones. The effects of income differences on the two principal components of population density tend to cancel each other, however; per household expenditures for housing tend to be greater in higher-income areas, and thus densities lower, but this is largely balanced by the greater value of housing output per square mile in the higher-income areas.

9 Population Density and Its Components on the South Side of Chicago

In the preceding chapter it was seen that the tendency for population density to decline with distance from the CBD results partly from the increase in the value of housing consumed per household and partly from the decline in the value of housing output per unit of land. When age of dwellings and the incomes of their inhabitants are added to the analysis, the tendency for population density to decline with distance persists, but there is some tendency for densities to be greater in areas of older buildings even when distance is held constant. Most of the decline in density with distance results from the decline in housing output with distance, for, when age and income are held constant, virtually all the variation of housing consumption with distance vanishes.

Several questions remain unanswered, however, by the analysis of the preceding chapters. First, how different is the variation in density and the output of housing per unit of land when variation in the proportion of total land area which is used for residential purposes is removed? Second, what accounts for the fact that the value measure of housing output shows no relation to age when holding location constant, while the physical measure of housing output shows a rather strong positive association with age? In like manner, what is responsible for the strong positive association between income and the value of housing output? Finally, does the high partial correlation between income and dwelling-unit condition reflect the effect of income on housing consumption, the effect of housing quality on the location of households by income, or both? In addition, there are several questions for research suggested by the theoretical analysis in Part I which remain unexplored. In particular, how are population density and its components related to local variations in accessibility to employment and shopping centers and to differences in marginal transport costs in different directions from the city center? Also, do density and its components vary as between white and Negro areas or with dwelling-unit condition, reflecting differences in housing prices as among such areas?

The best way to investigate questions such as these is by a much more detailed investigation of a single city than has previously been undertaken for many cities together. I have chosen to restrict my attention to the south side of Chicago for several reasons. Partly because of the long tradition in urban research in the social sciences at the University of Chicago, a wide variety of data is readily available for the Chicago area. Since I am more familiar with Chicago, and especially its south side, than with any other city, I felt that by concentrating my attention on it I would be less likely to overlook some important features. Furthermore, on Chicago's south side it is easier to differentiate between areas served by rapid transit or major highway facilities than in other parts of the city. And, finally, the low-income and Negro areas of the city tend to be concentrated on the south side. I realize, of course, that some of the variables considered might operate differently in other parts of the city or in other cities. But the similarity among cities observed so far suggests that different cities respond in similar fashion to important economic and other variables.

The present chapter contains an analysis of variation in population density and its components for 1950 and, mostly as a check on the earlier analysis but partly to make use of the greater variety of data provided by the 1960 census, for 1960 as well. The analysis of the determinants of housing quality and of the location of households by income groups is presented in the following chapter. After discussing the comparisons made and the data used in the first section, estimates for 1950 are presented in section two. The 1960 estimates are presented and discussed in section three, and the final section contains an examination of the residuals for the regressions for the two cross-sections and of their relationship to each other.

Comparisons Made and Data Used

As in Chapter 8, I shall examine variations in gross population density, GRODEN, two measures of housing consumption, VALHOU and PEROOM, and two measures of housing output per unit of land, VALAND and ONEFAM, in relation to location and to characteristics of dwelling units and of their inhabitants. Since dwelling-unit condition reflects not only the consumption of housing but also the incentive of owners to maintain their property, I shall examine it separately in the following chapter. I shall, however, examine net population density—population per square mile of land used for residential purposes, NETDEN—as well as gross density. In addition to distance to the CBD, DISCBD, I use measures of accessibility to local employment and shopping centers and to rapid-transit facilities as measures of location. Dwelling-unit condition as well as age of dwellings is included. In addition to income I use measures of race, occupation, education, size of household, and migration, mostly in the analysis of variations in housing consumption.

The variables GRODEN, VALHOU, DISCBD, AGEDUS, and INCOME are exactly as defined earlier for 1950, and the same data sources as previously described were used. The only differences for 1960 result from differences in the nature of the data presented in the 1960 census reports.[1] Data given by the 1960 housing census is for housing units rather than dwelling units. In addition to dwelling units as defined in the 1950 census, housing units include one-room dwellings without separate cooking facilities in rooming houses and some hotels. For small areas such as census tracts, the reported totals and characteristics for 1960 may differ substantially from those in 1950 because of the change from dwelling to housing units. In addition, there was less underreporting of characteristics for the 1960 housing census, especially for values of owner-occupied units. The oldest age-class of dwelling for which data is presented in the 1960 housing census tabulations is that built in 1939 or earlier, and so for 1960 AGEDUS is defined as the proportion of housing units built before 1940.[2] Another difference is in the income variable. The 1960 census presents median incomes by tract both for families and for families and unrelated individuals but gives distributions only for the former, whereas the 1950 census gave income data by tracts only for families and unrelated individuals. Since I needed to combine tracts and hence distributions in some cases, the income variables for 1950 and 1960 refer to somewhat different groups.[3] In the analysis for Chicago VALAND was defined as the value of housing output as described earlier divided by the land area used for residential purposes. I have also analyzed net density or population divided by residential land area.[4] The data on residential land area refer to 1960, but I doubt that residential land areas would have differed substantially in 1950, and, since only dependent variables were adjusted, measurement errors for 1950 would not bias the coefficients for that year unless these errors are correlated with some of the independent variables used. In view of the weak association between the proportion of land area

[1] Population data for 1960 are from U.S. Bureau of the Census, *U.S. Censuses of Population and Housing: 1960*, Final Report PHC (1)-26, Census Tracts, Chicago, Ill. (Washington, D.C.: U.S. Government Printing Office, 1962), table P-1. This volume is referred to hereafter as *Chicago Tract Statistics, 1960*. Data on the number of tenant-occupied units, average contract rent, number of owner-occupied units and their average value are from U.S. Bureau of the Census, *U.S. Census of Housing: 1960*, Series HC (3)-133, City Blocks, Chicago, Ill. (Washington, D.C.: U.S. Government Printing Office, 1961), table 2.

[2] From *Chicago Tract Statistics, 1960*, table H-1.

[3] Income data for 1960 are from *ibid.*, table P-1.

[4] Data on residential land area were obtained from the Department of City Planning, City of Chicago, and are unpublished.

which is residential and these independent variables (see Table 6, below), such a bias seems unlikely.

The other two dependent variables studied in this chapter were also somewhat different from those used earlier. PEROOM and ONEFAM are defined as described earlier for 1950, but both for 1950 and 1960 the square roots rather than logarithms of these variables were used, since this form appeared to result in more nearly homoscedastic simple regressions between these proportions and the more important independent variables. For 1960, data for a more complete breakdown of persons per room was given than for 1950, and I examined both the proportion of housing units with more than one and more than 0.75 persons per room;[5] the former only could be derived from the 1950 census reports. However, in most cases the proportion with more than one person per room appeared to be more satisfactory on statistical grounds as a measure of crowding, and PEROOM is defined this way for 1960 as well in all the comparisons presented unless explicitly noted to the contrary. The breakdown of housing units by number of units per structure also differs somewhat from that given for dwelling units for 1950. ONEFAM for 1960, therefore, refers to the proportion of units in one-unit structures only and differs from 1950 in that two-unit, semidetached structures are not included.[6]

All of the measures of density and its components are related to several measures of accessibility in addition to DISCBD. One pair of variables refers to accessibility to rapid-transit facilities. As was suggested in Chapter 4, population densities and housing output per unit of land might be expected to decline less rapidly in the vicinity of rapid-transit routes or express highways than elsewhere because of the lower marginal transport costs along such routes. The most important of such transit routes on Chicago's south side are the "L," (the elevated railroad of the Chicago Transit Authority), the Illinois Central suburban lines, and the Outer Drive, Stony Island Avenue, and the Calumet Expressway. I therefore included a dummy variable which takes the value 1 for a census tract within one mile of these facilities and 0 otherwise, designated RAPINT. Its coefficient measures the difference between the intercept of the regression for tracts within one mile of these rapid transit facilities and the intercept for all other tracts. A second such variable, RAPSLO, is defined as RAPINT multiplied by DISCBD, hence distance in miles to the Loop for tracts within one mile of the transit facilities described above and zero otherwise. Its coefficient measures the difference in the slope of the two regressions. I would expect it to have a positive sign in the density and

---

[5] Data are from *Chicago Tract Statistics, 1960*, table H-1.
[6] Data are from *ibid.*, table H-1.

VALAND regressions, indicating a smaller rate of decline along these rapid transit routes. Now, of course, there is no reason to expect that the influence of transit routes will be uniform within one mile and zero any further away. But if transit routes have the anticipated impact, I would expect densities and housing output to be greater within, say, one mile of rapid-transit routes than elsewhere, and there seemed to be no way that was obviously superior to the above procedure for an initial test of the effect of transit routes.

A second pair of accessibility variables might be termed measures of general accessibility. While the CBD is obviously the area of maximum concentration of employment and retail and service facilities and distance to the CBD an important component of accessibility to such facilities, it might be argued that accessibility to other such centers is important also. Probably the most widely used measure of generalized accessibility in spatial and location studies in demography, geography and economics is the so-called potential measure. Employment potential, say, might be defined for any areal unit i as employment in each areal unit j divided by distance from the areal unit j to the unit in question, i, summed over all units.[7] I was able to obtain a measure of manufacturing employment potential, MANPOT, and retail employment potential, RETPOT, both for 1950 from unpublished estimates made by Beverly Duncan for use in certain studies of hers. Natural logs of both were used, since in this form the potential measures seemed more nearly linearly related to the dependent variables used. Mrs. Duncan also has computed a potential measure for all other employment, but since it was virtually uniform for the area studied I have not used it.

The other four accessibility variables used are measures of location relative to local employment and shopping centers. From a map showing the number of major manufacturing establishments by square mile section for the City of Chicago in 1958 I classified census tracts into three groups by the number of such establishments in the square mile section in which the tract is located.[8] The threefold classification was described by two

---

[7] Obviously, some convention must be adopted for the distance from a unit to itself if it is included in the summation. For the measures used here the distance from a track to itself was taken to be one mile. The definition given in the text is often modified by taking either the numerators or the denominators in the ratios to be summed to various powers. The potential measure is based upon an obvious analogy with gravitation in physics. To my knowledge it has little a priori justification.

[8] Department of City Planning, City of Chicago, *Location Patterns of Major Industries in the City of Chicago* (Chicago: City of Chicago, 1960), map 3, p. 10. Major manufacturing establishments are defined as those employing 50 or more workers. This map shows the following breakdown by number of establishments: 0, 1 to 7, 8 to 20, 21 to 33, 34 to 36, and more than 36. Relatively few of the tracts in the sample I used fell into the last three classes, and so I combined them with the third class.

dummy variables, MANMAJ, for major manufacturing area, which takes the value 1 for any census tract in a square mile section containing eight or more major manufacturing establishments and 0 otherwise and MANMIN, for minor manufacturing area, which takes the value 1 for a census tract in a square mile section containing one to seven major manufacturing establishments and 0 otherwise. From a recently published study by Brian J. L. Berry, I obtained a list of the retail and service centers of different kinds for 1960 in the city of Chicago and adjoining areas.[9] Two dummy variables were used to describe location in relation to these centers. They are RETMAJ, for proximity to a major retail center, which takes the value 1 for census tracts within one mile of one of the groups of largest retail centers (Berry's *A* centers) and 0 otherwise, and RETMIN, for proximity to a minor retail center, which takes the value 1 for census tracts within one mile of one of the second largest class of centers (Berry's *B* centers) and 0 otherwise. Smaller centers were not included because the goods and services sold in them are much more widely available than those sold only in the larger two groups of centers.

For each of the dummy variables described in the paragraph above, the coefficient measures the difference between the average value of the dependent variable for all tracts having a particular characteristic and all other tracts. To the extent that households will pay more for housing services in the vicinity of such centers because of their favorable location, I would expect population density and the output of housing per unit land to be greater there, and the coefficients of the dummy variables would be positive. On the other hand, if households pay less because of undesirable neighborhood characteristics, the reverse would be true. The use of dummy variables to describe location in relation to local employment and shopping centers is admittedly a crude way to measure their influence, since there is no reason to expect that the effects of such centers on residential land use would be uniform for areas so defined and zero outside them. But for an initial test of the effects of such centers there seemed to be no obviously superior way to measure their effects, since little is known about these effects. Because the data for both manufacturing and retail centers refer to 1958 and 1960, the dummy variables might involve some measurement error for the 1950 comparisons. If so, their coefficients would tend to be biased toward zero, but I doubt that changes over a decade could have been of such great importance as to lead to a substantial bias on this score.

In addition to AGEDUS and INCOME, several other characteristics of dwellings and their inhabitants were included in the comparisons made here. As the analysis of Chapter 5 suggests, housing prices in Negro residential

---

[9] *Commercial Structure and Commercial Blight*, table 5.

areas may differ from those in other areas because of differences in the size of the Negro area and its rate of growth relative to the Negro demand for housing and its growth. The analysis of this earlier chapter also suggests that most census tracts will be occupied either by whites or by Negroes. Those few tracts with mixed population characteristics will be mostly ones in the process of shifting from occupancy by one group to the other. Furthermore, for those tracts occupied largely by Negroes it would seem likely that any whites remaining in the area would pay the Negro price for housing. For the tracts in the sample studied the concentration of tracts by percent population Negro was greatest for 5 percent or less and 80 percent or more.[10] I therefore described the racial composition of tracts using two dummy variables, NEGMAJ for percent Negro population 80 percent or more and NEGMIN for 5 to 80 percent. As with all other dummy variables of this variety, their coefficients measure the difference between the average value of the dependent variable or the level of the regression for designated tracts and all others. While, in principle, housing prices in the Negro area could be either greater or less than those in the white area, it is widely believed that Negroes pay higher housing prices than whites, and so a one-tail test for the Negro dummy variable coefficients seems appropriate in most cases.

It was argued in Chapter 6 that prices per unit of housing of comparable quality may vary as between areas of good- and poor-quality housing. If so, I would expect population density and the output of housing to vary between areas of different housing quality in the same direction as the variation in prices. I have used SUBSTD, defined in exactly the same way as before for both 1950 and 1960, as a measure of housing quality. It should be noted, however, that in the 1960 census, housing units were classified as dilapidated, deteriorating, and sound, while in 1950 dwelling units were classified as dilapidated and non-dilapidated. While the definition of dilapidation was the same for the two censuses, it is quite possible that some units classified as deteriorating in 1960 might have been classified as dilapidated in 1950 under the old classification. I therefore included an alternate measure of SUBSTD for some of the comparisons in 1960, the proportion of housing units deteriorating or dilapidated and/or without private bath. However, in virtually every case the definition of SUBSTD used for 1950 proved to be superior on statistical grounds. Hence, unless otherwise specifically noted, the variable SUBSTD in 1960 refers to the same classification of units as SUBSTD in 1950.

---

[10] Negro population data for 1950 are from *U.S. Census of Population: 1950*, vol. 3, table 1. Hereafter, this volume is referred to as *Chicago Tract Statistics, 1950*. For 1960 the data are from *Chicago Tract Statistics, 1960*, table P-1.

Most of the other variables measuring population characteristics were included only in the housing consumption comparisons, for reasons discussed in the following section. For each of them, in this chapter, the natural log of the proportion of the population possessing the particular characteristic was used, unless explicitly noted otherwise. One variable, the proportion of dwelling units which were owner-occupied or OWNOCC, was initially included in all the comparisons in order partially to account for the lingering effects of rent control in 1950 on residential land use.[11] To the extent it is effective, I would expect rent controls to hold prices of housing in controlled units below the levels they would otherwise reach and to increase the price of housing services in non-controlled units. Hence, the per household consumption of housing would tend to be greater than otherwise in controlled units and the output of housing smaller, the latter because owners of controlled units would have less incentive to maintain their properties in good condition. The reverse would be true for uncontrolled units, and, since owner-occupied units were uncontrolled, one might expect population densities and the output of housing to be greater the greater the proportion of owner-occupied units, and the per household of consumption of housing smaller. But the degree of home-ownership reflects other factors as well. As has been argued earlier, because of the federal income tax exemption to income from owner-occupied housing and federal mortgage programs, the price of housing services is lower to home owners than to others. In addition, since income from owner-occupied housing is not included in the census income data, for a given census reported median income the greater the proportion of dwellings owner-occupied the greater the true average income level. For both these reasons I would expect the average consumption of housing per household to increase with the degree of home-ownership. Finally, households with stronger than average preferences for housing as compared with other types of consumption may have a higher proportion of home-ownership, partly because of the tax and mortgage interest subsidies, so that home-ownership may be partly a surrogate for variables associated with above-average tastes for housing.

Two measures of household type, the proportion of population twenty-one years old or over who were sixty-five or over, AGEPER, and PERHOU as defined earlier were included in the housing consumption regressions.[12] The age variable was included primarily because the current incomes of

---

[11] Data are from *Chicago Tract Statistics, 1950*, table 3, and from *1960*, table H-1, respectively.

[12] Data on age of persons are from *Chicago Tract Statistics, 1950*, table 2, and from *1960*, table P-2. Data on persons per household for 1960 are from *Chicago Tract Statistics, 1960*, table P-1.

older households substantially underestimate the permanent income measure upon which they base their consumption; hence, one would expect housing expenditures to vary directly with AGEPER when current income is held constant.[13] Because, under rent control, increases in rentals were sometimes permitted with a change in tenant, one would expect average housing expenditures to be higher in 1950 in areas with a rapid turnover of population. As a partial control for such effects I included SAMHOU, defined for 1950 (1960) as the proportion of persons one year (five years) old or over who lived in the same unit in 1949 (1955) as in 1950 (1960),[14] and I would expect its coefficient to be negative for 1950. Finally, I included the proportion of the employed labor force reporting occupation who were in white-collar occupations—professional, technical, clerical, and sales, WHICOL, and the median years' schooling completed for the population twenty-five years old and over, SCHOOL.[15] These were included because housing consumption may be related to education and occupation as well as to current income. In the sociological literature such effects are frequently attributed to tastes associated with status, actual or that to which a household aspires. Alternatively, this association may reflect the fact that at any given current income level persons in the white-collar occupations and persons who are better educated are younger on the average and have higher expected incomes over their lifetimes.

As stated earlier, the comparisons in this chapter and the following one are restricted to census tracts in the south side of the city of Chicago. The south side is defined as the area south of 22d Street, the south branch of the Chicago River, and the Sanitary Drainage and Ship Canal. Since the measures of employment potential I wanted to include were available only for a sample of tracts in the Chicago area, the comparisons in this chapter were restricted to these tracts. This sample is roughly a 20 percent systematic sample of quasi-tracts (tracts or combinations of tracts) with a randomized starting point. Since tracts in Chicago are numbered roughly from north to south and east to west, a systematic sample tends to be a sample stratified by area of the city. Tracts for 1950 or 1960 were combined to make them as nearly comparable in area covered as possible, but there were some minor changes in boundaries between the two censuses whose effects could not be eliminated. From the total of all such tracts or combinations I eliminated all tracts or parts of combinations with fewer

---

[13] Reid, *Housing and Income.*

[14] Data are from *Chicago Tract Statistics, 1950,* table 1, and from *1960,* table P-1. Use of this variable was suggested to me by Margaret Reid.

[15] Occupational data are from *Chicago Tract Statistics, 1950,* table 2, and from *1960,* table P-3; the data on education from *Chicago Tract Statistics, 1950,* table 1, and from *1960,* table P-1.

than 100 persons in either 1950 or 1960 on the ground that such areas are devoted mostly to non-residential land uses. I also omitted any tracts in which I knew public housing projects to be located, since land-use intensity and other variables studied are probably quite different where public housing exists. The resulting sample contained sixty-seven observations. I used all of these rather than a smaller subsample because of the rather large number of variables I wished to include in some of the comparisons and in order to increase the extent to which intercorrelated variables would vary independently of each other and hence the precision of the resulting estimates.

Empirical Results for 1950

In this section the empirical findings for 1950 are presented. First I show the results for gross and net population density. I then present the analysis of variations in housing consumption, both as measured by expenditures per household and persons per room. This is followed by the comparisons of the output of housing per residential square mile, both value and physical measures. Finally, I show the results obtained when quadratic regressions in distance to the CBD are run.

When scatter diagrams were plotted, it was noticed that DISCBD and the two employment potential measures were quite highly intercorrelated. Subsequent computations revealed simple correlation coefficients of -0.84 and -0.98 between DISCBD and MANPOT and RETPOT, respectively, while for the two potential measures the simple correlation coefficient is 0.86. One would expect very high correlations between DISCBD and the potential measures if, outside of the CBD, employment were more or less uniformly distributed. This is because, under such conditions, a movement from any point in any direction would effect employment potential only through the increase in distance from the CBD; movement in a direction perpendicular to the movement along a radial from the CBD would bring one closer to certain employment places but farther from equally important ones. From the correlation coefficients presented above it is apparent that DISCBD and the employment measures are essentially measures of the same thing, general accessibility. The first step in my investigation, therefore, was to determine which, if any, yielded the best results.

The regression coefficients and R^2's for GRODEN and NETDEN as dependent variables are shown in Table 1. In all of these regressions the other independent variables included in equations (15) and (17), Table 2, were used as well. But since it made very little difference to the coefficients of the other variables included which of the measures of general accessibility were used, their coefficients are not shown separately. From Table

1 it is apparent that it makes very little difference in the proportion of explained variance which of the variables are used to measure general accessibility. For GRODEN, RETPOT does best, DISCBD next, the MANPOT's coefficient is insignificant, while for NETDEN manufacturing potential does best and DISCBD worst. The difference is probably due to the fact that when MANPOT differs from its average relationship with DISCBD it is because of local concentrations of employment where the fraction of land area used for residential purposes is much below average. When two or more measures of general accessibility are used in the same regression, the standard errors of the coefficients increase markedly, the coefficients themselves change radically, and R^2 increases very little—a sure sign of collinearity. Even though DISCBD does not do quite as well as the potential measures, I decided to use it in further comparisons for two reasons. First, the coefficient of DISCBD permits a much simpler interpretation. But, more important, computation of employment potential

TABLE 1

RELATION BETWEEN POPULATION DENSITIES AND VARIOUS ACCESSIBILITY
MEASURES, 1950[a]

EXPLANATORY VARIABLE	DEPENDENT VARIABLE EQUATION						
	GRODEN						
	(1)	(2)	(3)	(4)	(5)	(6)	(7)
DISCBD	−.096*	···	···	−.22*	.18	···	.049
	(.067)			(.098)	(.22)		(.23)
MANPOT	···	−.015	···	1.2	···	−1.2	−1.1
		(.50)		(.72)		(.66)	(.71)
RETPOT	···	···	1.0*	···	2.5*	2.0*	2.3
.			(.56)	···	(1.8)	(.76)	(1.8)
.							
.							
R^2	.64	.62	.65	.66	.65	.67	.67
	NETDEN						
	(8)	(9)	(10)	(11)	(12)	(13)	(14)
DISCBD	−.072*	···	···	.018	.13	···	.25
	(.046)			(.068)	(.15)		(.16)
MANPOT	···	.79*	···	.89*	···	.65*	.94*
		(.33)		(.50)		(.46)	(.49)
RETPOT	···	···	.76*	···	1.8*	.23	2.0*
.			(.39)		(1.3)	(.53)	(1.2)
.							
.							
R^2	.80	.82	.81	.82	.81	.82	.82

[a] In addition to those independent variables shown here, those others included in equations (15) and (17), Table 2, were included in all of the regressions. Their coefficients, however, showed remarkable stability in the different equations and, hence, were not shown here.
* Significant at the 1-tail 0.10 level.

is much more difficult and time consuming than measurement of distance to the CBD. Since DISCBD worked almost as well in the regressions, it seemed hardly worth the heavy additional cost involved for me or someone else to recompute potential for comparative studies of other years or cities.[16]

TABLE 2

RELATION OF POPULATION DENSITY TO ALL VARIABLES, 1950

EXPLANATORY VARIABLE	DEPENDENT VARIABLE (EQUATION)			
	GRODEN		NETDEN	
	(15)	(16)	(17)	(18)
DISCBD	−.096*	−.10*	−.072*	−.11*
	(.067)	(.064)	(.046)	(.049)
RAPINT	.58	.59	−.38	−.32
	(.58)	(.58)	(.41)	(.44)
RAPSLO	−.019	−.019	.072*	.073*
	(.067)	(.066)	(.046)	(.050)
MANMAJ	−.16	−.19	−.038	−.23
	(.22)	(.20)	(.15)	(.15)
MANMIN	−.069	−.12	.29	−.007
	(.33)	(.30)	(.23)	(.22)
RETMAJ	.27	.26	.22	.14
	(.20)	(.20)	(.14)	(.15)
RETMIN	.51†	.53†	.13	.25†
	(.20)	(.20)	(.14)	(.15)
AGEDUS	.55	.55	.77*	.76*
	(.50)	(.49)	(.34)	(.37)
INCOME	.38	.40	−.61	−.51
	(.77)	(.76)	(.54)	(.58)
NEGMAJ	.82*	.89*	−.11	.35
	(.49)	(.44)	(.34)	(.34)
NEGMIN	.086	.12	−.20	.007
	(.32)	(.30)	(.22)	(.23)
SUBSTD	−.024	−.010	−.019	.063
	(.15)	(.15)	(.11)	(.11)
OWNOCC	−.062	···	−.37	···
	(.17)		(.12)	
R^2	.64	.64	.80	.77

* Significant at the 1-tail 0.10 level.
† Significant at the 2-tail 0.10 level.

The regression coefficients for DISCBD and all other variables used in the analyses of population density are shown in Table 2. The regressions were first run including OWNOCC in an attempt to provide a partial control for the effects of rent control, and a positive coefficient for OWNOCC was anticipated. However, OWNOCC's coefficient is negative in both equations and three times its standard error in the second one. Large coefficients with wrong signs were also observed for OWNOCC in

---

[16] Results similar to those found here for an analysis of data for Washington, D.C., were obtained by Pendleton, "The Value of Accessibility."

the housing output regression in Table 4. Since OWNOCC tends to be strongly correlated with ONEFAM, it would appear that in the density and housing output regressions OWNOCC is merely another measure of land-use intensity. I recomputed the regressions with OWNOCC excluded, with the results seen in equations (16) and (18).

Densities, both gross and net, show a tendency to decline with distance from the CBD which is statistically significant at the 10 percent level in all the regression equations shown in Table 2, and NETDEN declines distinctly less rapidly in areas close to rapid-transit routes in equation (18). There is a tendency for densities to be below average near manufacturing centers and above average near retail centers in both equations (16) and (18); RETMIN's coefficient exceeds its standard error by half in both (16) and (18), and MANMAJ's does in (18). The coefficient of AGEDUS is positive in both (16) and (18), but half again as large and almost twice its standard error in the latter. This suggests indeed that in 1950 net population densities were above average in older areas but that a smaller fraction of land in these areas is devoted to residential uses.

Conversely, the coefficient of NEGMAJ is positive and twice its standard error in the gross density regression but less than half as large and about equal to its standard error in equation (18). It appears, therefore, that the greater gross population densities in areas largely inhabited by Negroes is partly due to the fact that a greater fraction of land is devoted to residential uses in these areas. Once this is removed in (18) there is considerable doubt, statistically, whether population densities are higher at all in Negro areas. Indeed, from (18) it would appear that housing prices are about 3 percent higher in Negro areas. NEGMAJ's coefficient in (18) is numerically about three times that of DISCBD's, and results given later in this chapter indicate that housing prices decline at the rate of about 1 percent per mile in south Chicago. Finally, note that unlike the case of DISCBD versus the employment potential measures, it makes considerable difference whether gross or net population densities are used as the dependent variable. More than three-fourths of the variation in NETDEN is explained in equation (18), but less than two-thirds of GRODEN's variation is accounted for in (16). More important, however, the coefficients of several variables differ markedly between (16) and (18). Since net density is clearly the more relevant variable for most of the analyses of Part I, it would appear desirable to use, if feasible, net densities and housing output per square mile of residential land in comparisons such as these.

The relation of housing consumption to the various explanatory variables is shown in Table 3. Regression coefficients for the value of housing expenditures per household are shown in equations (19) and (20), while those for PEROOM, a physical measure, are shown in (21) and (22). In equation

(19) expenditures tended to be noticeably greater in areas close to rapid-transit facilities, smaller in the vicinity of manufacturing areas, and above average, though not significantly so, close to the smaller retail centers. While I would expect that housing prices might vary in a similar manner, expenditures would vary directly with prices only if housing demand were inelastic; I suspect, therefore, that the variation of expenditures with these accessibility variables reflects something other than the effects of price variation. This suspicion tends to be borne out by equation (21), which

TABLE 3

RELATION OF HOUSING CONSUMPTION TO ALL VARIABLES, 1950

EXPLANATORY VARIABLE	DEPENDENT VARIABLE (EQUATION)			
	VALHOU		PEROOM	
	(19)	(20)	(21)	(22)
DISCBD	.030	.037	.0032	.0001
	(.022)	(.023)	(.0056)	(.0052)
RAPINT	.33†	.26	−.084†	−.046
	(.19)	(.18)	(.049)	(.040)
RAPSLO	−.033	−.032	.0057	.0043
	(.022)	(.020)	(.0056)	(.0046)
MANMAJ	−.26†	−.091	.063†	.030†
	(.071)	(.079)	(.018)	(.018)
MANMIN	−.48†	−.28†	.041	.006
	(.11)	(.11)	(.027)	(.025)
RETMAJ	−.080	−.028	−.004	−.008
	(.067)	(.061)	(.017)	(.014)
RETMIN	.093	.001	−.032†	.001
	(.068)	(.063)	(.017)	(.014)
AGEDUS	−.050*	−.63*	−.074*	−.000
	(.16)	(.20)	(.041)	(.044)
INCOME	.89*	.60*	−.33*	−.23*
	(.26)	(.24)	(.064)	(.054)
NEGMAJ	.66*	.78*	.024	.021
	(.16)	(.16)	(.041)	(.037)
NEGMIN	.077	.056	.055*	.002
	(.11)	(.12)	(.027)	(.029)
SUBSTD	.005	.030	.003	.000
	(.050)	(.053)	(.013)	(.012)
OWNOCC	.10†	.14	−.055†	−.058†
	(.055)	(.090)	(.014)	(.021)
AGEPER	· · ·	.23*	· · ·	−.11*
		(.11)		(.025)
PERHOU	· · ·	.065	· · ·	.11
		(.46)		(.11)
SAMHOU	· · ·	−1.6*	· · ·	−.088
		(.70)		(.16)
WHICOL	· · ·	.27	· · ·	.000
		(.21)		(.047)
SCHOOL	· · ·	−.052	· · ·	−.037
		(.47)		(.11)
R^2	.85	.90	.89	.94

* Significant at the 1-tail 0.10 level.
† Significant at the 2-tail 0.10 level.

shows less crowding or more rooms per person in the vicinity of rapid-transit routes and the smaller retail centers and fewer rooms per person in the vicinity of the larger local manufacturing centers. These variations in persons per room are all exactly the opposite to what one would expect if they reflected variations in quantity consumed due to price variations, since PEROOM should vary inversely with housing consumed and thus directly with price. In addition, equation (21) shows more structure space per person in older dwellings, but there is no apparent tendency for persons per room to vary with distance from the CBD as would be expected if variations in PEROOM reflected variations in housing prices. I therefore added a group of five variables reflecting household characteristics to see if the above-noted variations in housing consumption can be attributed to factors other than price.

From equations (20) and (22) it would indeed appear that the variations in housing consumption noted in the above paragraph are largely associated with household types. The coefficients of RAPINT fall in absolute value and become non-significant in equations (20) and (22). While the coefficients of MANMIN in (20) and MANMAJ in (22) are still too large to attribute to chance variation, they are much smaller numerically than the corresponding coefficients in (19) and (21), and the coefficients of the other local manufacturing and shopping center variables fall numerically in all but one instance. Finally, the coefficient of AGEDUS vanishes in (22), I suspect because older dwellings tend to be inhabited by older persons.

In equation (20) as well as in (19), housing expenditures per household tend to increase with distance, though the coefficient of DISCBD is not quite significant at the two-tail 10 percent level. Quantitatively the increase is quite small, however, being of the order of 3 to 4 percent per mile. The increase in VALHOU may reflect the fact that expenditures vary inversely with price because of an elastic housing demand, or that CBD and local worker households with above-average preferences for housing spend more for housing and live at greater distances from the city center. Both in (19) and (20) there is a strong tendency for per household expenditures to be smaller on older dwellings and to increase with income, as was found in Chapter 8. The income elasticity of housing expenditures in (19) is similar to values found in Chapter 8, but falls by about one-third in equations (20). This fall is to be expected, since holding occupation and education constant considerably reduces the fraction of income variability accounted for by permanent income differences, and increases the error in measured income. The results for PEROOM in (22) are also similar to those observed earlier in that DISCBD or AGEDUS have negligible coefficients, but income is strongly associated with structural space per person.

Turning to the other coefficients, NEGMAJ's coefficient is strongly positive in both (19) and (20); in fact, introducing variables describing household characteristics increases rather than reduces this coefficient. The positive coefficient, however, is not what one would expect if Negroes paid higher prices for comparable housing and the elasticity of housing demand were − 1 or smaller. Since introducing SAMHOU does not reduce NEGMAJ's coefficient, I do not believe it likely that the latter reflects the greater mobility of the Negro population or the possibility that Negroes were more strongly affected by rent increases permitted with a change in tenant by rent-control authorities. In addition, PERHOU'S coefficient is quite small in (20); therefore I do not believe the strongly positive coefficient of NEGMAJ is due to greater operating and depreciation costs resulting from larger numbers of persons per household in Negro areas. The coefficient of NEGMAJ, however, is only about half its standard error in equations (21) and (22); since PEROOM is in square root form and averaged about 0.4 in the tracts studied, NEGMAJ's coefficient implies that crowding may have been 10 percent greater in Negro areas. Of the other variables included, OWNOCC's coefficient is positive in the VALHOU regressions,[17] though not quite significantly so in (20), and negative in both (21) and (22); these suggest that owner-occupied households consume greater amounts of housing, given income levels and the other variables included. Likewise, older persons tend to consume more housing at given current income levels than others, as indicated by the positive coefficient of AGEPER in equation (20) and the negative one in (22). SAMHOU's coefficient tends to be negative in (20), which one would expect if controlled rentals were kept lower for dwellings whose tenants remained unchanged, but this variable's coefficient is actually negative in (22), which indicates a greater consumption in physical terms.

Let us now consider the housing output regressions in Table 4. As in the density regressions in Table 2, the coefficient of OWNOCC has the wrong sign if interpreted as reflecting the effects of rent control. Hence OWNOCC was eliminated in equations (24) and (26). Both of these indicate that housing output per unit of land declines with distance from the CBD; the coefficient in the ONEFAM regression is particularly strong, being three times its standard error in (26). The VALAND gradient in Table 4 is about equal in magnitude to the net density gradient in Table 2, but neither

---

[17] Note that VALHOU measures housing expenditures inclusive of the federal income tax saving. While the lower price of housing to home owners would not affect their housing expenditures after the tax saving had been deducted if the price elasticity of housing demand were − 1, the tax saving is of course positive. Hence, the positive coefficient of OWNOCC in the VALHOU equations is in no way inconsistent with a unit housing-price demand elasticity.

VALAND nor ONEFAM shows a significant tendency to vary less per mile in areas adjacent to rapid-transit facilities. VALAND is considerably smaller in the vicinity of manufacturing centers, and ONEFAM is greater, suggesting as did the density regressions that housing prices tend to be lower in the vicinity of such centers. Also, as in the density regressions, RETMIN's coefficient suggests that people are willing to pay more for housing located close to the smaller shopping centers. As was the case in Chapter 8, the value of housing output per unit land is no different in older areas than in newer ones, but the older areas clearly tend to have a smaller proportion of single-family dwellings. The coefficients of income are also similar to those observed earlier, though it is not very much larger than its standard error in the VALAND regressions. The coefficients of NEGMAJ behave in the output regressions as they did in the consumption regressions. For the value measure, VALAND, the coefficient is strongly positive, but in (26), while negative, it is only about equal to

TABLE 4

RELATION OF HOUSING OUTPUT TO ALL VARIABLES, 1950

EXPLANATORY VARIABLE	DEPENDENT VARIABLE (EQUATION)			
	VALAND		ONEFAM	
	(23)	(24)	(25)	(26)
DISCBD	−.032	−.082*	.021*	.039*
	(.052)	(.055)	(.010)	(.013)
RAPINT	.094	.16	.010	−.013
	(.45)	(.50)	(.091)	(.12)
RAPSLO	.024	.025	−.0054	.0059
	(.052)	(.057)	(.010)	(.014)
MANMAJ	−.39	−.63†	.033	.12†
	(.17)	(.17)	(.034)	(.04)
MANMIN	−.33	−.71†	−.016	.11†
	(.25)	(.26)	(.051)	(.06)
RETMAJ	.14	.038	−.012	.024
	(.16)	(.17)	(.031)	(.040)
RETMIN	.27†	.41†	−.060†	−.11†
	(.16)	(.17)	(.032)	(.040)
AGEDUS	.018	.007	−.22*	−.22*
	(.38)	(.42)	(.077)	(.10)
INCOME	.59	.71	.057	.015
	(.60)	(.66)	(.12)	(.16)
NEGMAJ	.53*	1.1*	.099	−.10
	(.38)	(.38)	(.077)	(.091)
NEGMIN	−.22	.036	.078	−.012
	(.25)	(.26)	(.050)	(.062)
SUBSTD	.011	.12	.003	−.033
	(.12)	(.13)	(.024)	(.030)
OWNOCC	−.47	· · ·	.16	· · ·
	(.13)		(.026)	
R^2	.67	.59	.88	.79

* Significant at the 1-tail 0.10 level.
† Significant at the 2-tail 0.10 level.

its standard error. And again, when the coefficients of DISCBD and NEGMAJ are compared, a rate of decline of housing prices of about 1 percent per mile suggests that housing prices are no more than 3 percent greater in Negro areas. Table 4, then, as with the density and PEROOM regressions, gives little solid evidence of a Negro price differential for housing.

TABLE 5

RELATION OF DENSITY AND ITS COMPONENTS TO DISTANCE,
QUADRATIC REGRESSIONS, 1950[a]

EXPLANATORY VARIABLE	DEPENDENT VARIABLE (EQUATION)			
	GRODEN	NETDEN	VALHOU	VALAND
	(27)	(28)	(29)	(30)
DISCBD	−.46*	−.59*	.15	−.57*
	(.34)	(.25)	(.10)	(.29)
DCBDSQ	.020	.027†	−.0060	.027†
	(.018)	(.014)	(.0055)	(.016)
RAPINT	.10	−2.2	.30	−1.9
	(1.4)	(1.0)	(.44)	(1.2)
RAPSLO	.06	.56*	−.019	.56*
	(.35)	(.26)	(.11)	(.30)
RSLOSQ	−.002	.027†	.0016	−.031†
	(.020)	(.015)	(.0067)	(.017)
.				
.				
.				
R^2	.65	.78	.91	.62

[a] In addition to those independent variables shown here, those others included in the last of the regressions for each of the dependent variables presented earlier were also included. Their coefficients differ very little in the linear and quadratic regressions and, hence, are not repeated here.
* Significant at the 1-tail 0.10 level.
† Significant at the 2-tail 0.10 level.

Finally, for the 1950 data, I tried including the square of distance, designated DCBDSQ and RSLOSQ, in the regressions. The results are shown in Table 5. The quadratic regressions in distance result in but little increase in R^2, and the coefficients of the quadratic terms are small for GRODEN and VALHOU. The quadratic terms are statistically significant for both NETDEN and VALAND, and each shows a decline in the gradient with distance for areas not located close to rapid transit facilities and no variation at all with distance for areas adjacent to rapid transit facilities. However, in all the regressions the coefficients of the other variables are virtually unaffected when the quadratic terms in distance are added.

EMPIRICAL RESULTS FOR 1960

To test the results for 1950, the regressions of the preceding section were run using 1960 data. The only further experimentation with forms of regression and variables included was the use of the alternative measures of dwelling condition and crowding mentioned earlier. The 1960 data not only provide a new sample to check the earlier results, but they are more suitable for several reasons. The effects of rent control had disappeared by 1960, and reporting of values for owner-occupied dwellings was more complete in the 1960 census. Also, the data on location of manufacturing and retail centers and on residential land area relate more closely to conditions in 1960, so that less measurement error is involved when using these variables. AGEDUS, however, now refers to dwellings built prior to 1940 rather than 1920 and may be less satisfactory for this reason.

TABLE 6

RELATION OF POPULATION DENSITY TO ALL VARIABLES, 1960

EXPLANATORY VARIABLE	DEPENDENT VARIABLE EQUATION		
	GRODEN	LANRES	NETDEN
	(31)	(32)	(33)
DISCBD	−.070*	.014	−.14*
	(.049)	(.014)	(.039)
RAPINT	.66*	.14	−.27
	(.46)	(.14)	(.37)
RAPSLO	−.041	−.020	.067*
	(.052)	(.015)	(.041)
MANMAJ	−.38	−.029	−.28
	(.24)	(.070)	(.19)
MANMIN	−.22	−.012	−.30†
	(.15)	(.045)	(.12)
RETMAJ	.14	.028	.18
	(.16)	(.046)	(.13)
RETMIN	.26	.085†	.010
	(.17)	(.049)	(.13)
AGEDUS	.43	.21†	−.35
	(.35)	(.10)	(.28)
INCOME	−.29	−.015	.11
	(.57)	(.17)	(.45)
NEGMAJ	.27	.021	.25
	(.28)	(.081)	(.22)
NEGMIN	−.072	−.029	.10
	(.25)	(.075)	(.21)
SUBSTD	−.028	−.032†	.28†
	(.054)	(.016)	(.098)
R^2	.59	.28	.71

* Significant at the 1-tail 0.10 level.
† Significant at the 2-tail 0.10 level.

In Table 6, coefficients for the gross and net density regressions in 1960 are shown, along with those using the proportion of land area that is residential, LANRES, as dependent. The results obtained are very similar to those for 1950. Both gross and net densities show a tendency to decline with distance from the CBD which is statistically significant at the 10 percent level, and this rate of decline is only about half as large in the vicinity of rapid-transit facilities for NETDEN. Also as in 1950, densities tend to be below average in the vicinity of manufacturing centers and above average near retail centers. Of these coefficients, however, only that of MANMIN in the NETDEN regression appears to be clearly different from zero. The coefficient of AGEDUS in the NETDEN regression is negative in 1960 rather than large and positive as in 1950; this negative coefficient may stem, in part, from the fact that AGEDUS now refers to dwellings built between 1920 and 1939, in addition to those built prior to 1920, and it may partly reflect an adjustment of the older housing stock to changed conditions that was delayed by the depression and war. The coefficient of NEGMAJ is positive and about equal to its standard error as before. Comparison of the coefficients of DISCBD and NEGMAJ suggests that housing prices may have been 2 percent greater in Negro residential areas in 1960. The coefficient of SUBSTD is over four times as large in 1960 as in 1950 and almost three times its standard error, indicating that in 1960 housing prices were higher in areas of poor-quality housing. The R^2's for the density regressions are about the same magnitude, though slightly smaller in 1960 than in the earlier year.

The housing consumption regressions are shown in the first two columns of Table 7. The coefficient of DISCBD in the VALHOU regression is even smaller for 1960 than for 1950; as in the earlier year, the manufacturing-area dummy variables have negative coefficients in the VALHOU regression, and both of them are statistically different from zero even though the household type variables are included. The coefficient of AGEDUS is significantly negative, though numerically smaller than in 1950, the income coefficient positive and numerically smaller. Both of the Negro area variables are significantly positive, but NEGMAJ's coefficient is only half as large as in 1950. The coefficients of OWNOCC and AGEPER are practically identical with the 1950 coefficients, but that of SAMHOU is very much smaller numerically. This last suggests that it was, indeed, primarily the effects of rent control that this variable showed in 1950. The residual effect of SAMHOU on VALHOU shown by (34) may reflect the possibility that a larger proportion of households who have not moved recently are out of equilibrium and, following a period of rising income, spend less on housing than they would if they were to move to new quarters.

The results using the physical measure of consumption, PEROOM, are also similar for 1960. Neither AGEDUS nor any of the accessibility measures have statistically significant coefficients for 1960, and in 1950 only the coefficient of MANMAJ was significant. The income coefficient is negative and more than twice its standard error but less than half as large numerically as in 1950.[18] Again, there is no statistically significant tendency for greater crowding in Negro areas, as would be expected if Negroes paid higher prices for housing of given quality. In (35) NEGMAJ's coefficient

TABLE 7

RELATION OF HOUSING OUTPUT AND CONSUMPTION TO ALL
VARIABLES, 1960

EXPLANATORY VARIABLE	DEPENDENT VARIABLE (EQUATION)			
	VALHOU	PEROOM	VALAND	ONEFAM
	(34)	(35)	(36)	(37)
DISCBD	.0085	.0044	−.14*	.036*
	(.013)	(.0036)	(.040)	(.014)
RAPINT	.022	.012	−.17	−.14
	(.12)	(.034)	(.37)	(.14)
RAPSLO	−.012	−.0039	.054*	.0054
	(.013)	(.0038)	(.042)	(.015)
MANMAJ	−.15†	.014	−.57†	.14†
	(.064)	(.018)	(.19)	(.07)
MANMIN	−.089†	.0053	−.45†	.11†
	(.043)	(.012)	(.12)	(.05)
RETMAJ	−.011	.0093	.082	.0044
	(.037)	(.011)	(.13)	(.046)
RETMIN	.019	.0005	.078	.033
	(.038)	(.011)	(.14)	(.050)
AGEDUS	−.43*	−.021	−.50	−.37*
	(.11)	(.031)	(.28)	(.10)
INCOME	.47*	−.095*	1.3	−.28
	(.16)	(.047)	(.46)	(.17)
NEGMAJ	.41*	.012	.64*	−.19*
	(.078)	(.022)	(.22)	(.082)
NEGMIN	.14*	.0097	.24	.043
	(.076)	(.022)	(.21)	(.075)
SUBSTD	−.033	.0062†	.10†	−.041†
	(.029)	(.0037)	(.043)	(.016)
OWNOCC	.13*	−.052*	⋯	⋯
	(.042)	(.012)		
AGEPER	.19*	−.025	⋯	⋯
	(.080)	(.023)		
PERHOU	−.048	.32†	⋯	⋯
	(.22)	(.063)		
SAMHOU	−.22†	−.053†	⋯	⋯
	(.094)	(.027)		
WHICOL	.036	−.028	⋯	⋯
	(.083)	(.024)		
SCHOOL	.54*	−.032	⋯	⋯
	(.27)	(.079)		
R^2	.93	.94	.54	.79

* Significant at the 1-tail 0.10 level.
† Significant at the 2-tail 0.10 level.

[18] Because of the decline in dwellings with more than one person per room over the decade, the mean value elasticities of PEROOM with respect to INCOME do not differ quite as much as the regression coefficients. The elasticity for 1950 was −1.2 as

again suggests that crowding is on the order of 10 percent greater in Negro residential areas once the effect of other variables is removed. However, the coefficient of SUBSTD is positive and significantly different from zero, suggesting as in the net density regressions that the price per unit of housing quality is greater in the areas of poor housing quality. The coefficient of OWNOCC is negative and too large numerically to attribute to chance, but several of the household-type coefficients differ from those obtained in 1950.[19]

The output-of-housing regressions shown in the last two columns of Table 7 also behave quite similarly to those for 1950. The coefficient of distance in both the VALAND and ONEFAM regressions shows a statistically significant tendency for the output of housing per square mile of residential land to decline with distance from the CBD, though the coefficient of DISCBD in the VALAND regression is somewhat more than one standard error larger in 1960, but for 1960, in contrast to the 1950 results, VALAND tends to decline significantly less rapidly with distance in areas adjacent to rapid-transit facilities. Because, as I have argued in Chapter 3, the elasticity of the value of housing per square mile is around +15, the coefficient of DISCBD in equation (6) implies that housing prices in south Chicago decline at the rate of about 1 percent per mile. Also as in 1950, both the physical and value measures show that residential land is less intensively used in the vicinity of manufacturing areas, but there is no longer a tendency for greater intensity of use in the vicinity of the smaller retail centers. The coefficient of AGEDUS is again strongly

---

compared with −0.58 in 1960; if only DISCBD and AGEDUS are included along with INCOME in the 1950 PEROOM regression, the INCOME elasticity is −2.5, which agrees with the values found for other cities in Chapter 8. It is not unreasonable, however, for the response of PEROOM (the proportion of units of lowest quality or quantity of housing per unit) to income changes to decline during a period of rising housing consumption.

[19] For comparative purposes another regression using the square root of the proportion of housing units with more than 0.75 persons per room as dependent was run. The R^2 was somewhat lower, 0.92 as compared with 0.94, and several of the coefficients differed from those in equation (35). In particular, AGEDUS had a significantly negative coefficient, the coefficient of SUBSTD was about one standard error greater numerically, AGEPER and WHICOL had significant negative coefficients, and the coefficient of PERHOU was much smaller and not significant. Thus, the specific results obtained for the crowding variable may depend rather strongly on the specific measure used. When the log of the proportion of housing units which were deteriorating or dilapidated and/or without private bath was used to measure SUBSTD, R^2 was about the same as in (35), but the coefficient of SUBSTD was also about one standard error larger. When the alternate measure of dwelling unit condition was used in the NETDEN, VALHOU, and VALAND regressions, the coefficient of SUBSTD was numerically smaller and insignificant, and R^2 was smaller in every case. It would thus appear that, if anything, the 1950 definition of condition is superior to the alternate one for the purpose of this study.

TABLE 8

RELATION OF DENSITY AND ITS COMPONENTS TO DISTANCE;
QUADRATIC REGRESSIONS, 1960[a]

EXPLANATORY VARIABLE	DEPENDENT VARIABLE (EQUATION)			
	GRODEN	NETDEN	VALHOU	VALAND
	(38)	(39)	(40)	(41)
DISCBD	.015	−.28*	.21†	−.12
	(.26)	(.20)	(.053)	(.21)
DCBDSQ	−.0049	.0079	−.012†	.0011
	(.014)	(.011)	(.0030)	(.011)
RAPINT	1.2	−1.3	.54†	−.48
	(1.1)	(.84)	(.21)	(.87)
RAPSLO	−.20	.37*	−.14†	.15
	(.27)	(.21)	(.052)	(.21)
RSLOSQ	.0094	−.018	.0075†	−.0066
	(.015)	(.012)	(.0030)	(.012)
⋮				
R^2	.60	.72	.95	.54

[a] In addition to the independent variables shown here, those others included previously were included here as well. Their coefficients differed very little in the linear and quadratic regressions in distance and, hence, are not repeated here.
* Significant at the 1-tail 0.10 level.
† Significant at the 2-tail 0.10 level.

negative in (37), but its coefficient in the VALAND regression is also negative. For 1960, the effect of income is similar to that found for other cities in 1950; the income coefficient is strongly positive in the VALAND regression and negative for ONEFAM, indicating a greater intensity of land use in comparably located higher-income areas. NEGMAJ has a positive coefficient in the VALAND regressions as in 1950, though it is numerically smaller. In 1960, the coefficient of NEGMAJ agrees with that in the value regression and indicates a greater intensity of land use in the Negro areas. This is the only instance where a physical measure of intensity of use for either 1950 or 1960 lends any firm support on statistical grounds to the hypothesis that housing prices are greater in Negro areas. Quantitatively, however, the results of (37) are similar to those for 1950; comparison of the coefficients of DISCBD and NEGMAJ implies that prices are about 5 percent higher in Negro areas. However, both in the value and physical measure of housing-output regressions the coefficient of SUBSTD indicates a significantly greater intensity of use in areas of poor-quality housing for 1960; these results are consistent with those observed in the NETDEN and PEROOM regressions. Also note that R^2 is a little smaller in the VALAND regression for 1960 than for 1950, but for ONEFAM it is about the same.

The final comparison of results for 1950 and 1960 is between the quadratic regressions in distance. For 1960, the results are shown in Table 8. As in 1950, neither of the quadratic terms was statistically significant in the GRODEN regression, and R^2 increases very little when the quadratic terms are added. Otherwise, the results are virtually the opposite to those for 1950. The quadratic terms are not statistically significant in either the NETDEN or VALAND regressions for 1960. On the other hand, none of the distance coefficients were significant in the VALHOU quadratic regression for 1950, but all are significantly different from zero for 1960. However, in no case did the quadratic regression result in a substantial improvement in R^2 except in equation (40). Because the behavior of coefficients is so different in 1950 and 1960, and because the fit is usually not much improved, it would seem that the quadratic regressions in distance do not improve the results very much.

EXAMINATION OF THE RESIDUALS FROM THE PRECEDING REGRESSIONS

Having presented the regression equations which relate density and its components to the accessibility measures as well as others suggested by my analysis in Part I, I now wish to examine the residuals from these regressions. The major reason for doing so is to check for the presence of important omitted variables and to determine if possible whether their omission has biased the coefficients presented. Unlike regressions using time-series data, there is no obvious way to order the observations and compute measures of serial correlation for a single sample. However, one can compare the estimated residuals by tract for a given dependent variable for 1950 and 1960. In addition, one can seek to determine whether the residuals show a systematic pattern by sector of the city.

Of the theories of city structure discussed in Chapter 1, greatest attention in this study has been given to the influence of distance from the center on residential land use. Some attention has been paid to the multiple-nuclei hypothesis in this chapter by including measures of location relative to local manufacturing and retail centers, but virtually none has been given to the sector hypothesis of Homer Hoyt. I now wish to examine the computed residuals from the NETDEN, VALHOU, and VALAND regressions to determine whether they differ systematically by sector. To do so, I divide the tracts in the sample into four approximately equal groups by drawing radials from the Loop. SECTR1 is the code name for that group of tracts lying closest to the lake, SECTR2 for the next closest, and SECTR4 for the group farthest from the lake and closest to the Sanitary Canal. As in Chapter 7, my examination is limited to the signs of the residuals, and inferences about the relationship among residuals are based upon chi-square tests applied to the numbers of residuals with plus and minus signs.

The residuals from the NETDEN regressions are compared in Table 9. The signs of the residuals vary greatly among the four sectors, and the pattern of signs is virtually the same for 1950 and 1960. The differences in residuals among sectors are highly significant, as indicated by the chi-square values shown at the foot of Table 9a. In view of the similarity by

TABLE 9a

NETDEN Residuals by Sector, 1950 and 1960

	SIGN OF RESIDUAL				
	1950		1960		TOTAL
	+	−	+	−	
SECTR1	14	3	15	2	17
SECTR2	8	9	6	11	17
SECTR3	6	10	5	11	16
SECTR4	5	12	3	14	17
Total	33	34	29	38	67
	$X^2(3) = 11$ Pr. $\cong$ 0.01		$X^2(3) = 20$ Pr. $<$ 0.001		

sector in the two years it is not surprising that the signs of the residuals for the two years are so much the same, as indicated by Table 9b. Here fifty-five of the sixty-seven residuals have the same sign in 1960 as in 1950, and the chi-square value shown indicates that correlation of residuals from the two regressions is highly significant.

TABLE 9b

NETDEN Residuals, 1950 versus 1960

	SIGN, 1960		
SIGN, 1950	+	−	Total
+	25	8	33
−	4	30	34
Total	29	38	67
$X^2(1) = 28$, Pr. $<$ 0.001			

The results are rather different for the residuals from the VALHOU regressions. As shown in Table 10a, there is little difference by sign among sectors, except for SECTR4 as compared with the other three. Such differences as do exist among sectors would result from chance variation in one out of every two samples or more. This result is rather surprising in view of the findings of previous research that sectoring tendencies tend to be most apparent in characteristics related to housing value. The conflict may be due to the fact that such sectoring as has been observed previously

TABLE 10*a*

VALHOU Residuals by Sector, 1950 and 1960

| | SIGN OF RESIDUAL | | | | TOTAL |
| | 1950 | | 1960 | | |
	+	−	+	−	
SECTR1	9	8	7	10	17
SECTR2	8	9	7	10	17
SECTR3	9	7	7	9	16
SECTR4	11	6	11	6	17
Total	37	30	32	35	67
	$X^2(3) = 1.1$ Pr. $\cong$ 0.8		$X^2(3) = 2.6$ Pr. $\cong$ 0.5		

TABLE 10*b*

VALHOU Residuals, 1950 versus 1960

| SIGN, 1950 | SIGN, 1960 | | |
	+	−	Total
+	26	11	37
−	6	24	30
Total	32	35	67
$X^2(1) = 16.8$, Pr. < 0.001			

is accounted for by explanatory variables included in the VALHOU regressions, income being the most likely one. Sectoring tendencies in median family income will be investigated in the following chapter. However, Table 10*b* indicates that there is a strong positive association between the VALHOU residuals for 1950 and 1960.

The results in Table 11*a* suggest that sectoring in the net density residuals results mostly from that in the VALAND residuals. Here, as in Table 9*a*,

TABLE 11*a*

VALAND Residuals by Sector, 1950 and 1960

| | SIGN OF RESIDUAL | | | | TOTAL |
| | 1950 | | 1960 | | |
	+	−	+	−	
SECTR1	12	5	12	5	17
SECTR2	8	9	9	8	17
SECTR3	5	11	5	11	16
SECTR4	5	12	6	11	17
Total	30	37	32	35	67
	$X^2(3) = 7.4$ Pr. $\cong$ 0.05		$X^2(3) = 6.5$ Pr. $\cong$ 0.1		

TABLE 11b

VALAND RESIDUALS, 1950 VERSUS 1960

SIGN, 1950	SIGN, 1960		
	+	−	Total
+	22	8	30
−	10	27	37
Total	32	35	67

$X^2(1) = 14$, Pr. < 0.001

great differences in the signs of the residuals are observed, and the pattern of signs by sector is virtually the same for the two years. As with VALHOU, the association between residuals for the two years is quite strong for VALAND. Hence, the correlation of residuals of NETDEN for the two years reflects a similar correlation of residuals for both VALHOU and VALAND. However, as shown by Table 12, there is little association between the computed residuals for VALHOU and VALAND in either 1950 or 1960. The last finding agrees with the earlier findings of this study that the determinants of the two components of population density are largely different.

I now wish to inquire whether the omission of variables suggested by the analysis of the residuals, or, perhaps, incorrect functional form or

TABLE 12a

VALAND VERSUS VALHOU RESIDUALS, 1950

SIGN, VALAND	SIGN, VALHOU		
	+	−	Total
+	16	14	30
−	21	16	37
Total	37	30	67

$X^2(1) = 0.08$, Pr. $\cong 0.8$

TABLE 12b

VALHOU VERSUS VALAND RESIDUALS, 1960

SIGN, VALAND	SIGN, VALHOU		
	+	−	Total
+	15	17	32
−	17	18	35
Total	32	35	67

$X^2(1) = 0.01$, Pr. $\cong 0.9$

correlated measurement errors, any of which might produce the kind of association between residuals just observed, have biased the regression coefficients reported earlier. One approach to this question is to include sector dummy variables in the VALAND regressions. Also, a paper by Lester G. Telser[20] suggests that if the residuals from a related regression are included, correlation between omitted and included variables will change the coefficients of the latter. My additional tests are summarized in Table 13.

The results of including the residual from the 1950 VALHOU regression, RVH050, in the 1960 regression are shown in equation (42). Not surprisingly, the coefficient of RVH050 is positive and highly significant, and R^2 rises from 0.93 to 0.96. The coefficient of RVH050 indicates that for a tract in which housing expenditures were 10 percent above average in 1950, they were about 4 percent above average in 1960. Thus, while deviations tend to persist, the 1960 deviations are considerably smaller than the corresponding 1950 ones. For the accessibility variables, the differences in coefficients between equations (34) and (42) are all small relative to their standard errors, and in each equation both MANMAJ and MANMIN are negative and significantly different from zero. The coefficient of AGEDUS is about one standard error smaller in (42) but still significantly negative. This is also true of the income coefficient. The decline in the latter may indicate that the omitted variables relate to permanent income differences among households; if so, holding them constant would reduce the fraction of the variability in measured income which relates to permanent differences and increase the bias in the coefficient of measured income. The only important changes in coefficients are the decline in NEGMIN's coefficient, which becomes non-significant in (42), and in that of SUBSTD, which now is significantly less than zero because of the decline in its standard error. Its coefficient is quite small, however. The calculated values of VALHOU from equation (42) are plotted against the observed values in Figure 1. Clearly, no departures from linearity or constant variance are suggested by the scatter.

The results when sector dummy variables are added to the VALAND regressions for 1950 and 1960 are shown in equations (43) and (44). When the sector variables are included, the coefficient of DISCBD increases numerically by about a standard error and becomes virtually identical with that for 1960. The only other important differences are the decline in the coefficient of MANMIN, which is now not quite significant statistically, and the increase in the coefficient of INCOME, now quite similar

---

[20] "Iterative Estimation of a Set of Linear Regression Equations," *Journal of the American Statistical Association* 59 (September, 1964): 845–62.

to that for the 1960 regression. Inclusion of the sector dummy variables raises R^2 from 0.59 to 0.70. For 1960, including the sector dummy variables makes RAPSLO's coefficient insignificant statistically. The latter result suggests that the rapid-transit variables used do not capture all the differences in transport costs which exist, and the sectoring of residuals reflects this shortcoming. The absence of sectoring in the VALHOU residuals is consistent with this interpretation, since earlier results show very little variation in housing expenditures attributable to accessibility itself. The only other difference of any consequence is the increase in the RETMAJ coefficient, which is now strongly positive. As for 1950, including the sector variables raises R^2 from 0.54 to 0.62 for the 1960 VALAND regression. Comparing the VALAND regressions in (43) and

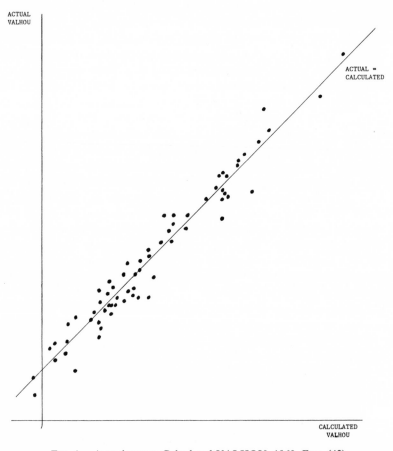

FIG. 1.—Actual versus Calculated VALHOU, 1960, Eqn. (42)

TABLE 13

RELATION OF HOUSING OUTPUT AND CONSUMPTION TO SECTOR VARIABLES
AND RESIDUALS FROM EARLIER CROSS-SECTION, 1950 AND 1960

EXPLANATORY VARIABLE	DEPENDENT VARIABLE (EQUATION)			
	VALHOU, 1960	VALAND, 1950	VALAND, 1960	
	(42)	(43)	(44)	(45)
DISCBD	.013	−.14*	−.14*	−.16*
	(.010)	(.054)	(.045)	(.024)
RAPINT	.054	−.53	−.16	−.22
	(.093)	(.54)	(.45)	(.23)
RAPSLO	−.016	.024	.023	.070*
	(.010)	(.060)	(.047)	(.025)
MANMAJ	−.15†	−.45†	−.37†	−.55†
	(.050)	(.16)	(.19)	(.12)
MANMIN	−.079†	−.39	−.30†	−.47†
	(.033)	(.24)	(.13)	(.076)
RETMAJ	−.017	.21	.23†	.10
	(.029)	(.17)	(.13)	(.077)
RETMIN	.014	.44†	.092	.23†
	(.030)	(.15)	(.14)	(.076)
AGEDUS	−.33*	.33	−.33	−1.1
	(.087)	(.42)	(.31)	(.18)
INCOME	.29*	1.0	1.3	.49
	(.13)	(.60)	(.44)	(.29)
NEGMAJ	.32*	.98*	.51*	.37*
	(.063)	(.38)	(.25)	(.14)
NEGMIN	.054	.086	.16	.005
	(.062)	(.23)	(.20)	(.13)
SUBSTD	−.022†	.028	.071†	.069†
	(.010)	(.12)	(.042)	(.026)
OWNOCC	.16*	...	...	...
	(.033)			
AGEPER	.15*	...	...	...
	(.064)			
PERHOU	−.16	...	...	...
	(.17)			
SAMHOU	−.23†	...	...	...
	(.074)			
WHICOL	.012	...	...	...
	(.065)			
SCHOOL	.69*	...	...	...
	(.22)			
RVH050	.41*	...	...	...
	(.074)			
SECTR2	...	−.27	−.29	...
		(.23)	(.19)	
SECTR3	...	−.85†	−.61†	...
		(.28)	(.20)	
SECTR4	...	−1.2†	−.54†	...
		(.28)	(.23)	
RVLD50	...	...	...	.67*
				(.069)
R^2	.96	.70	.62	.83

* Significant at the 1-tail 0.10 level.
† Significant at the 2-tail 0.10 level.

(44), if anything the sector dummy variables make the coefficients for the two years more consistent with each other. The coefficients of DISCBD and RAPSLO are now virtually identical. Of the accessibility variables, only the coefficients of RETMIN are markedly different. The income coefficients are now more nearly the same, but the coefficients of NEGMAJ still differ. The sector dummy variables are all negative, and those for sectors 3 and 4 significantly so. The one marked difference for their coefficients is the two-standard-error decline of SECTR4's coefficient in 1960. This may be due to the opening of the Congress Street (now Eisenhower) Expressway to the north of the Sanitary Canal, which may have improved SECTR4's accessibility to the Loop.

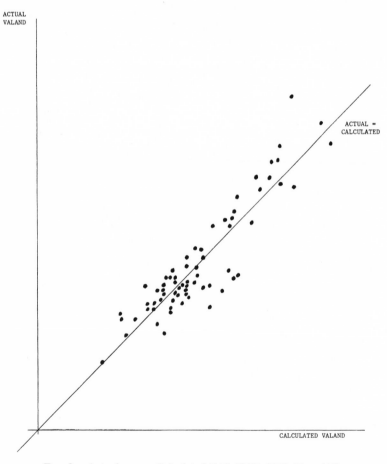

FIG. 2.—Actual versus Calculated VALAND, 1960, Eqn. (45)

TABLE 14

VALAND Residuals with Sector Variables Included,
1950 versus 1960

Sign, 1950	Sign, 1960		
	+	−	Total
+	23	11	34
−	7	26	33
Total	30	37	67

$X^2(1) = 15$, Pr. < 0.001

The signs of the residuals from the VALAND regressions with sector variables included are compared in Table 14. If anything, the association is stronger than before, and so sectoring would not appear to account for the correlation of the VALAND residuals for 1950 and 1960. Hence, I deleted the sector dummy variables and included the computed residual from the 1950 VALAND regression, RVLD50, in equation (45). This raises R^2 in the 1960 VALAND regression considerably. The coefficient of RVLD50 indicates a stronger degree of persistence of whatever effects the residuals in the VALAND regression represent than those in the VALHOU regression, equation (42). Comparing the coefficients of equation (45) with those of equation (36), Table 7, one sees that, except for RETMIN, the accessibility coefficients are virtually identical. The coefficient of AGEDUS is even more strongly negative, but the coefficient of INCOME declines sharply, though it remains positive. The actual values of VALAND and those calculated from equation (45) are shown in Figure 2. While there is perhaps a faint suspicion of positive curvature in the scatter of points, it is quite weak, and there is no indication of heteroscedasticity in Figure 2. Thus, it would appear that, whatever is responsible for the strong association over time in the residuals by census tract from regressions run earlier, the conclusions reached earlier are not seriously distorted.

Summarizing the results of this chapter, the more detailed analysis undertaken here tends to support the conclusions of the preceding chapter. There seems to be little reason to believe that the tendency for population densities to decline with distance can be accounted for mainly by the age of buildings, the income of their inhabitants, or other characteristics of either dwellings or inhabitants. The coefficients of DISCBD in the VALAND regressions suggest that in Chicago the decline in housing prices is of the order of 1 percent per mile, somewhat smaller but consistent in magnitude with that suggested for other cities in Chapter 8. As in other cities, in Chicago densities were positively associated with age of dwellings in 1950. But there is little relationship for 1960, suggesting that the pattern of intensity of land use may have adjusted to changed conditions during the fifties. There was no association between income and density for either 1950 or 1960 once other variables were held constant, which is also in agreement with the findings in Chapter 8. As in the other cities in 1950, the value of housing output per unit of land, too, was no larger in areas of older dwellings than in comparable newer ones. But both for 1950 and 1960 there was a significantly smaller proportion of one-unit dwellings in the older areas. I suspect this is because the demand for housing, and consequently housing prices, have fallen in older areas. Since the value of housing output was related to residential land area here, and the effects of rent control had presumably disappeared by 1960, the alternative explanations suggested in Chapter 8 are probably not responsible for the initially puzzling behavior of the age coefficients. These same considerations suggest that the above-average value of housing output in high-income areas results from higher prices for housing, and consequently greater land rentals, because of favorable neighborhood effects.

This chapter's analysis also suggests that population densities and the output of housing per unit of land, but not expenditures for housing per household, are related to other accessibility measures. In the net density regressions for both 1950 and 1960 and the VALAND regression for 1960, the relative rate of decline in the dependent variables is significantly smaller in the vicinity of rapid-transit routes than elsewhere. There was also a marked tendency for the intensity of land use to be less in the vicinity of local manufacturing centers, which might result from undesirable neighborhood characteristics in these areas. Conversely, there was a somewhat weaker tendency for land use intensity to be greater in the vicinity of local retail centers, which is consistent with, but does not lend strong support to, the hypothesis that housing prices are higher in the vicinity of these centers because of lower transport costs.

The other variables of interest for my analysis are the race and dwelling-unit condition variables. For both 1950 and 1960 the coefficients of NEGMAJ, the Negro area variable, were significantly positive in the VALHOU and VALAND regressions, but they were only half as large in 1960 as in the corresponding 1950 regression. With the exception of the ONEFAM regression for 1960, however, none of the NEGMAJ coefficients were statistically significant in the physical measure regressions—NETDEN, PEROOM, and ONEFAM. The latter results lend little support to the hypothesis that Negroes pay higher prices for housing of given quality because of racial segregation. More importantly, the quantitative estimates of the Negro price differential based upon comparisons of the coefficients of DISCBD and NEGMAJ in the NETDEN and ONEFAM regressions, though not very precise because of the statistical unreliability of the NEGMAJ coefficients, suggest that Negroes may pay housing prices that are from 2 to 5 percent greater. While such a differential is not necessarily a trivial one, it is far smaller than beliefs based upon the 30 to 80 percent differential in housing expenditures. Indeed, if Negroes did pay higher prices for comparable housing than whites, one would not expect a positive coefficient in the housing expenditure regressions, because it would appear that the price elasticity of housing demand is −1 or even smaller.

It has been suggested to me by some persons with whom I have discussed these findings that my failure to find the kinds of effects of higher Negro housing prices that I would anticipate is the result of a highly inelastic Negro housing demand. Closer examination, however, gives little reason for believing this to be so. As is well known, the strength of the income effect of a price change (note that money income is held constant in these comparisons) is greater the greater the fraction of a household's expenditure made on the commodity in question. If, as the VALHOU comparisons suggest, housing expenditures are larger in relation to income for Negroes, the income effect of a price change should be larger for them. The pure substitution effect of a change in housing prices depends upon the sub-stitutability of housing for other kinds of consumption. While Negroes as a group may have less knowledge of substitutes for housing because they are less educated, at given money-income levels Negroes have more education than whites and thus should be more knowledgeable. On both counts, then, there is reason to believe on a priori grounds that the relevant Negro price-elasticity of housing demand should, if anything, be numeri-cally greater, rather than smaller, than the elasticity for whites.

Even if for some unspecified reason the Negro demand for housing were perfectly inelastic, however, my findings cannot be explained away. With a perfectly inelastic Negro demand, there would be no differences between Negro and white housing consumption at given income levels, which is roughly consistent with my findings; and VALHOU's coefficient in 1960, equation (42), would imply that housing prices are about 30 percent greater for Negroes. NEGMAJ's coefficient is about the same magnitude in the VALAND comparison for 1960, equation (45). The perfectly in-elastic Negro-demand hypothesis, therefore, would imply that the output of housing per unit of land is no higher in the Negro residential area, despite the 30 percent price differential. Nevertheless, the analysis in Chapter 3 implies that the elasticity of the output of housing per unit of land with respect to price is of the order of +15. The coefficients of NEGMAJ in the NETDEN and ONEFAM comparisons, which are essentially zero as compared with these magnitudes, also imply that the output of housing per unit of land is no higher in Negro areas. Hence, to reconcile my findings with a Negro price differential of the order suggested by my VALHOU comparisons and the highly inelastic Negro-demand hypothesis, one also has to account for the failure of housing producers, many of whom are not Negroes, to respond to the Negro price differential.

Thus, I would interpret the differences in the value measures in Negro areas as reflecting some other factor. The decline in the coefficients from 1950 to 1960 may reflect the fact that under rent control rentals were less below the market equilibrium levels in Negro areas. But even in 1960, equations (42) and (45) indicate that expenditures were about one-third higher in the Negro areas. Such a difference is of an order of magnitude that might conceivably be explained by a greater importance of furnishings and utilities in contract rent in Negro areas or by higher operating costs for housing in these areas.

None of the 1950 regressions show significant coefficients for SUBSTD, the dwelling-unit condition variable. For 1960, however, in the NETDEN, PEROOM, VALAND, and ONEFAM regressions, the coefficients of SUBSTD are all statistically significant and all suggest that in 1960 housing prices are above average in areas of poor-quality housing. The extent of the price differences depends upon the elasticity of substitution between existing sites plus their structures and other factors in producing poor-quality housing. Even if this elasticity were quite small and the relative importance of these other factors small also, equation (45) would suggest that the elasticity of housing prices with respect to proportion substandard is no more than the coefficient of SUBSTD in equation (45), or about 0.07. Since about one-fourth of the dwellings were substandard on the average in the tracts sampled, the above reasoning suggests that prices of substandard housing were not more than 28 percent greater than those of other housing in 1960. An alternative interpretation of the coefficients of SUBSTD in the NETDEN, PEROOM, VALAND and ONEFAM regressions is that they reflect the effects of density or crowding on condition rather than the reverse. I shall examine this interpretation in the following chapter.

IO   *The Determinants of Dwelling-Unit Condition and the Location of Households by Income*

In Chapter 8 it was shown that the relative increase in the per household expenditure on housing with distance from the city center is about as great as the decline in the value of housing produced per unit of land. Further investigation showed, however, that most of the variation in expenditures on housing with distance vanishes when age of dwellings and incomes are introduced into the analysis. Also from Chapter 8 it was learned that the increase in median income with distance from the city center results mostly from the association of distance with the age and condition of dwellings. Doubt remains, however, whether the association of income and dwelling-unit condition results from the fact that low-income households spend less for housing than higher-income ones, and the quality of the dwellings they inhabit is thus adapted to their lower expenditures, or whether low-income households have less of an aversion to living in poor-quality housing, and are thus attracted to dwellings already in poor condition. Also, in Chapter 9 it was shown that in 1960 population density and related measures vary with housing quality in a way which suggests that slum housing is relatively expensive considering its quality. These results might alternatively be explained on the grounds that housing tends to deteriorate more rapidly in densely populated areas or in areas where there are relatively large numbers of persons per room.

In this chapter I will investigate the determinants of housing quality and the income levels of persons in different parts of the city and their interrelationships. I wish, in particular, to obtain evidence relating to the various theories of slums discussed in Chapter 6 and to the theories of household location by income level in Chapters 2 and 5. The first section reviews the ideas discussed earlier relating to these topics, presents the reasons for the comparisons made, and describes the data used. Next, the condition of dwellings and the income of families by census tract on Chicago's south side in 1950 are investigated. The third section presents comparisons of dwelling-unit condition among different central cities in 1950 as a check on the analysis within cities. Finally, as a further check on the analysis for

1950, variations in housing quality and income on the south side of Chicago for 1960 are examined.

COMPARISONS MADE AND DATA USED

As was argued in Chapter 6, most of the explanations commonly given for the existence of slums can be interpreted as relating to forces which increase the supply of poor-quality housing. I also suggested there that variations in housing quality might be better explained in terms of factors influencing the relative demand for poor-quality versus better housing. Here I will first summarize the factors affecting the relative demand for poor-quality housing and describe the demand variables I have used in my statistical analysis. Variables related to the supply of poor-quality housing will be discussed next. Finally, I will review the determinants of the location of households by income.

The principal determinant of housing consumption is income, and previous research has demonstrated that housing consumption varies at least in proportion to income whether comparisons are made over time, among different cities, or within a city at some given time. Since condition or quality is an important component of housing consumption, it might be expected that, as income increases, households will seek to obtain better-quality housing, and the demand for poor-quality housing will decline. In relating housing quality to income I have used the same measures of quality and income as have been used previously, SUBSTD and INCOME.[1] However, when scatter diagrams were plotted for census tracts on the south side of Chicago in 1950, it appeared that the relation was most nearly linear and homoscedastic if the natural log of proportion of dwelling units substandard was compared with income in natural units rather than with its log. For the various central cities studied this form of the relation appeared to be at least as suitable as any other. It is not surprising that the proportion substandard should decline at a decreasing absolute rate as income increases. Since a substandard dwelling is one below a level of certain quality, if the frequency distribution of dwellings were uni-model and not J-shaped, the above-noted behavior of the proportion substandard would occur once a certain level of average income and housing quality were reached. Therefore, for all of the comparisons made in this chapter, income is used in natural units rather than logs.

Another important variable affecting the consumption of housing, and hence dwelling-unit condition presumably, is the relative price of housing services. Thus, if the price of housing services declines with distance from

---

[1] The income variable used for the intercity comparisons was, in Chapter 7, designated CITINC to distinguish it from income for the whole of the urbanized area.

the city center and varies with accessibility to local manufacturing and shopping centers and rapid-transit lines, one might expect to find that dwelling-unit quality varies inversely with accessibility and housing prices. For this reason, all the accessibility variables used in Chapter 9, except for the measures of employment potential, will be included in the dwelling-unit condition comparisons for the south side of Chicago. In like manner, if Negroes pay higher prices for housing of given quality than do whites, one would expect to find a greater proportion of poor-quality dwellings in Negro areas. Also, a higher proportion of dwellings would be substandard in Negro areas if, as is sometimes alleged, segregation restricts Negroes to areas of the poorest housing quality. To take account of these possibilities I have included the dummy variable NEGMAJ and NEGMIN, described in the preceding chapter, in the condition comparisons of Chicago's south side. The last of the variables related to housing prices for the south Chicago condition comparisons is the proportion of dwelling units which are owner-occupied, OWNOCC, as defined in Chapter 9, but in natural units rather than logs. As argued previously in Chapters 5 and 9, the federal income-tax treatment of income from owner-occupied housing and federal mortgage programs tend to reduce the price of housing services to owners. Of course, because the census income data do not include the imputed income from owner-occupied housing, the greater the frequency of home ownership the greater the true level of income for any given census-reported income. The proportion of substandard dwellings would tend to vary inversely with owner occupancy for this reason too.

The major measure of housing prices included in the intercity condition comparisons is the index of residential construction costs, CONCST, described in Chapter 7. Unlike accessibility, which affects the price of housing services and hence the demand for structural features of housing within a city through its effect on land prices, CONCST refers directly to the cost of structural features. Hence, in the case of construction costs the effect of higher housing prices on the demand for structural features is not offset as in the case of higher land prices by the substitution of structures for land, but rather it is reinforced by the substitution of land for structures. Variations in the proportion of owner-occupiers among cities would have the same effect on prices paid for housing services and housing quality as variation within cities, and the variable OWNOCC used in the intercity comparisons is defined in the same way as the corresponding intracity variable.[2]

I have also included the proportion of the population which is Negro,

---

[2] Data on dwelling units by tenure for the various cities were obtained from *Census of Housing: 1950*, vol. 1, pt. 1, table 27.

POPNEG (described in Chapter 7), in the intercity condition comparisons. But the effects of the variations in housing prices paid by Negroes and whites on the proportion of dwellings substandard in the city as a whole are much more complicated than the effects as between white and Negro areas within a single city. If Negroes pay higher prices for housing than whites in all cities, the larger the Negro population the greater the fraction of households paying above-average housing prices. Under these conditions, however, the price paid for housing by whites and the quality of housing they inhabit would vary inversely with the relative size of the Negro population. The latter would tend to offset the decline in average quality for Negroes, so that average housing quality for the city as a whole would be roughly independent of the relative size of the Negro population.

But substandard housing refers to housing below a certain level of quality, and the proportion substandard may increase even though average quality remains unchanged. This is illustrated in Figure 1, which shows

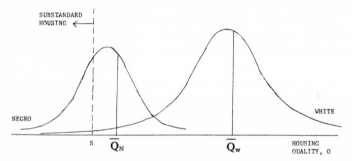

Fig. 1.—Distribution of Housing Quality According to Race

hypothetical functions indicating the number of Negro and white households inhabiting housing of any given quality, assuming each group pays the same price per unit. Substandard housing is any whose quality is less than S. Since Negroes typically have lower incomes than whites, the housing-quality functions for the two groups would look roughly like those in Figure 1, with the mean quality for Negroes, $\bar{Q}_N$, less than that for whites, $\bar{Q}_w$. If, now, the price of housing to Negroes increases and that to whites declines, the Negro quality distribution would shift to the left and the white distribution would shift to the right but by a smaller amount if the majority of the population is white. Under these conditions, unless the number of Negro households at S is less than the number of white households—which would be the case only if S cut the upper-tail of the Negro distribution—the shift of the Negro distribution would outweigh the opposite shift of the white distribution, and the proportion of all dwellings below S would increase. Thus, if Negroes pay higher prices than whites for housing, I would expect the proportion of dwellings substandard to increase with the relative size of the Negro population.

In addition to income and housing prices, the relative demand for poor-quality housing might depend on various population characteristics to which expenditures on housing were related in Chapter 9. Both in the Chicago and the intercity comparisons which follow I include persons per household, PERHOU, and AGEPER, the proportion of persons who are 65 years old or more.[3] The latter was included because the current incomes of older households may be below the permanent income on which their housing consumption is based; if this is so, I would expect SUBSTD to vary inversely with AGEPER. Also included in both kinds of comparisons are the measures of occupation and education, WHICOL and SCHOOL, which were used in Chapter 9.[4] These might be interpreted either as variables which reflect different tastes for housing or as differences in permanent incomes among households of equal current incomes, as argued earlier. Natural units were used, rather than logarithms as in the preceding chapter, of all the population characteristics noted above in this paragraph. Natural units for these variables together with proportion substandard in log form seemed to yield scatter diagrams which were more nearly linear and for which the variance of proportion substandard was more nearly constant. Finally, I included in the intercity comparisons a measure of unemployment, the proportion of the male labor force reporting length of employment in 1949 that worked twenty-six weeks or less, UNEMPT.[5] This last variable is included because the greater the level of unemployment for any given level of current income the higher is permanent income; I would therefore expect UNEMPT and SUBSTD to be inversely related.

Many factors might affect the relative supply of poor-quality housing. As discussed in Chapter 6, some writers have argued that older dwellings or neighborhoods are more likely to be in poor condition, either because of the ravages of time itself or because the demand for housing in older areas has fallen, and, consequently, buildings there have been allowed to deteriorate by their owners. Thus, AGEDUS, as defined in Chapters 7 and 8, was included in the intercity and Chicago comparisons. In the former an

---

[3] Data for the south side of Chicago are the same and from the same sources as described in Chapter 9. For the intercity comparisons it was more convenient to use the proportion of population aged 20 rather than those 21 who are over 65. In these comparisons, the data on PERHOU are from *1950 Census of Population*, vol. 2, pt. 1, table 86, and data on AGEPER are from *ibid.*, table 87.

[4] Data for the intercity comparisons are from *1950 Census of Population*, vol. 2, table 72, for WHICOL, and *ibid.*, pt. 1, table 86, for SCHOOL.

[5] The data refer to SMA's rather than cities and hence may be subject to some measurement error. They were obtained from *1950 Census of Population*, vol. 2, table 72.

additional measure of age, AGESMA, also as defined in Chapter 7, was included. A closely related reason, discussed in Chapter 6, is that the demand for housing has fallen in the vicinity of the older industrial centers, and housing has deteriorated in these areas as a result. The variables MANMAJ and MANMIN may thus reflect this fact. Still another reason is that with the coming of the automobile the demand for housing fell in areas closer to the city center. Since the fall in housing prices would vary inversely with distance from the CBD on this argument, I would expect the proportion of dwellings which are substandard to decline with distance. Finally, I included ONEFAM in natural units in the Chicago south-side comparisons on the grounds that, with the increase in incomes that has occurred since older areas were built up, and because of the federal income tax provisions and mortgage programs, the demand for single-family units has probably risen and that for multifamily units has fallen. If so, the fall in housing prices and the deterioration of buildings may be related to type of structure rather than to their age as such.

I have included several other variables suggested by many of the popular explanations for the existence of slums in the condition comparisons. One of the most important of these is crowding, as measured by PEROOM, which was defined earlier. It is commonly believed that crowding breeds slums, though I suspect that the association between SUBSTD and PEROOM results mainly from the fact that they are closely related aspects of the consumption of housing. Another variable related to crowding is population density, and so I have also included GRODEN in the condition comparisons.[6] The (natural) log form was used for both PEROOM and GRODEN, except that in Tables 8–11, where PEROOM is treated as dependent, the square-root form was used. Slums are also sometimes attributed to rapid turnover of population, although why rapid population turnover, or crowding for that matter, should lead to the deterioration of buildings has, to my knowledge, never been made clear. While frequent changes of tenant may impose great costs on property owners, there would seem to be no reason apart from rent controls why landlords could not charge higher rentals to cover the increased costs. It is possible, however, that recent immigrants or more mobile households generally have weaker preferences for housing and consume less of it and hence live in poorer-quality housing. Or rapid population turnover may merely be symptomatic of the fact that dwelling-unit condition in a neighborhood is deteriorating for other reasons. In any case, I included

---

[6] In the intercity comparisons GRODEN is the total population of the central city divided by its total land area or average gross density for the city as a whole. The data are from *1950 Census of Population*, vol. 1, table 17.

SAMHOU, as defined in Chapter 9, but in natural units, in an attempt to determine the extent to which dwelling-unit condition is associated with population turnover.[7]

Another factor frequently emphasized in discussions of slums is population growth. Rapid population growth is sometimes said to lead to deterioration of buildings, though as in the case of crowding and population turnover this may be merely symptomatic of other changes which lead to poorer housing quality, especially the growth of the low-income population of an urban area. On the other hand, where population grows at a relatively rapid rate, so does the demand for housing. Thus, housing prices are greater than otherwise[8] and the incentive for property owners to maintain their properties in good condition is greater. If this were so, one would find a smaller proportion of poor-quality units in areas of rapid population growth. In the Chicago comparisons I used the natural logarithm of the ratio of 1950 (1960) population to 1930 population by census tract, GROPOP, as a measure of growth rates.[9] For the intercity comparisons GROPOP is here defined as the natural log of the ratio of 1950 to 1900 SMA population.[10] Also included in the intercity comparisons was URBPOP as defined in Chapter 7, on the grounds that people may have more of an aversion to living in the central cities of the larger urbanized areas. A direct association between URBPOP and SUBSTD might be interpreted as reflecting the possibility that, given the census reported, money income, real incomes, and hence housing consumption are smaller because of the greater average distances which workers in the larger cities must travel to their jobs. Also, land rents and hence housing prices may vary directly with size of the urbanized area. Finally, MFGEMP, the proportion of the employed labor force reporting employment who were employed in mining and manufacturing, was included in the intercity condition comparisons because households might find living

---

[7] For the intercity comparisons the data are from *1950 Census of Population*, vol. 2, part 1, table 86.

[8] See my "The Demand for Non-Farm Housing," app. A, pp. 81–82.

[9] The 1930 population data were obtained from *Census Data of the City of Chicago, 1930*, ed. Ernest W. Burgess and Charles W. Newcomb (Chicago: University of Chicago Press, 1933), table 1. Prior to 1930, intracity population data for Chicago are much less comparable with the census tract population data for 1950 and 1960.

[10] Data are from Bogue, *Metropolitan Growth and the Conversion of Land to Non-agricultural Uses*, app. table 2, pp. 28–32. In this chapter I relate 1950 population to population in 1900 rather than in 1920 as I did in Chapter 7, partly to reduce the intercorrelation of GROPOP with AGEDUS. For my purposes here any measure of the long-term population growth rate will do, but the longer the period covered the less the ratio is due to random influences. For the comparisons in Chapter 7, however, growth following 1920, which is roughly the beginning of the auto era, seemed to be the relevant measure.

in the central cities of manufacturing areas less pleasant than in others.[11] If so, real incomes at any given census-reported money-income level would be lower, and, for this reason as well as because of the suspected unpleasantness itself, the demand for housing and thus housing prices would be lower in the areas where manufacturing is relatively more important.

Because the income level of the inhabitants of a census tract may be affected by as well as affect the quality of housing in the tract, the determinants of the location of households by income level are also examined empirically in this chapter. As was argued in detail in Chapter 2, if, as I would think likely, the income elasticity of housing demand is greater than that of the marginal cost of transport, the optimal location of higher-income CBD-worker households would tend to be at greater distances from the city center. For the same reason, more generally, the income level of households would vary inversely with housing prices and accessibility; I have therefore included all the accessibility measures in the analysis of income levels by census tract. As was found in Chapter 8, income by tract also varies inversely with the age of dwellings and their condition, as would be expected if higher-income households have a greater aversion to living in the vicinity of old housing and poor-quality housing. When scatter diagrams showing the relation of income to DISCBD, AGEDUS, and SUBSTD in 1950 were drawn, it was quite apparent that the level of the relationships differed as between Negro areas and others. Such a difference might be due to the fact of Negro residential segregation. Because of this finding I included the dummy variables NEGMAJ and NEGMIN among the determinants of location of households by income.

I also included two other variables which might be related to variations in the preferences of households by income level. These are GRODEN and ONEFAM, since it might be argued that higher-income households have greater preferences for space as compared with lower-income households. Higher-income households might also have stronger aversions to living in the vicinity of manufacturing and retail centers, and the appropriate accessibility dummy variables may reflect this fact. Finally, three variables were included in an attempt to correct deficiencies in the census-reported income measure. Since the latter omits income from owner-occupied housing, the true incomes of home owners would be greater than census-reported income. On this score one would expect INCOME and OWNOCC

---

[11] Data are from *1950 Census of Population*, vol. 2, pt. 1, table 91. This measure differs from that used in Chapter 7, which referred to males employed in manufacturing only, mostly because I had misgivings about the earlier measure. But since neither showed up very strongly I have not bothered to recompute the regressions using comparable measures of manufacturing employment for these different comparisons.

to be negatively related if location is based on true rather than census-reported income. Also, recent migrants and older households might tend to have current incomes which are below their permanent incomes. For this reason one might expect INCOME to be related positively to SAMHOU and negatively to AGEPER if households located in accordance with their permanent incomes.

As with the comparisons reported in Chapter 9, the intracity comparisons in this chapter are confined to that part of the city of Chicago south of 22d Street, the south branch of the Chicago River, and the Sanitary Drainage and Ship Canal. A different sample of tracts was used for the comparisons in this chapter, however. Because of the strong intercorrelation between variables such as distance, age of dwellings, and race, I wished to draw a sample in such a way as to get as much independent variation in these various variables as possible. Therefore, I grouped community areas (relatively homogeneous combinations of census tracts) into six groups on the basis of the variables noted above, which I anticipated would be related to dwelling-unit condition. The first two groups, one inhabited mainly by Negroes and the other mainly by whites, contains buildings built, for the most part, before 1920 and the lowest-income residents on Chicago's south side. The Negro area in 1950 was mostly north of 63d Street and east of State Street, the white area north of 55th and between Western Avenue and State Street. The third area, consisting of West Englewood, Englewood, Greater Grand Crossing, and Chatham, was an area of somewhat newer buildings and higher incomes in 1950; during the fifties most of this area switched from white to Negro occupancy. The last of the six groups consists of the highest-income areas on the south side: Hyde Park–Kenwood, which has a high proportion of buildings built before 1920; South Shore, Avalon Park, and Calumet Heights; and Beverly and the adjoining community areas in the far southwest part of the city. The southwest areas have a much lower proportion of dwellings built prior to 1920 than does Hyde Park–Kenwood. As with the sample used in Chapter 9, tracts were grouped for comparability between 1950 and 1960, and any tract with fewer than 100 persons or in which I knew of public housing projects was eliminated from the population of tracts sampled. A stratified random sample of approximately one-fifth of the tracts from each of the six groups was selected. A total of sixty-nine tracts was used in the comparison.

The cities used in the intercity comparisons were limited to central cities of urbanized areas of 100,000 persons or more for which the Boeckh residential construction cost index, CONCST, was available. Availability of the latter limited the intercity sample of forty-one observations. The resulting estimates would be more precise if a larger sample were used, but since CONCST tends to be positively associated with income, age, and city size, I wanted to include it to avoid bias in the coefficients of variables correlated with it.

TABLE 1

REGRESSION ANALYSIS OF SUBSTD, SOUTH SIDE OF
CHICAGO, 1950

EXPLANATORY VARIABLE	EQUATION		
	(1)	(2)	(3)
INCOME × 10^{-3}	−.63*	−.65*	−.27
	(.25)	(.25)	(.33)
DISCBD	−.039	−.033	−.067
	(.053)	(.056)	(.058)
RAPINT	−.58	−.51	−.59
	(.41)	(.44)	(.43)
RAPSLO	.11*	.10*	.11*
	(.060)	(.063)	(.061)
MANMAJ	.008	−.042	.083
	(.30)	(.32)	(.32)
MANMIN	−.39†	−.41†	−.38†
	(.19)	(.20)	(.20)
RETMAJ	.43†	.43†	.47†
	(.18)	(.18)	(.18)
RETMIN	−.38†	−.35	−.17
	(.22)	(.22)	(.23)
NEGMAJ	.49	.38	.32
	(.45)	(.48)	(.46)
NEGMIN	−.29	−.34	−.45
	(.34)	(.38)	(.39)
OWNOCC	.29	.11	.040
	(.47)	(.62)	(1.1)
AGEDUS	1.2*	1.3*	.86*
	(.44)	(.45)	(.46)
PEROOM	.072	.005	−.085
	(.26)	(.28)	(.28)
GRODEN	.018	.022	−.036
	(.11)	(.11)	(.11)
SAMHOU	−4.0*	−3.9*	−5.1*
	(1.6)	(1.8)	(2.8)
GROPOP	−.31	−.35†	.016
	(.19)	(.21)	(.26)
PERHOU	...	−.032	−.26
		(.22)	(.23)
AGEPER	...	−3.7	8.3
		(5.9)	(7.8)
WHICOL	...	...	−4.4*
			(2.3)
SCHOOL	...	...	.080
			(.13)
ONEFAM	...	...	−.54
			(.94)
R^2	.89	.89	.91

* Significant at the 1-tail 0.10 level.
† Significant at the 2-tail 0.10 level.

CHICAGO SOUTH-SIDE COMPARISONS FOR 1950

The comparisons of dwelling-unit condition and income level by census tract for Chicago's south side in 1950 are presented in this section. First, conventional least-squares regression equations with SUBSTD as the dependent variable are presented and discussed. These are followed by similar regressions with INCOME as the dependent variable. Last to be presented and discussed are two-stage least-squares regressions, in which SUBSTD and INCOME are treated as jointly dependent. As in previous chapters the regression coefficients are shown in the body of the table on the same line as the explanatory variable designated in the stub to which they refer, and the standard error is shown in parentheses below the coefficient to which it refers.

The SUBSTD comparisons are shown in Table 1. In both equations (1) and (2) the coefficient of income is strongly negative and suggests that the proportion of dwellings which are substandard declines by about two-thirds per thousand-dollar increase in income. The elasticity of SUBSTD with respect to INCOME, evaluated at the latter's mean value, for equations (1) and (2) is about -2.5, which agrees with the values found for other cities in Chapter 8. There is a slight tendency for the proportion substandard to decline with distance from the CBD, but SUBSTD actually increases with distance in the vicinity of rapid-transit facilities. In equation (1) there are fewer poor-quality dwellings in the vicinity of the smaller manufacturing and retail centers but more in the vicinity of the major retail centers. This pattern is hard to account for on the basis of variation in housing prices, since the analysis in the last chapter suggested that housing prices are below average in the vicinity of major as well as minor manufacturing areas and above average in the vicinity of both types of retail center. The manufacturing area coefficients also lend little support to the hypothesis that a higher-than-average proportion of dwellings are in poor condition in the vicinity of manufacturing areas because of unfavorable neighborhood effects or because of a decline in the demand for housing which is located near them.

In all the equations the coefficient of NEGMAJ is positive but small relative to its standard error, and the coefficient of NEGMIN is negative. These results lend little statistical support to the hypothesis that Negroes pay greater prices for housing than whites or that they are restricted to areas of poorest housing quality. If, as some of the findings of the following section imply, the price elasticity of SUBSTD is about 3.6, a coefficient for NEGMAJ of 0.40 would imply that housing prices are about 11 percent higher for Negroes, though on statistical grounds it might be anywhere from, say, 0 to 20 percent. More surprising to me is the fact that OWNOCC's coefficient is positive in all the equations, but it, too, is small compared with its standard error. The lack of a negative association between OWNOCC and SUBSTD may result from the fact that most home owners live in housing of considerably better quality than substandard housing. While the lower price for owners which results from the federal income-tax provisions and mortgage programs may well improve the quality of housing owners inhabit, much of this improvement takes place in the opposite tail of the housing-quality distribution from substandard housing.

Of the variables that I interpret as affecting the relative supply of poor-quality housing, both AGEDUS and SAMHOU have coefficients that lend strong support to the arguments discussed earlier. The coefficient of AGEDUS is two to three times its standard error and indicates that about three times as many dwellings built before 1920 are substandard. Since SAMHOU's value varies by no more than about 0.1 among census tracts, about half again as many dwellings were substandard in the areas of the smallest values of SAMHOU or the highest population turnover. The coefficient of GROPOP is negative in (1) and (2), significantly so at the two-tail 10 percent level in the latter. This last result indicates that, if anything, fewer units are substandard in tracts whose population has grown at above-average rates and it is consistent with the hypothesis that property owners have more incentive to maintain dwellings in good condition because prices are above average in these areas. On the other hand, the coefficients of PEROOM and GRODEN, while positive, are negligible as compared with their standard errors and lend little support to the hypothesis that crowding breeds slums.

Partly to see whether, as appears to have been the case in the household-expenditure comparisons in Chapter 9, the coefficients of the manufacturing and retail center variables in (1) reflect variations in housing consumption related to population characteristics, measures of the latter were introduced into equations (2) and (3). Introducing PERHOU and AGEPER alone in equation (2) has little effect on the coefficients of variables already included in equation (1), and R^2 is virtually unchanged. The coefficient of AGEPER, though numerically smaller than its standard error in (2), is consistent in sign with the implication of the permanent-income hypothesis mentioned earlier. When the measure of occupation is introduced in equation (3), however, WHICOL's coefficient is almost twice its standard error, R^2 rises to 0.91, and several of the other coefficients change considerably. This is particularly true of the coefficient of income, which falls by one and one-half standard errors and is no longer statistically significant. I suspect that this happens because, when occupation and education are introduced, the fraction of the variance in measured income which is due to permanent differences declines, and INCOME's coefficient is biased toward zero. Partly because I believe that occupation and education reflect mostly permanent-income differences and partly because their coefficients behave rather differently in other comparisons presented in this chapter, I have omitted them from the two-stage least-squares regressions presented later in this section. Finally, note that the coefficient of ONEFAM is negative but only half its standard error; in fact, virtually no change results when this variable is added separately to the regression. This result lends little support to the hypothesis that a higher proportion of multifamily units are substandard because of decline in the demand for the services of this type of dwelling.

TABLE 2

REGRESSION ANALYSIS OF INCOME $\times$ 10^{-3}
SOUTH SIDE OF CHICAGO, 1950

EXPLANATORY VARIABLE	EQUATION		
	(4)	(5)	(6)
DISCBD	.001	.014	.011
	(.030)	(.031)	(.031)
RAPINT	−.22	−.31	−.28
	(.24)	(.24)	(.24)
RAPSLO	.044	.054	.052
	(.034)	(.036)	(.035)
MANMAJ	−.23	−.14	−.18
	(.16)	(.17)	(.17)
MANMIN	−.11	−.10	−.17
	(.11)	(.11)	(.12)
RETMAJ	.12	.10	.10
	(.11)	(.11)	(.11)
RETMIN	−.074	−.12	−.13
	(.12)	(.13)	(.13)
AGEDUS	−.46*	−.49*	−.68*
	(.23)	(.23)	(.26)
SUBSTD	−.25*	−.26*	−.29*
	(.068)	(.068)	(.074)
NEGMAJ	−1.3†	−1.3†	−1.1†
	(.17)	(.17)	(.23)
NEGMIN	−.77†	−.77†	−.46†
	(.14)	(.14)	(.20)
GRODEN	· · ·	.11	.088
		(.061)	(.064)
ONEFAM	· · ·	.022	−.54
		(.28)	(.42)
OWNOCC	· · ·	· · ·	.74
			(.39)
SAMHOU	· · ·	· · ·	.11
			(.096)
AGEPER	· · ·	· · ·	1.0
			(2.7)
R^2	.91	.91	.92

* Significant at the 1-tail 0.10 level.
† Significant at the 2-tail 0.10 level.

The comparisons of INCOME by census tract are summarized in Table 2. None of the accessibility coefficients are very large relative to their standard errors, except perhaps the coefficient of MANMAJ in equation (4). The effect of AGEDUS on location by income seems, if anything, to be stronger than for cities examined in Chapter 8; the coefficients of this variable in Table 2 suggest that the income of the inhabitants of dwellings built prior to 1920 tended to be in the order of $500 smaller in 1950 than the income of those in newer dwellings. Income is even more closely associated with dwelling-unit condition, the coefficient of SUBSTD being about four times its standard error. The coefficients of SUBSTD in Table 2 indicate that a 10 percent increase in the proportion of dwellings substandard was associated with a reduction in median income of the tracts of from $25 to $30, or of about 7 to 8 percent of the mean value for the tracts in the sample. Thus, while highly significant statistically, the effects of dwelling-unit condition on the income of the households living there seem to be quite small quantitively. Because of the functional form of the relation between income and condition, the decline in income which results from an additional substandard dwelling is larger the smaller the number of substandard dwellings. This is quite reasonable, of course, since it would seem likely that the aversion to living in the vicinity of poor-quality dwellings would increase with income. The coefficients of the dummy variables for race are significantly negative. They indicate that, at a given income level as reported by the 1950 census, Negroes lived in newer and/or better-quality dwellings than whites, hardly the result one would expect if segregation restricted Negroes to areas of the worst housing. In equation (5), adding GRODEN and ONEFAM makes little difference to the results. Their coefficients surely do not indicate that the higher-income households have stronger preferences for space, since the coefficient of ONEFAM is quite small and that of GRODEN has the wrong sign. Likewise, introducing the variables which were meant to correct deficiencies in the census-reported income data makes little difference to the results, and only the coefficient of SAMHOU has the correct sign.

So far I have suggested several times that the income of a tract may both affect and be affected by the condition of dwellings in the tract. The time has now come to give explicit attention to the joint dependency of income and dwelling-unit condition. This possibility is illustrated in Figure 2, which shows two relationships between income and condition. The *A* curves show the adjustment of dwelling-unit condition to the income of its inhabitants, the *B* curve the influence of housing quality on the households living there. Suppose now that the *A* curve shifts upward to *A'*, showing a deterioration of housing quality from some factor apart from the income of its inhabitants, because of deterioration which accompanies the aging of the housing stock, say. The proportion of dwellings which are substandard thus increases from S_1 to S_2. Because of the deterioration in housing quality, lower-income households move into the area as some previous residents move out to better quarters, and the median income of residents of the tract declines from I_1 to I_2. It might also be argued that part of the decline in income is due to the adverse effects of the housing one inhabits on one's income. I find it hard to take this argument seriously, however, since the supposed adverse effects of poor-quality housing would probably show up only after a substantial time lapse, and the change in the inhabitants of deteriorating neighborhoods is all too obvious. The induced decline in income, of course, induces a further deterioration of quality, and so forth, but, if the B curve is steeper than the A curve, as drawn in Figure 2, the process is such that INCOME and SUBSTD converge over time to the new equilibrium position, I_3, S_3 in Figure 2.[12]

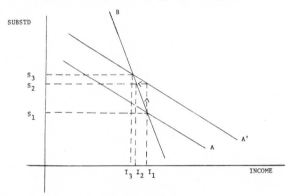

Fig. 2.—Joint Determination of Housing Quality and Income

It is well known, of course, that if two or more variables are simultaneously determined, as INCOME and SUBSTD may be, and if one or more are treated as independent in a conventional least-squares regression, the resulting estimates may be badly in error. It is also well known that if variables can be found which cause, say, the A curve in Figure 2 to shift or move to A' but does not cause the B curve to shift, consistent estimates of the parameters of the B curve may be obtained via the method of two-stage squares, and vice versa.[13] From the results shown in Tables 1 and 2 it

---

[12] Many passages written about slums can be interpreted as asserting that the equilibrium shown in Figure 2 is an unstable one and that a shift of the A curve will produce a continual decline in housing quality. The estimates in Table 3 suggest, however, that the slope of the B curve is about -5 and that of the A curve about -1, so that the equilibrium is indeed stable.

[13] This method has already been discussed in Chapter 7.

seems reasonable to suppose that RETMAJ, SAMHOU and GROPOP affect only the *A* curve, and MANMAJ, NEGMAJ and NEGMIN only the *B* curve. Also included in the analysis are DISCBD and RAPSLO, since I am especially interested in the relation of distance to quality and income for reasons detailed elsewhere, and AGEDUS, which would appear to have an important effect on both the *A* and *B* curves in Figure 2. Two-stage least-squares estimates of the two relationships were then computed. The first stage consisted of computing the conventional least-squares regressions of SUBSTD and INCOME separately on all the variables noted above in this paragraph. The second stage consisted, for the *A*-curve and similarly for the *B*-curve, of a conventional least-squares regression of SUBSTD on the value of income calculated from the first-stage regression and the actual values of the other variables on which SUBSTD was presumed to depend.

TABLE 3

TWO-STAGE AND CONVENTIONAL LEAST-SQUARES REGRESSIONS,
SOUTH SIDE OF CHICAGO, 1950

EXPLANATORY VARIABLE	DEPENDENT VARIABLE (EQUATION)			
	SUBSTD		INCOME $\times$ 10^{-3}	
	(7)[a]	(8)[b]	(9)[a]	(10)[b]
INCOME $\times$ 10^{-3}	$-.91$* (.15)	$-.81$* (.12)	$\cdots$	$\cdots$
SUBSTD	$\cdots$	$\cdots$	$-.20$* (.11)	$-.20$* (.060)
DISCBD	.055 (.039)	.045 (.037)	.024 (.026)	.024 (.020)
RAPSLO	$-.023$ (.022)	$-.021$ (.022)	.0097 (.013)	.0097 (.013)
AGEDUS	1.1* (.43)	1.3* (.39)	$-.51$* (.31)	$-.51$* (.22)
RETMAJ	.55† (.17)	.55† (.17)	$\cdots$	$\cdots$
SAMHOU	-2.6* (1.2)	-2.8* (1.2)	$\cdots$	$\cdots$
GROPOP	$-.30$† (.16)	$-.25$† (.15)	$\cdots$	$\cdots$
MANMAJ	$\cdots$	$\cdots$	$-.10$ (.14)	$-.10$ (.13)
NEGMAJ	$\cdots$	$\cdots$	-1.3† (.20)	-1.4† (.14)
NEGMIN	$\cdots$	$\cdots$	$-.78$† (.15)	$-.78$† (.14)
R^2	$\cdots$	.85	$\cdots$	.90

[a] Two-stage least-squares estimates treating SUBSTD and INCOME as simultaneously determined.
[b] Conventional least-squares estimates.
* Significant at the 1-tail 0.10 level.
† Significant at the 2-tail 0.10 level.

The two-stage least-squares estimates so obtained are shown in equations (7) and (9) in Table 3, the corresponding conventional least-squares estimates in equations (8) and (10). Clearly, there is little difference between the two sets of estimates. Thus, while it would appear that SUBSTD and INCOME are jointly determined in the manner illustrated in Figure 2, Table 3 suggests that the problem of least-squares bias is of little importance in this particular case. The R^2 in the reduced-form equations (not shown) was 0.86 for SUBSTD and 0.89 for INCOME.

TABLE 4

REGRESSION ANALYSIS OF SUBSTD AND VALHOU,

CENTRAL CITIES, 1950

EXPLANATORY VARIABLE	DEPENDENT VARIABLE (EQUATION)		
	SUBSTD		VALHOU
	(11)	(12)	(13)
INCOME × 10⁻³	−1.0*	−1.1*	4.5
	(.32)	(.34)	(7.7)
CONCST × 10²	1.7*	1.7*	−11
	(.61)	(.66)	(15)
POPNEG	.057	.12	31*
	(.75)	(.82)	(18)
OWNOCC	1.2	.57	34*
	(.78)	(.80)	(18)
AGEDUS	1.1	.93	18
	(1.1)	(1.2)	(28)
AGESMA	−.13	−.14	−.14
	(.040)	(.043)	(.97)
PEROOM	.38*	· · ·	· · ·
	(.17)		
GRODEN	−.19	−.25	1.5
	(.12)	(.13)	(2.9)
SAMHOU	−6.8*	−8.3*	50
	(2.7)	(2.8)	(63)
GROPOP	−.56†	−.67†	10†
	(.22)	(.23)	(5.2)
URBPOP	.28*	.34*	.02
	(.10)	(.11)	(2.4)
MFGEMP	.83	1.1	25
	(1.5)	(1.6)	(36)
PERHOU	−.47	.054	−6.9
	(.53)	(.52)	(12)
AGEPER	−6.2	−4.9	−.5
	(5.6)	(6.0)	(140)
WHICOL	.08	1.0	160*
	(2.7)	(2.8)	(64)
SCHOOL	−.11	−.16*	.37
	(.11)	(.11)	(2.5)
UNEMP	−3.1	−4.1	−120
	(2.9)	(3.2)	(71)
REGION	−.15	−.048	−8.0†
	(.17)	(.18)	(4.1)
R^2	.82	.78	.81

* Significant at the 1-tail 0.10 level.
† Significant at the 2-tail 0.10 level.

INTERCITY CONDITION COMPARISONS, 1950

My major reason for comparing housing quality in various central cities is to provide a check on the previous analysis among different areas of the same city. There is little reason to believe that differences in median income-levels among cities are much affected by the quality of their housing stocks, so that the problem of joint determination of income and dwelling-unit condition is not as severe as among different areas of the same city. Likewise, I find much less reason to believe that the demand for housing as among different cities is very closely related to the age of their dwelling units, as it might be among different parts of the same city. However, the relative income level of households and the relative demand for housing in the central city versus suburban areas might vary among metropolitan areas with the age and condition of the central-city housing stock. Most important of all, the greatest possible source of bias in the kind of estimates presented here is that which results from the omission of important explanatory variables that are correlated with those that are included. Since the kinds of possibly omitted variables are likely to be quite different as among cities than within any one of them, a comparison of the two types of regression estimates is likely to reveal important omissions. The other main reason for making intercity- as well as intracity-condition comparisons is that certain variables vary much more among different cities than within them. This is especially true of residential construction costs, but population growth rates as measured by GROPOP also vary much more among the various central cities studied here than among census tracts on Chicago's south side. Also, it is relatively easy to distinguish between the age of a city and the age of its dwelling units.

Table 4 presents conventional least-squares estimates of the determinants of dwelling-unit condition. Also shown is a regression equation with VALHOU, as defined earlier, but for the whole of the central city and in natural units rather than logs, as the dependent variable. Equation (13) was included as a check on the interpretation of some of the coefficients in the condition comparisons. The coefficient of INCOME in the condition regressions, equations (11) and (12), is highly significant statistically and of about the same magnitude, or even a little greater, than in the Chicago south-side comparisons presented in the previous section.[14] The coefficient

---

[14] The fact that the coefficient of INCOME in the VALHOU regression is small and less than its standard error is due, I believe, to the inclusion of variables such as SAMHOU, REGION, WHICOL, and SCHOOL, which reduce the fraction of the variation in INCOME that is due to permanent income differences. When the above noted variables are omitted, the coefficient of INCOME is 21 with a standard error of 6.5. The corresponding elasticity is $+1.0$, which agrees with values found earlier, in Chapters 8 and 9, for comparisons within cities.

of CONCST is also about three times its standard error in the SUBSTD regressions, and, while small relative to its standard error in the VALHOU regression, it is actually negative. This suggests that the price elasticity of housing demand is less than -1, and hence the elasticity of housing expenditures with respect to price is negative. The elasticities of INCOME and CONCST are quite similar numerically in the SUBSTD regressions, -3.2 and 3.6, respectively, in (12) if evaluated at the mean values of the variables. I previously found that the housing-demand elasticities of income and construction costs were about equal numerically,[15] so that the similarity of the elasticities here lends support to the belief that dwelling-unit condition largely reflects the demand for housing on the part of its inhabitants. The intercity income elasticity of housing quality is also quite similar to that found previously in this study from comparisons within cities.

The coefficients of POPNEG and OWNOCC in Table 4 are also similar to those found in the Chicago comparisons presented earlier, neither being both statistically significant and of the right sign in the condition regressions and both positive and significant in the VALHOU regression. As stressed before, it is hard to account for the greater-than-average expenditures by Negroes on the basis of their paying above-average prices for housing if the price elasticity of housing demand is -1. Furthermore, if Negroes paid above-average prices for housing in all cities, whites would pay below-average prices, and the two effects would tend to cancel out. Therefore, as I stated earlier, I am inclined to believe that the greater expenditures by Negroes result from a greater relative importance of furnishings and utilities in contract rent, higher costs of operation associated with Negro occupancy, or some similar factor affecting the rental expenditures of Negroes.

Turning now to the variables related to the relative supply of poor-quality housing, the coefficients of AGEDUS in (11) and (12) are quite comparable to the values found for the south side of Chicago in Tables 1 and 3. Here, though, the standard error is so much larger than previously that the coefficient is not statistically significant. The relatively large standard error is partly due to the relatively high intercorrelation of AGEDUS and GROPOP, but, in contrast with the within-city data examined earlier, the simple correlation coefficient between AGEDUS and SUBSTD is practically zero among cities. It is also interesting to note that the coefficient of AGEDUS is actually positive in the VALHOU regression, instead of negative and large compared with its standard error for the previous within-city comparisons. It would thus seem hard to sustain the

---

[15] "The Demand for Non-Farm Housing."

hypothesis that dwellings necessarily deteriorate in quality with age. Further complicating the relation of age to quality is the fact that the co-efficient of AGESMA is actually negative and three times its standard error. One possible explanation is that interest rates are lower in the older SMA's, many of which are important financial centers. But if this were so I would expect a positive coefficient for AGESMA in the VALHOU regression rather than the negative one observed.

Of the other relative supply variables, the coefficient of GRODEN is actually negative in the SUBSTD regressions, and the coefficient of SAMHOU is statistically significant and negative and of comparable magnitude to those found in Table 1, although a little smaller. Similarly, the coefficient of GROPOP is negative and two and one-half times as large as its standard error and about one standard error larger numerically than in the Chicago comparisons. The coefficient of URBPOP is positive and highly significant statistically, and it indicates that a sixfold increase in urbanized area size has about the same effect on dwelling-unit condition as a decrease in income of $500. If such a size difference meant one and one-half hour's additional travel time per working day, and workers valued time at $1.50 per hour, real income would be approximately $500 per year smaller in the larger city. But if this interpretation were correct, I would expect a negative coefficient for URBPOP in the VALHOU regression. Alternatively, a doubling of urbanized area size would have about the same effect on SUBSTD as a 10 percent increase in construction costs. Since land's relative share in the production of houses was about one-tenth that of non-land factors in 1950, and I would expect land rents to be roughly proportional to size, a doubling of size would have about the same effect on housing prices as a 10 percent increase in construction costs. Higher housing prices, however, would not affect expenditures on housing if the price elasticity of housing demand were unity. This interpretation, however, is not wholly satisfactory either, if quality refers primarily to struc-tural features, since higher construction costs would induce a substitution of land for structures, and higher land rents the reverse, in addition to their effect on housing prices. If, as a third alternative, living conditions in central cities became more unpleasant as size increased and the demand for, and hence condition of, central-city housing declined, I would expect VALHOU to be negatively related to URBPOP.

The greatest difference between the results obtained in the previous section and in Table 4 is in the coefficient of PEROOM. While the latter's coefficient was negligible in the Chicago comparisons, it is positive and more than twice its standard error here. Because the condition of dwellings and the space per person are different aspects of the consumption of housing, I suspected that the coefficient of PEROOM reflected the effects of omitted variables which influence the consumption of housing, and hence both SUBSTD and PEROOM. The calculated residuals from an earlier regression with SUBSTD dependent and the last four variables listed in Table 4 and PEROOM omitted were plotted against the residuals from a regression of PEROOM on the same set of independent variables. The scatter showed a strong association between the two sets of residuals. It was partly for this reason that the last four variables listed in Table 4 were added to the SUBSTD regression. Including them, as in equation (11), reduced the coefficient of PEROOM somewhat but failed to eliminate its effect. Comparing the coefficients of equations (11) and (12), one sees that it makes little difference to the coefficients of the other variables when PEROOM is excluded from the SUBSTD regression.[16] This observation is consistent with the hypothesis that the coefficient of PEROOM reflects the effects of correlated residuals in SUBSTD and PEROOM regression equations.

For a more conclusive test of the hypothesis that the coefficient of PEROOM is a proxy for omitted determinants of housing consumption and quality, I estimated the coefficients of the important determinants of SUBSTD using the method of two-stage least-squares. If my hypothesis is correct that the coefficient of PEROOM in (11) is due to least-squares bias rather than to the fact that crowding breeds slums, using the latter method of estimation should reduce or eliminate the coefficient of PEROOM in the substandard equation. The results presented in Chapter 9, as well as Margaret Reid's more comprehensive analysis of persons per room among various cities,[17] suggest that INCOME, OWNOCC, and PERHOU are important determinants of PEROOM. Miss Reid's work also suggests that crowding is greater the greater are construction costs and hence housing prices;[18] therefore CONCST was also included as a determinant of PEROOM. As a first step in the two-stage least-squares procedure, a conventional least-squares regression of PEROOM on the variables noted above plus GROPOP, AGESMA, URBPOP, and SAMHOU, variables which appear to have an important influence on SUBSTD, was run, and the calculated values of PEROOM were obtained. In the second stage, a conventional least-squares regression of SUBSTD on the calculated values of PEROOM and the other variables shown in Table 5 was run. The results shown in Table 5 indeed suggest that PEROOM itself has little effect on SUBSTD. In equation (15) the coefficient of PEROOM is 0.39, but the

---

[16] Deleting PEROOM has little effect on the coefficient of INCOME because, with all the other variables used in (12) included, the partial correlation coefficient of PEROOM and INCOME is essentially zero.

[17] *Housing and Income*, chap. 12, esp. table 61.

[18] *Ibid.*, p. 337.

two-stage least-squares estimate in (14) is only 0.15, three-fifths smaller, and is no longer significant statistically. None of the coefficients of the other variables in Table 5 differ very much as between equations (14) and (15). It would appear, therefore, that least-squares bias in the conventional least-squares regression presented earlier in Table 4 is confined mostly to the coefficient of PEROOM.

TABLE 5

TWO-STAGE AND CONVENTIONAL LEAST-SQUARES
REGRESSIONS, SUBSTD INTERCITY, 1950

EXPLANATORY VARIABLE	EQUATION	
	(14)[a]	(15)[b]
INCOME × 10^{-3}	−.67*	−.61*
	(.21)	(.20)
CONCST × 10^2	.72	.93*
	(.67)	(.62)
AGESMA	−.11	−.10
	(.036)	(.035)
PEROOM	.15	.39*
	(.24)	(.14)
SAMHOU	−2.9*	−2.5*
	(1.4)	(1.2)
GROPOP	−.56†	−.50†
	(.16)	(.15)
URBPOP	.15*	.11*
	(.093)	(.085)
R^2	⋯	.64

[a] Two-stage least-squares treating SUBSTD and PEROOM as simultaneously determined.
[b] Conventional least-squares.
* Significant at the 1-tail 0.10 level.
† Significant at the 2-tail 0.10 level.

CHICAGO SOUTH-SIDE COMPARISONS FOR 1960

As a further check on my results, the regression analysis of dwelling-unit condition and location of households by income for the south side of Chicago were repeated for 1960. The only additional experimenting done was the use of several variables made possible by the 1960 census data. These include the alternative measures of condition and crowding discussed in the preceding chapter and 1950-tract median income, in natural units and designated INCM50, to test for the existence of lagged adjustment in the location of households by income level and dwelling-unit condition. As in the second section, I present conventional least-squares regression equations with SUBSTD and then with INCOME as the dependent variable. These are followed by a two-stage least-squares analysis which treats SUBSTD, INCOME, PEROOM, and GRODEN as simultaneously determined. First, however, I would like to discuss briefly the matter of lag in the adjustment of income and condition to changing conditions.

It is obvious that, despite several dramatic instances of rapid neighborhood conversion to low-income residents and poor-quality housing, the residents and housing stock of an area usually change slowly over time. Buildings usually depreciate and deteriorate slowly and steadily, and old residents move out and new ones move in primarily with a change in job of the household head or when the composition of the household changes because of the death or retirement of its head, children leaving home, and so forth. One might thus expect that, everything else affecting location by income being the same, the greater the median income of a tract in 1950 the greater would it be in 1960. Further insight into the determinants of dwelling-unit condition can be gained by looking at its relation to the level of income a decade earlier. For example, suppose first that over the decade the income level of an area has declined but the condition of its housing stock has not yet fully adjusted to the new, lower income-level of its inhabitants. In 1960, dwelling-unit condition would be better than average for the income level of its current residents, or the proportion of dwellings substandard would tend to be smaller. Thus, given 1960 income, the greater the 1950 income of the area the smaller would be SUBSTD if housing quality deteriorated slowly over time when lower-income households move into an area. Conversely, if housing quality deteriorates first, and, in response to this, the income level of an area's residents declines but does not adjust completely by the end of the decade, there would be a greater proportion of dwellings substandard the higher the 1950 level of income relative to the 1960 level. The coefficient of 1950 income, here designated INCM50 and measured by the variable used to measure income in the 1950 comparisons, in the 1960 condition regression thus provides an alternative test of whether housing quality is primarily adjusted to the income level of its inhabitants or whether the reverse is true. Income a decade earlier could not be included in the 1950 comparisons because no tract income data are available from the 1940 census.

The conventional least-squares regressions with SUBSTD as the dependent variable are shown in Table 6. The most obvious and important difference when compared with the 1950 results is in the coefficient of INCOME. This coefficient was about ten times as large numerically in 1950 as in equations (16) and (17) and three times its standard error; in 1960, however, the coefficient of income no longer appears to be larger than its standard error. Conversely, the coefficient of PEROOM is three times its standard error in (16) and (17), even larger than in the 1950 intercity condition comparisons; it is still significantly greater than zero at the 0.10

TABLE 6

REGRESSION ANALYSIS OF SUBSTD, SOUTH SIDE OF
CHICAGO, 1960

EXPLANATORY VARIABLE	EQUATION		
	(16)	(17)	(18)
INCOME × 10^{-3}	−.069	−.054	−.20
	(.18)	(.21)	(.18)
DISCBD	−.015	−.0023	−.010
	(.085)	(.088)	(.076)
RAPINT	.26	.16	−.52
	(.60)	(.60)	(.58)
RAPSLO	.016	.036	.11
	(.094)	(.096)	(.088)
MANMAJ	.19	.15	−.47
	(.46)	(.46)	(.45)
MANMIN	−.14	−.26	−.60†
	(.31)	(.32)	(.30)
RETMAJ	.19	.14	.33
	(.29)	(.28)	(.26)
RETMIN	−.77†	−.72†	−.81†
	(.33)	(.33)	(.29)
NEGMAJ	−.074	.27	−.21
	(.58)	(.60)	(.52)
NEGMIN	−.040	.23	.13
	(.46)	(.47)	(.41)
OWNOCC	1.0	.76	.94
	(1.1)	(1.2)	(.95)
AGEDUS	.48	.23	1.6*
	(1.1)	(1.2)	(1.0)
PEROOM	1.8*	1.5*	.70*
	(.47)	(.49)	(.52)
GRODEN	.15	.14	.19
	(.19)	(.19)	(.17)
SAMHOU	.44	−.26	−.24
	(1.3)	(1.4)	(1.2)
GROPOP	−.41	−.24	−.28
	(.27)	(.28)	(.25)
PERHOU	−1.4†	−1.4†	−.74†
	(.34)	(.34)	(.35)
AGEPER	−1.1	−.19	−4.9
	(4.7)	(5.4)	(4.3)
WHICOL	⋯	.13	⋯
		(2.5)	
SCHOOL	⋯	−.35*	⋯
		(.23)	
ONEFAM	⋯	−.19	⋯
		(.80)	
INCM50	⋯	⋯	−1.1†
			(.31)
R^2	.83	.84	.87

* Significant at the 1-tail 0.10 level.
† Significant at the 2-tail 0.10 level.

level when INCM50 is added in equation (18), though only about half as
great as in (16) and (17). Unlike the calculations for 1950, the coefficient
of AGEDUS does not exceed its standard error except when INCM50 is
added, and the coefficient of SAMHOU is much smaller than in 1950 and

negligible in relation to its standard error. On the other hand, for 1960 the coefficient of PERHOU is significantly negative statistically. As in 1950, the coefficient of DISCBD is negative, but smaller numerically and again not statistically significant, and RAPSLO's coefficient is again positive though not significant. The coefficients of the manufacturing- and retail-area dummy variables are similar to their values for 1950, but MANMAJ's coefficient is negative in equation (18), that of RETMAJ is less strongly positive, and that of RETMIN more strongly negative. The 1960 results thus give even less support than the 1950 ones to the hypothesis that dwellings have deteriorated in the vicinity of manufacturing districts because of a decline in demand. The coefficient of NEGMAJ is again small relative to its standard error and actually negative in (16) and (18), the negative value implying that prices are about 6 percent lower in Negro areas. The coefficient of OWNOCC is again positive and about the size of its standard error, and the coefficient of GRODEN more strongly positive than before but not statistically significant. In one or two regressions run, however, the results of which are not shown here, the coefficient of GRODEN did just become significant at the one-tail 10 percent level. Again as in 1950, the coefficient of GROPOP is negative but not strongly significant. In equation (17) one sees that, as in the 1950 intercity comparisons and unlike the earlier comparisons for South Chicago, the coefficient of WHICOL is not significant, statistically or practically, but that for SCHOOL is. Finally, one sees that there is a rather strong negative relationship between INCM50 and SUBSTD; this indicates that, if anything, dwelling-unit condition adjusts over time to changes in the income level of its inhabitants rather than the reverse.[19]

The results of the conventional least-squares regression analysis with INCOME dependent are shown in Table 7. As for 1950 there is little relation between INCOME and the various accessibility measures except when INCM50 is added in equation (21), and most of the accessibility coefficients in (21) do not seem very sensible. The coefficient of AGEDUS is negative and significant as in 1950 though numerically larger, especially in equation (21). The fact that these coefficients are numerically larger may suggest that the aversion to older dwellings on the part of higher-income groups may increase as income does. The coefficients of SUBSTD in (19)

---

[19] When the alternative measure of condition, the log of the proportion of units deteriorating or dilapidated and/or without private bath, was used as dependent, the coefficients of most variables were about the same, but R^2 was slightly smaller than in (16). The same was true when the proportion of units with more than 0.75 rather than 1 person per room was used as a measure of crowding, though for the alternative measure of crowding the t-ratio was noticeably greater. When NETDEN, as defined earlier, rather than GRODEN, was used to measure population density, the latter's t-ratio was only about 0.5, but R^2 was about the same as in (16).

TABLE 7
REGRESSION ANALYSIS OF INCOME × 10^{-3}
SOUTH SIDE OF CHICAGO, 1960

EXPLANATORY VARIABLE	EQUATION		
	(19)	(20)	(21)
DISCBD	.052	.055	.024
	(.077)	(.077)	(.062)
RAPINT	.32	.26	1.0†
	(.56)	(.57)	(.47)
RAPSLO	−.090	−.074	−.16*
	(.081)	(.084)	(.066)
MANMAJ	−.20	−.082	.50
	(.41)	(.43)	(.35)
MANMIN	−.082	−.060	.44†
	(.25)	(.25)	(.22)
RETMAJ	−.21	−.24	−.36
	(.27)	(.27)	(.22)
RETMIN	.49	.41	.50†
	(.32)	(.34)	(.26)
AGEDUS	−.77*	−.77*	−1.5*
	(.53)	(.53)	(.44)
SUBSTD	−.27*	−.26*	.16
	(.11)	(.11)	(.11)
NEGMAJ	−1.8†	−1.8†	−1.1†
	(.30)	(.30)	(.27)
NEGMIN	−.84†	−.82†	−.67†
	(.30)	(.30)	(.24)
LANRES	···	.58	···
		(.72)	
INCM50 × 10^{-3}	···	···	1.2*
			(.21)
R^2	.79	.79	.87

* Significant at the 1-tail 0.10 level.
† Significant at the 2-tail 0.10 level.

and (20) are almost identical with the corresponding ones for 1950, though when INCM50 is added SUBSTD's coefficient becomes positive, and the coefficients of the Negro area dummy variables are practically the same as for 1950. Thus, the 1960 results are quite similar to those obtained for 1950.[20] For 1960 I also included LANRES, as defined in Chapter 9, to test the hypothesis that higher-income households have a stronger aversion to living in the vicinity of non-residential land uses. As seen in equation (20), its coefficient, while positive, is smaller than its standard error; quan-

---

[20] The results for 1960 were also similar to those for 1950 in that when GRODEN and ONEFAM were added to the variables shown in equation (19) neither was significant in the direction predicted by the hypothesis that higher-income households have stronger preferences for space and privacy, and all three of the variables introduced to correct for deficiencies in the census-reported income measure had the wrong sign. When the alternative measure of condition was substituted for the 1950 measure in equation (19), the *t*-ratio of the coefficient of SUBSTD and R^2 were only slightly greater.

titatively, the coefficient implies that in comparing tracts with three-quarters and one-quarter of their land area in residential uses, INCOME is only $300, or 2 percent, higher in the tract with the larger residential land area. When INCM50 was included in equation (21), the results were rather different. As noted above, several of the other coefficients changed markedly, especially that of SUBSTD, R^2 rose from 0.79 to 0.87, and the coefficient of INCM50 was five times as large as its standard error. It would thus appear that there is a strong tendency for relatively high-income areas to remain so over time.

For the 1960 data I repeated the two-stage least-squares analysis which treated SUBSTD and INCOME as simultaneously determined. Because I suspected that the positive and significant coefficient of PEROOM in the condition comparisons for 1960 was the result of the same kind of least-squares bias that showed up in the intercity condition comparisons, PEROOM was treated as simultaneously determined in the two-stage least-squares analysis as well.[21] Also, since in some of the SUBSTD regression equations I ran, which are not shown here, the coefficient of GRODEN was positive and barely significant, I decided to treat it as jointly dependent also. PEROOM and GRODEN were also treated this way in order to determine whether the significantly positive coefficients of SUBSTD in the density comparisons for 1960 reflected least-squares bias rather than above-average housing prices in areas of poor-quality housing. In the first stage of the analysis SUBSTD, INCOME, PEROOM, and GRODEN were regressed in turn on all the other previously used variables that I felt might have a significant effect on one or more of the jointly dependent variables. These explanatory variables included all the accessibility measures, AGEDUS, the Negro population dummy variables, OWNOCC, PERHOU, AGEPER, SAMHOU, GROPOP, and INCM50.[22] Examination of the anticipated and estimated values of the coefficients of the four regression equations, each of which has one of the variables treated as jointed determined written on the left-hand side, indicated that the rank condition for identification of each of the equations shown below in Tables

---

[21] Because PEROOM was treated as a dependent variable in these comparisons, the square-root rather than log form was used. As pointed out in Chapter 9, the square-root form seemed more nearly to equalize the residual variance of PEROOM.

[22] Both measures of condition and of crowding were used alternatively as dependent in these reduced-form regression equations. In each case, the regression using the 1950 measure as dependent had the larger R^2. Considering this result, as well as other comparisons made earlier, there appears to be no very strong reason for believing that the alternative measures of condition and crowding that can be constructed from the 1960 census tract data are superior to the measures used for the 1950 comparisons. For this reason, the 1950 measures were used in the two-stage least-squares regressions which follow.

8 through 11 is probably satisfied. The calculated values of the simultaneously determined variables as well as the values of various combinations of predetermined variables were used in the two-stage least-squares
regressions whose coefficients are shown in Tables 8 through 11. Also
shown for each of the dependent variables is the conventional least-squares
regression corresponding to the two-stage least-squares regression that
seemed to be the most satisfactory.

TABLE 8

TWO-STAGE AND CONVENTIONAL LEAST-SQUARES REGRESSIONS
SUBSTD, SOUTH SIDE OF CHICAGO, 1960

EXPLANATORY VARIABLE	EQUATION			
	(22)[a]	(23)[a]	(24)[a]	(25)[b]
INCOME × 10^{-3}	−1.0*	−.71	−1.3	.049
	(.59)	(.66)	(1.1)	(.18)
DISCBD	−.082	−.030	−.0092	.090
	(.10)	(.097)	(.11)	(.067)
RAPSLO	−.054	−.060	−.073	−.066
	(.049)	(.047)	(.055)	(.035)
RETMAJ	· · ·	.52†	.31	.69†
		(.31)	(.44)	(.23)
NEGMAJ	· · ·	· · ·	−1.0	· · ·
			(1.4)	
NEGMIN	· · ·	· · ·	−.63	· · ·
			(1.0)	
AGEDUS	−.75	−.30	−1.5	.83
	(1.7)	(1.6)	(2.5)	(1.0)
PEROOM	1.2	2.3	−2.2	3.6*
	(5.4)	(7.8)	(10.8)	(2.6)
GRODEN	−.78	−.69	−.32	−.075
	(.34)	(.31)	(.62)	(.14)
SAMHOU	· · ·	−.34	−2.4	−.69
		(1.7)	(3.6)	(.99)
GROPOP	−.25	−.21	−.44	−.24
	(.35)	(.33)	(.48)	(.25)
PERHOU	−1.5†	−1.5†	−1.0	−.70†
	(.53)	(.59)	(.91)	(.32)
INCM50 × 10^{-3}	.010	−.16	−.13	−.94*
	(.52)	(.49)	(.54)	(.27)
R^2	· · ·	· · ·	· · ·	.81

[a] Two-stage least-squares estimates treating SUBSTD, INCOME, PEROOM and
GRODEN as simultaneously determined.
[b] Conventional least-squares estimates.
* Significant at the 1-tail 0.10 level.
† Significant at the 2-tail 0.10 level.

The coefficients of the SUBSTD equation are shown in Table 8. Comparison of the coefficients in the first three columns estimated by two-stage
least-squares with the conventional least-squares estimates in the last
column reveals several important instances of least-squares bias. Most
important, perhaps, is in the case of the coefficient of income, which is the
same magnitude as that found for 1950 and statistically significant in (22)

when estimated by the two-stage least-squares method but small and positive when estimated by conventional least-squares. Conversely, the coefficient of PEROOM is statistically significant in equation (25) but much smaller numerically, unstable, and not statistically significant when estimated two-stage least-squares in (22) through (24). Also interesting is the fact that the coefficient of AGEDUS is positive though smaller than its standard error in (25) and negative in (22) through (24), whereas the apparent significance of INCM50 in (25) would seem to be due to least-squares bias.

Otherwise the coefficients seem to agree with what was found in Table 6. In particular, the coefficients of DISCBD, GROPOP, and SAMHOU are negative but not statistically significant, that of GRODEN is even more negative in the two-stage than in the conventional least-squares regression, and the coefficient of PERHOU is significantly negative and more so in (23) than in (25). Note, too, that when the Negro-area dummy variables are included in (24) their coefficients are actually negative and absurdly large numerically. The R^2 in the SUBSTD reduced-form equation was 0.86. Probably because collinearity becomes a serious problem in the two-stage regressions shown in Table 8, many of the coefficients shown are not, by themselves, very reliable statistically. But their general consistency with the results previously presented in this chapter suggests to me that differences in dwelling-unit condition are primarily the result of differences in the incomes of their inhabitants.

Differences between the two-stage and conventional least-squares estimates of the other three equations are much less important than for estimates of the SUBSTD equation presented above, and collinearity is not much of a problem. None of the coefficients in equations (27) and (28) in Table 9, which are estimates of the determinants of location by income, differ by more than about one standard error from each other except for the coefficients of PEROOM. Again, in Table 9 there is no tendency for household income to increase with distance from the city center, but income varies inversely with the age of the dwellings. As in the last of the regressions shown in Table 7, the coefficient of condition is not of any significance, but income in 1960 tended to be greater the greater was income in 1950. The negative and significant coefficient of PEROOM would seem to suggest that higher-income households have an aversion to living in the vicinity of those households occupying little space per person. If PEROOM is included among the independent variables in equation (21), its coefficient has a t-ratio of -3.6, and R^2 increases from 0.87 to 0.89. The coefficients of the Negro area dummy variables fall numerically to -0.55 and -0.28, the latter for NEGMIN becoming non-significant, and those of several of the accessibility variables decline by about one standard error. It appears, therefore, that a good part of the tendency, which was apparent earlier in Tables 2 and 7, for Negroes to inhabit housing which is newer and of better quality for their incomes was due to the omission of PEROOM from the regression equations. But Table 9 also suggests that a part of this tendency may be due to least-squares bias, since the coefficients of the Negro-area dummy variables in equation (27) are only about one-tenth as large numerically as those in the corresponding conventional least-squares regression, equation (28). R^2 in the reduced form for INCOME is 0.90.

TABLE 9

Two-Stage and Conventional Least-Squares
Regressions INCOME × 10^{-3}, South Side of
Chicago, 1960

Explanatory Variable	Equation		
	(26)[a]	(27)[a]	(28)[b]
DISCBD	−.049	−.020	−.0082
	(.054)	(.060)	(.051)
RAPSLO	−.023	−.028	−.030
	(.027)	(.028)	(.027)
MANMAJ	. . .	.32	.32
		(.29)	(.27)
RETMIN	. . .	.32	.41†
		(.25)	(.21)
AGEDUS	−1.1*	−1.4*	−1.6*
	(.46)	(.49)	(.40)
SUBSTD	−.15	−.050	.057
	(.15)	(.18)	(.094)
NEGMAJ	−.12	−.026	−.31
	(.41)	(.41)	(.32)
NEGMIN	−.006	−.024	−.23
	(.29)	(.29)	(.25)
INCM50 × 10^{-3}	.39*	.46*	.67*
	(.24)	(.25)	(.18)
PEROOM	−7.2*	−7.3*	−5.6*
	(1.9)	(1.9)	(1.4)
GRODEN	−.16	−.16	−.043
	(.20)	(.23)	(.12)
R^2	. . .	. . .	.88

[a] Two-stage least-squares estimates treating SUBSTD, INCOME, PEROOM and GRODEN as simultaneously determined.
[b] Conventional least-squares estimates.
* Significant at the 1-tail 0.10 level.
† Significant at the 2-tail 0.10 level.

There are few instances of least-squares bias to be found in the estimates of the PEROOM (which is in square-root form here) equations in Table 10. Comparing equations (30) and (32) one sees that the coefficient of SUBSTD is less than one standard error smaller in the two-stage than in the conventional least-squares regression. Because it is treated as jointly dependent in (30), its standard error in much larger, however. It would

TABLE 10

TWO-STAGE AND CONVENTIONAL LEAST-SQUARES REGRESSIONS
PEROOM,[c] SOUTH SIDE OF CHICAGO, 1960

EXPLANATORY VARIABLE	EQUATION			
	(29)[a]	(30)[a]	(31)[a]	(32)[b]
DISCBD	.0044	.0001	.0007	.0007
	(.0030)	(.0030)	(.0034)	(.0026)
RAPSLO	−.0043	−.0032	−.0034	−.0030
	(.0020)	(.0019)	(.0020)	(.0017)
AGEDUS	· · ·	−.098*	−.097*	−.093*
		(.028)	(.029)	(.026)
INCOME × 10⁻³	−.036*	−.041*	−.046*	−.026*
	(.019)	(.018)	(.024)	(.0062)
NEGMAJ	· · ·	· · ·	−.010	· · ·
			(.034)	
NEGMIN	· · ·	· · ·	−.013	· · ·
			(.026)	
SUBSTD	.007	.009	.007	.012†
	(.015)	(.014)	(.016)	(.0046)
OWNOCC	−.13*	−.15*	−.14*	−.21*
	(.050)	(.047)	(.051)	(.038)
PERHOU	.084†	.079†	.078†	.090†
	(.028)	(.026)	(.028)	(.013)
AGEPER	−.41*	−.15	−.13	−.31*
	(.19)	(.19)	(.20)	(.17)
SAMHOU	−.10*	−.087*	−.11*	−.062*
	(.052)	(.048)	(.076)	(.044)
GRODEN	.004	.003	.000	.0056
	(.016)	(.015)	(.018)	(.0063)
R^2	· · ·	· · ·	· · ·	.92

[a] Two-stage least-squares estimates treating SUBSTD, INCOME, PEROOM, and GRODEN as simultaneously determined.
[b] Conventional least-squares estimates.
[c] In square-root form.
* Significant at the 1-tail 0.10 level.
† Significant at the 2-tail 0.10 level.

appear, therefore, that the greater crowding observed in areas of poor-quality housing in 1960 in Chapter 9 is not because crowding breeds slums but may well be because housing prices were above average in poor-quality housing areas. When one compares the coefficients of INCOME in (30) and (32), it would appear that, if anything, the conventional least-squares estimate is biased somewhat toward zero. It is also interesting to note that the coefficients of AGEDUS are strongly negative in Table 10. This might be accounted for by below-average housing prices in areas of older housing. The coefficient of OWNOCC is also somewhat smaller in (30) than in (32). The fact that the coefficients of OWNOCC and especially AGEPER are numerically smaller in the two-stage than in the conventional least-squares regressions tends to support the hypothesis that permanent income is a better measure than census-reported current income of the variable upon which housing consumption is based. When INCOME is treated as simultaneously determined, as in (29) through (31), the bias due to measurement error is eliminated, and its coefficient becomes numerically larger. At the same time, the coefficients of AGEPER and OWNOCC, which pick up part of the permanent income effect in the conventional least-squares regression, no longer do so in the two-stage least-squares regressions. Finally, when the Negro-area variables are included in equation (31), their coefficients are both negative as they were in the SUBSTD comparison in Table 8, though quite small. This result lends no support whatsoever to the hypothesis that housing prices in Negro areas are above those in white areas. In PEROOM's reduced form $R^2 = 0.93$.

Two-stage and conventional least-squares estimates of the population density equation are shown in Table 11. Because the results appeared to differ when gross and net densities were used in Chapter 9, both measures

TABLE 11

TWO-STAGE AND CONVENTIONAL LEAST-SQUARES REGRESSIONS,
POPULATION DENSITY, SOUTH SIDE OF CHICAGO, 1960

EXPLANATORY VARIABLE	DEPENDENT VARIABLE (EQUATION)			
	GRODEN		NETDEN	
	(33)[a]	(34)[b]	(35)[a]	(36)[b]
DISCBD	−.10	−.10*	−.057*	−.061*
	(.085)	(.062)	(.033)	(.032)
RAPINT	.70	.63*	.19	.22
	(.63)	(.45)	(.24)	(.23)
RAPSLO	−.10	−.084	.027	.025
	(.092)	(.066)	(.035)	(.034)
MANMAJ	−.62	−.69†	−.009	−.030
	(.46)	(.33)	(.18)	(.17)
MANMIN	−.59†	−.25	−.16	−.19†
	(.35)	(.20)	(.14)	(.11)
RETMAJ	.31	.28	.034	.055
	(.30)	(.22)	(.12)	(.11)
RETMIN	.22	.35	.062	.0089
	(.38)	(.26)	(.15)	(.23)
AGEDUS	−.72	−.16	−.023	.086
	(.79)	(.46)	(.30)	(.24)
INCOME × 10⁻³	−.88*	.059	−.059	−.068
	(.56)	(.13)	(.21)	(.067)
NEGMAJ	.80*	.89*	.29*	.30*
	(.56)	(.34)	(.20)	(.18)
NEGMIN	.50*	.44*	.21*	.30*
	(.37)	(.26)	(.14)	(.14)
SUBSTD	−.28	.083	.13	.070
	(.29)	(.090)	(.11)	(.046)
PEROOM	−11	−2.0	−.15	−.005
	(4.7)	(.69)	(1.8)	(.36)
R^2	...	.61	...	.79

[a] Two-stage least-squares estimates treating SUBSTD, INCOME, PEROOM and density as simultaneously determined.
[b] Conventional least-squares estimates.
* Significant at the 1-tail 0.10 level.
† Significant at the 2-tail 0.10 level.

were used here as well. For analyzing the determinants of the intensity of residential land use, net density is the more relevant measure; like GRODEN, NETDEN is in natural log form and is identical with the measure used in Chapter 9. Comparing the coefficients of SUBSTD in (35) and (36) one sees that the two-stage estimate is about one standard error larger than the conventional least-squares estimate, which is itself virtually identical with that found for 1960 in Chapter 9. It appears, then, that the earlier coefficient reflects the effect of above-average housing prices in areas of poor-housing quality rather than the influence of population densities on housing quality. In Table 11 the coefficients of the Negro-area variables are about the same magnitude as observed in Chapter 9 for 1960, but because of their smaller standard errors they are both statistically significant here. The quantitative implications for the Negro housing-price differential are similar to those noted in Chapter 9, however; comparing the coefficients of NEGMAJ and DISCBD in (35), a 5 percent differential is again implied. Finally, note that there is virtually no difference of any significance, statistical or practical, between the two-stage and conventional least-squares estimates in equations (35) and (36). It would appear, therefore, that the estimates presented in Chapter 9 are not subject to serious least-squares biases. The R^2's in the reduced-form equations for GRODEN and NETDEN are 0.68 and 0.89, respectively—comparable with but even higher than those found in Chapter 9 for 1960.

TABLE 12*a*

SUBSTD RESIDUALS BY SECTOR, SOUTH SIDE OF CHICAGO, 1950 AND 1960

| | SIGN OF RESIDUAL | | | | |
| | 1950 | | 1960 | | |
	+	−	+	−	Total
SECTR1	7	10	10	7	17
SECTR2	9	8	6	11	17
SECTR3	7	10	12	5	17
SECTR4	9	9	8	10	18
Total	32	37	36	33	69

| $X^2(3) = 0.76$ | $X^2(3) = 4.98$ |
| Pr. $\cong$ 0.90 | Pr. $\cong$ 0.20 |

As a further step in the analysis of dwelling-unit condition and the location of households by income, I examined the residuals from the Chicago south-side regressions for sector variation and for correlation over time. Sectors were defined in much the same way as in Chapter 9, but, because a different sample of tracts was used here, the radials from the Loop separating tracts into sectors were drawn a little differently. Table

12*a* shows the signs of the computed residuals from the SUBSTD regressions, equation (7) for 1950, and equation (23) for 1960, by sectors. In neither of the two years does there appear to be significant differences by sector, and the pattern of signs by sector appears to be rather different for the two years. There appears to be a positive association between the residuals for 1950 and 1960, as shown by Table 12*b*, but this association

TABLE 12*b*
SUBSTD RESIDUALS, SOUTH CHICAGO,
1950 VERSUS 1960

SIGN, 1950	SIGN, 1960		
	+	−	Total
+	20	12	32
−	16	21	37
Total	36	33	69
$X^2(1) = 2.55$		Pr. > 0.10	

is decidedly weaker than that observed for VALHOU and VALAND in Chapter 10. As Table 13*a* shows, there is also little tendency toward sectoral differences in the residuals from the INCOME regressions, equation (9) for 1950 and equation (27) for 1960. There is, again, little association between the income residuals for 1950 and 1960 in Table 13*b*, but this fact is not surprising since INCM50 was included in the 1960 regressions. Finally, as shown in Table 14, there is actually a rather strong positive association between the residuals in the SUBSTD and INCOME regressions for 1950 and for 1960. A positive association, of course, is quite the contrary to what would be expected if some important determinant of dwelling-unit condition and the income of the residents of an area had been omitted from the comparisons. On the whole, there does not

TABLE 13*a*
INCOME RESIDUALS BY SECTOR, SOUTH SIDE OF CHICAGO, 1950 AND 1960

	SIGN OF RESIDUAL				
	1950		1960		
	+	−	+	−	Total
SECTR1	10	7	12	5	17
SECTR2	11	6	7	10	17
SECTR3	7	10	9	8	17
SECTR4	8	10	8	10	18
Total	36	33	36	33	69
	$X^2(3) = 2.63$		$X^2(3) = 3.57$		
	Pr. $\cong$ 0.50		Pr. $\cong$ 0.30		

TABLE 13*b*

INCOME RESIDUALS, SOUTH SIDE OF CHICAGO,
1950 VERSUS 1960

SIGN, 1950	SIGN, 1960		
	+	−	Total
+	21	15	36
−	15	18	33
Total	36	33	69

$$X^2(1) = 1.14$$
$$\text{Pr.} \cong 0.30$$

appear to be any strong departure from randomness in the condition and income residuals. The actual and calculated values of SUBSTD and INCOME from equations (23) and (27) are plotted in Figures 3 and 4, respectively. There appears to be little tendency for the residual variance in either (23) or (27) to vary along the regression plane. Neither scatter appears to have any noticeable non-linearity.

As a final comparison I reestimated the SUBSTD regressions for the south side of Chicago for both 1950 and 1960 using conventional least-squares, retaining only the more important explanatory variables. I did so

TABLE 14*a*

SUBSTD VERSUS INCOME RESIDUALS, SOUTH SIDE OF
CHICAGO, 1950

SIGN, SUBSTD	SIGN, INCOME		
	+	−	Total
+	21	11	32
−	15	22	37
Total	36	33	69

$$X^2(1) = 4.33 \qquad \text{Pr.} < 0.05$$

TABLE 14*b*

SUBSTD VERSUS INCOME RESIDUALS, SOUTH SIDE OF
CHICAGO, 1960

SIGN, SUBSTD	SIGN, INCOME		
	+	−	Total
+	25	11	36
−	11	22	33
Total	36	33	69

$$X^2(1) = 9.00 \qquad \text{Pr.} < 0.01$$

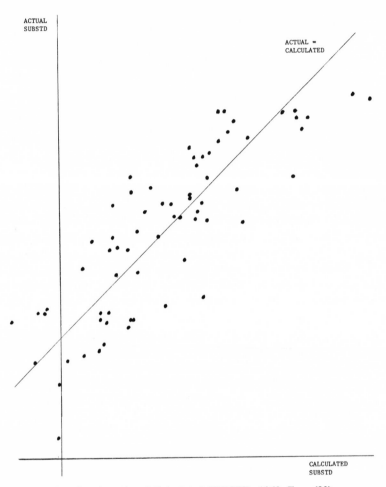

Fig. 3.—Actual and Calculated SUBSTD, 1960, Eqn. (23)

in order that the results would be less contaminated by the effects of variables that I consider extraneous. As a test for the linearity of the partial regression of dwelling-unit condition on income, this being, in my opinion, by far the most important of the explanatory variables, I included a variable LOWINC. The last takes the same value as INCOME for values below the median for all tracts and zero otherwise. The coefficient of LOWINC gives the difference in the linear approximation to the slope of SUBSTD on INCOME as between the lower and upper halves of the income range. I made this test for linearity primarily because of the vulgar belief, which amazingly has been voiced to me upon several occasions by professionally trained economists, that the only effects of increasing the incomes of lower-income groups would be to increase these groups' expenditures for liquor and automobiles. The results of the comparisons are summarized in Table 15. Only two things need to be commented upon: First, the coefficients of INCOME are each quite similar to values shown in previous regressions, and in each of the years the "*t*"-ratio of the INCOME coefficient is about −6. And second, the difference between the coefficients of INCOME in the lower and upper ranges of the income distribution is truly negligible in each of the years. It would appear, then,

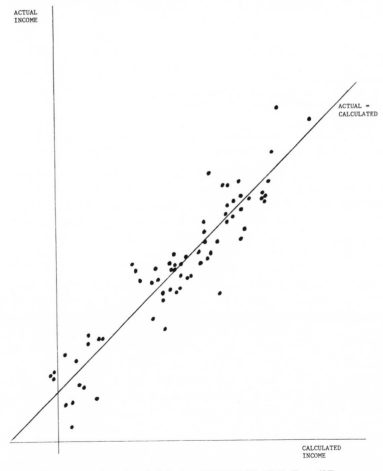

FIG. 4.—Actual and Calculated INCOME, 1960, Eqn. (27)

TABLE 15

FURTHER REGRESSION COMPARISONS OF SUBSTD,
1950 AND 1960

Explanatory Variable	1950 (37)	1960 (38)
INCOME × 10^{-3}	−.74*	−.61*
	(.12)	(.11)
AGEDUS	1.2*	. . .
	(.41)	
RETMAJ	.51*	.72*
	(.17)	(.27)
PERHOU	. . .	−.58†
		(.24)
SAMHOU	−2.6*	−.88
	(1.2)	(1.0)
GROPOP	−.18	−.22
	(.15)	(.15)
LOWINC	.026	.0045
	(.067)	(.057)
R^2	.85	.70

* Significant at the 1-tail 0.10 level.
† Significant at the 2-tail 0.10 level.

that the effects of increased incomes on housing condition within the lower half of the distribution is the same as in the upper half or as between them.

To summarize the results of this chapter, the one variable to which the proportion of dwelling units was most consistently and strongly related is INCOME. The only exception was in the conventional least-squares regressions for 1960 in Table 6, but the two-stage least-squares analysis presented in Table 8 suggests that the apparent lack of an effect of income on housing quality in the conventional least-squares regressions is the result of least-squares bias. Not only do slums appear to be associated mainly with poverty, but the analysis presented here indicates that housing quality improves dramatically as the incomes of the lower-income groups increase. While the elasticities of the proportion of dwelling units substandard vary somewhat according to the method of estimation and data used in the comparisons, all are numerically quite large. For the Chicago comparisons in 1950 the implied income elasticities are −2.5 and −3.2 in equations (2) and (7), respectively, while for 1960 the elasticity implied by equation (23) is −4.6; the intercity comparisons for 1950 yield elasticity estimates of −3.2 in equation (12) and −2.0 in equation (14). Much of the difference for the different sets of data results from differences in the mean values of income at which the elasticities are evaluated. The form of the relationship, with proportion substandard in logs and income in natural units, is such that the elasticities increase numerically as income increases.

The high elasticity of dwelling-unit condition with respect to income, when coupled with the substantial differences in income that exist at a given time or over time, imply very large differences in condition. On the south side of Chicago in 1950, median income by tract varied from about 2 to 5 thousand dollars, and differences of this magnitude together with the INCOME coefficient shown in equation (7), Table 3, imply that the proportion of dwellings substandard would be only about 6.7 percent as large in the highest income tracts as in the lowest. In 1960 the variation is even more striking. INCOME in the latter year varied from about 4 to 10 thousand dollars, so the coefficient in (23), Table 8, implies that the proportion substandard would only be 1.5 percent as large in the highest income tracts. Among cities in 1950, INCOME varied from about 2 to 3.5 thousand dollars; in the latter case the proportion substandard would be only about 37 percent as large as in the former, according to the intercity income coefficient in Table 5. This same coefficient together with an average increase in income of from about 3 to 4 thousand dollars in real terms during the fifties would imply that in 1960 the proportion substandard would be only one-third as large as in 1950. The practical significance of income differences for housing condition is thus striking indeed.

Dwelling-unit condition was also seen to be very sensitive to housing prices in the intercity comparisons, where the elasticity of SUBSTD with respect to construction costs was estimated at about $+3.6$ in Table 4. In addition, the positive association between SUBSTD and urbanized area shown in Table 4 might well reflect the increase in housing prices due to the increase in land prices with city size, since, as was shown in the third section, the coefficient of URBPOP was about the value one would expect if this is what URBPOP's coefficient reflects. No statistically significant association between SUBSTD and DISCBD was found for the Chicago comparisons, but the weak association may be because the variation of housing prices with distance is small. If, as argued in Chapter 9, housing prices decline by about 1 percent per mile, an elasticity of SUBSTD with respect to price of $+3.6$ would imply a coefficient of DISCBD of -0.036 in the SUBSTD equation. Values of -0.033, equation (2) for 1950, and -0.030, equation (23) for 1960, agree quite closely in view of their rather large standard errors. Note, too, that the INCOME and CONCST elasticities estimated here are quite consistent with national changes in the proportion of dwellings which were substandard during the 1950's. During that decade real median family income increased at about the rate of 3 percent per year, while real construction costs rose at an average annual rate of 1 percent. If the income and price elasticities of SUBSTD are each equal to 3.5 numerically, the proportion substandard would have declined at the rate of 7 percent per year or by 50 percent during the decade. In fact, for the central cities studied in Chapter 7, the proportion substandard fell from 0.20 in 1950 to 0.11 in 1960.

Despite the above evidence for the large response of dwelling-unit condition to housing prices, none of the comparisons in this chapter give much support to the hypothesis that a higher proportion of Negroes than whites inhabit substandard housing when other variables are taken into account—income, I suspect, being the most important of these. These results reinforce the strong doubt I expressed at the end of Chapter 9 that racial segregation of Negroes results in markedly higher housing prices for them. The results also cast doubt upon the idea that segregation restricts Negroes to areas in which housing quality is poorest. Rather, the results of this chapter strongly imply that the reason Negroes inhabit poorer-quality housing than whites is that the incomes of Negroes are lower. While discrimination in employment may contribute to the poverty of Negroes generally, it does not appear that discrimination in housing does to any practically significant extent.

Turning now to variables affecting the relative supply of poor-quality housing, there appears to be little truth in the homily that crowding breeds slums. No association between PEROOM and SUBSTD was found for South Chicago in 1950, and the statistically significant and positive coefficients of PEROOM in the other comparisons appear to be largely the result of least-squares bias. Because poor housing quality and little space per person are both aspects of a low per household consumption of housing, the least-squares estimate of the PEROOM coefficient tends to reflect the effects of the correlation of residuals in the condition and crowding equations. It is because poor dwelling-unit condition and crowding are closely related aspects of a low consumption of housing that the two are so closely associated. And because crowding can increase very quickly as occupancy of a neighborhood passes to lower-income groups, but quality deterioration takes longer, it is probably a natural mistake to infer that crowding causes slums. In this regard it is also interesting to note that none of the comparisons made here indicate that housing is of poorer quality in more densely populated areas once the effects of other variables have been removed.

Evidence on the relationship of age of dwellings to housing quality is much less clear cut. There was a strong negative association between AGEDUS and SUBSTD for the south side of Chicago in 1950; in fact, about three times as many dwellings were substandard among buildings built prior to 1920 than among those built in later years. The intercity comparisons for 1950 indicated that the effect of age of dwellings was about the same among different cities as within them, but because of its high standard error the coefficient of AGEDUS is not very precise. Furthermore, there was no tendency at all for the per household expenditures on housing to vary inversely with age of dwellings among various central cities as within them, and the coefficient of AGESMA was actually strongly negative in the intercity condition comparisons. Finally, in only one of the equations presented for Chicago in 1960, (18), was the coefficient of AGEDUS significant and of the same magnitude as for 1950, and comparison of equations (23) and (25) suggests that the positive coefficient of AGEDUS in 1960 may result to an important extent from least-squares bias. In equation (23), the two-stage least-squares estimate was actually negative.

Now, the difference in coefficients for 1950 and 1960 may result partly from the fact that in 1960 AGEDUS includes dwellings built between 1920 and 1939 as well as those built before 1920. It may also reflect the possibility, suggested in Chapter 9 to explain similar differences between the coefficients of AGEDUS in the comparison of population density and its components, that adjustments of residential land use to changed conditions of the era of automobile transport may not have been fully completed by 1950 because of the depression of the 1930's and the war and readjustment from it during the 1940's. Another possible explanation is that a higher proportion of older dwellings were subject to rent controls and that the reduction in the incentive for property owners to maintain their dwellings in good condition brought about by rent control led to a more rapid rate of quality deterioration for older dwellings.

To test the hypothesis that housing is of poorer quality in areas of rapid population turnover, I included SAMHOU in the condition comparisons. This variable had negative and statistically significant coefficients of roughly the same magnitude in the two comparisons for 1950, but its coefficient was negligible for 1960. The latter, plus the fact that in the VALHOU regressions in Chapter 9 the coefficient of SAMHOU was much less negative in 1960 than in 1950 and quantitatively not very important, casts some doubt on the explanation that migrants have weaker preferences for housing. The behavior of SAMHOU's coefficient might also be largely the result of rent control. While costs of maintenance and operation might well be greater in areas of more rapid population turnover, this need not lead to deterioration of housing if landlords can charge greater rentals to cover the higher costs. They may have been prevented from doing so, however, during the period of rent control. It was also found in this chapter that housing tends to be of better quality rather than the reverse in areas of rapid population growth; this was especially true among the various central cities in 1950. The only other variable to show a consistently positive association with SUBSTD was the major retail-center dummy variable for Chicago. This may be because, due to the rapid growth in surburban shopping centers, the demand for housing in the vicinity of similar centers in the central city has declined. This explanation is merely conjecture, however. The other non-residential center variables showed a negative association with SUBSTD. Thus, there is little evidence of poorer-than-average housing quality in the vicinity of industrial areas.

The location of households by income level was also examined for both 1950 and 1960 for the south side of Chicago. In general, the results tend to substantiate the conclusions drawn earlier, in Chapter 8. With age of dwellings and their condition included in the analysis there tends to be little association of INCOME with DISCBD; in equation (5) for 1950 median income tended to increase by about $14 per mile, whereas an increase of about $24 per mile for 1960 is indicated by equation (21). INCOME was quite strongly negatively associated with age of dwelling, as suggested by the hypotheses that higher-income households have stronger preferences for newer housing or that older dwellings are more cheaply converted to lower-income occupancy. Equation (5) indicates that in 1950 the median income of the inhabitants of dwellings built before 1920 tended to be about $500 lower, and in 1960 the inhabitants of dwellings built before 1940 had incomes which were about $1,500 lower, as equation (21) indicates. The much larger coefficient of AGEDUS in 1960, despite the inclusion of housing built from 1920 to 1939, suggests that preferences for newer housing or conversion-cost differentials increase as income does. This latter observation may help explain the weak tendency, which was found in Chapter 7, for density gradients to decline numerically as income increases.

Both for 1950 and 1960, the coefficient of SUBSTD in the INCOME equation was estimated at about -0.25 and was at least twice its standard error; the corresponding elasticities are about -0.07 and -0.04 for 1950 and 1960, indicating that the effect of dwelling-unit condition on the median income of a tract is quantitatively quite small. In addition, when income level in 1950 was included among the determinants of income in 1960, the coefficient of SUBSTD became positive. In Table 9, however, it was found that even with incomes a decade earlier included, there was a strong negative association between PEROOM and INCOME, suggesting that it may be the character of the occupants rather than poor housing quality itself that the higher income households seek to avoid. It makes little practical difference, however, since crowding and SUBSTD are so highly correlated, and both are primarily the result of low incomes. Some of the comparisons seemed to suggest that, if anything, Negroes tended to inhabit housing which was newer and in better quality considering their income level, but in the two-stage least-squares analysis for 1960 with

PEROOM and INCM50 included this effect vanished. The strongly positive coefficient of INCM50 in the 1960 income comparisons suggest a lag of considerable length in the adjustment of the location of households by income. Finally, no significant effects in the income regressions were found either in 1950 or in 1960 when GRODEN and ONEFAM were included, so that there again seems to be little support for the hypothesis that higher-income households inhabit housing containing more space and privacy relative to the structural features of housing.

11 Housing Prices and Race on the South Side of Chicago

In Chapters 9 and 10 several comparisons of land use intensity and housing consumption in Negro areas versus others were made. On the whole, I failed to find the kinds of differences one would expect to exist if Negroes paid greater prices per unit of housing because of limitations on the residential area available to them imposed by their residential segregation. In Chapter 9, per household expenditures for housing were found to be significantly greater in Negro areas both in 1950 and 1960. However, since it would appear that the price elasticity of housing demand is -1 or even larger numerically, higher housing prices would not result in greater expenditures on housing by Negroes. The greater expenditures might result from higher operating costs for Negro housing or because inclusion of payments for furnishings and utilities in average contract rent is more important for Negroes. I also found that expenditures on housing per square mile of residential land were greater in Negro areas, by about the same relative amount as expenditures per household were, but this too might be due to cost differences or differences in the relative importance of furnishings and utilities included in average contract rent. On the other hand, most of the comparisons of physical magnitudes—population density, proportion of units which are single-family, and the proportion of units which are substandard or crowded—failed to show any practically important differences between Negro and other areas. For this reason, I doubt that housing prices paid by Negroes are much different than those paid by whites if the effects of quality differences are eliminated.

Because of the importance of the relation of housing prices to race, and because the conclusions I draw from the evidence described above are so different from prevailing views, I shall present some additional evidence in this chapter. This is a comparison of changes in average contract rent and median value of housing during the 1950's among areas occupied by whites and those occupied by Negroes throughout the period, with changes taking place in areas occupied by whites in 1950 and by Negroes in 1960. Although many changes can, admittedly, take place in the housing stock of an area over a ten-year period—some dwellings are demolished, new ones are built, and new units are created from conversions—I suspect that there is much less relative variability in the quantity of housing per dwelling in a given area over a decade than among widely separated areas of the city at a given time. Furthermore, by including certain other variables in the analysis one can hope to reduce still further the variation of quantity of housing per dwelling. Therefore, I believe that differences in average contract rent and median value in given areas over time more nearly reflect differences in price per unit of housing than differences among areas at a given time. If there is a differential in housing prices associated with race as such and not some related factor, I would expect rents and values to rise more rapidly in census tracts which change from white to Negro occupancy over the period than in similar tracts which remained in white occupancy throughout. Furthermore, by comparing changes in rents and values in areas occupied by whites and by Negroes throughout the period, one might obtain a measure of the change in the racial differential over time. In the first section of this chapter I will describe the comparisons made and data used in more detail. The results of the comparisons are presented in the second section.

COMPARISONS MADE AND DATA USED

The area of Chicago studied here is the central part of the south side, bounded roughly by 55th and 91st Streets and by Western Avenue and the Illinois Central tracks. More specifically, it consists of all the community areas known as Washington Park, Chatham, West Englewood, Englewood, Greater Grand Crossing, and Auburn Gresham, and those parts of Woodlawn south of 63d Street and west of the Illinois Central tracks and those west of Cottage Grove Avenue.[1] In 1950, Washington Park was inhabited primarily by Negroes, and Negroes were beginning to move into the Woodlawn area. During the fifties Englewood, Greater Grand Crossing, and Chatham shifted largely to Negro occupancy, while West Englewood and Auburn Gresham remained mostly in white occupancy.

For the comparisons made in this chapter, a census tract is considered to be occupied by whites if the Negro population is 20 percent or less of the total population,[2] and by Negroes if the white population is 20 percent or

---

[1] Census tracts in the Woodlawn area which are east of Cottage Grove Avenue and north of 63d Street were omitted because property values in these might have been affected by the expansion of the University of Chicago and by the Hyde Park urban redevelopment.

[2] For 1950 the population data were obtained from *Chicago Tract Statistics, 1950*, table 1. The population data for 1960, as well as all other data for 1960 used here, are from City of Chicago, Department of City Planning, *Population and Housing Characteristics: 1960*, advance table PH-1, 1960 Census (City of Chicago, March, 1961).

less. In the study area, a total of thirty-five tracts were occupied by whites
in both 1950 and 1960, and fifteen were occupied by Negroes in both years.
Nineteen tracts were occupied by whites in 1950 and by Negroes in 1960.
Fifteen of the eighty-four tracts or combinations of tracts in the area
studied did not fall into one of these three categories, and these were not
included in the comparisons. As in the comparisons described earlier,
tracts were combined for comparability as between 1950 and 1960 where
necessary, and any tracts in which I knew public housing to be located were
eliminated.

In many of the comparisons presented below, tracts which changed from
white to Negro occupancy during the decade are described by a dummy
variable, CHANGE, and Negro occupied tracts by another dummy
variable, NEGRO. As I argued earlier, in Chapter 9, because of the high
degree of residential segregation of Negroes in Chicago and other cities,
most census tracts will be inhabited largely either by whites or by Negroes.
Few tracts will exhibit mixed characteristics, and most of these will be in
the process of shifting from white to Negro occupancy. Since I am not
interested here in what happens when a few Negroes move into a previously
white area, or in the transition from white to Negro occupancy, I omitted
the tracts with intermediate Negro population in either of the two census
years. Furthermore, it seems possible that movement of a few Negroes into
an area would have relatively little effect on housing prices but that once
an area has come to be largely occupied by Negroes any remaining whites
would have to pay the Negro price for housing. For these reasons, the
relevant comparisons for my purposes would seem to be between areas
largely occupied by Negroes and those largely occupied by whites. My
empirical definition of "largely" was derived from inspecting the scatter
diagram relating the percent population that was Negro in 1950 to the
percentage Negro 1960. In one pair of comparisons, however, the percent population Negro for 1950 and for 1960, PNEG50 and PNEG60,
were substituted for the dummy variables described above.

The principal reason for comparing rents and values in the same area at
different times rather than among different areas at the same time is to
reduce the confounding of differences in rents and values—due to differences in quantity of housing per unit or to differences in location and
neighborhood characteristics—with differences in the price per unit of
housing paid by whites and Negroes. Certainly, all dwellings in the area
studied are not of the same quality, as evidenced by the fact that there was
considerable variation in average rents and values among census tracts in
the area studied both in 1950 and 1960. But to the extent that quality differentials remain constant in relative terms over time, their effects are
eliminated by comparing relative changes in rents and values between

1950 and 1960. Also, dwellings depreciate over time, but to the extent that depreciation takes place at a constant relative rate,[3] the comparisons made here eliminate its effects. Another factor affecting rents and values over the decade in all areas is war and postwar rent controls. In the area studied, average contract rents of tenant-occupied dwellings increased about 90 percent during the fifties, but the median value of one-unit, owner-occupied dwelling increased only about 40 to 60 percent on the average. In an attempt partly to remove the effects of a differential degree of relaxation of rent control in 1950, I included the proportion of the population one year old or over that lived in the same house in 1950 as in 1949—SAMHOU, as defined earlier—since rents tended to increase with a change in tenant during the period of rent control. I would expect SAMHOU to be positively associated with the relative increase in average contract rent over the decade, for the smaller the change in tenants prior to 1950 the greater the effects of the removal of controls on rentals during the fifties.[4]

Certain other factors might affect rents and values reported by the census differently in different areas as defined by the race of their residents. The first of these is conversion of existing dwellings to smaller ones as an area changes from white to Negro occupancy. Since Negroes generally have lower incomes than whites, they tend to occupy less space per person, and, since smaller units generally rent for less than larger ones at any given time, conversions to smaller units might cause the observed change in rentals in changed-occupancy areas to underestimate the racial differential. I shall attempt to remove the effects of conversions by including the ratio of housing units in 1960 to dwelling units in 1950 in the tract, UNITS, in my comparisons of relative changes in rents and values.[5] Conversions, of course, would tend to increase the number of dwellings in a tract, but other changes in the housing stock such as new construction and demolitions also affect the relative change in the number of units. New construction, in particular, might produce a positive association between relative increases in rents and values and UNITS, but there was little new construction in the study area during the fifties.[6] The relative change in rents and values

---

[3] See Grebler, *et al.*, *Capital Formation in Residential Real Estate*, app. E, pp. 377–82.

[4] I am indebted to Margaret G. Reid for this suggestion.

[5] The 1950 data are from *Chicago Tract Statistics, 1950*, table 3.

[6] See City of Chicago, Department of City Planning, *1958 Residential Construction and Trends, 1950 to 1958* (City of Chicago, August, 1959). Note, too, that the change from the dwelling unit to the housing unit by the Census Bureau means that the 1960 data include one room quarters without separate cooking facilities in rooming houses and some hotels. Since these latter would probably rent for less than other housing units at any given time, their inclusion for 1960 tends to impart a negative association between the relative change in average contract rents and UNITS. The relative change in values, however, would not be affected by the changed definition.

might be affected by shifts from the tenant-occupied to the owner-occupied stock or vice versa. The effect of such shifts on values would depend upon whether the poorer- or better-quality owner-occupied units were involved; one can think of reasons why either might be the case. However, since owner-occupied units typically contain a greater quantity of housing than tenant-occupied units, shifts from the owner-occupied to tenant-occupied stock would most likely lead to an above-average increase in average contract rentals. To take account of such shifts, in addition to UNITS as defined above, I included the ratio of the number of units reporting average contract rents in 1960 to the number in 1950, RENUNI, in the rent comparisons, and the ratio of owner-occupied units reporting values in the two census years, OWNUNI, in the value comparisons.[7]

Another factor that might be expected to accompany the change from white to Negro occupancy and might have a differential effect on relative changes in rents and values is crowding. Crowding or increases in the number of persons per dwelling unit, here designated POPUNI, might take place with changed occupancy partly because Negroes tend to have larger families but mostly because doubling is one way to reduce housing expenditures to levels appropriate to the lower incomes of Negroes. Now, to the extent that crowding is indicative of quality deterioration which is not severe enough to be reflected in the proportion of units substandard, one would expect that crowding would be inversely associated with the relative change in rents and values. However, to the extent that operating and/or maintenance costs increase with increases in the number of persons per dwelling unit, crowding would be positively associated with average contract rents. Failure to include it in the latter case would mean that relative increases in changed-occupancy tracts compared with white tracts would overestimate the differential on account of race itself. But an increase in operating and/or maintenance costs would not affect values if gross rents were raised to cover the increased costs.[8]

Finally, when occupancy changes in a neighborhood, the condition of dwelling units might deteriorate and contract rents and values rise less than they would have done through the racial differential alone. This is because Negroes generally have lower incomes than whites and, as was shown in the preceding chapter, dwelling-unit condition is strongly related to

---

[7] Data for 1950 are from *Chicago Tract Statistics, 1950*, table 3.

[8] It makes no difference whether or not increased maintenance is actually performed. If crowding increases the rate of depreciation of a building but greater expenditures for maintenance are not made to offset this, the cost of depreciation would show up as smaller rentals and net income from the building in future time periods. By not making expenditures for maintenance, the owner of a building changes the time pattern of the stream of net incomes from it but does not necessarily alter its present value.

income. I shall attempt to eliminate the effect of changes in dwelling-unit condition by including two variables, the proportion of dwelling units which were substandard in 1950, as defined earlier but here designated SUB50, and the ratio of units substandard in 1960 to those in 1950, RATSUB. As was noted earlier, units were classified into two groups in 1950 and three in 1960 on the basis of condition. While the definition of dilapidated was the same for the two censuses, it is possible that some units classified as deteriorating in 1960 would have been classified as dilapidated in 1950. Furthermore, the condition variables defined above may fail wholly to eliminate the effects of quality deterioration in changed-occupancy areas.

The comparisons to be presented in the next section are made using conventional regression analysis with the variables described above treated as independent. Separate regressions using average contract rent in 1960 relative to 1950, AVCNRN, and the median value of one-unit, owner-occupied units in 1960 relative to 1950, MEDVAL, were run in turn as dependent variables.[9] As was pointed out earlier, census-reported contract rent includes payment for furnishings and utilities. If there is a differential change in the extent to which such payments are included in rents in different areas, the race differentials estimated here might be distorted. But there would seem to be no way to remove the influence of differential changes in furnishings and utilities from the comparisons. Census value-data are based on owners' estimates of the value of their property. While there would seem to be little bias in owners' estimates of value, discrepancies between owner's and appraiser's estimates of the value of a given home would seem to be quite large.[10] Therefore, medians for tracts with a small number of reported values are likely to be unreliable. For this reason, tracts with fewer than 100 units reporting values in either 1950 or 1960 were not included in the value comparisons. The twenty-one of sixty-nine tracts thus omitted include all but one of the Negro tracts, so that it was not possible to include the Negro tracts in the value comparisons or to infer anything about the change in the race differential in house values between 1950 and 1960. The value comparisons are therefore based on forty-seven observations rather than the whole sixty-nine used in the rental

---

[9] The 1950 data on rents are from *Chicago Tract Statistics, 1950*, table 2, and data on values from *ibid.*, table 3. I used median rather than average values because the latter for 1960 were not available to me when the analysis was begun. The difference between relative average and relative median values does not seem important enough to me to redo the comparisons now that the block statistics for 1960 are available. Since most Negroes are tenants, the race differential in rents is of by far the greater practical importance.

[10] See Leslie Kish and John B. Lansing, "Response Errors in Estimating Value of Homes," *Journal of the American Statistical Association* 49 (September, 1954): 527.

comparisons. Finally, it should be noted that all the variables included in the analysis of this chapter are measured in natural units.

EMPIRICAL FINDINGS

The results of the comparisons described earlier are presented in this section. The basic comparisons using the variables described in section one are shown in Table 1. Tables 2 and 3 show the results when certain additional variables are used, and Tables 4 and 5 show the results obtained when separate regressions are run for the white, Negro, and changed-occupancy areas. As in the previous chapters, the coefficient of each of the variables for any particular equation is shown in the row and column of the table which corresponds to the particular variable and equation, and the estimated standard error of any particular coefficient is shown below it in parentheses. Because the constant term of intercept is of interest here, it and its standard error are also included in the first line of the various tables.

TABLE 1

RELATIVE CHANGE IN RENTS AND VALUES, 1950–60

EXPLANATORY VARIABLE	DEPENDENT VARIABLE (EQUATION)			
	AVCNRN		MEDVAL	
	(1)	(2)	(3)	(4)
Constant	1.89	−.30	1.38	.80
	(.34)	(.79)	(.023)	(.41)
CHANGE	.031	−.011	.21*	.13*
	(.057)	(.078)	(.042)	(.066)
NEGRO	−.12†	−.029	· · ·	· · ·
	(.061)	(.093)		
UNITS	· · ·	.40	· · ·	.11
		(.26)		(.22)
POPUNI	· · ·	.71*	· · ·	.23
		(.31)		(.33)
SUB50	· · ·	−.013	· · ·	.84†
		(.25)		(.34)
RATSUB	· · ·	−.023	· · ·	.028
		(.043)		(.042)
SAMHOU	· · ·	1.4*	· · ·	· · ·
		(.78)		
RENUNI	· · ·	−.12	· · ·	· · ·
		(.24)		
OWNUNI	· · ·	· · ·	· · ·	.15†
				(.067)
R^2	.072	.37	.35	.52

* Significant at the 1-tail 0.10 level.
† Significant at the 2-tail 0.10 level.

The constant term in equation (1) of Table 1 indicates that, in tracts remaining in white occupancy in 1960, average contract rents rose about

89 percent from 1950. The coefficient of CHANGE, which is the difference between the relative rental increase in changed-occupancy and white tracts, indicates that average contract rents rose by about 3 percentage points more, or 92 percent, in tracts that changed from white to Negro occupancy during the fifties. Rents in tracts in Negro occupancy throughout the period rose by only about 77 percent over the decade, however, as indicated by the coefficient of NEGRO. The standard error of the coefficient of CHANGE indicates that the difference between the average percentage increase in rents in white and changed-occupancy tracts is probably small. But the Negro area dummy variable's coefficient suggests that these areas probably had somewhat smaller increases in rentals. In equation (3), the median values of one-unit, owner-occupied dwellings rose about 38 percent on the average in white tracts, as indicated by the constant term in equation (3). The coefficient of the changed-occupancy variable, however, implies that values rose about 59 percent on the average in tracts in which occupancy changed from white to Negro. There can be little doubt that the increase in average values was greater in changed-occupancy tracts, since CHANGE's coefficient in (3) is about five times its standard error.

When the other variables discussed in the first section are added to the regression equations, as in (2) and (4), the results are not markedly different. As in equation (1), the coefficient of CHANGE in (3) is numerically small in comparison with its standard error, but it has become negative. Examination of regression equations obtained by adding variables one by one indicates that the change of sign takes place when POPUNI is added, so that the slight tendency for contract rents to rise more in changed-occupancy areas apparently reflects increased crowding rather than a race differential per se. The fact that the coefficient of POPUNI is positive and more than twice as large as its standard error tends to support the increased cost hypothesis, especially since the coefficient of this variable is small in the value regression, but not the hypothesis that crowding reflects quality deterioration not captured by the conditional variables. In (2), the coefficient of the Negro area variable is much smaller numerically and no longer statistically significant. The decline in this coefficient appears to result mainly when SAMHOU is introduced. Thus, equation (2) gives little indication of a race differential as such in contract rents for either 1950 or 1960.

In equation (4), the coefficient of CHANGE is decidedly smaller than in (3) but still about twice as large as its standard error. The change in the value of this coefficient occurs mainly when SUB50 is added to the analysis. The latter's large positive sign might result from the increase in the price of poor-quality relative to good-quality housing during the fifties which was indicated by the analysis of Chapter 9. But while part of the greater relative increase of values in tracts switching to Negro occupancy was due to dwelling-unit condition rather than a racial differential per se, it would appear that there is a differential in the prices paid by whites and Negroes for one-unit, owner-occupied housing. Assuming no change in the number of units, condition, or crowding (i.e., UNITS = OWNUNI = RATSUB = POPUNI = 1) and that the percent of units substandard is equal to the mean value for all tracts used in estimating equations (3) and (4), or 6.3 percent, equation (4) implies that median values would have risen about 37 percent on the average in tracts remaining in white occupancy. For tracts changing to Negro occupancy values would have risen about 50 percent on the average under the same conditions, so that the race differential in 1960 for one-unit, owner-occupied houses was about $(1.50/1.37) - 1$ or about 10 percent as compared with the estimate of 15 percent implied by equation (3).

After obtaining results similar to those described above, several other variables were suggested to me by persons with whom I communicated my results. Results obtained when these variables are included are shown in Tables 2 and 3. First, it was suggested that the comparisons might be distorted by boundary effects of the type already discussed in Chapter 5. If Negroes prefer to live close to whites, prices on the Negro side of the boundary between white and Negro areas might be greater than in the interior. And, if whites prefer not to live close to Negroes, they will be induced to do so only if housing is especially cheap for them there. A similar price pattern might result from certain dynamic effects on housing prices. It might be argued, for example, that in white areas contiguous to Negro areas a few Negroes might already have "penetrated." The latter could result in a decline in demand for housing in the area by whites and a temporary depression of rents and values. At the same time, rents and values might be temporarily high in the Negro areas contiguous to white areas if Negroes recently moving into them had paid premium prices to acquire the area.

Either kind of effect in 1950 would imply that my procedure under-estimates the racial differential in 1950 if the Negro tracts are close to the 1950 but not the 1960 boundary, since the racial differential is the difference between prices in the interiors of the Negro and white areas. However, these effects on changed-occupancy tracts would mean that I have over-estimated the 1960 race differential. The numerator of my estimate is the (adjusted) average of prices paid by Negroes in 1960 divided by prices paid by whites in 1950 in the same changed-occupancy tracts. The effects described in the above paragraph would imply that prices paid by Negroes in 1960 are too high in my changed-occupancy tracts and that prices paid by whites in 1950 are too low relative to the correct ones. Finally, these effects imply that prices are lower in white tracts close to the 1960 boundary between white and Negro areas than in the interior of the white area; this, too, would tend to make my estimate of the Negro-white differential in 1960 too large.

TABLE 2

FURTHER TESTS, AVCNRN COMPARISONS, 1950–60

EXPLANATORY VARIABLE	EQUATION			
	(5)	(6)	(7)	(8)a
Constant	−.27	−.72	−.36	.14
	(.83)	(.88)	(.79)	(1.3)
CHANGE	−.023	−.021	· · ·	.078
	(.10)	(.079)		(.088)
NEGRO	−.038	.024	· · ·	· · ·
	(.11)	(.11)		
PNEG50	· · ·	· · ·	−.034	· · ·
			(.13)	
PNEG60	· · ·	· · ·	−.031	· · ·
			(.086)	
UNITS	.37	.42	.40	.17
	(.30)	(.26)	(.26)	(.27)
POPUNI	.69†	.83 †	.79†	.16
	(.32)	(.33)	(.31)	(.46)
SUB50	−.0034	−.14	−.081	.14
	(.26)	(.28)	(.26)	(.49)
RATSUB	−.024	−.021	−.022	.037
	(.045)	(.043)	(.043)	(.056)
SAMHOU	1.4*	1.7*	1.4*	2.6*
	(.80)	(.83)	(.78)	(1.0)
RENUNI	−.093	−.13	−.13	−.94
	(.27)	(.24)	(.24)	(.43)
WHIBDY	−.0061	· · ·	· · ·	· · ·
	(.066)			
CHABDY	.018	· · ·	· · ·	· · ·
	(.086)			
VACRAT	· · ·	1.8	· · ·	· · ·
		(1.6)		
R^2	.38	.39	.37	.28

a Using only those 47 tracts used in the comparison of relative change in median value.
* Significant at the 1-tail 0.10 level.
† Significant at the 2-tail 0.10 level.

Using the data for the study area described earlier it was not possible to differentiate between boundary and interior tracts as of 1950. However, I did test for boundary effects in 1960 by including two new variables: WHIBDY, which takes the value 1 for a white tract which is contiguous to or touches the 1960 boundary of the Negro area and 0 otherwise, and CHABDY, which takes the value 1 for a changed-occupancy tract which is contiguous to the 1960 boundary and 0 otherwise. The effects of including these two variables in the rent and value regressions are shown in Tables 2 and 3, equations (5) and (9), respectively. All the boundary tract coefficients are small relative to their standard errors, that of CHABDY in the value regression has the wrong sign, and including the boundary tract variables has little effect on the other coefficients. These results, then, suggest that the boundary phenomena had no important effects on the data for census tracts in the area studied, though they might have been more important if data for blocks were examined.

TABLE 3

FURTHER TESTS, MEDVAL COMPARISONS, 1950–60

EXPLANATORY VARIABLE	EQUATION		
	(9)	(10)	(11)
Constant	.88	.88	.75
	(.45)	(.42)	(.40)
CHANGE	.13*	.14*	...
	(.079)	(.066)	
PNEG60	...	...	.14*
			(.072)
UNITS	.063	.092	.11
	(.25)	(.22)	(.22)
POPUNI	.21	.19	.27
	(.35)	(.34)	(.32)
SUB50	.87†	.97†	.83†
	(.36)	(.37)	(.34)
RATSUB	.028	.025	.030
	(.043)	(.042)	(.042)
OWNUNI	.15†	.15†	.15†
	(.069)	(.067)	(.067)
WHIBDY	−.023	...	...
	(.049)		
CHABDY	−.0092	...	...
	(.068)		
VACRAT	...	−1.5	...
		(1.7)	
R^2	.53	.53	.52

* Significant at the 1-tail 0.10 level.
† Significant at the 2-tail 0.10 level.

Another problem that arises relates to my interpretation of the effects of crowding or increases in population per dwelling. I have suggested that the increase in rents associated with increases in population per dwelling results from increases in operating and/or maintenance costs associated with more intensive utilization of dwellings. But it might be argued that an increase in population per dwelling is symptomatic of an increase in the demand for housing relative to its supply. The results of such an increase would be a rise in rentals and, consequently, some doubling-up of families and individuals into single dwelling units.[11] Since one would expect an increase

---

[11] This interpretation is frequently placed upon the fact that population per dwelling is generally larger in Negro areas and increases as an area changes from white to Negro. See, for example, Otis Dudley Duncan and Beverly Duncan, *The Negro*

in housing demand relative to supply and the resulting increase in rentals to be accompanied by declining vacancy rates, the increased-demand interpretation of crowding can be tested by including a measure of the change in vacancy rates in the analysis. Probably because of rent controls and the postwar housing shortage, there were very few vacancies in the study area in 1950; in fact, in several of the tracts no vacancies whatsoever were reported in the 1950 census. Therefore, I use as my measure of change in the vacancy rate the number of available vacant housing units divided by the number of all housing units as reported in the 1960 census and designate this variable VACRAT. When this variable is added to the regressions, equations (6) and (10), Table 2 and 3, respectively, its coefficient has the wrong sign in the rent regression, its coefficient is numerically smaller than the standard error of the coefficient in each of the regressions, and there are no important changes in any of the other coefficients— especially the coefficient of POPUNI. I conclude, therefore, that the increased-demand interpretation of crowding is not borne out by my data.

Up to now I have simply averaged the relative change in rents and values in white, changed-occupancy, and Negro tracts as defined earlier to obtain my estimate of the Negro housing price differential. But one might argue that the relative changes in rents or values in such tracts will depend upon the percent of the population that is Negro. If, for example, rents and values rise only for those dwellings actually occupied by Negroes in changed-occupancy tracts as I have defined them, then the relative change in rents and values would be an increasing function of percent population Negro in 1960 and a decreasing function of percent population Negro in 1950. On the other hand, it seems quite possible that when Negroes "invade" an area, they tend to occupy the poorer-quality housing and remaining whites the better housing. If the price of the better-quality housing has been rising relative to that of the poorer, as might well be the case during a period of rising incomes, then the Negro price differential might tend to be hidden by the change in the quality differential. The poorer-quality argument, too, suggests that instead of dummy variables I should use percent population Negro to measure occupancy characteristics.

For these reasons I have recomputed regressions (2) and (4) using PNEG50, the proportion of the population which was Negro in 1950, and PNEG60, the proportion of the population which was Negro in 1960, to measure occupancy characteristics, instead of the dummy variables NEGRO and CHANGE. However, since in most of the white and changed-occupancy tracts PNEG50 is less than 0.01, only PNEG60 was included in

---

Population of Chicago (Chicago: University of Chicago Press, 1957), p. 9. As shown earlier, however, crowding depends critically on income and also on family size.

the value regression. One sees from equation (7) in Table 2 that the coefficient of PNEG60 has the sign opposite to that implied by the hypotheses in the above paragraph, both coefficients are smaller than their standard errors, and the coefficients of the other variables are virtually the same as the corresponding ones in equation (2), Table 1. In like manner, the coefficient of PNEG60 in equation (11), Table 3, is practically identical with that of CHANGE in equation (4), Table 1; on the arguments of the above paragraph the coefficient of PNEG60, which is the relative increase in value for 100 percent Negro occupancy in 1960, is the appropriate measure of the Negro differential. All the other coefficients of equations (7) and (11) are practically the same, and R^2 is actually a little smaller in equation (11) before rounding. Thus, I conclude that by using dummy variables to measure occupancy characteristics I have not biased my measure of the Negro housing price differential downward.

Because of the differences in some of the coefficients between equations (2) and (4) I refitted the rent regression using only those forty-seven tracts to which the value regressions were fitted. (This, of course, made it necessary to drop the Negro area variable.) The results are shown in equation (8), Table 2. In contrast with equation (2), the coefficient of CHANGE in (8) is positive, though still smaller than its standard error, and it implies that contract rents rose about eight percentage points more in tracts which switched to Negro occupancy during the decade. When the race differential in contract rent for 1960 is evaluated using the method described above for values, equation (8) implies a differential of about 4 percent, still noticeably smaller than that for values. The only other important difference in the coefficients is the drop of the coefficient of POPUNI from 0.71 in (2) to 0.16 in (8), the latter being only about one-third its standard error. This last result suggests that the increase in contract rents with increased crowding occurred mainly in the Negro area.

Because of the difference in coefficients between equations (2) and (8), as another test I ran separate regressions for each of the groups of tracts as defined by racial characteristics. Whereas in comparisons made so far, only the level of the regression plane was allowed to vary as among areas, in these latter the slopes can vary among areas as well. The results for contract rents are shown in Table 4 and those for values in Table 5. It is readily apparent on inspecting Table 4 that the only really important differences in the slope coefficients are those between the Negro area and the other two; the differences between equations (12) and (13) are all small relative to the standard errors of the respective coefficients.[12] The coefficients of POPUNI

---

[12] Except, perhaps, for the coefficients of RENUNI, which have the wrong sign in both (12) and (13).

confirm the suspicion just expressed that the increase in contract rents with increased crowding takes place mostly in the Negro area; the coefficient in (14) is three times its standard error, but in (12) and (13) the coefficients are quite small. The tendency for contract rents to increase with

TABLE 4

SEPARATE REGRESSIONS, AVCNRN, 1950–60

EXPLANATORY VARIABLE	AREA (EQUATION)		
	White (12)	Change (13)	Negro (14)
Constant	.31	.25	1.68
	(1.6)	(1.8)	(1.1)
UNITS	.20	−.32	1.2
	(.30)	(.53)	(1.1)
POPUNI	.12	.28	.97†
	(.83)	(.39)	(.32)
SUB50	−.55	−.0034	−.11
	(.73)	(.70)	(.16)
RATSUB	.051	−.014	.15
	(.063)	(.067)	(.086)
SAMHOU	2.5*	2.4	−1.6
	(1.1)	(1.9)	(1.2)
RENUNI	−1.0	−.42	−.69
	(.59)	(.52)	(.92)
R^2	.36	.53	.97
Number of Observations	35	19	15

* Significant at the 1-tail 0.10 level.
† Significant at the 2-tail 0.10 level.

TABLE 5

SEPARATE REGRESSIONS, MEDVAL 1950–60

EXPLANATORY VARIABLE	AREA (EQUATION)	
	White (15)	Change (16)
Constant	1.37	1.17
	(.55)	(1.2)
UNITS	.17	−.19
	(.22)	(.64)
POPUNI	−.48	.28
	(.52)	(.72)
SUB50	.71	.72
	(.51)	(.63)
RATSUB	.017	.063
	(.038)	(.23)
OWNUNI	.64†	.15
	(.075)	(.19)
R^2	.27	.37
Number of Observations	33	14

† Significant at the 2-tail 0.10 level.

a change in tenant prior to 1950, however, appears only in the white and changed-occupancy areas, since SAMHOU's coefficient is actually negative in the Negro area regression. From a covariance analysis it would appear that the differences in slope coefficients among the three areas seen in Table 4 are too great to attribute to chance variation. The mean additional sum of squares attributable to the separate regressions is over three and one-half times as large as the pooled estimate of residual variance, but because the residual variance appears to be very much smaller for the Negro area regression, the usual F test is not appropriate. When the average increase in contract rent for the three areas is estimated by substituting UNITS = RENUNI = POPUNI = RATSUB = 1 and SAMHOU = 0.89 and SUB50 = 0.14, the latter two being the average values for all sixty-nine tracts in the area studied, one finds increases of 80, 92, and 90 percent in the white, changed-occupancy, and Negro areas, respectively. The first two of these would imply a Negro differential in average contract rent of a little under 7 percent for 1960. The difference in coefficients among the various areas thus makes little difference for my estimate of the racial differential in tenant-occupied housing prices.

In contrast with the average contract rent regressions, there would seem to be no important differences in the coefficients of the median value regressions as among white and changed-occupancy areas which are in-dicated in Table 5. For the relative change in median value, the mean additional sum of squares attributable to the separate slope estimates is less than half as large as the pooled estimate of residual variance. The residual variance of the changed-occupancy tracts appears to be about three times as large as in the white tracts, however, so that the usual F test is not strictly valid. But the small additional explanatory power of the separate regressions is clearly not very convincing evidence of differences in the true slopes. If the increase in median values is estimated as was done earlier in connection with the estimates in equation (4), Table 1, I find an average increase of 29 percent in the white tracts and 52 percent in the changed-occupancy tracts. The implied race differential in prices of single-family, owner-occupied units is about 18 percent, which as in previous comparisons is distinctly greater than that for tenant-occupied units.

As a final test, I compared the signs of the residuals from the contract rent regression (8) and median value regression (4), both of which were fitted to the forty-seven tracts for which enough values were reported for reliable estimates. This comparison is summarized in Table 6. Clearly there is little relationship between the two sets of estimated residuals; a positive association would be expected if some important common deter-minant of rents and values had been omitted. In fact, a switch of only two negative rent residuals would produce as perfect an agreement as could be obtained from an odd number of observations, and a difference as great or greater than seen in Table 6 would be expected in about three out of every five samples if, in fact, the residuals were independent. There is little evidence, then, that my results have been distorted by the omission of some important variable. The actual and calculated values of AVCNRN from equation (8) are plotted in Figure 1, those of MEDVAL from equation (4) in Figure 2. In neither case does there seem to be any clear-cut departure from linearity and constant residual variance.

TABLE 6

COMPARISON OF RESIDUALS, AVCNRN AND MEDVAL

AVCNRN EQN (8)	MEDVAL, EQN. (4)		
	+	−	Total
+	8	8	16
−	13	18	31
Total	21	26	47

$$X^2 = 0.27 \qquad Pr. \cong 0.6$$

In summary, from the comparisons presented here it would appear that the race differential itself in tenant-occupied housing prices is small and of uncertain direction. Comparisons made using equations (8) and (12) and (13) yielded estimates of 4 and 7 percent, while from equation (2) the differential was negative, if anything. These findings agree quite closely with inferences drawn from comparisons made in Chapters 9 and 10. There, in only two of the several comparisons of physical magnitudes that were made was any very conclusive evidence found for the hypothesis that Negroes pay greater prices not offset by cost differences for housing of comparable quality than whites. Equation (9.37), Table 9.7, showed significantly fewer one-family dwellings in comparable Negro areas. Comparing the coefficient of NEGMAJ with that of DISCBD and assuming the response to a given price change is equal in two cases, a Negro differential of about 5 percent in housing prices is implied, since previously I have shown that housing prices tend to decline at the rate of about 1 percent per mile from the CBD. Similarly, in the analysis of net population densities in equations (10.35) and (10.36), Table 10.11, density was about 30 percent higher in Negro areas. Compared with the coefficient of DISCBD, a race differential of around 5 percent is again implied. Other comparisons based upon NEGMAJ coefficients which are not statistically significant suggest even smaller differentials.

My analysis also suggests that the race differential in the prices of one-unit, owner-occupied dwellings may be larger than that for tenant-occupied housing, being of the order of 10 to 20 percent. Such a difference, of course, if it exists, is a substantial one for those who must pay it, since it is about half to the same size as the income tax subsidy to home owners, but it is of small practical importance since most Negroes are renters. In the city of Chicago in 1950, for example, there were more than seven times as many Negro renters as owner-occupants of one-unit dwellings.[13] There are several reasons, however, why the differential in values I have suggested might be an overestimate. Although, in some of the tracts used in the comparisons made here, one-unit, owner-occupied dwellings were about as numerous as tenant-occupied ones, in most they were only a small proportion of the housing stock. Thus, the control variables I used may not have done a very good job of eliminating extraneous factors from the

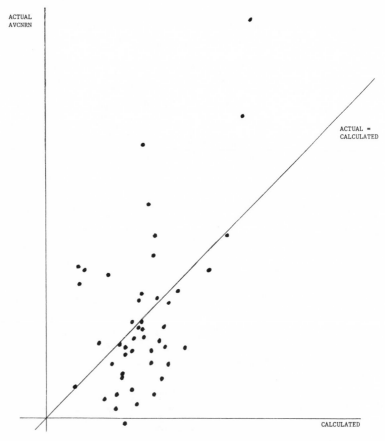

Fig. 1.—Actual and Calculated Values of AVCNRN, 47 Obs., Eqn. (8)

[13] *Chicago Tract Statistics, 1950*, table 3.

house-value comparisons. My estimate of the differential does not differ considerably, however, when these control variables are excluded for the contract rent comparisons. Second, the census value data are owners' estimates, and in a period of rising housing prices the estimates of recent buyers could be less downward biased than others; as a result, the racial differential would be biased upward by the comparisons I have made, since recent buyers would be relatively more numerous in changed-occupancy tracts. The study by Kish and Lansing cited earlier, however, would appear to discredit this hypothesis. Finally, it seems likely that a large proportion of Negro buyers in changed-occupancy tracts purchased their homes on contract-for deed.[14] If so, and if these buyers agreed to pay

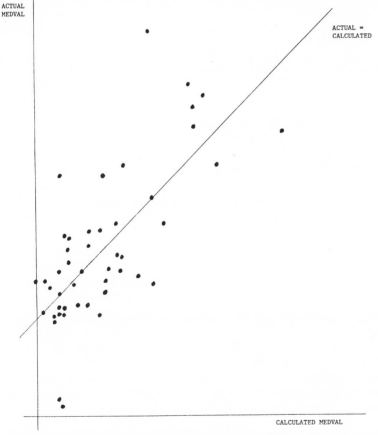

FIG. 2.—Actual and Calculated Values of MEDVAL, 47 Obs., Eqn. (4)

[14] A study by the Chicago Commission on Human Relations, "Selling and Buying Real Estate in a Racially Changing Neighborhood, A Survey," reported that in the one block in the Englewood area studied, most Negro buyers had done so.

off a balance larger than the value of their property as a substitute for a higher contract-interest rate, as when a bond is issued at a discount or a commercial bank requires a borrower to maintain a compensating balance, the Negro owner estimates might be based upon the balance they agreed to pay the seller rather than the market value of their property. If this is true, I may well have overestimated the race differential in values, for the study of house values I cited in Chapter 5, in which a large number of physical and other characteristics were carefully controlled, found that house values were actually about 20 percent lower in the interior of the Negro area than in the white area during the middle fifties.[15]

If the Negro differential in housing prices were really larger for one-unit, owner-occupied houses, the difference can be readily explained in terms of the analysis of Chapter 5. There it was argued that the race differential varies directly with the relative rate of growth of Negro demand for housing and inversely with the rate at which housing passes from white to Negro occupancy near the Negro area boundary. Now, home ownership tends to increase most rapidly in the middle range of the income distribution, since in the upper part most households already are home owners. It is quite possible, therefore, that in a period of rapidly rising incomes the relative demand for home ownership by the lower-income group would grow more rapidly. In addition, it seems quite likely that white home owners would move out of an area less rapidly than white renters as the Negro area approaches them. Home owners tend to move less frequently than renters for reasons other than a change in the character of their neighborhood and generally have greater attachments to their area of residence in the form of friendships, knowledge of employment and shopping opportunities, preferences for schools, and the like. In addition, movement by home owners from a racially changing neighborhood may entail a capital loss if the white demand for housing in the area has declined, and whites have few opportunities for contacting possible Negro buyers; renters, however, have no such problem. For both reasons, then, a greater differential in one-unit, owner-occupied housing seems quite consistent with the analysis of residential segregation in Part I.

Although my analysis suggests that the effects of residential segregation on the price of housing to Negroes is minor, the comparisons in this chapter suggest two other reasons why Negroes may spend more for housing than whites. The first of these is crowding. It would seem reasonable on a priori grounds that gross rentals would tend to increase with

---

[15] Martin J. Bailey, "Effects of Race and Other Demographic Factors on the Values of Single-Family Houses," This study was of houses in the University of Chicago neighborhood, and it is conceivable that whites are willing to pay more of a premium for housing in such an area than are Negroes.

increases in the number of persons per unit if operating and/or maintenance costs do. My empirical analysis of contract rents tends to support this hypothesis, at least for Negro areas. Since Negroes tend to live under more crowded conditions, mostly because of their lower incomes, partly because of larger family sizes, but not because of race as such, it seems reasonable to expect that they would spend more for housing on this account. And second, the results of this chapter, too, would seem to imply that substandard housing is more expensive relative to its quality than better housing. In none of the comparisons made in this chapter was there a significant tendency for contract rents or values to decline with an increase in the proportion of dwelling units substandard. The comparisons made in Chapter 9 suggest that the price per unit of housing on the south side of Chicago was greater in poor-quality housing areas in 1960, though not in 1950. Thus, the increase in the price of poor- relative to good-quality housing over the decade may have counteracted the tendency for rents and values to decline with quality deterioration. In addition, the coefficient of SUB50 in the value comparisons was positive and large; this also might be accounted for by a relative increase in the price of poor-quality housing in the 1950's. Negroes typically have lower incomes than whites and live in poorer-quality housing on the average for this reason, not because of race as such. If the estimates of Chapter 10 are correct, they may tend to pay higher prices for housing on the average than whites because poorer-quality housing is relatively expensive both for Negroes and whites.

PART III

Conclusions and Implications

12 An Appraisal of the Theoretical Analysis

Having completed the discussion of my empirical findings, I now wish to reexamine the theoretical analysis contained in Part I. In Part II I described those implications of my empirical findings which seemed apparent without extended discussion, and I do not wish merely to repeat those comments here. Rather, I wish to draw together pieces of evidence from the various chapters of Part II, to determine which of the many hypotheses discussed in Part I seem to have empirical relevance, and to assess the consistency of the determinants of residential land use which I believe are of major importance with the magnitudes of some of the co-efficients found in Part II. In so doing I will first reconsider some of the determinants of the relative demand for housing in different parts of the city. Next, I will reexamine forces affecting relative housing supply. In this chapter's final section I will discuss the effects of factors such as size, income level, and home-ownership subsidies on urban spread or decentralization. Chapter 13 will consider some of the implications of these and other findings of this monograph for public policy toward cities.

THE RELATIVE DEMAND FOR HOUSING IN DIFFERENT PARTS OF CITIES

Throughout this study I have stressed the importance of transport costs as a determinant of the spatial pattern of housing demand. In this section I will first discuss various pieces of evidence relating to the impact of transport costs on the pattern of demand. Next, using the empirical results from my detailed study of Chicago, I will estimate the magnitude of marginal and total transport costs and compare my estimates with those from other studies. I will then consider the effects of a household's income on its optimal location. Finally, I will examine the effects of home-ownership subsidies on relative housing demand in different parts of the city.

Economists and others have long suspected that improvements in transportation tend to increase the relative demand for housing at greater distances from the city center. Until quite recently, however, there has been little good empirical evidence to substantiate this belief. One important bit of evidence is Winsborough's finding that, while the population density gradient of the city of Chicago has been declining over the whole of the period from 1860 to 1950, the greatest percentage changes occurred during the 1880's—the period of great building of rapid transit facilities—and the 1920's.[1] The latter, of course, was the decade during which automobile transportation became widespread. In another previously cited study,[2] Herbert Mohring demonstrated that the sales prices of undeveloped land in the Seattle area tend to decline with distance from the city center, as would be anticipated from the increase of transport costs. Similarly, William C. Pendleton has demonstrated a significantly negative effect of distance from the city center on the sales prices of single-family, FHA financed houses in the Washington, D.C., area.[3]

The evidence presented in Part II provides two important additional pieces of evidence confirming the influence of transport costs on relative housing demand within an urban area. First, the comparisons made in Chapter 7 strongly suggest that, among a large number of U.S. cities both in 1950 and in 1960, the spread of residential population varies inversely with car registrations per capita. My interpretation of this finding is that both density gradients and automobile ownership reflect the influences of differences in the cost of automobile transportation. Secondly, when separate density gradients for areas close to and farther from rapid transit and express highway facilities on the south side of Chicago were estimated, the former was markedly smaller than the latter. Such a finding is to be anticipated, of course, on the basis of the hypothesis that the rate of decline of housing prices in a city is influenced by the marginal costs of transport. At first glance it might seem difficult to understand the remarkable similarity of the estimated density gradients for 1950 and 1960 for Chicago's south side in view of the obvious decentralization of population that occurred during the fifties in Chicago as in other cities. Because separate density gradients were estimated for areas presumably differing in marginal transport costs, but for each of which there were no marked changes in transport facilities during the fifties, the stability of the estimated density gradients for the south side of Chicago is not at all surprising. Indeed, this finding suggests that the decentralization occurring during the fifties because of a reduction in marginal transport costs was largely the result of building new facilities, especially express highways.

In Chapter 2 I suggested that the marginal costs of transport could be estimated by multiplying the price gradient by a household's expenditure

---

[1] Winsborough, "A Comparative Study of Urban Residential Densities."
[2] "Land Values and the Measurements of Highway Benefits."
[3] "The Value of Accessibility."

on housing [equation (2.3′)]. In Chapter 3 it was demonstrated that the price gradient can be obtained by dividing the relative change in value of housing produced per unit of land by the elasticity of this quantity with respect to price [equation (3.10)]. I also pointed out in Chapter 3 that this elasticity is of the order of +15, so that the VALAND gradient of 0.15 per mile for the parts of the south side of Chicago remote from rapid-transit facilities implies a decrease of housing prices of the order of 1 percent per mile in these areas. On the average, for the tracts included in the Chicago sample, expenditures for housing were $59 ($111) in 1950 (1960). The theory developed in Part I thus implies that marginal transport costs were $0.59 ($1.11) per mile per month per household in 1950 (1960). Assuming that the average household with a member employed in the CBD makes forty-two trips per month and that the average speed of travel at the mean distance of tracts from the Loop—about 7.8 miles—was thirty miles per hour, the above in turn implies marginal transport costs of $0.42 ($0.79) per hour per household in 1950 (1960).

From my knowledge of the area it would seem reasonable to expect that substantial numbers of CBD workers residing about eight miles from the Loop on Chicago's south side used some form of public transportation. If so, the marginal costs of transport for them would be wholly time costs. The average census-reported income for tracts in the Chicago sample was about $3,530 ($6,510) per year in 1950 (1960). On the further assumption that about 0.8 of this was income from earnings and that household members worked 2,000 hours per year, marginal costs of transport would have been about 0.3 times average hourly earnings both for 1950 and 1960 for households with CBD workers using public transportation.[4] Furthermore, the constancy of marginal transport costs relative to earnings, or the fact that marginal transport costs rose by almost the same percentage as average income—88 as compared with 84 percent—suggests that the income elasticity of marginal transport costs is about equal to unity.

The implications of this study for the marginal costs of transport agree quite well with the findings of other studies based upon quite different data. Beesley recently reported the results of a study based upon cost of the work-trip choices actually made by British civil servants employed in central London, compared with the cost of the alternative which would have been selected if they did not choose their usual mode.[5] He found that

---

[4] Of course, marginal transport costs may have differed among households, and certainly not all CBD worker households eight miles from the Loop on Chicago's south side were public transportation users. The analysis of Chapters 2 and 4, how-ever, suggests that CBD worker households with higher (lower) marginal transport costs would locate closer to (farther from) the Loop, other things being the same, than the average household to which the above calculations refer.

[5] M. E. Beesley, "The Value of Time Spent in Travelling: Some New Evidence."

a value of time of about one-third their average hourly earnings maximized the number of cases for which the total cost of the mode habitually used was smaller than that for the best alternative. From a regression analysis of the sales prices of undeveloped land in the Seattle area in relation to distance from downtown Seattle and other variables for the period 1949–55, Mohring determined that the value of an hour's travel time is approximately $0.58–0.65 (in 1947–49 prices), if a discount rate of 10 percent per year is used.[6] Similarly, Pendleton, from his analysis of the resale prices of FHA financed houses in the Washington, D.C., area in relation to 1959 driving time and variables describing variations in the houses themselves for the period around 1960, estimated the hourly value of travel time saved at around $0.75 (in 1960 prices).[7] The agreement of my findings with the studies mentioned above is remarkably close. All these estimates seem quite low, and, indeed, Pendleton has pointed out that his and Mohring's do not even cover automobile operating costs (the automobile being probably the predominant commuting mode in the areas they studied).[8] However, the fact that my estimate of marginal transport costs agrees so closely with those made by others using quite different data would seem to lend strong support to the theoretical analyses of Chapters 2 and 3 and to my estimate of the elasticity of the value of housing output per unit of land with respect to price.

The data for the south side of Chicago also yield useful information on the magnitude and elasticity of the total transport costs of CBD worker households. Assuming that marginal transport costs are invariant with distance, the variable component of transport costs for CBD worker households located 7.8 miles from the Loop would be $0.59 ($1.11) × 7.8 × 12 = $55 ($104) per year. If, in addition, public-transit riders paid fares of $0.15 ($0.25) per trip in 1950 (1960) and made 500 CBD work trips per year, annual fixed transport costs would be about $75 ($125), yielding total transport costs of $130 ($229) in 1950 (1960). Since income exclusive of the value of time was $3,530 ($6,510), total transport costs for CBD work trips amounted to 0.037 (0.035) of income as usually defined in 1950 (1960), and a much smaller fraction of income inclusive of the value of time. Furthermore, since the variable component of transport costs appears to be about 40 percent of total costs for the average Chicago south-side household and the elasticity of marginal transport costs with respect to income is about unity, the elasticity of total transport costs with respect to income is of the order of 0.4. The term $1 - \rho_T E_{T,y}$, which, as one sees

[6] Mohring, "Land Values and the Measurements of Highway Benefits," p. 248.
[7] Pendleton, "The Value of Accessibility," p. 58.
[8] *Ibid.*, p. 59.

from Chapter 2, is the factor by which a given relative increase in the money-wage income of CBD worker households is multiplied to obtain the increase in their real consumption, is almost unity.

I now wish to consider the relation of income differences to differences in the optimal location of households at a given time. One of the facts of U.S. cities most obvious to the casual observer is that, on the average, higher-income households tend to live at greater distances from the city center. The comparisons presented in Chapter 8 clearly suggest both a close simple association and a strong quantitative response of median tract income to distance from the CBD. These same comparisons also suggest, as do the more detailed comparisons for the south side of Chicago presented in Chapter 10, that the relation between income and distance is due largely to their common relation to the age of buildings in a neighborhood. For, when age of buildings is added to the comparisons, there is but a negligible partial relationship between income and distance and a strong negative one between income and age of buildings. The most reasonable explanation to me for this relationship is that older dwellings are more cheaply converted to lower-income use than newer ones as the total population of a city grows. An alternative explanation, which is, in fact, largely another way of saying the same thing, is that higher-income households have a preference for newness as such, and, hence, the relative earnings of older dwellings are higher the lower the income level of their occupants. But, in any event, it seems quite clear empirically that there is little relation between census-reported income and distance from the CBD on pure locational grounds—the balance between savings on the purchase of a given quantity of housing and additional transportation expenditure.

Is the analysis of Chapter 2 consistent with my empirical finding? It would appear from the preceding discussion that the elasticity of marginal transport costs with respect to income is about unity for the south side of Chicago. Thus, with an income elasticity of housing demand as low as $+1$, the $-qp_k$ and T_k curves described in Chapter 2 would shift upward by about the same amount with an increase in income, and the household's optimal location would remain unchanged. However, from the estimates cited earlier, the income elasticity of housing demand may be substantially larger than unity, in which case higher-income CBD worker households would have an incentive on purely locational grounds to live farther from the CBD. The increase in the income of CBD worker households with distance is given by equation (2.15); substituting the values $E_{q,p;C} = -1$ and $T_{kk} = 0$ suggested in Chapter 4, it becomes

$$\frac{\partial y^*}{\partial k} = \frac{-[(p_{kk}/p_k) - (p_k/p)]}{\{E_{q,y;R}(1 - \rho_T E_{T,y}) - E_{T_k,y}\}} \tag{1}$$

The numerator of (1) can be readily evaluated by recalling that the investigations in Chapters 8 and 9 revealed little or no systematic tendency for the relative change in the value of housing produced per square mile per mile to vary with distance. For this reason

$$\frac{\partial^2}{\partial k^2}\left(\frac{pQ}{L}\right)^* = \left(1 + \frac{\rho_N}{\rho_L}\sigma\right)\frac{\partial}{\partial k}\left(\frac{p_k}{p}\right) + \left(\frac{p_k}{p}\right)\frac{\partial}{\partial k}\left(1 + \frac{\rho_N}{\rho_L}\sigma\right) = 0$$

and

$$-\frac{\partial\left(\frac{p_k}{p}\right)}{\left(\frac{p_k}{p}\right)} = -\left(\frac{p_{kk}}{p_k} - \frac{p_k}{p}\right) = \frac{\frac{\partial}{\partial k}\left(1 + \frac{\rho_N}{\rho_L}\sigma\right)}{\left(1 + \frac{\rho_N}{\rho_L}\sigma\right)}, \tag{2}$$

or, in words, the effects of the relative change in the price gradient on the curvature of the VALAND-distance relationship is just offset by the relative change in the elasticity of VALAND with respect to price. In Chapter 3 I argued that, since the Chicago price gradient is about 1 percent per mile in those areas remote from rapid transit facilities, the change in the elasticity of VALAND with respect to price is about 0.7 per mile and its average value about $+15$. The expression (2) is thus about equal to 0.05. Thus, for an $E_{T_k,y} = 1$ and $E_{q,y;R} = 1.5$, equation (1) implies a relative increase in the money income of CBD worker households of 0.1 per mile, or an absolute increase of \$353 (\$651) per mile in 1950 (1960).

The values just cited are, of course, far higher than the increases in census-reported income observed in the Chicago comparisons of Chapter 10. It was also pointed out in Chapter 2, though, that the money incomes of locally employed worker households must decline by an amount equal to their expenditures on housing multiplied by the price gradient [equation (2.26)]. Given average monthly expenditures on housing of \$59 (\$111) in 1950 (1960) and a price gradient of 1 percent per mile, the annual incomes of locally employed worker households would have had to decline by about \$7 (\$13) per mile on the south side of Chicago. Now, according to data gathered by the Chicago Area Transport Study, approximately 280 thousand persons are employed in the Loop area of Chicago, or about 10 percent of the total of about 2.5 million reported in the 1960 census for the Chicago urbanized area. Combining the predicted income changes for CBD worker and local worker households, the predicted income change per mile becomes $0.1 \times 353 + 0.9 \times (-7) = 29$ (53) dollars per mile in 1950 (1960). These predicted values agree fairly closely with coefficients of \$24 per mile (with a standard error of 20) and -20 (60), which are observed for 1950 and 1960, respectively, in Tables 3 and 9 of Chapter 10. Therefore, if the income elasticity of housing demand were as large as 1.5, the observed variation of income attributable to pure locational influences could be explained by taking local employment into consideration.

At this point it is interesting to consider the relative increase in expenditures on housing per household with distance that an income elasticity of housing demand of 1.5 and the other numerical values described in the above two paragraphs would imply. Using equation (4.21), which gives the increase in expenditures by CBD worker households resulting from the tendency for those with larger incomes to locate at greater distances from the CBD, one finds a value of 15 percent per mile. Now, since local workers of the same class defined by wage rate earned at a given location have the same real incomes everywhere, the housing expenditures made by their households would be the same everywhere. Thus, for all households taken together, the relative increase in per household expenditures on housing on the south side of Chicago would be only 1.5 percent per mile. Such an increase would make only about one-tenth as large a contribution to the density gradient as the decline in the value of housing produced per unit of land with distance. Of course, the relative contribution of changing housing expenditures to the density gradient might be greater in other cities, especially in those cities where the fraction of CBD workers is greater. However, from the Chicago comparisons it would still appear that the principal locational influence on density gradients is that operating through differences in the intensity of housing output.

The final topic I wish to consider in this section is the effect of home-ownership subsidies on the location of households. In Chapter 9 I found an elasticity of housing expenditures with respect to percentage of owner-occupancy of about 0.15. Since, in 1960, an average of about 60 percent of the dwelling units in the tracts studied were owner-occupied, an elasticity of 0.15 implies that owner-occupants spend about 25 percent more on housing than others similarly situated. In Chapter 5 I suggested that the combined effects of the federal income-tax advantage to home ownership and federal mortgage programs would be to increase housing expenditures by 35 percent at most. Thus, my estimate of 25 percent greater expenditures by home owners is of a magnitude which might be attributable to these programs.

Now, if producers of single-family and other housing had different production functions, the different house types would be built in disjoint annular areas surrounding the CBD, with single-family houses, being the most land-intensive, in the outermost area. Under these conditions, the increase in the relative demand for single-family housing brought about by home-ownership subsidies would, in effect, be an increase in the demand for housing produced in the outer annular area. The outer area would, in turn, expand both inward toward the CBD and outward beyond the previous city limits, and the area of the city having the flatter residential land rental and density gradients would thus become a larger fraction of the city's total area. But there is a second, less obvious, effect of home-ownership subsidies on the location of households. From equation (2.3'), it can be seen that, with the increase in expenditures on housing brought about by home-ownership subsidies, the housing price gradient must be proportionately smaller numerically than before at the household's new equilibrium condition. Because of the second-order or stability location of locational equilibrium, the housing price gradient is numerically smaller at greater distances from the CBD. On account of this second factor, then, home-ownership subsidies will also lead to an increase in housing demand in the outer parts of the city relative to its inner zones. I shall return, in the final section of this chapter, to examine the quantitative implications of these effects upon urban decentralization.

THE RELATIVE SUPPLY OF HOUSING IN DIFFERENT PARTS OF THE CITY

Both from the empirical findings of Chapters 8 and 9 and from the discussion in the preceding section it seems clear that variations in the per household consumption of housing resulting from pure locational forces are quite small. Rather, any long-run tendency for population densities to decline with distance from the CBD would seem to result almost wholly from the decline in the intensity of housing output with distance. In this short section I was to examine two very important factors bearing on long-run variations in housing output as among different parts of a city. These are the nature of the production functions of producers of housing and variation in the fraction of total land area that is used for residential purposes.

In Chapter 4 I indicated that the rise in land's share of the value of housing output which accompanied the increase in land values relative to construction costs during the 1950's is inconsistent with the simplest hypothesis about housing-production functions, namely that all producers of housing have the same Cobb-Douglas functions. I suggested two possible alternatives to account for the rise in land's relative share: (1) that all producers of housing have the same production function, characterized by a less than unit elasticity of substitution of land for non-land factors; and (2) that housing producers have Cobb-Douglas productions differing in the exponent of land. In most of my interpretations I have, perhaps unconsciously, relied on the first of these, and I now wish to discuss my preference for it. This preference is based upon two considerations, the curvature of the relation between VALAND and distance, on the one hand, and the changes in the spread of residential population with increasing city size on the other.

I argued in Chapter 4 that if all CBD worker households are not identical, the price gradient must decline numerically with distance from the CBD for stability of locational equilibrium. I also pointed out that such a decline in the price gradient would induce a positive curvature in the relation between the log of housing output per square mile and linear distance. However, no such positive curvature was, in general, observed in the density-distance and VALAND-distance functions estimated in Part II. There were, of course, more instances of positive than of negative curvature among the density-distance relationships estimated in Chapter 7, but the difference between the number of occurrences is not statistically significant. In addition, in those instances where the curvature was statistically significant in a particular sample, both for the density-distance functions in Chapter 7 and the VALAND functions in Chapter 8, negative curvatures were more numerous than positive ones. Finally, in Chapter 9 when quadratic functions were fitted to the Chicago south-side data, quite different curvatures were found for the 1950 and 1960 comparisons.

Now, the different Cobb-Douglas functions hypothesis also implies a positive curvature for the VALAND-distance function. This is because, if they are to locate anywhere at all, those producers whose rental gradients are steeper must locate closer to the city center. They are, according to equation (3.5), the producers for whom land's share is smaller. The smaller land's share, in turn, the greater is the elasticity of the value of housing produced per square mile with respect to price, as equation (3.10) indicates. The decline in VALAND per mile would therefore tend to be greater closer to the CBD if the different Cobb-Douglas function hypothesis were correct. If all producers had the same production function, with a less than unit elasticity of substitution, however, land's relative share declines with distance along with the decline in residential land rentals, and the elasticity of VALAND with respect to price increases with distance. This increase, in turn, would impart a negative curvature by itself and offset the effects of a decline in the price gradient. Since a positive curvature to the density-distance and VALAND-distance functions was not generally observed, the same function—less than unit substitution-elasticity hypothesis—seems clearly preferable.

The strong tendency for the residential population to become more spread out as the size of a city increases, noted in Chapter 7, also favors the less than unit substitution-elasticity hypothesis. As indicated in the paragraph above, on the different Cobb-Douglas hypothesis housing output is more responsive to price changes closer to the city center. Thus, with the increase in housing demand and hence price which accompanies a growth in population, the output of housing and residential population would grow more rapidly closer to the CBD and population would become more rather than less concentrated. On the less than unit substitution-elasticity hypothesis, in contrast, output would be more responsive at greater distances from the CBD, and residential population would become less concentrated with an increase in size.

Evidence on the variation of the fraction of land area used for residential purposes is partly direct and partly indirect. In the Chicago comparisons in Chapter 9 I examined the fraction of land area which is residential and found virtually no relationship between it and any of the accessibility measures included in the regressions. Similarly, the coefficients of all the accessibility variables in corresponding gross and net density regressions in Chapter 9 were practically the same. In Chapter 4 I suggested that, if anything, there is some presumption that the fraction of land which is residential should increase with distance from the CBD. But, since the fraction is bounded from above by unity, the rate of increase must eventually decline, producing a negative curvature in the density- and VALAND-distance functions. As was pointed out earlier, however, this negative curvature was not generally observed. An increase in the fraction of land used for residential purposes with distance, though, might be responsible for those instances of strong negative curvature which were found in Chapters 7 and 8. Finally, in Chapter 7 I found that, while the total land area of the city responds in about the degree expected if the same pattern of population-density decline with distance prevails in the suburbs as in the central city, the fraction of urbanized-area population responds much less than would be expected to increases in area population or reductions in the central-city density gradient. A smaller fraction in the suburbs of total land which is residential, perhaps because a larger fraction of land is withheld from current urban uses for future development, might account for the finding noted in the previous sentence. All in all, though, there do not seem to be sufficient grounds for abandoning the analytically simpler constant-fraction land residential hypothesis in the analysis of applied urban land problems.

On Some Determinants of Urban Decentralization

In this section I wish to assess the quantitative impact of certain determinants of urban decentralization. In particular, I wish to determine whether the differential response of housing output in different parts of the city can account—as I have suggested earlier it might—for the tendency for cities to become more spread out as they grow larger. I also will try to account for the effects of increases in income on the density gradient. Finally, I will try to determine the effects of subsidies to home ownership upon the spread of population in urban areas.

The differential response of housing output to an increase in demand depends both upon the rise in housing prices and upon differences in the elasticity of housing supply with respect to price. With, say, a 10 percent increase in a city's population, housing demand would rise by 10 percent. The resulting price increase, of course, is equal to the shift in demand divided by the supply elasticity less the demand elasticity. In Chapter 3 I demonstrated that for an elasticity of substitution of 0.75 and a relative share for land of 0.05, the elasticity of housing supply per unit of land is a little over +14. With the growth in population the demand for land for other urban uses would increase as well, so that there is no presumption that the fraction of the city's previous land area used for residential purposes would increase. From the estimates presented in Chapter 7, though, the urbanized area's land area would increase by about 5 to 10 percent with the 10 percent population increase. On balance, then, the elasticity of housing supply for the city as a whole is probably about +15, and with a demand elasticity of −1, the price of housing would rise by 10/16 ≃ 0.6 percent.

Also in Chapter 3 I argued that the change in the elasticity of the value of housing produced per square mile per mile would be about 3.6 times the rental gradient or 72 times the price gradient. The latter, I suggested in Chapter 8, averaged about 2 percent per mile in U.S. cities in 1950. Hence, the elasticity of the value of housing produced per square mile would vary by about 1.5 per mile, or from about 7.5 to 22.5 over a ten mile range. With the 10 percent population increase, then, the value of housing produced would increase 4.5 to 13.5 percent over this same range. But, with a unit elastic-demand curve for housing, the rise in housing prices would leave expenditures for housing everywhere unchanged, and thus the price gradient would remain unchanged. The only effect upon the density-distance function is therefore that of the differential output response to a price increase which is proportionately the same everywhere.

Letting the subscripts B and A denote values before and after the population change, respectively, one has

$$e^{-10g_A} = \frac{D(10)_A}{D(0)_A} = \frac{1.135 \; D(10)_B}{1.045 \; D(0)_B} = 1.085e^{-10g_B}$$

or $g_A - g_B = -0.008$. Since the density gradient estimates shown in Table 7.1 average around 0.3, the implied elasticity of the density gradient with respect to population is about −0.27, as compared with the estimated value of −0.47 (with a standard error of 0.13) from Table 7.10. Since the "t"-ratio for the difference between these two values is about −1.5, the evidence would seemingly suggest that the differential response of housing output to price changes cannot explain the whole of the tendency for cities to become more decentralized as they grow larger.

The research reported in this monograph provides little in explanation of other factors which may bring about increased decentralization with size. Two conjectures come to my mind, however. In discussing the optimal location of households by income in the first section of this chapter I pointed out that pure location factors might lead to an increase in the money income of CBD worker households on the order of $300 to $600 per mile and to a resulting relative increase in the per household expenditure on housing of CBD workers of about 15 percent per mile. For locally employed worker households of a given wage class, however, the per household expenditure on housing is invariant with distance. If, then, there is a reduction in the ratio of CBD of locally employed workers with increased city size, there would be a reduction in the increase in per household housing expenditures, and a decline in population densities, with distance. Secondly, if the number and size relative to the CBD of non-CBD employment concentrations increase as population grows, in accord with my discussion of the effects of these centers in Chapter 4 the overall rate of density decline would become smaller relative to the rate of decline around any one of the centers separately. In view of the fact that the future population growth of American cities is likely to be great enough to produce decentralization of great practical importance, further investigation of the relation between size and spread would seem to be an important topic for research.

In Chapter 7 I found that, while it is not very well estimated, the elasticity of the density gradient with respect to urbanized-area income is about -0.63. Since, at current rates of income growth, real income can rise by one-third during a decade, such an elasticity implies a density gradient reduction of 20 percent per decade. It is thus quite important to understand the nature of the forces producing decentralization as income grows. This study has suggested many possible explanations for such an association. The growth in income, of course, increases the total demand for housing in a city in a way quite similar to an increase in population and thus may lead to a differential expansion in output in different parts of the city. Secondly, if the income elasticity of housing demand exceeds that of marginal transport costs, the price gradient will decline with a growth in income, or housing prices will increase more in the outer parts of cities. Finally, in Chapter 5 I suggested several forces, including stronger preferences for space relative to structures, stronger preferences for home ownership or for single-family dwellings, and increased incentives to home ownership as housing consumption increases, which might increase the relative demand for housing in the outer parts of cities as income increases. I now wish to inquire into the quantitative contributions of these various forces for decentralization.

Not surprisingly, the answer depends critically upon the size of the income elasticity of housing demand. If this elasticity were as low as $+1$, a 10 percent increase in income would have the same effect upon housing demand and the density gradient, through the output expansion effect alone, as a 10 percent increase in population. Furthermore, the price gradient would remain unchanged, because expenditures for housing would increase by the same relative amount as marginal transport costs. These two factors, then, would produce an elasticity of the density gradient with respect to income of only -0.27, and the bulk of the effect of income growth on decentralization would have to be accounted for by other forces, such as the taste factors discussed in Chapter 5. On the other hand, if the income elasticity of housing demand were as large as $+1.3$, housing demand would increase by 13 percent, and the output expansion effect alone would cause a decline in the density gradient of $1.3 \times 2.7 = 3.5$ percent. Furthermore, the price gradient would decline by 3 percent, the 10 percent increase in marginal transport costs being more than offset by a 13 percent increase in expenditures on housing. Thus, the VALAND and density gradients would each decline by about 6.5 percent, implying an income elasticity of the density gradient of -0.65. Hence, if the income elasticity of housing demand were $+1.3$ or larger, the factors discussed in Chapter 5 would make no contribution at all to increased decentralization. It would seem, then, that a finer determination of the income elasticity of housing demand than is currently available would be necessary to settle the issue.

Finally, I wish to discuss the likely quantitative impact of federal subsidies to home ownership on urban decentralization. Since, as noted in the previous section, there is no evidence for the different production-function hypothesis, there is no reason on the supply side of the market to expect that increased decentralization of population will result from the increased demand for home ownership. However, by increasing expenditures for housing relative to marginal transport costs by 25 percent, the price gradient must be 25 percent smaller than in the absence of the subsidy in the home owner's new equilibrium location. If all households were the same and none had any preferences for renting versus ownership, with the institution of the subsidy all households who were not home owners would become so, and the price gradient would fall by 25 percent throughout the city. In addition, with the 25 percent increase in demand for housing, because of output-expansion effect the density gradient would decline by $25 \times (-0.27) = 7$ percent. On balance, then, the density gradient would decline by about one-third, or from an average of 0.3 for all American cities in 1950 to 0.2. The effects upon the fraction of the urbanized area's population contained inside the central city and the land area of the former could then be readily evaluated from the results of Chapter 7.

Despite the fact that federal home-ownership subsidies reduce the relative price of housing by at least 25 percent to home owners, in the United States in 1960 only about 60 percent of all dwellings were owner-occupied. This is probably because for many households—especially lower-income and younger ones and those that move frequently—the costs of owner-occupied housing are very high relative to the costs of renting. As noted in the first section, the increased housing expenditures of home owners require that they locate in the outer parts of the city where the price gradient is smaller. Thus, as illustrated by Figure 1, households that are renters after the subsidy is instituted would tend to inhabit the area of the city closer to the CBD, or from 0 to k_1 miles in Figure 1. Because there is

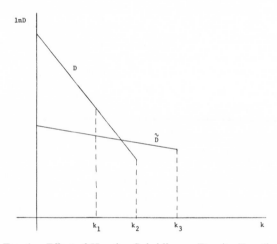

Fig. 1.—Effect of Housing Subsidies on Density Function

no increase in the quantity of housing demanded by renters, there is no change in the price gradient and no output expansion effect in the renter area. The distribution of population up to a distance of k_1 miles from the CBD would, therefore, be given by the old density-distance function, D.

Now, in Chapter 4, equation (4.12), it was shown that the fraction of the total population of a city living not more than k_1 miles from the CBD, P_1/P, is given by $f(D_1, k_1)/f(D_1, k_2)$, where $f(D_1, k) = 1 - (1 + D_1 k)e^{-D_1 k}$, D_1 is the density gradient, and k_2 is the radius of the city. For the forty-six American cities whose population distributions were studied in Chapter 7, the median values of the necessary parameters were approximately $D_1 = 0.3$ and $k_2 = 6.0$. Hence, $f(D_1, k_2) \simeq 0.54$, and if $P_1/P = 0.40$, one finds by trial and error that $k_1 \simeq 2.9$ miles.

For the 60 percent of the city's households who are home owners after the subsidy is instituted the slope of the log density-distance function must be about one-third smaller, or that of $\tilde{D}$ in Figure 1. At the boundary separating the renter and home owner residential areas, population densities are 25 percent smaller on the home owner side. While the subsidy lowers the price of housing net of the subsidy to home owners, it does not affect the price per unit of housing received by producers of owner-occupied relative to renter housing. Thus, because producers of the two types of housing would appear to have the same production functions, residential land rentals and the output of housing per square mile of land are the same on either side of the boundary of k_1. Because of the subsidy, though, the per household consumption of housing is a fraction $\phi = 0.25$ greater to the right of k_1. Thus, at k_1

$$\tilde{D}(k_1) = \tilde{D}_0 e^{-\tilde{D}_1 k_1} = (1 - \phi)D(k_1) = (1 - \phi)D_0 e^{-D_1 k_1}$$

or, using (4.11),

$$\tilde{D}_0 = \frac{(1 - \phi)D_1{}^2 P e^{-(D_1 - \tilde{D}_1)k_1}}{\xi f(D_1, k_2)}. \tag{3}$$

Further, since the per household consumption of housing has increased for home owners, and population densities have fallen, the radius of the city must increase from k_2 to k_3, the latter being that value of k for which

$$\left(\frac{P - P_1}{P}\right) = \int_{k_1}^{k_3} \frac{\tilde{D}_0}{P} e^{-\tilde{D}_1 k} \xi k \, dk = \frac{\xi \tilde{D}_0}{P \tilde{D}_1{}^2} [f(\tilde{D}_1, k_3) - f(\tilde{D}_1, k_1)]. \tag{4}$$

Upon substituting (3) into (4),

$$\left(\frac{P - P_1}{P}\right) = (1 - \phi)(D_1/\tilde{D}_1)^2 \frac{e^{-(D_1 - \tilde{D}_1)k_1}}{f(D_1, k_2)} [f(\tilde{D}_1, k_3) - f(\tilde{D}_1, k_1)] \tag{5}$$

Inserting the appropriate values already noted, (5) becomes

$$0.6 = 0.75 \left(\frac{0.3}{0.2}\right)^2 \frac{e^{-0.1(2.9)}}{0.54}$$
$$\times [(1 + 0.2 \times 2.9)e^{-0.2(2.9)} - (1 + 0.2 k_3)e^{-0.2 k_3}],$$

which reduces to

$$(1 + 0.2 k_3)e^{-0.2 k_3} \simeq 0.63. \tag{6}$$

Again by trial and error one finds that a $k_3 \simeq 6.5$ miles satisfies (6). Hence, the effect of the 25 percent subsidy is to increase the land area of the urbanized area by about $(6.5/6.0)^2 - 1$ times, or by about 17 percent. This is somewhat smaller than the 23 percent increase expected upon the basis of the predicted DENGRA coefficient in Table 7.15 if all households would become home owners as a result of ownership subsidies.

For the forty-six U.S. cities studied in Chapter 7 the median radius of the central city was about 4.4 miles. One sees, then, as Figure 1 illustrates, that the effect of home-ownership subsidies is to reduce the population in roughly the outer third of the central city and to increase population in the suburban parts of the urbanized area. How big is this effect? Prior to the subsidy the central city's fraction of the urbanized area population is given by $f(0.3, 4.4)/f(0.3, 6.0) = 0.70$. Following the subsidy the central city population is the fraction 0.40 who are renters plus the fraction of the urbanized area population who live at distances of from 2.9 to 4.4 miles in the home-owner ring. The latter, obtained from the right member of (5) by substituting 4.4 for k_3, is about equal to 0.25. Thus, the subsidy would tend to reduce the central city population to 0.65, or by $(0.05/0.7) \times 100 \simeq 7$ percent. Allowing, however, for the attenuation of forces making for decentralization into the suburbs by multiplying by the ratio of the actual to predicted DENGRA coefficients in Table 7.13 (0.22/0.52) reduces the predicted decline to 3 percent. The expected effect of home-ownership subsidies on the central city's fraction of the urbanized area population is thus rather small, but their effect on the land area used for urban purposes is of considerable practical importance.

13   *Implications for Public Policy*

In commenting upon John Neville Keynes's distinction between positive (what is) and normative (what ought to be) economics, Milton Friedman stresses that "normative economics...cannot be independent of positive economics."[1] This is so because any policy recommendation necessarily rests upon some positive conclusion as to why a problem exists and how the recommendation made will ameliorate it. Friedman adds:[2]

> I venture the judgment, however, that currently in the Western world, and especially in the United States, differences about economic policy among disinterested citizens derive predominantly from different predictions about the economic consequences of taking action—differences that in principle can be eliminated by the progress of positive economics—rather than from fundamental differences in basic values, differences about which men can ultimately only fight.

Nowhere, in my opinion, is Friedman's judgment so well illustrated as in the area of public policy toward urban problems. Governmental programs such as subsidized rapid transit, urban renewal, and a variety of housing subsidies receive enthusiastic support from persons of widely different political views who are sincerely interested in solving urban problems. In my view, these and many related programs are seriously deficient. At best they contribute little to solving the basic urban problem, which is poverty, and many actually tend to intensify poverty and waste resources. This view of mine is not based upon values different from those held by persons supporting the programs to which I object. Like them, I am a strong believer in measures designed to promote economic efficiency and equality. Rather, the positive analysis of the supporters of current programs seems wanting—sometimes naive, frequently unsound logically, and almost invariably lacking in empirical support.

---

[1] "The Methodology of Positive Economics," p. 5.
[2] *Ibid.*

Now, I would be the last person to argue that my positive conclusions are so firmly established that there is no room for legitimate difference in interpretation of a priori argument or empirical judgment. I would insist, however, that the evidence of this monograph and its implications for public policy deserve to be taken seriously and not ignored simply because they conflict with previously held beliefs. Therefore, in this chapter I wish to appraise some of the more important current and contemplated governmental programs in the light of the findings of this monograph. First, I will summarize my positive conclusions relating to the twin problems of suburban sprawl and urban blight. In the second and third sections I consider in turn the implications of my findings for governmental programs which relate to these two problems.

SUMMARY OF RELEVANT POSITIVE FINDINGS

Of all the forces making for urban decentralization during the 1950's, lower marginal transport costs, as reflected in increased car registrations per capita, have been by far the most important quantitatively. As noted at the close of Chapter 7, during the fifties CAREGS increased from 0.26 to 0.35, and such an increase would have been sufficient to account for a decline in the central-city density gradient from a 1950 median value of 0.30 to 0.13. The increase in CAREGS would also have led to a decline in the population of central cities by about 14 percent and to an increase in the land area used for urban purposes of around 47 percent. The increase in city sizes, which averaged about 30 percent during the fifties, also had important effects. An increase of this magnitude would, according to the estimates of Chapter 7, have reduced the density gradient by 15 percent and increased land area by almost 25 percent. It would, however, have led central-city population to grow at only a slightly slower rate—27 percent— than the urbanized area's.

My analysis at the close of Chapter 12 suggests that federal housing subsidies have been an important factor in urban decentralization. It would appear that these subsidies would reduce the density gradient by as much as one-third in the outer parts of the city inhabited by home owners and increase the typical city's land area by around 17 percent. While the effects of urbanized area income on density gradients are uncertain statistically, the estimated DENGRA elasticity in Chapter 7 together with a decade increase in real income of one-third would lead to a 20 percent reduction in the central-city density gradient.

This monograph has produced practically no evidence that urban decentralization has been the result of physical or social conditions in the central city. Of the physical indicators related to DENGRA in Chapter 7, only the proportion of the central city's dwelling units which are substandard gave much indication of influencing the density gradient. Not only were its effects quite uncertain on statistical grounds, but the decline in proportion substandard during the 1950's, which averaged from 0.20 to 0.11 in the cities studied, would actually have led to increased centralization. From the results of Chapter 7 it would appear that, with increases in the central-city population which is Negro, housing demand grows more rapidly in the outer parts of the central city than in its inner zones. Neither an increase in the proportion of central-city dwelling units that are substandard nor an increase in the fraction of its population that is Negro would appear to reduce the central-city population or increase the land area of the urbanized area, however.

To an important extent it appears to me that the forces influencing the distribution of an urbanized area's population between the central city and its suburbs are very much the same as those which affect the spread of population within the central city itself. Two important exceptions should be noted, however. First, with a fall in the average income level of the central city relative to its suburbs, the central-city population tends to decline and the urbanized area's land area to increase. Although there is no direct evidence, the best explanation for this phenomenon is, I believe, the increased tax burden on higher-income households and business firms in the central city to which an influx of lower-income households leads. And, second, it appears that the central city's population declines less in response to forces making for an increased spread of population within its borders than one would expect if population distribution between the central city and its suburbs were merely an extension of that within the central city. Thus, my analysis gives little evidence that suburbanization of population has been carried too far.

Turning to the determinants of the quality of the central city's housing stock, it appears to me that differences in the proportion of dwellings which are substandard within or among different cities at a given time and over time in a given place can best be explained on the basis of differences in the relative demand for poor- versus good-quality housing. By far the most important determinant of the condition of dwelling units is the income level of their inhabitants. Not only is the association between condition and income quite close, but the quantitative response of condition to income changes is very strong indeed. The estimates made in Chapter 10 suggest that the elasticity of the proportion of dwelling units substandard with respect to income is of the order of -3.3, or that with a 10 percent increase in income—which can occur in three or four years—the proportion of dwellings substandard would decrease by one-third. In Chapter 10 I also found that among different cities in 1950 the elasticity of condition with respect to construction costs is of opposite sign but the same order of magnitude as that with respect to income. Since my earlier studies showed the income and price elasticities of housing demand to be about the same numerically, this similarity of the magnitude of the dwelling-unit condition elasticities lends support to the hypothesis that dwelling-unit condition is determined primarily by conditions of demand.

On the whole there seems to be little evidence that variations in the relative quantities of poor- and good-quality housing are importantly affected by differences in their relative supply. In my opinion, the positive association between poor dwelling-unit condition and crowding is largely due to the fact that they are closely related aspects of the low-income demand for housing. Strong support is lent to this interpretation by the fact that, when estimated by the method of two-stage least-squares, the coefficient showing the effect of crowding on condition falls drastically and becomes statistically insignificant. For the year 1950 there was a strong tendency for a higher proportion of dwellings substandard to be found in areas with above-average age of dwellings and rates of population turnover. Neither effect showed up at all strongly in 1960 for the south side of Chicago, however. Until further evidence is available I am inclined to attribute the 1950 results to the effects of rent control. Among the other variables which might be interpreted as reflecting differences in the relative supply of housing of different qualities, no evidence was found that above-average population densities lead to an above-average proportion of substandard dwellings. When the effects of income differences are controlled for, the proportion substandard was below average in areas of above-average rates of population growth. Finally, my results suggest that dwelling-unit condition has negligible effects upon the income level of persons inhabiting these dwellings. Hence, the association between income and condition cannot be explained by the hypothesis that slums exist for reasons other than low-income demand and that lower-income households are attracted to or higher-income ones are repelled from an area by its poor-quality housing.

My analysis gives little support to the view that Negroes pay higher prices for housing of comparable quality than whites do. I do find that expenditures for housing by Negroes are higher at a given income level, but with a price elasticity of housing demand of unity or larger, price differences cannot account for such expenditure differences. My examination of population densities and other physical magnitudes, as well as my comparison of changes in median rents in Chicago south-side tracts remaining in white occupancy during the fifties versus those changing to Negro occupancy, suggests to me that in Negro areas rental housing prices are no more than 5 percent higher than in comparable white areas and perhaps less. Furthermore, my examination in Chapter 10 of the effects of race on dwelling-unit condition suggests that at given income levels the proportion of dwellings in Negro areas which are substandard is no higher than in white areas. This finding lends no support to the widespread view that the residential segregation of Negroes restricts them to areas of poorest housing quality. Rather, it would seem that the low average quality of Negro housing is due primarily to the low incomes of the inhabitants.

PROGRAMS RELATING TO URBAN DECENTRALIZATION

While it has been an avowed aim of public policy to reduce urban decentralization, largely through the federal urban renewal program, on balance governmental programs have almost certainly encouraged decentralization. By reducing the proportion of a central city's dwellings which are substandard, urban renewal might tend to increase the numerical rate of population-density decline within the central city itself. This possibility tends to be counterbalanced, though, by the fact that many more low-income households are displaced by renewal projects than are replaced by higher-income households in the renewal area.[3] In addition, my results suggest that the distribution of population between the central city and its suburbs is not appreciably affected by dwelling-unit condition in the central city, contrary to the widespread belief of supporters of renewal programs. At the same time my results suggest that decentralization has been encouraged to a substantial degree by improvements in transportation, to which the building of urban expressways—largely with federal funds— have probably been of principal importance, and by federal home-ownership subsidies.

If, as is widely believed, decentralization of population had occurred largely because of undesirable physical conditions in the older, more central parts of cities, then improvement of transportation facilities might tend to moderate decentralization in the future. In the absence of improved transportation, some business firms might also be induced to relocate to outlying areas for better access to potential customers and employees. There is virtually no empirical evidence to support the view that decentralization has occurred because of deterioration of the central city, however. Rather, decentralization of population has occurred to an important extent because of transportation improvements, and these improvements thus provide indirectly the very incentive for decentralization of business firms which they are designed in part to counteract.

In recent years, the development and improvement of rapid-transit facilities through federal subsidy has received strong support. This support

---

[3] Anderson, *The Federal Bulldozer*, p. 67, estimates that, as of March 31, 1961, 126,000 dwellings had been eliminated by urban renewal and replaced with 28,000.

probably derives from concern over rush-hour congestion on urban highways and the belief that rapid transit would be a technologically more efficient means of commuter travel. Congestion, however, is not so much a technological problem as an economic one; it arises largely because of a failure to impose a charge for the use of a scarce resource. Even if preferable on other grounds, congestion would still be a problem on rapid-transit routes if fares are set too low—witness the New York City subway system during rush hour. And to the extent that subsidized rapid-transit systems are technologically more efficient than highways, they will merely be more efficient in encouraging decentralization. I realize, of course, that building more highways and rapid-transit facilities may well be justified by th⌐ saving of resources for other uses that they might permit. There seems to be little reason, though, to anticipate by so doing that one might slow down urban decentralization.

Subsidies to home ownership in the form of the federal income-tax advantage and federal mortgage programs have probably tended substantially to reduce population-density gradients in the outer parts of cities and to increase the land area that urbanized areas occupy. As I will argue in more detail in the following section, there is little evidence to suggest that consumption of housing at the expense of other commodities ought to be encouraged. Much more important, however, is the fact that, being geared largely to home ownership, these subsidies tend to benefit the higher-income groups primarily and thus to increase inequality.

Another group of programs that is receiving increasing scholarly and popular support comprises various suburban development programs. Prominent among these are proposed federal subsidies for the building of new towns. Support for these programs stems largely, I believe, from the hope that, in avoiding the undesirable physical conditions of past urban development by means of proper planning, they will prevent future deterioration and decentralization. There is little evidence, however, that current decentralization results to any important degree from physical deterioration of the older parts of cities which proper planning might prevent. Rather, by encouraging the flow of new resources into suburban development and thus reducing the price of housing there relative to that in the central city, the subsidization of new towns and related programs would surely encourage decentralization currently.

At this point the reader may ask what policies I would recommend to reverse the tide of decentralization. Apart from the elimination of federal home-ownership subsidies and the kind of municipal fiscal reform discussed below, I see no need to attempt to halt decentralization. Because of the development of the automobile and other transport improvements, the older, more accessible parts of cities have lost a part of the comparative advantage they once enjoyed for the production of many commodities. For promotion of economic efficiency there is no more reason to reverse the resulting changes than to impose a protective tariff on cotton textile products in order to overcome the loss of comparative advantage the domestic industry may once have enjoyed. A little less than half of the tendency for cities to decentralize as they grow in size seems explainable on the basis of a differential output response resulting from the fact that production of housing is more cheaply expanded in the outer parts of cities. Likewise, the tendency for density gradients to fall with a growth in income would seem to result partly from the factor just noted and partly from the desire of households to minimize their costs of housing plus transportation by locating farther from the CBD. By reversing decentralization occurring from increased population and incomes one would, in effect, be preventing savings in the production and consumption of housing that might otherwise occur, and thus the national income would be made smaller than it otherwise would be.

Given current municipal fiscal relationships, decentralization does pose a serious problem. In our society some of the most significant income and wealth redistributing functions are performed by local governments through their role in providing for public education and health and hospital services to the lower-income population, and welfare services of many kinds. At the same time, local governments have been dependent to an important extent upon taxes raised from their own residents for the support of these functions. With the growth in the absolute size of the lower-income population in central cities, the tax burden of higher-income households and business firms increases if a given level of public services per capita is to be maintained. With the higher central-city tax burden, those so affected have additional incentives to choose suburban over central-city locations. The analysis of Chapter 7 does indeed suggest that the lower the average income level of the central city relative to its suburbs, the smaller is the central city's population and the larger is the land area occupied by the urbanized area. In the future there is every reason to believe that the absolute size of the lower-income population in central cities will continue to grow, since, as seen from Chapter 10, the age of dwellings and previous income level of the residents of a part of the city are the principal determinants of its current household-income level. If so, one can anticipate an even greater stimulus to decentralization because of the municipal fiscal problem.

Until now the typical answer to the fiscal problems of central cities has been federal grant-in-aid funds for specific purposes. The greatest disadvantage of this method of overcoming the problem is that it encourages too much expenditure for certain purposes and too little for others. If local governments are allowed free rein in designing programs for which they are required to pay only some fraction, say one-third, of the costs, they have the incentive to push expenditures on them to the point where the marginal benefits are only one-third of the marginal costs. It is probably for this reason that the federal government has retained a substantial degree of control over specific local projects. Such controls result in delays and impose additional administrative costs. And it is quite difficult for federal legislation and administrative regulation to allow for all exceptions warranted by genuine differences in local conditions. Another answer to the municipal fiscal dilemma which is gaining increased support is the colonization of lower-income persons in suburban areas and the discouragement of their migration from rural areas in the South to large cities. Colonization has the disadvantage of incurring greater housing costs than would otherwise be incurred. Discouragement of migration is likewise inefficient in that it prevents the movement of labor from areas of lower to higher marginal productivity.

Given that it is desirable for local governments to retain functions such as support of public education, a far more efficient means of dealing with the municipal fiscal problem is federal and/or state tax-sharing with municipalities. If individuals and business firms had to pay the same taxes regardless of their location, the fiscal incentive for decentralization would be eliminated. Such tax-sharing schemes would also eliminate the inefficiencies inherent in grants-in-aid for specific programs. Each city, having to bear the full marginal costs of each project, would have no incentive to overspend, and the need for federal control of local projects would largely be obviated. Finally, regional development projects could be evaluated on their own merits without regard to the extraneous issue of the fiscal problem arising from continued in-migration into large cities.

PROGRAMS RELATING TO CENTRAL-CITY HOUSING QUALITY

Public concern over the quality of housing in central cities has grown so great that almost any program that gives any hope of quality improvement is warmly embraced. Yet, because it is not widely realized that the basic cause of poor-quality housing is the poverty of its inhabitants, many such programs have accomplished little, since they have done nothing to raise the incomes of the poor. Indeed, as I will argue below, some have probably even reduced the real income of the poor. In addition, many housing programs are economically inefficient because they stimulate housing in the wrong way.

In discussing government housing policies it is convenient to consider separately demolition, policies such as stricter code-enforcement which raise the cost of producing poor-quality housing, and housing subsidies, despite the fact that certain actual government programs such as public housing contain elements of more than one of these categories. By demolition I mean any policy which tends to decrease the supply of poor-quality housing by shifting the curve horizontally. In contrast, code-enforcement and similar cost-increasing policies reduce the supply of poor-quality housing by shifting the supply curve vertically. By housing subsidy I mean any policy which reduces the price low-income households pay for housing relative to its marginal costs of production.

Immediately following demolition, the average housing quality for the city will improve because of the removal of poor-quality dwellings from the housing stock. With this removal, the price of poor- relative to good-quality housing rises, since demolition does nothing to affect the relative demand for housing of the different qualities. The rise in the relative price of poor-quality housing, in turn, will increase the profitability of conversion, and some previously existing good-quality housing will be converted to smaller units and allowed to deteriorate over time. If the long-run relative supply curve of poor-quality housing were perfectly elastic—that is, if there were no differences among structures in their cost of conversion from good- to poor-quality housing—then in the long run the relative quantities of poor- and good-quality housing would be the same as they were prior to the initial demolition. The long-run effect of demolition, then, would be wholly to relocate poor-quality housing.

I argued in Chapter 6, however, that there is good reason to suppose that the long-run relative supply schedule of poor- versus good-quality housing is less than perfectly elastic. It seems likely that older dwellings in general and dwellings in multifamily structures are more cheaply converted to poor-quality use. In addition, I would anticipate that the relative earnings in good- versus poor-quality use would be higher for single-family dwellings and dwellings on large lots than for other house types. Under these conditions, even in the long run, slum clearance would bring about some reduction in the relative quantity of poor-quality dwellings. But at the same time the price of poor- relative to good-quality housing would remain above its level prior to demolition. While some households who in the absence of demolition would have lived in poor-quality housing will be induced by its relative price increase to inhabit better-quality housing instead, others will remain in poor-quality housing and consume less of it than they otherwise would have done. Thus, although demolition probably leads to a long-run reduction in the proportion of poor-quality dwellings, it lowers the average quality of poor-quality dwellings. And, with a less than perfectly elastic long-run relative supply curve, clearance makes the poor even poorer, relative to higher-income groups, by raising the relative price of poor-quality housing.

Now, many persons would object to my conclusion by pointing out that, in fact, federal law often requires that persons displaced by demolition be relocated in better-quality housing. While official reports would seem to indicate that such relocation has been accomplished, Hartman has pointed out that these reports may both understate the average quality of dwellings prior to demolition and overstate the average quality of dwellings to which former residents of the area have been relocated.[4] But any before-and-after comparisons of the housing quality inhabited by the area's predemolition residents are likely to be seriously deficient for two reasons. The relevant group to compare is the whole of the lower-income population, not merely the area's former residents. It is quite possible for all of the area's former residents to be better housed after relocation and for other lower-income households to be more poorly housed. And second, in any comparison I have seen, housing quality has been studied within a relatively short time after relocation. Since quality deterioration may take several years, re- study of quality at a later date would probably reveal lower average housing quality than initially.

Despite its adverse effects upon the distribution of income by reducing the real consumption opportunities of the poor, demolition might be justifiable on grounds of economic efficiency. Many of the explanations for slums which I discussed earlier in Chapter 6 in effect assert that the market has produced too much poor-quality housing in American cities relative to the low-income demand for it. This, of course, is equivalent to asserting that the price per unit of housing service is lower in slums than in other areas or that the intensity of residential land use and population densities are likewise lower. My examination of the Chicago south-side area yields no evidence whatsoever that such is the case. Indeed, for 1960 there was some suggestion, admittedly not very strong, that the price per unit of housing as well as population densities are actually higher in slum areas than in similarly situated non-slum areas. Proponents of demolition also frequently suggest that such programs may be justified on the basis of external effects on the values of surrounding properties, though to my knowledge none has presented any very convincing arguments in support of that position. As Bailey points out, however, to the extent that the length of the perimeter of the slum area is unchanged by demolition, demolition merely shifts the locations of the external effects and not their total.[5] Thus, apart from other factors to be discussed below in connection with housing subsidies, there seems little reason to believe that slum clearance can be justified on the basis of economic efficiency either.

---

[4] Chester Hartman, "The Housing of Relocated Families."
[5] Bailey, "Note on the Economics of Residential Zoning and Urban Renewal."

While some persons have come to realize that demolition has adverse effects upon the poor, few realize that the long-run effects of measures which raise the cost of producing poor-quality housing are equally, if not more, injurious to lower-income groups. Among the latter are measures such as stricter code-enforcement, the rent strike, and public receivership of slum dwellings. In the short run such measures may improve the housing of the poor by allowing the quasi-rents which would otherwise accrue to the owners of poor-quality dwellings to be appropriated and used either for quality improvement or for reducing the unit price of poor-quality housing. Such actions, however, reduce the relative earnings of dwellings in poor- as compared with good-quality use. For this reason, in the long run fewer dwellings will be converted to poorer-quality dwellings as the low-income population grows, and some may be reconverted to good-quality ones. The net effect of cost-increasing policies is thus to reduce the housing opportunities of the poor. This will be the case even with a perfectly elastic relative supply schedule of poor-quality housing. For, by shifting this supply curve vertically rather than horizontally, code enforcement, for example, directly raises the long-run equilibrium relative price of poor- versus good-quality housing. Although they are less readily apparent than the effects of demolition, the effects upon the lower-income population of cost-increasing programs are if anything even more harmful.

Unlike the policies discussed thus far, housing subsidies tend to benefit the poor even in the long run by increasing their real consumption opportunities. Such subsidies are inefficient, however, in that they increase the real incomes of their recipients by no more than an income subsidy whose annual cost to the government is the same would do. For, if the cost of the housing subsidy were given as an income subsidy, its recipients could if they wished spend the whole of the increase in their incomes on housing. If they were to choose to spend only a part of their additional incomes on housing, one would presume that they preferred the expenditure pattern they had selected for themselves. Certain housing subsidies, especially those involving loans at below market interest rates, are further deficient in that they lead producers of housing to use more capital and less current expenditure in producing housing services than market conditions warrant. Interest-rate subsidies would be economically efficient only if it were demonstrated that market rates of interest charged lower-income borrowers exceed the alternative earnings of capital funds invested in other uses plus any additional costs of and allowance for risk in lending for low-income housing.

Two additional arguments might be used to justify housing subsidies in preference to general income subsidies. The first, which is pure paternalism, is that the poor are unable to spend their incomes in their own best interest. A more serious argument is that by inhabiting poor-quality housing the poor impose costs upon other members of society. For example, it is argued that crime, disease, and delinquency rates all tend to be higher in slum areas than elsewhere. Such an argument, of course, is exceedingly naïve, since the obvious association between crime, disease, and delinquency rates and housing quality by no means implies any causal relationship. I am aware of only one careful study of the problem, which compared the experience of pairs of low-income households of similar economic and demographic characteristics in which one member of the pair lived in public housing and the other in private.[6] Apart from characteristics which obviously related to the increased housing consumption afforded by the public housing subsidy, the differences between the publicly and privately housed families were minor. Of course, the families were studied only for a period of less than three years, and a longer period might be required for the beneficial effects of public housing to be revealed. Until such effects can be demonstrated, however, there would seem to be no grounds for preferring housing to general income subsidies.

In view of the strong response of housing quality to increased incomes found in Chapter 10, a general income subsidy would be surprisingly effective in eliminating substandard dwellings. On the south side of Chicago in 1950, in the lowest-income areas median incomes of census tracts averaged around $2,000 per year, and around 40 percent of all dwellings were substandard. According to the estimates of Chapter 10, a 10 percent income subsidy—$200 per family per year—would lead to a reduction of the proportion of dwellings substandard of one-third or from 40 to 27 percent. Thus, in a census tract with 1,000 households the subsidy would cost approximately $200,000 per year, and the additional expenditure for housing it induced would result in about 130 units' being improved so as to be removed from the substandard category. Thus, the general income subsidy would cost approximately $130 per month per substandard dwelling eliminated. By way of comparison, Nourse has estimated that the average monthly subsidy per public housing unit during the 1950's was about $115 plus utilities furnished without cost to tenants.[7] Of course, under public housing the average increase in housing consumption per family rehoused would be greater than under the income subsidy, but the latter would improve the housing quality of a greater number of families. The income subsidy would also permit lower-income families to increase their expenditure on food, clothing, and medical care. With the substantial growth in incomes that has occurred since 1950,

---

[6] Daniel M. Wilner and others, *The Housing Environment and Family Life.*
[7] Hugh O. Nourse, "The Effect of Public Housing on Property Values in St. Louis," p. 434.

substandard dwellings would be more costly to eliminate now, both because a given percentage income-increase now represents a roughly 50 percent larger absolute increase and, the proportion of substandard dwellings being much smaller now than in 1950, because a given percentage reduction would be a smaller absolute one. Still, in view of its other advantages, a general income subsidy to lower-income households appears to me to be an attractive alternative to housing subsidies for improving the real consumption opportunities of the poor.

Glossary of Variable Names

The following gives brief definitions of the various variables used in the empirical comparisons in Part II, their units of measure where these are not obvious from the definition, and the functional form used if it is other than natural form. For a more detailed description and/or motivation for inclusion of these variables in the various comparisons the reader should refer to the text discussion. Numbers in parentheses refer to the chapter where used. For the first chapter in which any given variable is used, a full description is presented. For succeeding chapters, only differences from earlier usage are noted explicitly.

AGEDUS
- (7) proportion of the central city's dwelling units which were built prior to 1920, for 1950
- (8) same, census tracts
- (9) same, and proportion of housing units in the census tract built prior to 1940, for 1960
- (10) same

AGEPER
- (9) proportion of the population 21 years old or older who were 65 or over, 1950 and 1960, in natural logs
- (10) same, but in natural units, and for intercity comparisons the proportion of population age 20 over 65

AGESMA
- (7) number of decades since the SMA first attained a population of 50,000
- (10) same

AVCNRN
- (11) average contract rent in census tracts in 1960 relative to 1950

CAREGS
- (7) car registrations per capita in principal SMA counties, 1950 and 1960

CHABDY
- (11) 1 if a racially changed occupancy tract which is contiguous to the 1960 boundary, 0 otherwise

CHANGE
- (11) 1 if tract changed from white to Negro occupancy during the decade, 0 otherwise, 1950 to 1960

CITINC
(7) median income of families and unrelated individuals (families) in dollars per year, central city of the urbanized area, 1949 (1959)

CNTPOP
(7) natural log of the central city population, 1950 and 1960

CONCST
(7) measure of residential construction costs for 1949, using the Boeckh index for brick structures
(10) same

DCBDSQ
(9) square of DISCBD

DENCIT
(7) average population density of the central city in persons per square mile, 1950 and 1960

DENGRA
(7) natural logarithm of the estimated population density gradient

DISCBD
(8) distance to the CBD in miles
(9) same
(10) same

GRODEN
(8) census tract gross population densities, 1950, in natural logs
(9) same, 1950 and 1960
(10) same

GROPOP
(7) proportion of the SMA's population growth that took place since 1920, for 1950 and 1960
(10) for Chicago south-side comparison (intercity comparisons) natural log of the ratio of 1950 or 1960 population to 1930 population (natural log of ratio of 1950 to 1900 SMA population)

INCM50
(10) 1949 tract median income of families and unrelated individuals

INCOME
(8) median income of families and unrelated individuals in 1949, in dollars per year, for the tract, in natural logs
(9) same, and of families in 1959
(10) same, but in natural units

LANRES
(9) proportion of land area which is residential, 1960
(10) same

LNAREA
(7) natural log of the urbanized land area in square miles, 1950 and 1960

LOWINC
 (10) takes the same value as INCOME for values below the median for all tracts and zero otherwise

MANCIT
 (7) proportion of the SMA manufacturing employment located in the central city, 1947 and 1958

MANMAJ
 (9) 1 if a census tract in a square mile section containing 8 or more major manufacturing establishments, 0 otherwise
 (10) same

MANMIN
 (9) 1 if a census tract in a square mile section containing 1 to 7 major manufacturing establishments, 0 otherwise
 (10) same

MANPOT
 (9) manufacturing employment potential, 1950, in natural logs

MEDVAL
 (11) median value, for census tracts, of one-unit, owner-occupied units in 1960 relative to 1950

MFGEMP
 (7) proportion of urbanized area manufacturing employment (male) in manufacturing, 1950
 (10) proportion of the employed labor force reporting employment who were employed in mining and manufacturing, 1950

MILINE
 (7) miles of line of local transit systems per square mile of urbanized area

NEGMAJ
 (9) 1 if Negro population 80 percent or more of total, 0 otherwise, census tracts, 1950 and 1960
 (10) same

NEGMIN
 (9) 1 if Negro population 5 to 80 percent of total, 0 otherwise, census tracts, 1950 and 1960
 (10) same

NEGRO
 (11) 1 if a Negro occupied tract (Negro population of 80 percent or more), 0 otherwise, 1950 and 1960

NETDEN
 (9) net population density—population per square mile of land used for residential purposes, 1950 and 1960, in natural logs
 (10) same

ONEFAM
 (8) proportion of dwelling units in the census tract which were in single-family structures, 1950
 (9) same, 1950 and 1960, in square root form
 (10) same, but in natural units

OWNOCC
  (9) proportion of dwelling units which were owner-occupied, 1950 and 1960, in natural logs
  (10) same, but in natural units

OWNUNI
  (11) ratio of the number of owner-occupied units in the tract reporting values in 1960 to the number reporting values in 1950

PASCAR
  (7) passengers carried per vehicle mile operated by local public transit systems, 1950 and 1960

PERHOU
  (8) total population in households divided by the number of households, census tracts, 1950, in natural logs
  (9) same, 1950 and 1960
  (10) same, but in natural units

PEROOM
  (7) proportion of dwelling units with more than one person per room, central cities, 1950
  (8) same, census tracts, 1950, in natural logs
  (9) same, 1950 and 1960, in square root form
  (10) same, natural logs except Tables 8–11 where square root form was used

PNEG50
  (11) proportion of the population in the tract which was Negro in 1950

PNEG60
  (11) proportion of the population in the tract which was Negro in 1960

POPNEG
  (7) proportion of the central city population which was Negro, 1950 and 1960
  (10) same

POPUNI
  (11) ratio of persons per dwelling unit in 1960 to those in 1950 by tracts

RADCEN
  (7) average distance in miles from the CBD to the boundary of the central city

RAPINT
  (9) 1 if a census tract within one mile of designated important transit routes, 0 otherwise
  (10) same

RAPSLO
  (9) RAPINT multiplied by DISCBD
  (10) same

RATSUB
  (11) ratio of dwelling units in census tracts substandard in 1960 to those in 1950

REGION
(7) 1 for urbanized areas in the South (of Washington, D.C.) and West (of Saint Louis, Mo.), 0 otherwise
(10) same

RENUNI
(11) ratio of the number of units in the tract reporting average contract rents in 1960 to the number in 1950

RETCBD
(7) proportion of SMA retail sales in the central business district, 1954 and 1958

RETMAJ
(9) 1 if a census tract within one mile of one of the groups of largest retail centers, 0 otherwise
(10) same

RETMIN
(9) 1 if a census tract within one mile of one of the second largest class of retail centers, 0 otherwise
(10) same

RETPOT
(9) retail employment potential, 1950, in natural logs

RSLOSQ
(9) square of RAPSLO

RVHO50
(9) computed residual from the 1950 VALHOU regression

RVLD50
(9) computed residual from the 1950 VALAND regression

SAMHOU
(7) for 1950 (1960), the proportion of persons 1 year (5 years) old or over who lived in the same dwelling unit in 1949 (1955) as in 1950 (1960)
(9) same, but census tracts, in natural logs
(10) same, but in natural units
(11) same, 1950, in natural units

SCHOOL
(9) median years schooling completed for the census tract population 25 years or over, 1950 and 1960, in natural logs
(10) same, but in natural units

SECTRI-4
(9) four approximately equal groups of tracts constructed by drawing radials from the loop

SMAMFG
(7) natural log of manufacturing production worker employment in the SMA, 1950 and 1960

SUBSTD
(7) proportion of central city dwelling units substandard (dilapidated and/ or without private bath), 1950 and 1960
(8) same, census tracts, 1950, in natural logs
(9) same, 1950 and 1960
(10) same

SUB50
(11) proportion of dwelling units in census tract which were substandard in 1950

UNEMPT
(10) proportion of the SMA male labor force reporting weeks worked in 1949 who worked 26 weeks or less

UNITS
(11) ratio of housing units in 1960 to dwelling units in 1950 in the tract

URBINC
(7) median income of families and unrelated individuals (families) in 1949 (1959) in dollars per year in the urbanized area

URBPOP
(7) natural log of the urbanized area population, 1950 and 1960
(10) same

VACRAT
(11) number of available vacant housing units in the census tract divided by the number of all housing units as reported in the 1960 census

VALAND
(8) value of housing produced in the census tract, in dollars per month per square mile of land, 1950, in natural logs
(9) same, but land used for residential purposes only, 1950 and 1960

VALHOU
(8) average value of housing consumed in dollars per household per month in the census tract, 1950, in natural logs
(9) same, 1950 and 1960
(10) same, but in natural units and for the whole of the central city

VEHMIL
(7) vehicle miles operated per mile of local transit system line, 1950 and 1960

WHIBDY
(11) 1 if a white tract which is contiguous to or touches the 1960 boundary of the Negro area, 0 otherwise

WHICOL
(9) proportion of the employed labor force reporting occupation who were in white-collar occupations—professional, technical, clerical, and sales, 1950 and 1960, in natural logs
(10) same, but in natural units

180CIT
(7) 1 if "waterfront" city, 0 otherwise

Bibliography

Anderson, Martin. *The Federal Bulldozer: A Critical Analysis of Urban Renewal, 1949–62.* Cambridge, Mass.: M.I.T. Press, 1964.

Alonso, William. "A Theory of the Urban Land Market." *Papers and Proceedings of the Regional Science Association* 6 (1960): 149–58.

Bailey, Martin J. "Effects of Race and other Demographic Factors on the Values of Single-Family Homes." *Land Economics* 42 (May, 1966): 215–20.

———. "Note on the Economics of Residential Zoning and Urban Renewal." *Land Economics* 35 (August, 1959): 288–92.

Becker, Gary S. *The Economics of Discrimination.* Chicago: University of Chicago Press, 1957.

Beesley, M. E. "The Value of Time Spent in Travelling: Some New Evidence." *Economica*, new series 32 (May, 1965): 174–85.

Berry, Brian J. L. *Commercial Structure and Commercial Blight.* Chicago: Department of Geography, University of Chicago, 1963.

Bogue, Donald J. *Metropolitan Growth and the Conversion of Land to Nonagricultural Uses.* Oxford, Ohio: Scripps Foundation, 1956.

———, and Harris, Dorothy L. *Comparative Population and Urban Research via Multiple Regression and Covariance Analysis.* Oxford, Ohio: Scripps Foundation, 1954.

Burgess, Ernest W. "The Growth of the City." In *The City*, by Robert E. Park, Ernest W. Burgess, and Roderick D. McKenzie. Chicago: University of Chicago Press, 1925.

Chicago Commission on Human Relations. "Selling and Buying Real Estate in a Racially Changing Neighborhood, a Survey." Chicago, June 14, 1962. (Processed.)

Clark, Colin. "Urban Population Densities." *Journal of the Royal Statistical Society*, series A, 114 (part 4, 1951): 490–96.

Davis, Otto A. "Economic Elements in Municipal Zoning Decisions." *Land Economics* 39 (November, 1963): 375–86.

———, and Whinston, Andrew B. "The Economics of Urban Renewal." *Law and Contemporary Problems* 26 (Winter, 1961): 105–17.

Duncan, Beverly, and Hauser, Philip M. *Housing a Metropolis—Chicago.* Glencoe, Ill.: The Free Press, 1960.

Duncan, Otis Dudley, *et al. Metropolis and Region.* Baltimore: Johns Hopkins Press, 1960.

———, and Duncan, Beverly. *The Negro Population of Chicago.* Chicago: University of Chicago Press, 1957.

Friedman, Milton. *Capitalism and Freedom.* Chicago: University of Chicago Press, 1962.

————. "The Methodology of Positive Economics." In *Essays in Positive Economics.* Chicago: University of Chicago Press, 1953.

Garrison, William, L., et al. *Studies of Highway Development and Geographic Change.* Seattle: University of Washington Press, 1959.

Goode, Richard. "Imputed Rent of Owner-Occupied Dwellings under the Income Tax." *Journal of Finance* 15 (December, 1960): 504–30.

Grebler, Leo, Blank, David M., and Winnick, Louis. *Capital Formation in Residential Real Estate: Trends and Prospects.* Princeton, N.J.: Princeton University Press, 1956.

Gries, John M., and Ford, James, eds. *Slums, Large Scale Housing, and Decentralization.* Report of the President's Conference on Home Building and Home Ownership. Washington: U.S. Government Printing Office, 1932.

Harris, Chauncey D., and Ullman, Edward L. "The Nature of Cities." *The Annals of the American Academy of Political and Social Science* 242 (November, 1945): 7–17.

Hartman, Chester. "The Housing of Relocated Families." *Journal of the American Institute of Planners* 30 (November, 1964): 266–86.

Hicks, John R. *The Theory of Wages.* New York: Peter Smith, 1948.

Hoover, Edgar M. *The Location of Economic Activity.* New York: McGraw-Hill Book Company, 1948.

————, and Vernon, Raymond. *Anatomy of a Metropolis.* Cambridge, Mass.: Harvard University Press, 1959.

Hoyt, Homer. *One Hundred Years of Land Values in Chicago.* Chicago: University of Chicago Press, 1933.

————. *The Structure and Growth of Residential Neighborhoods in American Cities.* Washington: U.S. Government Printing Office, 1939.

Johnson, Thomas F., Morris, James R., and Butts, Joseph G. *Renewing America's Cities.* Washington: Institute for Social Science Research, 1962.

Kain, John F. "The Journey-to-Work as a Determinant of Residential Location." *Papers and Proceedings of the Regional Science Association* 9 (1962): 137–60.

Kitagawa, Evelyn M., and Bogue, Donald J. *Suburbanization of Manufacturing Activity within Standard Metropolitan Areas.* Oxford, Ohio: Scripps Foundation, 1955.

Klaman, Saul B. *The Postwar Residential Mortgage Market.* Princeton, N.J.: Princeton University Press, 1961.

Lösch, August. *The Economics of Location.* Translated from the 2d rev. ed. by William H. Woglom with the assistance of Wolfgang F. Stolper. New Haven, Conn.: Yale University Press, 1954.

Malone, John R. "A Statistical Comparison of Recent New and Used Home Buyers." Unpublished Ph.D. dissertation, Graduate School of Business, University of Chicago, 1963.

Marshall, Alfred. *Principles of Economics.* 8th ed. New York: Macmillan Company, 1920.

Mohring, Herbert. "Land Values and the Measurement of Highway Benefits." *Journal of Political Economy* 49 (June, 1961): 236–49.

Moses, Leon N. "Towards a Theory of Intra-Urban Wage Differentials and Their Influence on Travel Patterns." *Papers and Proceedings of the Regional Science Association* 9 (1962): 53–63.

———, and Williamson, Harold F., Jr. "Value of Time, Choice of Mode, and the Subsidy Issue in Urban Transportation." *Journal of Political Economy* 71 (June, 1963): 247–64.

Muth, Richard F. "The Distribution of Population within Urban Areas." In *Determinants of Investment Behavior*, ed. Robert Ferber. New York: National Bureau of Economic Research, 1967, pp. 271–99.

———. "The Demand for Non-Farm Housing." In *The Demand for Durable Goods*, ed. Arnold C. Harberger. Chicago: University of Chicago Press, 1960.

———. "The Derived Demand Curve for a Productive Factor and the Industry Supply Curve." *Oxford Economic Papers*, new series 16 (July, 1964): 221–34.

———. "Economic Change and Rural-Urban Land Conversions." *Econometrica* 29 (January, 1961): 1–23.

———. "Interest Rates, Contract Terms, and the Allocation of Mortgage Funds." *Journal of Finance* 17 (March, 1962): 63–80.

———. "The Spatial Structure of the Housing Market." *Papers and Proceedings of the Regional Science Association* 7 (1961): 207–20.

Nourse, Hugh O. "The Effect of Public Housing on Property Values in St. Louis." *Land Economics* 39 (November, 1963): 433–41.

Oi, Walter Y., and Shuldiner, Paul W. *An Analysis of Urban Travel Demands.* Evanston, Ill.: Northwestern University Press for the Transportation Center of Northwestern University, 1962.

Pascal, Anthony H., "The Economics of Housing Segregation." In *Abstracts of Papers Presented at December 1965 Meetings*. New York: Econometric Society, 1965.

Pendleton, William C. "The Value of Highway Accessibility." Unpublished Ph.D. Dissertation, Department of Economics, University of Chicago, 1963.

Perry, Clarence Arthur. *The Rebuilding of Blighted Areas: A Study of the Neighborhood Unit in Replanning and Plot Assemblage.* Architectural and Planning Studies under the Direction of C. Earl Morrow. New York: Regional Plan Association, 1933.

Ratcliff, Richard U. *Urban Land Economics.* New York: McGraw-Hill Book Company, 1949.

Reid, Margaret G. *Housing and Income.* Chicago: University of Chicago Press, 1962.

Schmid, Calvin F., and Miller, Vincent A. *Population Trends and Educational Change in the State of Washington.* Seattle: Washington State Census Board, 1960.

Sobotka, Stephen P. "Union Influence on Wages: The Construction Industry." *Journal of Political Economy* 61 (April, 1953): 127–43.

Subcommittee on Urban Redevelopment of the President's Advisory Committee on Government Housing Policies and Programs. *A Report to the President of the United States.* Washington: U.S. Government Printing Office, 1953.

Taeuber, Karl E. "Negro Residential Segregation, 1940–60: Changing Trends in the Large Cities of the United States." Paper read at the annual meetings of the American Sociological Association, 1962.

Turvey, Ralph. *The Economics of Real Property*. London: George Allen and Unwin, 1957.

U.S. Bureau of the Census. "Quality of Housing: An Appraisal of Census Statistics and Methods," Response Research Branch Report no. 66-16, Second Draft, April, 1966. (Processed.)

U.S. Housing and Home Finance Agency. *Fourteenth Annual Report*. Washington: U.S. Government Printing Office, 1961.

Valavanis, Stefan. "Lösch on Location." *American Economic Review* 45 (September, 1955): 637–44.

Walker, Mabel L. *Urban Blight and Slums*. Harvard City Planning Studies 12. Cambridge, Mass.: Harvard University Press, 1938.

Wilner, Daniel M., *et al. The Housing Environment and Family Life*. Baltimore: Johns Hopkins Press, 1962.

Wingo, Lowden, Jr. *Transportation and Urban Land*. Washington: Resources for the Future, Inc., 1961.

Winnick, Louis. "Rental Housing: Problems for Private Investment." In *Conference on Savings and Residential Financing, 1963 Proceedings*, ed. Leon T. Kendall and Marshall D. Ketchum. Chicago: U.S. Savings and Loan League, 1963.

Winsborough, Halliman H. "A Comparative Study of Urban Residential Densities." Unpublished Ph.D. dissertation, Department of Sociology, University of Chicago, 1960.

Index

Accessibility characteristics, other, 86–93, 238. *See also* MANMAJ; MANMIN; MANPOT; RAPSLO; RETMAJ; RETMIN; RETPOT
Age of dwellings. *See also* AGEDUS; Household location
condition, 116–17, 280–81
population density, 99, 205, 237–38
price of housing, 95, 203, 238
production of housing, 95–96, 203–4, 237–38
rental of land, 95–96
tastes, 98–99
Age of persons, 100–101. *See also* AGEPER
AGEDUS,
DENGRA, 156
described, 151–52, 194, 208, 245
GRODEN and NETDEN, 195–96, 218, 225
INCOME, 201–2, 254, 265
SUBSTD, 198, 251–52, 259, 264, 269
VALAND and ONEFAM, 202–4, 222, 227–28, 237
VALHOU and PEROOM, 196–98, 220, 225, 233, 271
AGEPER, 213–14, 225, 245, 252, 271–72
AGESMA, 147, 151, 162, 246, 260
Alonso, William, 6 n., 30 n.
Anderson, Martin, 124 n., 327 n.
Automobile transport. *See* CAREGS; Dwelling condition; Transport costs
AVCNRN, 289

Bailey, Martin J., 110 n., 111–12, 132 n., 166 n., 302 n., 332
Becker, Gary S., 107 n., 109, 110 n.
Beesley, M. E., 309–10
Berry, Brian J. L., 84 n., 131 n., 211
Blank, David M., Grebler, Leo, and Winnick, Louis, 187 n., 287 n.
Block-busters, 110
Bogue, Donald J., and Kitagawa, Evelyn M., 163 n.
Budget constraint, 21, 38, 43
Building and occupancy codes, 115, 119–20, 134, 330–31, 333. *See also* Zoning
Burgess, Ernest W., 5, 6
Butts, Joseph G., Johnson, Thomas F., and Morris, James R., 116 n.

Capital market imperfections, 120
CAREGS, 147, 153, 161, 162, 163, 167, 169, 171, 172, 175, 176, 180–82
Census data on dwelling condition and quality, 125 n.
Central business district (CBD)
described 3–4, 7
growth, 98, 118
highest-order shopping center, 84
principal employment center, 21
Central city
definition, 3 n.
fiscal problems, 170, 329–30 (*see also* CITINC)
population, 75–77, 164–66, 322 (*see also* CNTPOP)
radius, 75–76 (*see also* RADCEN)
Central place theory, 84, 154
CHABDY, 293–94